NOT EVEN A SPARROW FALLS

NOT EVEN A SPARROW FALLS

THE PHILOSOPHY OF STEPHEN R. L. CLARK

Daniel A. Dombrowski

MICHIGAN STATE UNIVERSITY PRESS • *East Lansing*

Michigan State University Press
East Lansing, Michigan 48823–5202

06 05 04 03 02 01 00   1 2 3 4 5 6 7 8 9

LIBRARY OF CONGRESS CATALOGING-IN-PUBLICATION DATA
Dombrowski, Daniel A.
Not even a sparrow falls : the philosophy of
Stephen R. L. Clark/ by Daniel A. Dombrowski.
p. cm.
Includes bibliographical references and index.
ISBN 0–87013–549–x (alk. paper)
1. Clark, Stephen R. L. I. Title. B1618.C57 D65 2000
192—dc21 99–050947

Book and cover design
Sharp Des!gns, Lansing, Michigan

Cover photograph is used courtesy of Stephen R. L. Clark

Visit Michigan State University Press on the World Wide Web at:
www.msu.edu/unit/msupress

#433129

CONTENTS

VI

❧

ABBREVIATIONS

AJ = *From Athens to Jerusalem*

AM = *Aristotle's Man*

AT = *Animals and Their Moral Standing*

CP = *Civil Peace and Sacred Order*

GW = *God's World and the Great Awakening*

MR = *The Mysteries of Religion*

MS = *The Moral Status of Animals*

NB = *The Nature of the Beast*

PS = *A Parliament of Souls*

PREFACE

SINCE THE MID-1970S AN AMAZING PHILOSOPHER HAS BLAZED ACROSS THE PHILO-sophic sky. His name is Stephen R. L. Clark. He has authored twelve books (seven of them by Oxford University Press or Clarendon Press) and dozens of articles (many of which are in the most prestigious journals). His books have been reviewed and a few of the articles have received comment, but as a whole Clark's work has not been carefully assessed by philosophers. The purpose of the present book is to bring together all of Clark's works to date for the purpose of patient examination and evaluation. I think it is fair to say that I am an admirer of Clark's work, but it will become evident in the course of this book that my admiration is not necessarily synonymous with my agreement with him on some important issues.

There are at least two obstacles that will face me throughout this book. First, Clark has not only written a great deal, he has written a great deal in three areas of philosophy that at least initially seem quite far apart: philosophy of religion, the status of animals, and political philosophy. My experience has been that philosophers who are familiar with one of Clark's areas of interest, say the moral status of animals, are not familiar with the detailed work he has done in other areas, say in philosophy of religion. My procedure will be both to let Clark speak for himself and to analyze his views. It must be admitted, however, that even when I have let Clark "speak for himself," I have interpreted him by choosing this quotation rather than that and by putting his views in certain configurations of my choosing rather than in others. Nevertheless, I am confident that a reader of this book will gain a firm grasp of Clark's concepts as they are spread across his writings, such that a misunderstanding of his entire philosophy, which is very likely if only one or two of his works is read, can be avoided.

The second obstacle, in addition to the synoptic one, is that of determining in any particular work of Clark's which stance is his own among the many ideas that he floats with varying degrees of seriousness and with various rhetorical goals in mind. An indication of the difficulty can be seen in the following:

> I am an Aristotelian on Mondays and Wednesdays, a Pyrrhonian Sceptic on Tuesdays and Fridays, a Neo-Platonist on Thursdays and Saturdays and worship in the local Episcopalian church on Sundays. . . . I add that I am strongly influenced by Mahayana Buddhism. . . . (MS, 4–5)

If there were more days in the week we could add to this statement that sometimes Clark is a pragmatist and sometimes an anarchist.

I would like to emphasize that it is difficult to overcome the second obstacle without having overcome the first. It is only when one has read a great deal of Clark that one can get a lens with a wide enough angle to see how these apparently contradictory positions are rendered consistent by him. There are contradictions in Clark, but not nearly as many as some readers think, in that an occasional reader may be tempted to look for arguments in Clark in the microcosm which are more readily found in the macrocosm. He is, to use Thomas Nagel's categories, a philosopher who is often locally obscure (albeit thought-provokingly so) but globally clear. Some philosophers may wonder whether it is fair of Clark to make so many demands of them. I have no desire to take a stand on this issue; my concern is to make sure that we take Clark on his own demanding terms, so that we can fairly evaluate his strong points and criticize him on the weak ones. It should also be noted that if Clark made himself easier to read he would be only half as witty and, I think, when he is at his best, only half as profound.

The three major parts of the book are meant to treat what I take to be the three major foci of Clark's work: God, animals, and the polis. I have isolated each of these topics from the others to the extent that this is possible. As I have previously indicated, in order to understand Clark's political views one needs to understand his views on religion and animals; in order to understand his view on religion, one must understand his views on animals and politics; and so on. Each of the three parts of this book is, in turn, divided into three chapters, making a total of nine. The first three chapters cluster around religious issues.

Chapter one introduces Clark's approach to religion, an approach that is built on certain controversial methodological theses that concern his concepts of tradition, language, and argument. He holds that one can have too much as well as too little confidence in human reason, and that reason, properly understood, rests on faith. Whereas chapter one is largely expository, chapter two is much more argumentative on my part. I argue that Clark's theism, which can be described as a version of dipolar theism, nonetheless leans quite heavily in the direction of traditional monopolar theism (i.e., toward God as supreme Being as opposed to supreme Becoming). I also argue that, although a great deal can be learned from Clark (say, regarding religious ceremony and sacrament and regarding the positive features of a contemporary version of polytheism), there are problems created by the paradoxical way in which he treats the centripetal and centrifugal forces that energize his thought and that provide it with its fundamental tension. The most important of these problems, theodicy, is treated in chapter three. Here we can see at once both Clark's awesome originality (e.g., in his defense of divine command theory) and his willingness to be saddled with the traditional problem of theodicy found in the Abrahamic religions (a problem largely due to a belief in divine omnipotence). That is, in this chapter we will be frustrated by Clark's choice to pull in the reins on his considerable abilities.

The second part of the book deals primarily with animals. Chapter four treats Clark's courageous and insightful contemporary version of Aristotelianism, a version that continues Aristotle's project of a biologized (or ethologized) philosophy. In particular, I concentrate on how our animal inheritance affects our views of gender issues and violence. Clark's moderate view of ethology sees animals as ethical but not moral, a view that provides partial continuity with human ethics and morality. Chapter five, however, shifts from a view of animals and human beings as ethical or moral agents to a view of them as moral patients. Two arguments for animal "rights" (the scare quotes are essential here) are explored, arguments that I will defend with Clark against his critics, some of whom are animal rightists themselves. Clark's use of these arguments—from sentiency and from marginal cases—differs from that of other thinkers who defend animals in that he places them within the context of a *philosophia perennis* and of a theistic metaphysics, and against the background of his own traditionalist political principles. Chapter six moves beyond the issues surrounding animals as either agents or patients to a consideration of the place of animals and humans within the natural environment in general. Clark's critique of (liberal) universalism, and his defense of a (conservative) concern for historical, tradition-bound communities makes his treatment of environmental ethics distinctive. That is, Clark is a conservationist regarding politics, religion, and the natural environment. Finally, it is worth noting at the outset the irony that gives rise to the title of this book: Jesus' sardonic instruction to rely upon the God who cares even for the fall of a sparrow is usually quoted so as to license the killing of sparrows and other animals who are not human (AT, 4). Clark would not grant this license.

The final three chapters cluster around political issues. Chapter seven examines Clark's distinction between true community and mere society, the latter of which is the lair of liberalism. Clark's critique of liberalism, wherein he emphasizes that we were communal before we were human, is only partial, however, in that Clark is sometimes closer to liberalism than he wishes to admit. It is unclear whether Clark's own view of politics is more theocratic or anarchistic, but to the extent that he defends anarcho-capitalism he counteracts his best efforts at political philosophy, efforts that consist of an alternative to contemporary society not from the left or right but from below, from the perspectives of premodern theistic wisdom and of ethologized Aristotelianized philosophy. In chapter eight I treat the differences between good and bad ethology as they affect one's political views as well as what Clark takes to be the defects in utilitarianism in the effort to preserve and strengthen political community. This chapter also introduces the key issue treated in chapter nine: the World Soul. Here Clark views the cosmos as a polis; in fact, he views it as a polis deserving of more allegiance than that which is due, if any is due, to the nation-state. This chapter will make it possible to treat in detail the integral link in Clark's thought between politics and religion and to recapitulate Clarkian thought in general.

I have avoided a chronological treatment of Clark's writings because in the twenty-five years since the publication of his first book (AM), his thought, even if it has developed in many ways, still clusters around the three main topics mentioned previously: God, animals, and politics. Each of his books deals with all three of these topics, even if some books deal primarily with animals (MS, NB, AT), some primarily with God (MR, AJ), and some primarily with political issues, as in his trilogy titled *Limits and Renewals* (CP, PS, GW). No doubt, Clark will continue to publish works that will make worthwhile reading, but the recent completion of this trilogy, a monumental intellectual effort in its own right, marks a logical spot to pause so as to evaluate his work thus far and to provoke Clark to pick up several (apparently inconsistent) threads lying about his work published thus far. My hope is also that through the present work scholars will have an opportunity to catch up with Clark's work before he moves on to new projects, to understand what he has accomplished, and to become dialectically engaged with his thought so as to determine where it is strong and where it is weak.

Karl Popper has argued that the intellectual life progresses by means of two sorts of procedure: bold hypotheses and severe criticisms of these hypotheses. If Popper is even remotely close to accurate about what causes intellectual progress, then Clark has done his share of the work to bring about such progress. Very few philosophers in the last generation have been as bold as he has been in the development of theories or of proposed solutions to philosophical problems. Boldness is an intellectual virtue because it is an expedient way of getting at the truth. If any mere hypothesis is stated in philosophy, there is usually no assurance that it is true or false, or even if it makes any sense. However, if a bold hypothesis is stated (i.e., one that has a greater possible truth content than a mere hypothesis) then the author of the hypothesis is out on a limb that can more easily be sawed off, if the hypothesis is defective. If a bold hypothesis is stated and it cannot be easily criticized, then the hypothesis should be taken seriously as one that, even if not true, has at least taken an asymptotic step toward the truth. That is, Clark has several bold hypotheses on the table. This book is an attempt to determine how many of them can remain on the table after criticism. In any event, it is worth noting that neither intellectual boldness nor criticism are individually sufficient for intellectual progress to occur. However, it may well be that each is necessary for it to occur. If this is true, then Clark is truly a philosopher worthy of our consideration.

The need for the present book becomes apparent when one reads Clark's recent interpreters in the 1990s, even those who are favorable to what he has tried to do in his philosophy. For example, Lewis Ayres favors Clark's attempt to rebuild an openly classical understanding of our world, and he likes the texture of Clark's work, where there is ironic juxtaposition of argument pointing to the inconsistencies of all forms of "rationalistic" modernism (or postmodernism). Yet he notes, correctly, I think, that because of the breadth of Clark's attack the simplistic criticisms that Clark has thus far received are not sufficient to the task of an evenhanded appraisal of Clark's work. Likewise, Oliver

O'Donovan approves of Clark's "unrepentant Hellenism," and he thinks that Clark will eventually be generally seen as a philosopher who is very important for our generation, but the furious intensity of some of Clark's polemics as well as the broadness of some of his brush strokes sometimes get in the way of our ability to appreciate his greatness as a thinker. Finally, John Rist seems to agree with Clark that the modernist view that the *philosophia perennis* is outmoded is merely fashionable, and that contemporary orthodoxy in philosophy has not really been argued for. Yet he wishes that Clark's arguments against the opponents to the *philosophia perennis* did not resort to the extent that they do to academic name-dropping or to so rapidly leaping from topic to topic. One of the purposes of the present book is to counteract the impression that many have, including Rist, that Clark's many attacks are like the behavior of a mad gunman in a restaurant, spraying bullets in every direction.[1]

PART I

GOD

AN APPROACH TO RELIGION

INTRODUCTION

In this chapter I would like to introduce Clark's approach to religion. This approach, as we will see, is built on certain controversial methodological theses that Clark vigorously defends, theses that concern his concepts of tradition, language, and argument. Although I will briefly criticize some aspects of Clark's approach to religion, the primary purpose of this first chapter is to get Clark's major concepts on the table so that they can be analyzed in detail later. Hence there will unavoidably be some unsubstantiated jumps in this chapter that will, I hope, be avoided in subsequent chapters.

A TRADITIONALIST APPROACH TO RELIGION

In order to understand the thought of Stephen R. L. Clark, one must first come to terms with his approach to religion, an approach that starts from ordinary experience rather than from scholastic arguments for or against the existence of God. This approach requires a William Jamesian view of the field, with a wider-angle lens than that to which most philosophers are accustomed. Still, as we will see, Clark includes in his approach (and much more frequently than his critics admit) a great deal of tight philosophical argumentation. His overall view is that it is only part of the task of philosophy to criticize and to find fault with arguments, especially arguments with conclusions that no one has any serious interest in rejecting. "The real aim of philosophy," he thinks, "is not to destroy, but to understand and explore." His hope is that by laying out the possibilities in religion, politics, our relations with animals, and so on, we may have an accurate map, at least, with which to begin to explore in detail the terrain of these regions (MR, viii–ix).

Clark does not restrict what it is to "be religious" to any particular religion. The generic point he wishes to make can be put negatively: to be irreligious is to be disinclined to believe that anything but human pleasure and pain much matter. In fact, there can be whole "ages of irreligion," which are often mistakenly called "ages of doubt." Clark feels that this latter designation is inaccurate because the irreligious can be every bit as complacent as religious believers. Contemporary irreligion is based on the dominant self-perception that one has a duty to believe only what it is "reasonable" to believe. As we will see, Clark does not think that there are sufficient reasons to support this supposed duty. These vague characterizations of the religious and the irreligious are dangerous, however, in that they can easily lead to the smug belief that one can reach the essence of religion without practicing any particular religion. Intellectuals are often reluctant to be associated with the sort of people to be found in any worshipping community, yet the imagined bypassing of the disputes and idiosyncracies of competing religions has usually resulted in the establishment of still other sects. To be religious, Clark thinks, is to practice some religion or other (MR, 3–5).

One of the reasons why some people refuse to take any particular religion seriously is that they assume that the religious believer is really doing something other than what he claims to be doing (e.g., he is really prolonging a childlike desire for a father to take care of him, etc.). To Clark, however, religious believers by and large mean by religious ceremony and creed roughly what they say they mean, and he believes it is incorrect to suppose that all or most religious groups mean just the same things, even if there is some sense in which they do the same things. Clark's instructive example goes as follows: Imagine two different tribes that regularly perform rain dances, one of which assumes that the rain dance is a necessary condition for the subsequent rain, and the other of which assumes not that it will not rain if the dance is not performed, but that they will not receive the rain in the proper (thankful) frame of mind if the dance is not performed. That is, Clark is intent on making particular religions more plausible to us by showing us that in most (Clark overstates the case when he says "all") religious traditions there are both literalists (the rain-makers) and symbolists (the rain-blessers), and that it is counterproductive to religion if one insists that only one group is "really" religious (MR, 6).

Common to both Clark's understanding of religion and his understanding of animals is his critique of behaviorism, to be detailed later. Here I would like to emphasize the fact that an exclusive concern for religious behavior may well leave one without a clue as to what religion is all about:

> Husband, lover, ritual priest and Tantric mystic may all be "having sex," but to understand only that much is to understand very little. If "religiosity" lies in the emotion and attitude of the agents it can only be detected by our perceiving their actions with their eyes and minds. . . . We have to "participate" in the action. (MR, 7)

Once we imaginatively enter, in this R. G. Collingwoodian way, into the minds of religious believers, we can come to understand what it means to profane something—that is, to use something for merely practical purposes or immediate ends: "What is sacred is not for use. It hardly follows, of course, that what is useless is sacred" (MR, 9). Clark uses the term "sacred" here in a wide sense, in that even a craftsman's tools may, *in a sense*, be sacred if they are used to produce goods that contribute something positive to the divine life. To profane the tools of one's trade is to intentionally use them for purely mundane purposes. This difference in intent or attitude is difficult for behaviorists to appreciate.

The rites of religion can be understood as ways of linking our ordinary lives to that of the sacred *cosmos,* which exists beyond human contrivance and without our aid. The sacred may be used in a peculiar way, in that people can be very practical about religious objects and institutions, and hence it is a mistake to assume that "primitive" humanity lived or lives in a religious haze. Churches and cemeteries can perform practical functions for a community and still be lineaments of a sacred *cosmos*. Our very lives are half-sacred to us, in that, being gifts, they are not our own:

> The sacred permits itself to be used, on its own terms, but is not ordinary, not accessible, not defenseless. . . . The sacred cosmos . . . exists beyond human contrivance, and without our aid. The rites of religion can be understood as ways of linking our ordinary lives to that cosmos. . . . In understanding "the sacred," therefore, it is unwise to suppose that this is an emotional category and nothing more. . . . Equally "the sacred" need not reside in a response of awe. Books,

5

animals, rites and people are sacred because they are set aside from ordinary careless use, but it is not necessarily true that what is sacred is experienced to be profoundly significant. . . . It is probably unwise to follow William James (in other respects a fine observer) in supposing that the essence of religion is to be found in the religious enthusiast. . . . Causes served *only* by enthusiasts—political, military, literary, or religious—do not survive and spread. All causes need a mass of nonenthusiasts. (MR, 10–11)

Religious enthusiasts, in contrast to more sober religious believers, are rather rare, but so are philosophers. One of the most controversial features of Clark's philosophy of religion is his concerted effort to highlight the unnaturalness of philosophical speculation in religion, speculation that, he thinks, tends to undermine, amplify, and expand on religious tradition, but which cannot *live within* such a tradition. That is, there is a fundamental tension in Clark's work, to be explored throughout this book, between his own rather ambitious activity as a speculative philosopher, on the one hand, and his conservative defense of religious and political tradition, on the other. Clark's response to this tension seems to be that it is only a particular sort of philosophy that causes problems, that sort which leads to a casual and unthinking relativism (MR, 12). This response is, in part, on the mark, but the tension is equally caused by Clark's rather extreme defense of tradition, as I will show.

Most current philosophical analysis and speculation leads to relativism, he thinks, because of the dogma that suggests that we ought not to believe anything that cannot be *proved*. Of necessity this dogma leads to agnosticism: where nothing is taken for granted, nothing can ever be established. But it is not necessarily the case that all hell will break loose if nothing can ever be established. In fact, relativistic agnosticism can easily lead in Humean fashion to a pseudoconservativism or a conventionalism that Clark would criticize:

Lacking any argument to convince him (Hume) that he was rationally bound to believe even that food would not poison him or that the sun would rise tomorrow, he was happy to forget argument and rely instead upon irrational conviction, strengthened by good food and company. Those who begin as enthusiasts for understanding may end as lazily conventional. (MR, 13)

Clark is well aware of the fact that he will be criticized for having too thin a commitment to reason in religion, an awareness that compels him to find a niche, if not a place of prominence, in his thought for the traditional arguments for the existence of God. In addition to this niche there is his admonition against too bland an acceptance of whatever a cleric says, because bland acceptance leads to bad believers. The point seems to be to philosophize with moderation, not with the intention of proving religion a nullity, nor of proving it a necessity, but "merely" of using reason to *understand* religion. Clark is reluctant to give a larger role to the traditional arguments for the existence of God, for the historical—not philosophical—reason that they have plainly not been central to religion:

> For a philosopher to concentrate on those arguments and ignore the living con-
> text within which speculative philosophers have elaborated their theories is to
> run the risk of missing the point entirely. (MR, 14)

It is Clark's hope that by helping us to understand the terrain in religion, by functioning as a worthy mapmaker for us, he will help us to obtain the results promised in religion. We will attempt to determine whether Clark can deliver on this pragmatic promissory note.

It is certainly no easy task to try to reconcile the two poles that are in fundamental tension in Clark's thought: he is both a philosophical enthusiast for understanding and an apologist for even the most apparently irrational religious experiences, like "conversion" and "baptism in the Spirit." But this is what I will attempt to do, *to the extent that* such reconciliation is possible. Clark himself very often tries to bring these two poles in his thought together by showing that the supposed bifurcation between Western reason and Eastern mysticism is unfair to both the "Western," Abrahamic religions of the book (Judaism, Christianity, and Islam) and the Eastern religions. That is, to understand the great religions of the world is *already* to have come to grips with the fact that religion by its very nature *requires* some sort of rapprochement between reason and faith (MR, 15–17).

What matters to believers in the Abrahamic religions is that one is part of a sacred history, a history that can be understood in various ways: through memory and ceremonial painting (as in "primitive" religions), through reason, and through sacred texts. Yet the importance of this last source need not mean that one has to believe that Moses wrote the Pentateuch, that Gabriel mouthed the Koran word for word to Mohammed, or that Joseph Smith ever had any oracular golden plates. The importance of the sacred texts lies in the fact that they depict the religious history of a people who were (as we are, at least metaphorically) dislocated

7

and dispossessed, exiled and defeated. Clark's point here is not to reduce the history of religion to various political, economic, and social realities, but to point out the dependence human beings have on God, a dependence that is amply illustrated in the Bible, for example (MR, 18–19).

In order to understand the biblical figures, we once again need to think ourselves into other skins, an act of imagination that, for example, could enable us to understand the religious impulse involved in Abraham's (or better, Terah's) leaving Ur, even if it were true that his family would have left Ur anyway because of changing economic conditions. There is no necessary incompatibility in Clark between natural and sacred history, as there is in many versions of agnosticism as well as in extreme dualistic versions of theism (MR, 20).

If one assumes the sufficiency of naturalistic explanations, then there is no need to posit sacred explanations as fifth wheels. For example, we do not need to have recourse to an extraterrestrial, Galactic Empire in order to explain the relics and stories of ancient religions. Clark's peculiar response to this objection consists of an analogy between ufologism (belief in UFOs) and theism to the effect that ufologists and theists may well live more imaginatively, and hence more happily, than those who never glance beyond the confines of their local community to wonder about what might be going on in the sky. Obviously this sort of defense of theism needs greater rational support, but here Clark alerts us to the fact that in addition to looking for rational argumentation in defense of theism, we should also be on the lookout for the pragmatic benefits of theism, benefits that are not irrelevant in the evaluation of a view of the world. We should be wary of the parsimonious consequences brought about by the new clerics of the contemporary world who would try to convince us that the world can be explained *simpliciter* through natural causes (MR, 20–24).

Even if we do not suppose that there are extraterrestrial visitors or divine causes, we should be humbled by the realization that many things in nature happen unexpectedly, and on this evidence alone we should be hesitant to claim that theism is a mistake. Sacred historians, as Clark uses the term, do not have to include any events that might not also appear in natural histories; ordinary events need not be incompatible with what religious believers think happened. *Within* the world of nature it is possible to locate oneself in a sacred setting, where it is possible to have contact with realities that are normally hidden:

> No amount of merely naturalistic enquiry will reveal this meaning, any more than chemical analysis of a human brain will reveal the thoughts that issue in speech. . . .

8

The divine realm is not understood as an explanation of material and human events which are otherwise inexplicable, but rather as the giver of meaning to events that are, in their own right, entirely ordinary. Not all religious will agree to this description of the situation; some will prefer to take as "literal" a view of their sacred texts. . . . The Bible is the Word of God—if so it is—not because no human being could have written the texts it contains . . . but because the writings can be understood as a whole, beyond any human intention of the writers. What the Bible *qua* sacred text means is not merely what its human authors meant . . . a communication floating on the water of natural, historical events. (MR, 25–26)

In actuality the issue is a bit more complicated than this for Clark. In addition to a religious ontology there are at least two other views regarding the natural world. The relationship between scientific truth, on the one hand, and the ordinary secular truth of common sense, on the other, is just as complex as that between religious ontology and naturalistic ontology in general. An indication of the fact that science and common sense are competing forms of naturalism can be seen in the realization that even if there were sufficient causes in nature for human action which could be discovered by science, there would still be a pragmatic need to punish criminals.

The pragmatism that Clark defends could more accurately be described as an emphasis on the praxic implications of commonsensical beliefs and of theories that are veridical, true-in-fact. That is, Clark's pragmatism does not include the belief that truth, conceived of as what is really the case, independent of our experience and investigations, is too far afield for us. It does include the "agreement with the result of the most rigorous imaginable intrasubjective, dialectical examination of our most important experiences" (AJ, 24). It is not enough that our conclusions are warranted by the rules of our intellectual community; these rules can, in fact, be impediments. We should join ourselves to, or continue to participate in, an intellectual community because it *works* in establishing the agreement mentioned in the above quotation.

Clark doubts whether our intellectual lives can have the beneficial consequences we desire from them without their resting on a certain faith. To tell a consistent story does not prove the story true, and no amount of empirical evidence ever *determines* us to believe anything. In order to do this we need some premise regarding the likeliest way of producing sufficient evidence; we also need a nonempirical premise about the nature of things before we can *argue* about the nature of things (AJ, 26–28). It is because of an underlying assumption on our part (a certain sort of faith on our part) that the world in general is intelligible that we can come to understand particular things. It is partially because of this faith that we can have insight regarding, and get inside the skins of, other human beings, animals, and protein molecules:

> It is always a slight shock, so used are we to supposing that Galileo was a martyr to pure observational science, when we realize that Galileo thought of himself as a Platonist, and formed his theories not on the basis of observations but of rational insight. Similarly Einstein: "There is only the way of intuition which is helped by a feeling for the order lying behind the appearance." That feeling for order is explicable in a Platonic universe by the postulate that we, being immortal spirits, saw the pattern to which things were made. . . . We do not find the universe wholly alien; we are of a piece with the nature of things. (AJ, 31–32)

Our thought is, at its best, receptive to the pattern by which things are made, and if we are to take our thought seriously it can only be due to a certain faith or ungrounded intuition (these terms are interchangeable for Clark). This intelligible pattern by which things were made is identified by the gospel-writer John as the *Logos* that lights every person and that provides the root for the flowering of reason (AJ, 32–34).

This flourishing of *logos* in intellectual virtue consists of a certain mean. On the one hand, "those who pursue absolute consistency by refusing to entertain all propositions that conflict with their ruling hypotheses are bigots," whereas, on the other hand, "those who devise merely ad hoc solutions to apparent contradictions, never admitting that one or other thesis must by now have been refuted, are fanatics"(AJ, 181). Intellectual virtue consists of both the effort to be consistent *and* the effort to save the phenomena of religious experience. As we will see, many of Clark's critics can claim greater consistency than Clark only because of the restricted range of phenomena that they are willing to examine. The good intellectual, according to Clark, does not expect his or her conceptual scheme to be *perfectly* consistent:

> The good intellectual holds fast to the law of non-contradiction, as the condition of all rational discourse, but does not take it for granted that she can infallibly detect a contradiction. We have now no complete and perfect theory about the world, no single perspective from which (uniquely) all other perspectives can be understood. . . . What is real are the manifold perspectives. (AJ, 181–82)

Clark's point here is neither to encourage a gut response to issues nor to promote social prejudice. Philosophers have a duty to explore the mind's landscape and to map out the possibilities for those who follow. But,

> much of the intelligible universe is quite unintelligible to us. There are those who prefer to stay in the well-lighted places, driving the fog back step by anxious step. Others, of whom I am—obviously—one, prefer to strike out across country, trusting that we can at least make a rough map of the territory, that there will be moments of clarity. . . . Our sketch-maps are not intended to be definitive doctrinal statements, and if others assume that we whole-heartedly believe the tales we tell, and never believe the opposite, they are likely to feel disappointed. . . . We are as prone as anyone else to fall in love with our own creations, and interpret critical comment as a reflection on our integrity or virtue, but it is almost as exasperating (ungracious as this seems) to receive uncritical praise, as if one were wholly to be identified with the thesis one has offered. (AJ, 206–7)

Clark often gets into trouble with his critics because of the inability of the latter to take him with a grain of salt when he is ironic. His hope is to use his intellectual endeavors to dispel at least *some* of the aforementioned fog without developing an inflated confidence in human reason along the way. Equally dangerous as intellectual hubris, however, is too little confidence in human reason:

> To suppose that the universe is "just as chance would have it," that our capacities and fundamental categories are generated solely by the selfish gene, that there are no absolute values, that human beings are the only value in a universe devoid of value, that "God" is the name of something like the Loch Ness Monster, and the like are the doctrines of insanity. . . . If a friend reveals that she really does doubt that the world is intelligible, or suspects that she is the only conscious being in the world, one's immediate reaction (even as a philosopher who has explored these possibilities) is to wonder about her diet, her recent history, whether she has the flu. (AJ, 208)

Once again, Clark reminds us here of William James.

When we come to find the world less obvious than it seemed, we can begin to pursue philosophy. The world intermittently becomes less obvious to us because it is of a much greater scope than our perspectival experience of it

(NB, 1). Hence the modern dogma that no one ought to believe anything more than he or she can demonstrate on the basis of personal knowledge is inadequate both on pragmatic grounds (in that we could not survive on such a parsimonious basis) and because it presupposes that it is the world's job to conform to us (a biological impossibility) rather than the other way around: "We simply cannot reconstruct anything remotely resembling the body of information by which, perforce, we all live, on the basis of logically self-evident principle" (CP, 7). Living within a sea of testimony, we find that the very possibility of demonstrating anything itself rests on our having been initiated into the techniques and presuppositions of the testifying community. It is significant that the modern dogma mentioned previously—that we believe only that which we can prove—is called by Clark the Clifford Principle, after W. K. Clifford, the opponent to James's pragmatism. Clark's own view is closer to Hans Georg Gadamer's (or Edmund Burke's), to the effect that the onus of proof is on those who wish to subvert received wisdom, although Clark is quick to point out that such subversion is neither impossible nor irrational. This conservative view also has its problems, as we will see, but this much can be said in its favor: no one in religion, nor even in philosophy of religion, now hopes to deliver on the Cartesian promissory note that encouraged us to doubt everything so as to eventually build up a whole system of religious beliefs (CP, 7–9, 18).

Clark asks the following rhetorical questions:

> Am I to believe in my wife's fidelity and virtue, for example, only if those alleged characters have been subjected to destructive testing? Few of us entirely admire folklore heroes who "test" their wives! Am I to trust my fellow researcher's veracity only if I have arranged for her to be tempted into falsifying her results for financial or professional gain? . . . The very claim that only scientifically validated propositions may legitimately be believed is itself something that lies beyond scientific validation. If it is false we should obviously not believe it . . . but if it is true we should also not approve it. . . . In sum: the rules of scientific method—whatever they may be—no more define reality than the rules of legal evidence. Many undoubted truths may not be admitted in court; many equally clear truths cannot be the object of scientific reason. . . . They transcend the little provinces of human meaning that we delimit as scientific. (CP, 12–13)

The methodology at work here is meant to apply not only to the understanding of religion, but also to the understanding of animals. For example, those who fail to admit that animals feel pain, because it has not been "scientifically" proven that they do, demonstrate a prejudice by insisting that they are entitled to assume that animals do not feel pain even though this belief is equally indemonstrable by science. Richard Rorty, for example, suggests that there are no factual issues at all involved in the determination of who "has feelings." However, a being who screams or twitches when poked with a sharp object gives us evidence of *something*; compare Rorty's view that "having feelings" can be attributed to a being solely on the basis of its potential for membership in *our* linguistic community. As in religion, in the consideration of animals some people exhibit a myopic refusal to admit the existence of a world larger than the society of human beings (cp, 13). That is, a dogmatic *human*ism is equally objectionable to theists and to those who think that animals deserve moral respect.

It is certainly true that some traditional beliefs and practices (especially some beliefs and practices regarding animals) come to seem false; hence even Clark admits that not all "well-established" beliefs are true:

> But it does not follow that long-established beliefs and practices have no greater claim on our practical and theoretical allegiance than newly minted ones. They have the signal advantage that they are there, that their ramifications have, to some extent, been explored, that we have some idea of what they really amount to. Old doctrines are not true merely because they are old, any more than new ones are true because they are new: but it is not absurd to suggest that the old ones have our prior allegiance, that they do not need to establish themselves on just the same terms as new theories, that they have, as it were, the benefit of the doubt. . . . Why should it not be true both that we have lost a great deal of what our predecessors knew, and that we are beginning to find out things that they did not? (cp, 14–15)

Clark's view is precisely that defended by Josiah Royce:

> Whenever I have most carefully revised my moral standards, I am always able to see . . . that at best I have been finding out, in some new light, the true meaning that was latent in old traditions. . . . Revision does not mean mere destruction. . . . Let us bury the natural body of tradition. What we want is its glorified body and its immortal soul.[1]

There is considerable skepticism on Clark's part as to whether there are very many significant truths about life that have been noticed for the first time in the last hundred years, after millions of years of growth and exploration. Our perception, affection, and anticipation were in the making throughout the evolutionary ages, an inheritance that makes it possible today to turn on lights and replace fuses even if some of us cannot understand the principles of electricity. It would be odd to claim that someone was a normal human being even if that person did not know to remove his or her hand from a hot object, yet it is quite normal to claim ignorance of metaphysical or scientific truths (CP, 16, 18). Because the roots of reason lie in faith, Clark's position on religion can legitimately be called, as Fergus Kerr claims, an *ethics* of belief or an elaboration of the values implied in our beliefs. That is, in Clark we find an imaginative alternative to the "austere climate of tight-lipped rigour" preferred by most other philosophers in the analytic tradition.[2]

The similarities between Clark and Gadamer or Burke also obtain when he is compared to W. B. Yeats or John Henry Newman. With Yeats he agrees that one should believe whatever has been believed in all countries and periods, and reject any part of it only after much evidence; and with Newman he agrees that we should *begin* by believing everything that is passed down to us from tradition.[3] Clark is serious in his claim that this is where we should begin but not end. Interpretation, he thinks, even interpretation of well-known classics, is, in a way, a type of re-creation. Although we may not be able to have interpretations which are dispassionate, we should be able to have interpretations in which we see things straight (AM, 6, 11). In our scholarly pursuits in religion we should purge

> ourselves of bias and dishonesty to achieve that lucid condition of which we catch elusive sight from afar. Someone who has not heard, half-heard the call of that distant divinity may find the chase inane, and for him all that follows can at best only be an example for sociological research, if he should bother. (AM, 10)

It is appropriate at this point to note that in order to understand Clark's thought well one needs to read a lot of it. For example, it is quite easy to criticize Clark's conservativism in *Civil Peace and Sacred Order* and in several of his articles as being too obsequious to the past, if these are seen in isolation from *Aristotle's Man*. The latter work has received the opposite criticism, to the effect that his appropriation of Aristotle is too "gutsy" and that his use of Aristotle includes some "extravagant ingredients."[4] Gerard Hughes is a bit more judicious. He claims that Clark's book is "irritating to read, but both a pleasure and a challenge to reread." The challenge is that in order to adequately criticize Clark one needs to articulate a whole "philosophy of life" in response to Clark's. Clark rejects the hermeneutical stance that exhibits a "studied literalism" regarding an ancient text like Aristotle's or like the Bible. Such a literalism, Clark thinks, is both impossible in principle and barren in practice. Hence (and herein can be found Clark's gutsiness), the interpretive philosopher re-creates not only his own Aristotle but his own self in the act of interpretation. This re-creation must, of course, be based on the text, but not on a simple exegesis on the models of Ross, Ackrill, or Hintikka. Clark offers a *speculative* view of the world *based* on Aristotle (both emphases are needed). Despite the fact that there is little in the way of traditional Aristotle scholarship in Clark, it is very hard to read him at any length without finding a citation of Aristotle ornamenting his prose. Furthermore, there are always premises and conclusions in Clark's work, but these are on such an enormous scale that they are often not noticed by scholars, as Hughes suggests.[5]

I. N. Robins does a fine job of isolating Clark's principles of interpretation regarding the past, whether that be the religious past or the (Aristotelian) philosophical past: (1) We can understand past philosophers only in terms of what makes sense to us; (2) We should often explain the meaning of philosophical positions in terms of what they later developed into (a delightfully Aristotelian view in its own right); (3) There is no one correct original system of Aristotle (or of Christianity, etc.) that we might recapture; and (4) Any interpretation of the past must be of value in the philosophical development of the interpreter. Once one comes to terms with these Clarkian principles, one is in a better position to tolerate his allusive suggestions, which are often intended more to provoke reflection than to expound or support argument.[6]

LANGUAGE

Integral to Clark's methodology as a philosopher is a conception of language as the central fact of human existence: everything we do and experience is suffused with language. Yet the chief error of humanity lies in thinking that words *capture* a reality, because events are always more than any words could say: "Words convey more than they say, and never say all that there is" (MR, 49). Not even true statements can provide every detail. Hence Clark in many ways thinks that poetic utterances are more accurate than legal or scientific utterances, because the poet is self-conscious of the fact that he creates or evokes a rich reality, whereas the lawyer or scientist may insist that he means nothing more than he has strictly said. In practice, however, scientific utterances do evoke extra meanings, as in Bohr's model of the atom, where it is claimed that atoms are in certain ways *like* solar systems, and it is not obvious that science could survive without these types of utterance (MR, 50).

Religious utterances are usually thought to be more like poetic utterances than like the supposed matter-of-fact utterances of science. In order for discourse to be not only poetic but also religious it must evoke an appropriate sort of emotion, an emotion that is often not evoked if the poetic splendor of religious language is translated or interpreted. Even abstract propositions in religion, say with respect to divine omniscience, are valued not so much for the precise truths they convey as for their moral and emotional influence. In actuality almost any discourse is unlike the merely "scientific." If our statements do not so much report as at least partially create or evoke their own realities, however, then some philosophers will no doubt become relativists. Clark's theory, by way of contrast, is that although the truth to which we approximate is not wholly extralinguistic, it is at least partially so. The world within which human minds take shape is already suffused with order (MR, 51–52). Clark claims the following regarding the "anti-realist"—that is, the relativist:

> The difficulties we experience in saying what it is for religious utterances to be true are matched by more general difficulties, and that we cannot take it for granted that we have any clear cases where the truth of a statement rests simply on its "correspondence" with an extra-linguistic reality. In practice all statements that are labelled "true" are so labelled simply as being, in the context, the right thing to say, the usable formula, the helpful and inspiring rule. Our failure to find any way of understanding how a statement might "correspond" to an extra-linguistic reality, as a mirror-image "corresponds" to its original, has led some thinkers down the anti-realist road. But even the most sanguine anti-realist will concede that words are not the world, that changing the way we speak of things does not change the way things *are*. (MR, 53)

Antirealism, as Clark uses the term, is an extreme type of magic, in that for the antirealist "the way things are" consists solely of how we speak of them. If this is true, then changing the way we speak of things ought to (magically) change the things. What is obviously true in some cases (as that this piece of paper is worth five apples if enough people say it is) the magician/antirealist

16

takes to be true of everything. By way of contrast, Clark is only partly a magician. As an Anglican he does not think that it is *only* because people say that a wafer is the Christ that it is so, even if it is largely the case that there is *something* magical about (Searlian) ceremonies that make husband and wife or that transfer property. The strange magics found in exotic cultures should not occlude our vision of our own magics. That is, there are magical roots to many "facts" in Western religion and culture as in the above examples. The point I am trying to make is that for Clark it is not merely the "soft facts" in religion and philosophy (e.g., that courage is a virtue) that have a magical component (MR, 53–54).

Even "science" and "scholarship" are magical in effect, because what the intellectual elite say tends to make current thought and practice, whether these are in conflict with reality or not, seem obvious and natural. In the final analysis, however, Clark's position is that whereas some particular "facts" may be revealed as cultural artifacts, a generalized antirealism or relativism is defective on pragmatic grounds because if there is no extralinguistic reality, and we can change what is real merely by changing the way we speak, then there is no guarantee that it will not be an Orwellian tyrant who will fix the future. In other words, relativists should not assume that if everyone were a relativist then an open society would ensue (MR, 54–55).

The partial magicalism/relativism/antirealism that Clark adopts consists of: (1) the rejection of the notion that *anything* is as it is, whether we like it or not; and (2) the rejection of relativism as an absolute truth, because if it is true then there is at least one truth that does not depend on us, and so it is false. The upshot of this latter rejection is that Wittgensteinian fideists, who have made a momentary alliance with the extreme magicians, have contradicted themselves by defending both the brash assertion of the will to control all things by the way we speak of them and (hubris-hating) piety (MR, 56).

Far more accurate than the attribution of Orphic abilities to human beings, abilities whereby speaking about something brings it to life, is the attribution of such abilities to God. According to the biblical narrative of creation, God *said* that there should be light, and there was. Artificial and logically exact languages of human beings aspire to an accuracy which, if there is a God, only God could have. We know that "a cabbage" is not a cabbage, but God's speech has exactly this effect. One of the goals of religious believers is to find out what God has said, an effort that is usually thought to be exhausted by ritual or prophecy. But science also, when it describes the world as accurately as possible, gives us a vicarious experience of divine speech and ordering of the world. Even without direct, divine revelation, we cannot be debarred from an understanding of the traces of divine speech manifest in the natural world if we carefully scrutinize that natural world (MR, 57–58).

Science is not the sole interpreter of divine speech, however. Clark puts ritual and prophecy on an equal footing with science in this regard. By prophecy he means the gift of tongues or glossolalia, which relies neither on ritual nor on scientific reason. Speaking a language given to one by God, he thinks (and apparently Clark speaks here from personal experience), does not involve a hysterical loss of self-control, because such a language often exhibits a faint resemblance to known languages. No apologia on Clark's part will convince most contemporary philosophers that the "gift" of tongues should be taken seriously. It should be noted, however, that Clark's view here is consistent with his belief that words do not really capture the world in some sort of one-to-one correspondence. To state the forms of things accurately we sometimes need a poetic or religious (in this case, Pentecostal) language:

> If what matters in religious utterance is simply the awakening in us of a love and awe directed at the rationally incomprehensible Beginning, the proper speech may well be deliberately nonsensical. (MR, 60)

The elusiveness of deity noticed by Clark has very often been dealt with either through negation or through discourse about God in strictly abstract terms, terms that leave the concrete nature of God unexplained and perhaps inexplicable. That is, it is one thing to know *that* God exists, another to claim to know *how* God exists with omniscience, omnipresence, and so on. To merely say that God exists is an abstract claim that leaves unspecified what the divine actuality is like qualitatively at any particular moment. Regarding divine actuality our literal descriptions are always false, yet from this fact the conclusion is rarely drawn that we should keep quiet about God. Despite the fact that we do not have a language even about everyday things which can do full justice to a realistic metaphysics, we still use such language all the time to warn, reprove, and chat; likewise, it makes sense to continue to talk about God, even if such talk sometimes misleads us (MR, 60–62).

The inadequacies of religious language are less of a problem for Clark than they would be for many thinkers, and this due to what we have seen to be Clark's peculiar version of pragmatism. The best avenue to the divine consists of the life well lived; our goal should therefore primarily be the Jamesian one of service and only secondarily the desire to intellectually take hold of divinity. This desire is precisely what Buddhists have tried to overcome altogether. Clark's pragmatism (and his Buddhism) is peculiar in that it is integrally connected with his conservativism:

> We come as close as we may to an appreciation of the One by participating in the religious tradition, by using the words and following the commands laid down for us. We are always in danger on two sides: on the one hand, we may slip away from the proper traditional speech and come to speak of things not as God would have us speak but as our desires and prejudices prompt us; on the other, we may forget that the speech ordained for us is not itself the One, but only our best pointer. (MR, 64)

An essential part of the tradition that Clark wishes to preserve in the Abrahamic religions is the religious truth found in the Bible. Yet the written word is vulnerable to readers, as Plato indicates in the *Phaedrus*, because books cannot respond to the reader's questions. Authors are often baffled by the blatant misreadings of their work, hence Clark thinks it important to remind us that "to read anything with decent openness is to be changed a little, even if it is only to see that some possible world is not for us" (MR, 65). The biblical texts are a bit like Platonic forms because they can be copied or interpreted in many ways, most of which are predictably defective in some manner or other. Only rarely will a critic understand the text better than the author. It should be emphasized that Clark is not encouraging us to consult the Bible as an oracle, as some people have read Virgil or the Book of Changes. Rather, he is alerting us to the fact that to interpret the Bible discursively is not necessarily to abandon a reverential awe before the text (MR, 65–67).

The goal of pious biblical interpretation is to gain an occasional insight. Clark isolates at least two ways in which these insights can receive metaphysical backing. In one interpretation, they are nonempirical, neoplatonic, or Jungian archetypes; in the other, less radical, view, they are tendencies in conspecifics to respond in similar ways to similar experiences. Although Jung himself wavered between these two interpretations, Clark prefers the first, though not to the exclusion of the second. Insightful biblical scholars are not threatened by the attempt to understand the *logos* through science, when science is conceived of as an effort to find the forms behind the phenomena. The important things to remember, however, are that: (1) there is never any exact "correspondence" between human theory and reality, even if our most penetrating access to reality comes through theory; and (2) there is no scientific demonstration that does not rest on strictly indemonstrable principles, as in Einstein's belief that the one unintelligible fact about the universe is that it is intelligible. Hence, in Clark's view it makes sense to say that not only does science not contradict religion, it requires religion (MR, 68–71).

METAPHYSICAL THEISM

Clark can easily be misinterpreted here. His view tends toward fideism without falling headlong into it. Just as there is a place for science within a religious view of the world, so also there is a place for the traditional arguments for the existence of God, as long as these are not assumed to provide the core of religious belief and are not abstracted away completely from religious prayer and practice. Although only a few religious believers have ever approached religion from some perspective outside the complex of ritual and personal devotion, it would be odd if religious tradition had no rational explanation of the world to offer; hence the need for arguments for the existence of God and for the explanatory function of creeds. These arguments, especially the argument that suggests that the world has a designer, provide for religion the helpful function of moving from local to global explanation, a move that signals a reduced appeal to miracles. Unsophisticated believers use the gods to explain particular events, especially odd ones, in nature. More sophisticated believers invoke God to explain the whole system of nature. That is, Clark is critical of those theologians who have retreated altogether from rational arguments for the existence of God and from global claims. Those who have abandoned all metaphysical pretensions and all attempts to explain the world through religion would reduce religion to a mere coping mechanism with which to negotiate our way through a frightening world. While this is certainly one of the purposes of religion, Clark believes, it should not be considered its only one (MR, 122–24).

The chief contribution that Clark makes to a contemporary formulation of the argument from design is to point out that the following two key premises in the argument are in danger of contradicting each other: (1) signs of goal-directed order occur only as a result of creative intelligence (as in a watch); and (2) signs of goal-directed order occur in the absence of a detectable, finite intelligence (as in a cardiovascular system). Clark agrees that from these premises we should conclude that there is a nonfinite (or better, nonfragmentary, in that God in *some* sense must be finite in order to relate to particular creatures here and now) creative intelligence at work. Yet the apparent contradiction must be resolved, a resolution that hinges on the realization that we do not always experience goal-directedness in culture or in nature, but when we do there can be no plausible way to account for it short of some governing intelligence (MR, 125).

Many biologists have unwittingly confirmed this realization by abandoning explanation in terms of final causes precisely because they thought it committed them to belief in divine providence. Clark's agreement with these biologists is a qualified one, however. Consider that Aristotle's teleological explanations did not commit him to providential design. Our allegiance to teleological explanation does not in itself entail a belief in a creative God, in that

> It may simply be that this is the sort of universe that does naturally exist, as being the one that most effectively sustains itself. Other, non-self-sustaining universes may, as it were, have emerged by the million from the happy nothing, but been lost too soon for consciousness. Our world is the least self-sustaining universe that can sustain conscious life. (MR, 126–27)

What makes the argument from design work is that in order to explain the universe *with beings like us in it* we need to avail ourselves of the divine as an explanatory hypothesis. Our very notion of causality derives from our experience of volition because the only true causes intimately known to us are our own wills, and we know that we did not will conscious beings into existence.

Thus, even though religion has rarely been adopted simply because of its abstract explanatory hypotheses, it does not follow that there are no distinctive explanatory theses in religion (MR, 129). Nor does it follow from the presence of rational arguments for God in religion that sacred texts are epiphenomenal fifth wheels. These texts are those that have struck generations as being crucial for an understanding of religion:

> There is never likely to be any contradiction between "scientific" and "religious" understanding. Science, on this account, seeks only regularities and the cosmic grammar: religion seeks to read the text, guided by the conviction that nothing will in the end be merely accidental. (MR, 132)

Clark's theodicy, as we will see, contains a partial retreat from this claim in the sense that some (painful) events *are* accidental. The point to be made here, however, is that by reading a sacred text correctly (which does not entail that we have extratextual evidence regarding the author's intention) we come to learn a divine grammar as important as that found in nature or in rational arguments for God's existence.

Some will no doubt criticize Clark because by merely placing rational arguments within a larger religious whole, rather than making them the foundation of religion, he has played into the hands of those who defend the view which suggests that belief in God is analogous to belief in Santa Claus. Surprisingly, however, Clark does not take this view to be a canard; a belief in Santa Claus, in his view, does, in fact, "bear an uncomfortable resemblance to purported religious beliefs" (MR, 220). If Santa Claus is construed as a personification of parental love for children, then "to reject his existence is to deny that earthly parents love to give good gifts to their children" (MR, 221). If one asks why some children get gifts from Santa Claus while other children starve, Clark offers the following spiritualized (rather than allegorized) version of the Christmas story: we sometimes receive gifts that are gratuitous or that are due to no earthly artifice. That is, Santa Claus is not unrelated to real religion, in that traditional religion provides the context within which dreams of Santa Claus and of grace are checked (MR, 222).

Religious experience is an entry into the world of religious tradition; it consists of being seized by the inwardness of such tradition. Only those who misunderstand this inwardness go out of their way to insist that there is really no Aphrodite. For Clark, Aphrodite is a real presence or mood in the world, and religious tradition is built out of this and other presences. Some of the things that we think are unreal or dreams are in fact drowsy awakenings to the real (MR, 222–23). As we will see in a later chapter, Clark not only believes that religion is reasonable, but also that one particular metaphysical system (i.e., neoplatonism) best expresses this reasonableness. The phenomenal universe, he thinks, is the actualization in time of an ideal project that is best grasped as a cosmic community united in love (i.e., by Aphrodite). This neoplatonism places human beings on two levels, or better, it sees us in two different lights. There is the ordinary level of competitive individualism and material interest, on the one hand, and the "original" level of divine conciliarity, on the other:

One of the reasons for the "decline" of religious faith among the half-educated masses and the more self-opinionated intelligentsia is the failure of churchmen to understand and unfold the riches of their metaphysical heritage. Once religion is reduced to the level of sentimental moralism on the one hand, and equally sentimental ritualism on the other, it is hardly surprising that a lot of people lose interest. When it is understood that there is something to be said for a hard metaphysical theism we can at least get a sensible discussion going. (MR, 247)

As noted previously, one of the difficulties involved in getting contemporary thinkers interested in metaphysical theism lies in the wide acceptance of the following false dichotomy: either we adopt a rational point of view by refusing to believe *anything* without sufficient evidence, or we take the blind leap of faith which is historically dependent on certain versions of Protestantism. On this account both reason and faith are distorted. It is comparatively easy to say that to have a reason for believing in Q one must produce some other proposition P that implies the truth of Q, but Clark asks in an Aristotelian way about the status of P. If this is what is meant by rationality, then every belief, according to Clark, requires an infinite number of prior justifications. He is not convinced by one response given to this objection in modern philosophy, that there are some privileged beliefs that require no prior justification, such as the self-evident axioms of logic or the immediate pronouncements of sense experience. As is well known, "self-evident" does not mean "evident to all" (MR, 246–48).

Much more agreeable to Clark is the (Aristotelian) effort to found knowledge not on any privileged set of self-evident propositions but on the consensus reality of suffering humanity. That is, the rule that we should believe only what is "self-evident" or what can be inferred from what is self-evident must give way in practice to a more generous rule: that we should accept common discourse until we have reason to dismiss it. "We cannot get outside our whole system of belief in order to check it against reality, or find an unquestionable starting point from which we could rationally reconstruct that system" (MR, 249). By continuing to believe until there is reason to withhold belief we are not giving absolute support, he thinks, to conservative forces in society, although Clark is easily open to the charge that his procedure gives *something* of a carte blanche to reactionary forces in a society. In any event, Clark seems to think that our object of ridicule in contemporary society should not so much be a church's claim to infallibility as those who are entirely credulous of what they are told through the electronic media.

If rationalism is an unviable project, as Clark thinks it is, we are not reduced to arbitrary faith, as many Protestant thinkers have held. Rather, demonstration takes its beginnings from indemonstrable premises which are not the choice of any individual will. Clark has no qualms about claiming that these indemonstrable premises are apprehended through "faith," "intellectual intuition," or "*nous*," all of which amount to the same thing, he thinks, and all of which he differentiates from what are often claimed to be self-evident principles. Although we have no independent proof of the universe as rational, we have to think that it is in order to survive or in order to do science; this is the intellectual equivalent to the dictum in religion that wisdom begins in "fear of the Lord"—that is, in a respectful obedience to that which is. The fundamental premise of religion is also the fundamental premise of reason: that that which is has authority over us (MR, 250–52). Apollo, conceived of as deductive reasoning, has his place in religion, but he is not absolute in the cosmos. The pious, even though they are sometimes diverted into parodies of religion, are nonetheless willing to agree with Pascal's wager: when life is uncertain we must calculate our gains and losses. We stand to win a prize of happiness in religion that makes the gains of irreligion seem trivial. It is safer, he thinks, to assume that what we do will have profound repurcussions than not to assume this, for by assuming this we lose nothing (MR, 258–59).

The effort to move philosophy of religion from its home in Athens to its roots in Jerusalem (or better, to Alexandria, in that Clark is a neoplatonist) is a difficult one for some because it involves an admission of "faith." Yet even those who find their world an obvious one such as no rational being could reject may, in ages of social change or migration, find that what they hold most dear can intelligibly be denied. Rationalism in the generic sense of the term, which includes rationalism per se as well as empiricism, consists of the hope of securing some rationally indubitable principle even if this principle includes empirical claims. Once the impossibility of indubitability is noticed there is a temptation to run to the opposite, skeptical extreme. Of the two, Clark seems more at home with skepticism than with rationalism. Although the Skeptic (à la Sextus Empiricus) denies that there are "indicative signs," which purport to lead us from appearances to reality, he does admit that there are "suggestive signs," which provide us with that pragmatic evidence that is propaedeutic to a meaningful life, as when the appearance of smoke suggests fire (AJ, vi, 19, 21–23).

Although Clark is closer to skepticism than to rationalism, ultimately he rejects a strong version of skepticism in favor of his own brand of pragmatism/fideism:

> Our epistemological (and ethical) standards rest in the end on principles which can be proved neither by logical analysis nor by observation. These principles are accepted on faith alone. I have argued further that if we are to remain settled in our epistemological faith we must suppose that the universe is not one to which consciousness is alien, but one founded on the very patterns to be found also in our intellect. In theological language, the world was made by the same Logos that enlightens every intellectual creature. (AJ, 35)

Clark's epistemology obviously depends to a great extent on memory or on the Greek *aletheia*. Yet this epistemology is quite different from Heidegger's obscure attempt to sever one's tie to the usable past so as to recover (invent?) a more distant one:

> This perspective on truthfulness offers a contrast to the cult of sincerity which is given a sophisticated expression in Heidegger's association of *aletheia* with "lack of concealment." Sincerity of speech and manner is not the same as honesty, and it has traditionally been honesty, living in accordance with remembered laws, that has been esteemed. (AJ, 35)

If one desires the truth one has no alternative but to put one's faith in the reliability of our common intellect. Heidegger's mistake, according to Clark, consists (despite his followers' protests to the contrary) in his psychologizing tendency, in that he desires us to be *aletheis* in the sense of being out in the open or sincere. Clark doubts if honesty is the same thing as sincerity because the latter issues in the injunction to "say what you *really* think," an injunction which, in turn, usually produces either "aphasia or a jumble of half-digested slogans" (AJ, 36). *Aletheia*, Clark notes, is not a quality of people so much as it is a name for reality. "The intellectual enterprise is not directed towards self-expression, but to discovery" (AJ, 36). Yet even this emphasis on discovery (of the truth) can be perverted, say, if we develop a fetish for truths which serve no biological, ethical, or religious goal (AJ, 39).

Confidence in the power of human reason to find out the truth embodies an unadmitted metaphysical system, a system concerning which we can have objective knowledge, with "objectivity" referring, at the very least, to a faith in the possibility of agreement among separate individuals. This faith can be coherently maintained only if the world is founded, however imperfectly, on a principle of order. In effect, Clark is attempting here to use Peirce's "neglected" argument for the existence of God: the rapid progress in the sciences indicates the instinctive ability of human beings to invent new hypotheses capable of bearing the test of experience; this must mean that the human mind is in a deep way attuned to the nature of things, and our best explanation of this attunement is through a theistic hypothesis (AJ, 73).

One of the reasons why the attunement between human ability to know scientifically (admittedly, for Clark, a limited sort of knowing) and the knowability of the world is sometimes taken for granted is that we spend much of our time preoccupied with our own identities or with verbal quibbles. When words get in the way of knowing rather than help the effort to know, we are benefited by a deliberate, disciplined silence, a silence for which religion has several famous recipes. Language is essential for providing us with a range of concepts with which to articulate religious experience, but it cannot be used to develop didactic arguments that give us knowledge worth having because divine reality eludes such a use of argument. Clark notes the irony in those Westerners who criticize his supposed anti-intellectualism yet are fascinated with Buddhism, which is usually associated with the belief that enlightenment dawns when we stop trying to dichotomize. Similarly, some commentators try to make Buddhist doctrine intelligible by portraying it as a type of self-realization, yet criticize the Christian experience of salvation for being so. The point I am trying to make here is that Clark's careful demarcation of the epistemological limits of language and intellect receives support from sources far beyond Tertullian (AJ, 75–76, 79).

Newman was correct, Clark thinks, to say that argument can only lead to notional rather than real assent, and real assent is what we give to our everyday affairs regarding, for example, the existence of other minds:

> Those who find themselves unable to disbelieve in God, though they lack any conclusive argument for the truth of their belief, may at least take comfort that no one else is in much better a case by rational standards. (AJ, 87)

That is, it is not only the clinically depressed who live under a cloud, but also those who take philosophy a bit too seriously (AJ, 86–88).

Reason rests on faith, even with respect to items as fundamental as the law of contradiction, a law that rests on a faith that reality is indeed amenable to human discourse. For example, it is much more difficult to apply the law than to state it, because what appear to be a pair of contradictory statements may very well turn out to be compatible under some hitherto unimagined conditions. As before, Clifford's Rule (that one should never believe anything without adequate evidence), which in effect leads to extreme skepticism, must give way to something resembling Chisholm's Rule (that we should continue to believe what we "naturally" do until sound evidence turns up to the contrary); later I will examine in detail Clark's concept of natural belief. Here we should note that Clark bases his view on Aristotelian principles:

> It is the mark of reason to know that not all things can be proved by reason: "The starting point of reasoning is not reason itself but something greater. What then could be greater than rational knowledge or the human intellect but God?" (AJ, 94)[7]

Philo goes even further than Clark or Aristotle in claiming that the path of learning is actually *inferior* to knowing God through direct inspiration; Clark is claiming only that reason lies on the path of inspiration and that reason is not at variance with faith.

The importance of reason in Clark's philosophy becomes obvious when it is realized that it is a necessary, if not sufficient, condition for any real assent that is "proper." The ideal philosopher, for Clark, is something like the medieval saint-thinker, or better, like the ancient sage-thinker, whose profession grew out of the still more ancient craft of the inspired prophet-poet-sage:

> Philosophy is not the enemy of faith: if we permit it, it will lead us to that place from which we see that Love which moves the sun and other stars. (AJ, 95)

The position that Clark defends can be called an "ethics" of belief because the alternatives to this position have a difficult time accommodating, or explaining the origins of, any rules of evidence. For example, consistent materialists cannot claim that their arguments are ones that anyone *ought* to accept, because the rules of evidence that the materialist uses are not themselves established by appeal to material objects. To say that one does not care whether what one says is really true, or whether the rules of evidence by which one arrives at what one says are true, is to request that one's arguments not be taken seriously. To be "taken seriously," one needs to be up front about those elements one has taken on faith, elements that we ought to continue to take on faith unless there are countervailing reasons of prudence, charity, fidelity, consistency, or explanatory depth (AJ, 96, 99).

Sometimes we have to act on the assumption either that P is true or that not-P is true without having final grounds for dismissing either option, and when these praxic situations are considered we are in a position to appreciate Clark's own appreciation of James:

> If we believe that no bell in us tolls to let us know for certain when truth is in our grasp, then it seems a piece of idle fantasticality to preach so solemnly our duty of waiting for the bell.[8]

These bells are usually alleged to come in one of two modes of reasoning, induction and deduction, concerning which Clark says the following:

> Neither mode can get started without some initially established claims to serve either as the first premises of the deduction or as the explananda of the induction. Whence do they receive their warranty? Aristotle, not unreasonably, concluded that not everything can be a matter for proof, that some things are perceived or intuited without further evidence. Unfortunately, neither logical self-evidence nor indubitable sense-perception seems sufficient to generate the starting points of reasonable enquiry. (AJ, 100, 102–3)

Or again:

> The notion that we must take our start in epistemology from a set of unprovable but not self-evident propositions that are the ones "anyone would take for granted" either dissolves into social relativism of the familiar kind or else rests upon a strong notion of "the natural" which cannot be equated simply with "what happens." (AJ, 106)

It is Clark's task, therefore, to explicate what he means by "the natural," a task that is not as forlorn as the epigoni of G. E. Moore have assumed.

THE NATURAL

A preliminary consideration of Clark's concept of "the natural" would have to include a notice of the claim that to believe something is, strictly speaking, to believe that it is true. It is not coherent to say that "I believe *P*, but not that *P* is true." However,

> Epistemological rules cannot require us to believe all and only what is "proved by reason" or established by "the testimony of the senses," both because the rule is pragmatically self-refuting and because nothing worth believing can be proved by reason or the senses. At first sight it seems plausible to suggest that we are entitled to believe what comes *naturally*, a set of "basic beliefs," unless and until some argument is produced against theism. But there seems to be no agreed list of such basic beliefs. . . . Unless we have reason to believe that "*naturally* arising beliefs" are likely to be largely accurate, we can feel no reasoned confidence in the beliefs we find it *natural* to have. Pantheism, of course, is in practice the conviction that what comes *naturally* is right (and so leads to Protagorean relativism, that declares all appearances accurate). . . . *Naturalism* begets sceptical relativism. . . . If there is any escape we must find some acceptable guidance. (AJ, 108)

That is, Clark's Aristotelian defense of "the natural" does not commit him to an uncritical *natural*ism or to pantheism.

Myriad thoughts naturally pass before our mind's eye, so the question regarding what we are to believe amounts to the determination of which thoughts we will allow to grow. Belief consists more in the selection of naturally arising thoughts and imaginings ("an exhausting whirlwind") than in their creation: "Only those who have never attempted to organize their thoughts find it easy to believe that they themselves own those thoughts" (AJ, 109). There are many thoughts that "pop up" that we must, on reflection, refuse. One is enlightened when one knows how and when to engage in such a refusal without the help of a primer. In order to reach such a state of enlightenment one must go through a period of informal initiation, Clark thinks, a period that relies heavily on the notion of "ceremonial truth." For example, discourse itself, as we have seen, partially determines who is married to whom and whether a particular sexual relationship is adulterous. Clark holds that a religious statement partially derives its truth from the necessity of its affirmation if the particular religious tradition is to continue; hence the truth value of a religious claim is partially dependent on the tradition from which it arises. It is through a sort of habituation to ceremonial truth that we learn how to select appropriate natural thoughts and desires (AJ, 110, 112, 116).[9]

Ceremonial truth is not to be denigrated because it evokes sentiment, awe, and love, for even intellectual discourse about God, Clark thinks, has as its ultimate aims the same things. We cannot conceive what it is to *be* God; it is much easier to state that God is not subject to mortal limitations. From the difficulty of stating what the divine nature is in itself, however, Clark does not infer that religious discourse requires no intellectual effort. In effect, religious ceremony and intellectual efforts to understand God require each other, and naive believers should be reminded that they play into the hands of agnostics or atheists when they push the importance of religious ceremony to the point that it altogether crowds out rational reflection in religion (AJ, 183–84, 188).

The commitment on Clark's part to the role of reason in religion is obvious not only in his aforementioned use of the argument from design, but also in his defense of the ontological argument. His entry into the argument is idiosyncratic even on Clarkian standards. He asks why fantasies regarding Galactic Empires in science fiction "speak to our condition," on the one hand, and why they are beside the genuinely religious point, on the other. These fantasies take us beyond mundane concerns, and hence our interest in them, but these fantasies, like medieval belief in angelic hierarchies, are beside the point because their possible truth must be qualified by their possible falsehood (AJ, 190).

> No being that is of a kind that comes into existence, or that could exist only in some possible worlds, can be responsible for its own existence. . . . A contingent being, one that exists if and only if something else is the case, is not what theists are talking about. That being than which nothing more perfect can be conceived is not one whose existence and character is dependent on something else beyond its own control. A perfect being, if it exists at all, must exist "of necessity.". . . If the most perfect being does not exist it can only be because there is some flaw in the very concept, because it simply does not make sense. . . . Conversely, if it does make sense to speak of God (the One, the most perfect being), then God does exist. . . . This argument, of Anselm's, is, I believe, entirely valid, though it is open to determined atheists to deny that talk of God makes sense. What is not possible is to admit that such talk makes sense and yet deny that God, so understood, exists. The One towards whom theists look is not identical with any contingent being. (AJ, 191)

One does not need to give assent to the ontological argument in order to do mathematics, but, according to Clark, if there were no good reason to believe in God there would be no reason to expect that mathematical science would apply to the world. Whether or not God exists, or better, whether or not we can even conceive of the nonexistence of God, is not a matter of indifference in religion or in the intellectual life in general. Obviously there are some who can live life with equanimity without believing in God, but the question is whether their disbelief in God is intelligible (AJ, 196, 199, 200–201):

> But though there is something unintelligible about an obdurate rejection of the One, it is not difficult to understand the act, nor is it quite a contradiction in itself to say that the One is not to be revered. It is, of course, false. If the One is not to be revered, then nothing is or can be. . . . Those who have noticed the shadow of the One upon the world, who have had their attention drawn momentarily aside from mundane matters, who have glimpsed the Unborn and Indestructible of which even the best that they conceive is far too small, "must" respond by worship. . . . If the One, the Logos, and the Life are real then we have obligations that are not the product of our own legislation. (AJ, 202)

It should be reiterated that Clark's central point is the one emphasized in the epistle by St. James (and by the philosopher William James) to the effect that our moral and volitional responses are our best route to the recognition of divinity. However, "it is a refusal of the talents given us to refrain from intellectual examination of the world" (AJ, 204). Clark is bothered by such anodynes as "Life is a great mystery which we cannot understand." On the contrary,

> we are meant to understand as much as we possibly can; but "understanding" does not necessarily mean transforming the subject into matter for disinterested contemplation. (AJ, 204)

God *is* mysterious to Clark the neoplatonist, but, as Plotinus illustrated, it takes a great deal of intellectual effort to be fully cognizant of this fact.

Clark's use of the ontological argument is peculiar (I do not say "false" or "unproductive"), not only because he introduces it in contrast to domination by a Galactic Empire, but also because he connects it to his "epistemological argument" for theism, that is, to Peirce's neglected argument. Is it just by chance that the world is intelligible to us? Clark thinks not. The best explanation of this intelligibility, as we have seen, is provided by the postulate that the universe and the human mind both issued from the same cause, a God who exists necessarily. An obvious objection to this view would be that if human consciousness evolved successfully through nature, it is not surprising that it is capable of understanding this very nature. As we will see, however, Clark, despite his heavy dependence on a biological and naturalized view of human nature, denies the possibility that human consciousness could evolve. That is, Clark has a faith that the world is intelligible to us because we are created with the patterns of the world in us. Staudenbauer sums up well Clark's view:

> Knowledge cannot be grounded in self-evident or indubitable premises, therefore it "needs" the "prior belief" that the world is intelligible to the human mind. And this "intelligibility thesis" needs the Logos theory for its support. But the Logos theory is held by faith. Therefore knowledge "needs" or "rests on" faith.[10]

All "genuinely religious" believers hold the ontological argument, even if it is held in spite of themselves if they are not philosophers. All believers imply, Clark thinks, that God could not be contingent, because nothing that is worth being called "God" could depend for its existence on factors not of divine contrivance.[11] Ordinary religious believers are realists about God—that is, they are sure that God always exists, a constancy that, as before, assures the continued efficacy of realism in science. Intellectuals are often offended at being expected to believe the same things as nonintellectuals, a type of cultural snobbery that Clark rejects even if he is also opposed to the use of rhetoric to hide the absence of philosophical reasoning.[12]

Clark's use of inegalitarian reason to defend the egalitarian beliefs of ordinary religious believers fits well with his belief that the truth of an utterance in religion is made evident in its usefulness, its capacity to awaken and direct piety. Clark is on weaker ground, however, when responding to Don Cupitt's claim that to conceive of God in traditional terms like king, conqueror, or loving despot is defective. The weaknesses in Clark's views that stem from his traditionalism will be treated at least twice later in the book: (1) In the next chapter I will discuss in depth the problems involved in accepting in an uncritical way the traditional concept in the Abrahamic religions of God as an omnipotent monarch; and (2) Toward the end of the book I will criticize Clark's MacIntyre-like assumption that modern liberal society is only a collection of nomadic citizens who have banded together for mutual protection; it is not the case, I will claim, that rootlessness and romantic disaffection are the only alternatives to the traditional belief in God as eternal.[13]

I have no strong objection to Clark's view that the standard of correctness in theological utterance is not its recognizable correspondence with an objectively known reality (although Clark's use of the arguments for the existence of God indicates that such correspondence is not a matter of indifference to Clark or to any intellectual religious believer) but its capacity to awaken religious "spirit." Nor do I object to Clark's view that religion is largely a work of the imagination (as are law, morality, architecture, and science), in that it is not composed (à la positivism) of "plain" facts open to "plain" sight:

> Is it analytically true that all facts must be plain facts, or is it merely inductively certain (from an inspection of presently recognized truths) that they are? Neither alternative is satisfactory: the claim that all facts are plain amounts to no more than a covert recommendation to trust only those supposed truths that can be admitted without endangering our own perception of ourselves as masters of the world. . . . That "truth" itself is one we should have doubts about. . . . Our grasp of divine truths also comes through disciplined devotion. . . . To say that there are no laws not of "our" making is hardly to promote the virtues of sound reasoning.[14]

The house we inhabit is that of imagination, and the imaginings concerning which we have the greatest confidence are those that provide the best and/or simplest explanation of what is *already* agreed to be fact. These imaginings are "basic" in the sense that they are almost impossible to think away or destroy. A paradoxical feature of Clark's thought lies in his belief that our imaginings, even those essential to understand the already agreed to, need to be re-educated regarding "the great structures of traditional religion, the larger house." This paradox can be resolved, however, if we remember his aforementioned claim that any worthwhile preservation of a tradition must consist in a re-creation of that tradition. This re-creation presupposes a turning within rather than a trust in "outward things." Clark is well aware of the fact that in putting his point this way he runs the risk of being interpreted in social idealistic terms only (i.e., God is just what "we" say God is), or of being interpreted as defending ideas of God that are merely the effects of neurophysiological excitation. These mistaken interpretations, Clark thinks, are due to the assumption that the house of imagination is built by us. However, as we will see at the end of this book, human imagination originates in a "centre which is everywhere (and whose circumference is nowhere)." We are parts of a divine whole.[15]

It is not surprising to learn that the following view in Clark proceeds quite smoothly from one of the dominant themes in the history of spirituality: by turning within one learns that the individual is a part of a cosmic whole and that the individual is not only not the absolute creator of value but is in fact in need of release from the petty devils of rage, greed, and ennui. This interpenetration of the mesocosm and the cosmos as a whole confirms, in Clark's mind, the Buddhist insight that "salvation" has been here all along, although he puts this insight in theistic terms: "If God is not 'now' victorious then prophesies of His eventual success can only be more or less unreasonable hopes."[16] Likewise, our moral obligations are not gratuitous fictions that we have invented, but are obligations literally owed to (a cosmic) Someone. The God to whom these obligations are owed must at least be possible, and if possible then necessary, per the ontological argument. By denying this and other arguments for the existence of God the agnostic or atheist takes away the ground for moral obligation. As a consequence, it would make sense for the agnostic or atheist to say that moral duties are merely social constructs or neurophysiological excitations.[17] That is, in a rare agreement with Kant, Clark makes it clear that God is needed to make sense of our very strong inclination to believe that we are morally obligated.

We are alerted by Clark himself to his "radical conversion back to Christianity," to his three years of training for the nonstipendiary Scottish Episcopal priesthood, and to his baptism "in the Spirit," experiences that were instrumental in his finding "more truth in old-fashioned religion than good liberal intellectuals usually allow."[18] Yet Clark would agree that even if we start by believing in the truths of traditional religion, or if we are converted to believing in them, these truths must, if challenged, be defended. It is not my intention in this book to challenge the legitimacy of Clark's belief in the *existence* of God. Because the arguments for the existence of God play an ancillary role in Clark's philosophy, those who are primarily interested in *detailed* argumentation in favor of God's existence are better served by reading Charles Hartshorne, Richard Swinburne, or Alvin Plantinga. Rather, in the next chapter I will be interested in the connection between Clark's traditionalism and what he conceives to be the *mode* of God's existence. Further, in later chapters I will be concerned with the extent to which disbelief in God is the root of our confusion and degradation in epistemology as well as in morals. I can well understand that people who believe the world to be the product of blind and indifferent powers should think that it can be given value only by our wishes. . . . Only if the pattern of things is a pattern imprinted in our hearts—as of course the founding fathers of modern science, like Galileo, actually believed—can we rationally expect to find that pattern.[19]

In my critique of Clark's thought I will exhibit various sorts of response— for example, admiration regarding his stance on duties owed to animals, amusement regarding his belief in fairies, and skepticism regarding his critique of liberalism. Yet even where I disagree with Clark, I respect him as a profound, thought-provoking philosopher. His critique of liberalism, for example, is both bothersome and cleverly nuanced. One cannot lightly dismiss Clark even where one disagrees with him. Consider that he starts his critique from the phenomenologically accurate observation that undergraduate responses to moral issues are notoriously defective; to ask even bright students to justify their beliefs on experimentation on embryos, on eating animals, or on discrimination against foreigners is to invite rhetorical indulgence. This indulgence is a consequence, Clark thinks, of the modern dogmatic condemnation of all moral condemnations. This modern dogma is no idle theory for those who torture and rape children, for those who practice what strong relativists preach. Clark's "conservativism" is open-minded in the sense that he is willing to accept support even from Noam Chomsky to the effect that by accepting the presumption of legitimacy of debate on certain issues one has already lost one's humanity.[20]

Civil questions can be broken down into technical and ideological components. Problems in the former area cannot be solved by philosophic reason. It is the task of the philosopher, however, to elevate ideological disputes on how to respond to technical problems, data, and solutions to a level beyond mere rhetorical trickery or disengenuous manipulation. Rhetoric itself is not a disreputable craft; in fact, Clark thinks that philosophers would do well to assimilate philosophic discussion to artistic discussion by "telling a fresh story" regarding other approved stories. Regarding this fresh story, he says the following:

Part of our self-identity as philosophers has been the conviction that we will not be taken in, that we will follow the argument only where it leads, that we will not be caught out with ungrounded premises or credulous of received opinion. But it is obvious to us all that not even philosophy can be conducted on this basis.

We have to start from our received opinions, from the world of common day, and cannot ground all argument upon strictly indubitable dicta. In one sense, there are no such indubitabilia (not even that I exist); in another, there are far more than Descartes allowed (as that I have two hands, and that some acts are sins). . . . Some of the greatest of our philosophical texts are not strictly composed of arguments at all, moving by strict logic from clear premises to their conclusions: many of the texts we read with profit amount to rhetorical redescriptions of the world.[21]

CONCLUSION

As I have indicated, this first chapter has been designed to introduce Clark's approach to religion and to the major components of his philosophy. These components include the following: (1) a critique of too much as well as too little confidence in human reason; (2) an insistence that reason, properly understood, rests on faith; (3) a criterion for evaluating philosophical arguments that weighs not only an argument's consistency but also its range of application and efficacy; (4) an attempt at rapprochement between the natural and the sacred; (5) an attempt to understand the differences between poetic/religious and "scientific" uses of language; and (6) an attempt to resolve the tension between tradition in religion and politics, on the one hand, and speculative, path-blazing philosophy, on the other. My aim in the rest of this book is to analyze in detail and, where appropriate, to criticize these concepts.

CHAPTER 2

DIPOLAR THEISM

INTRODUCTION

The primary purpose of the previous chapter was to introduce many of the key ideas in Clark's philosophy; only secondarily was I concerned with showing the consistency of those ideas or with judging their adequacy. In the present chapter I would like to be a bit more critical, specifically with respect to the effect that the traditional Western view of God has had on Clark. His stance would seem to be that we should accept the traditional view until we find serious defects in it. I suggest that there are, in fact, defects in it, defects that are quite severe.

CONFLICTING EVIDENCE

As we have seen, Clark thinks that the standard arguments for God's existence are not to be taken seriously out of context: they are largely ways of pointing out connections between different ritual elements. Yet these arguments perform another function that is largely unnoticed by Clark, in that they say something not only about God's existence but also about God's actuality—that is, about the mode of God's existence. Clark in some sense accepts that God is an omnipotent being who is also omniscient in the sense that God knows in minute detail what will happen in the future; that God is eternal and nonmaterial in the sense that

God does not change as do material things; and that God is a supernatural Creator in the sense that God transcends the limitations found in natural creatures. Clark is certainly aware of the fact that Hindus will criticize this conception of God as having too strong a commitment to divine "otherness," and Clark makes an effort to avoid the view that God is *so* transcendent that we could not have a personal, friendly relationship with this supreme being. Yet Clark is much more worried that our view of God might be too friendly and too personal, a view whose defects are easily seen when believers expect God to have a hand in every twist and turn of their personal lives. In some sense, he thinks, God must be above the minor details (MR, 44, 112–13, 129).

As we will see, one reason why it is not wise to attribute to God too much of a hand in the particulars of the world is that God would then seem to be responsible for particular evils. Clark acknowledges "the powerful impulse" to seek a compromise solution to the debate between deism and "sectarianism," with the latter signifying the belief that God is responsible for the minute details of our lives:

> It may be that the right way forward is to take account of both impulses, but we should not equate that synthesis with a murky and unprincipled compromise—unprincipled because there is no way of defining just why the Creator should be concerned with nothing below a certain size. . . . Deism is the explanatory element of religion in its most emaciated form. . . . "Worshipping" such a one involves no service . . . but mere admiration of indifference. . . . In practice, of course, deists do not worship their inactive Creator, but abandon "religion" in favor of secular humanism or the like. . . . At the other, and perhaps more traditionally religious extreme, sectarian enthusiasm detects a divine meaning in the most seemingly trivial event. (MR, 130–31)

It seems that Clark is here leaning toward the sectarian end of the spectrum, an interpretation of Clark that is supported by the following quotation:

> To be convinced of God is to perceive as God perceives: not the "God's eye view" of cosmic aeons, in which individuals fall into insignificance, but the more divine outlook, for which nothing is accidental, no individual lost. Where this view differs from the typical sectarians', eager to see God in the downfall of an enemy or the success of a business venture, is that it does not contain God's purposes in ours. (MR, 133)

Yet the issue is not so simple. Regarding the split between immanentists and transcendentalists, which is not exactly the same split as that between sectarians and deists but is close to it, Clark says the following:

> Immanentists regard things as they are as just what they ought to be; transcendentalists who follow a conquering divinity think that they may eventually be as they ought to be. (MR, 141)

Here, if I understand Clark correctly, he sides with the transcendentalists.

On the one hand, Clark believes in a God of infinite personal love who values each particular being, a theme that is pervasive in the Abrahamic religions, especially Christianity, and peculiar to them. Judaism and Islam, however, are suspicious of Christianity's exaltation of a creature to godhead and of its need for an incarnation in order to insure that God knows us from within (MR, 228–29). Abrahamic believers, in general,

> find it difficult to maintain any sense of our own worth in a universe where no one else values us. . . . The Christian priest reported to have said "I know I exist, because I know God loves me" expressed the theistic answer to Descartes' erroneous claim to know that he existed because he indubitably thought. (MR, 230)

On the other hand, Clark offers the following qualified defense of divine immutability, transcendence, and eternity:

> Much religious and philosophical thought seems directed to this possibility: that the Divine is absolutely unchanging. . . . This doctrine, taken in abstraction from the whole religious field, results in paradoxical conclusions: a god who does not know anything of its creatures' experiences, and is never affected by them. Such a being is . . . far beyond or below anything we can conceive to be personal. . . . Even this doctrine is not without religious merit, but it is as well to remember that the timelessness and changelessness of the Divine are religious notions, to be understood within the context of prayer and worship. Changelessness is a matter of absolute fidelity and reliability rather than simply never being different, in any respect, from one moment to another. "Timelessness" rather connotes the irrelevance of period, age or date to God: He has no special time any more than He has any special place. (MR, 242)

The family resemblance between the deism-sectarianism contrast and the divine transcendence-divine immanence contrast extends to the timeless deity-changing deity contrast (sometimes misrepresented as a contrast between Hellenic and Hebraic conceptions) and the God the Father-God the Son contrast. Clark's judicious desire to save the phenomena of religion is exhibited in his attempt to preserve *both* the timeless aspects of deity (God as infinite, eternal, and transcendent) and the "in time" aspects of deity (God as finite and immanent, so as to be responsive). I have no quibble with Clark's desire to have both—indeed, I think it counts in his favor that he is, in some sense, a dipolar theist—but I think he should be criticized for: (1) eschewing polar equality in his dipolar theism by leaning too far in the direction of divine transcendence; and (2) assuming that these two poles cannot be shown to be rationally compatible, but must be counted as constituting a paradox (MR, 245). These two criticisms will be my foci in the remainder of this chapter. That is, I will try to show that the process philosophies of A. N. Whitehead and Charles Hartshorne can help to bring together these two poles without paradox.[1]

At times Clark comes close to an adequate resolution of this "paradox," for example when he invokes Aristotle in the following way:

> The good man and the man who sees the world as it is are the same, for to see the world as it is is to see the form within the material. . . . Aristotle's mysticism, his reliance on the intuition of the divine, differs from some accounts of more overtly mystical thinkers in that he recognizes the reality of change and development. . . . The principles of being are evidenced over time. (AM, 200)

As I will argue, I am not convinced that Clark has interpreted Aristotle correctly here. Yet I think that Clark is on the right track in suggesting that God's "timelessness" consists not in a Boethian *totum simul* but in the ability to exist through *all* of time, as opposed to our inability to do so.

For Clark there are many important ideals in life that we cannot unite but must preserve. Hence, regarding God the greater danger is not that we will err by trying to preserve all of the complex concepts attributable to deity, but rather that we would present a "narrow and one-sided" view of God if we gave up altogether on the attempt to preserve complexity.[2] When Clark tries to bring together these complex features, however, he expends very little effort to render them consistent; he is more than willing to rest content with the claim that "genuine religion rests in awe and obedience" (AJ, 185):

Of God Himself we can say nothing, even that He exists. . . . But if that [awe
and obedience] is the proper response it is inevitable that some images will be
appropriate, some not. . . . To be inscrutable, dispassionate, impassible, changeless, and without particular nature is, for creatures, to be something less than
human, less than mammalian. What is meant in saying that God is these things
[is] to deny that any image is His equal. (AJ, 186)

This quotation exhibits both Clark's refusal to render compatible the two poles
in his own dipolar theism and his preference for the changeless pole. Two routes
are approved by Clark: the ineffable route that looks toward the transcendent
One, and the route to the divine through the Logos, the pattern that the One
eternally begets. Yet because we cannot get to the One directly, the Logos is, in
effect, God for us (AJ, 187).

There is an interpretation of an ancient Greek pattern, due largely to Plato's
Phaedo, that stresses the radical separation of the divine from the phenomenal
realm of our experience; this separation is opposed by a Hellenistic pattern that
consists of a greater degree of divine immanence. Yet Clark is quick to point out
that by the time of the neoplatonists there was a perceived need to return to an
emphasis on divine transcendence, as in Philo's belief that Abraham followed
his vocation precisely by abandoning the Chaldaean identification of the visible
world with God. Both the Chaldaean and the Abrahamic views are somewhat
compelling; we are indeed "at home" in the world, but we will not be at home
in it forever (CP, 163, 165):

A merely natural and uncontentious God offers no standard from which to reject
the way things sometimes are. A merely ideal or trans-natural God is unattain-
able. (CP, 168)

DIPOLAR THEISM

It will be to our advantage to be as clear as we can on what we mean by the term
"God." In this effort we will be able to see more clearly the strengths and weaknesses of Clark's view of God, a view that lies between a traditional, monopolar
view and a process, dipolar view. I will use the term "God" to refer to the
supremely excellent or all-worshipful being. A debt to St. Anselm is evident in
this preliminary definition. It closely resembles St. Anselm's "that than which
no greater can be conceived."

The ontological argument is not what is at stake here. Even if the argument fails, which both Clark and I would doubt, the preliminary definition of God as the supremely excellent being, the all-worshipful being, or the greatest conceivable being seems unobjectionable. To say that God can be defined in these ways still leaves open the possibility that God is even more excellent or worshipful than our ability to conceive. This allows me to avoid objections from traditional theists, mystics, or Clark who might fear that by defining God I am limiting God to "merely" human language. I am simply suggesting that when we think of God we must be thinking of a being who surpasses all others, or else we are not thinking of God. Even the atheist or agnostic would admit this much. When the atheist says, "There is no God," he is denying that a supremely excellent, all-worshipful, greatest conceivable being exists.

The excellent-inferior contrast is the truly invidious contrast when applied to God.[3] If to be invidious is to be injurious, then this contrast is the most invidious one of all when both terms are applied to God, because God is only excellent. God is inferior in no way. Period. To suggest that God is in some small way inferior to some other being is no longer to speak about God but about some being that is not supremely excellent, all-worshipful, or the greatest conceivable. The dipolar theist's major criticism of traditional theism is that it has assumed that all contrasts, or most of them, when applied to God are at least somewhat invidious, as in Clark's preference for God as unchanging.

Let us assume that God exists. What attributes does God possess? Consider the following two columns of attributes in polar contrast to each other:

one	many
being	becoming
activity	passivity
permanence	change
necessity	contingency
self-sufficient	dependent
actual	potential
absolute	relative
abstract	concrete

Traditional theism tends toward oversimplification. It is comparatively easy to say, "God is strong rather than weak, so in all relations God is active, not passive." In each case, the traditional theist decides which member of the contrasting pair is good (on the left), then attributes it to God, while wholly denying the contrasting term (on the right). Hence God is one but not many, permanent but not changing, and so on. This leads to what Hartshorne calls the monopolar prejudice. Monopolarity is common to both traditional Western theism and pantheism, with the major difference between the two being the fact that traditional theism admits the reality of plurality, potentiality, and becoming as a secondary form of existence, "outside" God (on the right), whereas in pantheism God includes all reality within itself. Common to both traditional theism and pantheism is the belief that the categorical contrasts listed above are invidious. The dilemma these two positions face is that either the deity is only one constituent of the whole (traditional theism)—a view that Clark *should*, given his belief in the World Soul, find anathema—or else the alleged inferior pole in each contrast (on the right) is illusory (pantheism).

However, this dilemma is artificial. It is produced by the assumption that excellence is found by separating and purifying one pole (on the left) and denigrating the other (on the right). That this is not the case can be seen by analyzing some of the attributes in the right-hand column. At least since St. Augustine, traditional theists (though perhaps not Clark) have been convinced that God's eternity means not that God endures through all time, but that God is outside of time altogether, and is not, cannot be receptive to temporal change. St. Thomas Aquinas (following Aristotle, who was, it should be noted, the greatest predecessor to traditional theism) identified God as unmoved. Yet both activity and passivity can be either good or bad. Good passivity is likely to be called sensitivity, responsiveness, adaptability, sympathy, and the like. Insufficiently subtle or defective passivity is called wooden inflexibility, mulish stubbornness, inadaptability, unresponsiveness, and the like. "Passivity" per se refers to the way in which an individual's activity takes account of, and renders itself appropriate to, the activities of others.[4] To deny God passivity altogether is to deny God those aspects of passivity that are excellences. Or, put another way, to altogether deny God the ability to change does avoid fickleness, but at the expense of the ability to lovingly react to the suffering of others, whether human or animal.

The terms on the left side also have both good and bad aspects. Oneness can mean wholeness, but also it can mean monotony or triviality. Actuality can mean definiteness, or it can mean nonrelatedness to others. What happens to divine love when God, according to St. Thomas, is claimed to be *pure* actuality? God ends up loving the world, but is not intrinsically related to it, whatever sort of love that may be. Self-sufficiency can, at times, be selfishness.

43

The trick when thinking of God is to attribute to God all excellences (left and right sides together) and not to attribute to God any inferiorities (right or left sides). In short, excellent-inferior, knowledge-ignorance, or good-evil are invidious contrasts; but one-many, being-becoming, and the like are noninvidious contrasts. Evil is not a category and hence it cannot be attributed to God. It is not a category because it is not universal, and it is not universal because animals cannot commit it, even if they can be its victims. That is, both animals and God can feel evil but they cannot commit it, God because of the supreme goodness in the divine nature, animals because of their ignorance of moral principles.[5]

Within each pole of a noninvidious contrast (for example, permanence-change), there are invidious or injurious elements (inferior permanence or inferior change), but also noninvidious, good elements (excellent permanence or excellent change). The dipolar, process theist does not believe in two gods, one unified and the other plural. Rather, he believes that what are often thought to be contraries are really mutually interdependent correlatives, as Hartshorne indicates:

> The good as we know it is unity-in-variety or variety-in-unity; if the variety overbalances, we have chaos or discord; if the unity, we have monotony or triviality.[6]

Supreme excellence, to be truly so, must somehow be able to integrate all the complexity there is in the world into itself as one spiritual whole, as Clark would agree. The word "must" indicates divine necessity, along with God's essence, which is to necessarily exist. The word "complexity" indicates the contingency that affects God through decisions made by creatures. In the traditional theistic view, however, God is identified solely with the stony immobility of the absolute, implying nonrelatedness to the world. God's abstract nature, God's being, may in a way escape from the temporal flux, but a living God is related to the world of becoming, which entails a divine becoming as well, if the world in some way is internally related to God. The traditional theist's alternative to this view suggests that all relationships to God are external to divinity, once again threatening not only God's love, but also God's nobility. A dog's being behind a particular rock affects the dog in certain ways, and thus this relation is an internal relation to the dog, but it does not affect the rock, whose relationship with the dog is external to the rock's nature.[7] Does this not show the superiority of canine consciousness, which is aware of the rock, to rocklike existence, which is unaware of the dog? Is it not therefore peculiar that God has been described solely in rocklike terms: pure actuality, permanence, having only external relations, unmoved, being and not becoming?

One may wonder at this point why traditional theism has been so popular among theists (including, *to a certain extent*, Clark) when it has so many defects. Hartshorne suggests at least four reasons, none of which establish the case for traditional, monopolar theism: (1) It is simpler to accept monopolarity than dipolarity; that is, it is simpler to accept one and reject the other of contrasting (or better, correlative, noninvidious) categories than to show how each, in its own appropriate fashion, applies to an aspect of the divine nature. Yet the simplicity of calling God "the absolute" can come back to haunt the traditional theist if absoluteness precludes relativity in the sense of internal relatedness to the world.

(2) If the decision to accept monopolarity has been made, it is simpler to identify God as the absolute than to identify God as the most relative. Yet this does not deny divine relatedness, nor that God, who loves all, would therefore have to be related to all, or to use a roughly synonymous term, be relative to all. God may well be the most relative of all as well as the most absolute of all, in the sense that, and to the extent that, both of these are excellences. Of course, God is absolute and is relative in different aspects of the divine nature.

(3) There are emotional considerations favoring divine permanence, as found in the longing to escape the risks and uncertainties of life. Yet even if these considerations obtain, they should not blind us to other emotional considerations, like those that give us the solace that comes from knowing that the outcome of our sufferings and volitions makes a difference in the divine life, which, if it is all-loving, will certainly not be unmoved by the suffering of creatures, even nonhuman creatures.

(4) Monopolarity is seen as more easily compatible with monotheism. Yet the innocent monotheistic contrast between the one and the many deals with God as an individual, not with the dogmatic claim that the divine individual itself cannot have parts or aspects of relatedness with the world.

In short, the divine being becomes, or the divine becoming is. God's being and becoming form a single reality, and there is no reason, as Clark suggests, that we must leave the two poles in a paradoxical state. As Hartshorne puts the point:

> There is no law of logic against attributing contrasting predicates to the same individual, provided they apply to diverse aspects of this individual.[8]

The remedy for "ontolatry," the worship of being, is not the contrary pole, "gignolatry," the worship of becoming:

> God is neither being as contrasted to becoming nor becoming as contrasted to being; but categorically supreme becoming in which there is a factor of categorically supreme being, as contrasted to inferior becoming, in which there is inferior being.[9]

In process theism the divine becoming is more ultimate than the divine being only for the reason that it is more inclusive, an inclusiveness that is essential to support Clark's defense of the World Soul, to be discussed in the last chapter. That is, to the extent that Clark adheres to traditional, monopolar theism he has a difficult time justifying his adherence to belief in God as the World Soul.

The process theism with which Clark sometimes flirts, and which I am defending through the thought of Hartshorne, is: (1) *dipolar*, because excellences are found on both sides of the previously mentioned contrasting categories (i.e., they are correlative and noninvidious); (2) a *neotraditional* theism, because it relies on the belief that the traditional theists (especially St. Anselm) were on the correct track when they described God as the supremely excellent, all-worshipful, greatest conceivable being, but the traditional theists did an insufficient job of thinking through the logic of perfection; (3) a process theism, because it sees the need for God to *become* in order for God to be called perfect, but not at the expense of God's always (i.e., permanently) *being* greater than all others; and (4) a theism that can be called *panentheism*, which literally means "all in God." God is neither completely removed from the world—that is, unmoved by it—as in traditional theism, nor completely identified with the world, as in pantheism. Rather, God is: (a) world-inclusive, in the sense that God cares for all the world, and all feelings in the world—especially suffering feelings—are felt by God; and (b) transcendent, in the sense that God is greater than any other being, especially because of God's love. Thus, we should reject the conception of God as an unmoved mover not knowing the moving world (Aristotle, I allege, contra Clark's interpretation of Aristotle); as the unmoved mover inconsistently knowing the moving world (traditional theism); and as the unmoved mover knowing an ultimately unmoving, or at least noncontingent, world (Stoics, Spinoza, pantheism).[10]

Two objections may be raised by the traditional theist that ought to be considered. To the objection that if God changed God would not be perfect, for if God were perfect there would be no need to change, there is this rather obvious reply: in order to be supremely excellent God must at any particular time be the greatest conceivable being, the all-worshipful being. At a later time, however, or in a situation where some creature that previously did not suffer now suffers, God has new opportunities to exhibit divine, supreme excellence. That is, God's perfection does not merely allow God to change, but requires God to change.[11]

The other objection might be that God is neither one nor many, neither actual nor potential, and so forth, because no human concept whatsoever applies to God literally or univocally, but at most analogically. The traditional theist would say, perhaps, that God is more unitary than unity, more actual than actuality, as these are humanly known. Yet one wonders how traditional theists, once they have admitted the insufficiency of human conceptions, can legitimately give a favored status to one side (the left side) of conceptual contrasts at the expense of the other. Why, if God is more simple than the one, is God not also more complex, in terms of relatedness to diverse actual occasions, than the many? Analogical predication and negative theology can just as easily fall victim to the monopolar prejudice as univocal predication. "To be agent and patient is in truth incomparably better than being either alone."[12] This is preeminently the case with God, and a human being is vastly more of an agent and patient than is an ape, which is more of both than a stone. Stones can neither talk nor listen, nor can they decide for others or appreciate others' decisions.

SACRED AND NATURAL HISTORY

Reading Clark requires a great deal of tolerance of his alternation between dipolar theism and traditional monopolarity. For example, he sometimes doubts the compatibility of natural and sacred history because natural events carry, of themselves, no moral; there is no sacred meaning in the facts of history as such because they are outside of deity (MR, 26–27). By stipulating that "natural history" excludes a sacred dimension, Clark is left with the Augustinian project of trying to explain how the natural and the supernatural interact, although Clark's solution to the problem is somewhat different from Augustine's:

Any natural history must leave divine purpose out of it. . . . Does it follow that to consider matters from the standpoint of naturalistic history is to deny the importance of the sacred dimension? It is not clear that it should. The sacredness of an event is not to be identified with its natural properties, any more than the sacredness of a sacred cow resides in her biological properties. . . . It is not entirely clear that ordinary historians should always be so ascetic. The idea that we ought to try to understand all human history "without affect," without forming any judgment of its significance and moral worth, is really nonsensical. To describe human beings as if they were no more than matter in motion . . . sacred history need not constitute a rival explanation for what has happened, but rather a different way of identifying what has. (MR, 28–29)

Sacred "history" (or better, sacred explanation) is not unreasonable, nor is it necessarily an offense to historical consciousness, according to Clark. This claim can make sense only from the perspective of dipolar theism, because an eternal God outside of history who guides or controls history is an offense to a truly historical point of view.

The view that Clark opposes is the following:

Natural history understands us as we are, quite ordinary primates with the gift of language and an easily disturbed psycho-social system. To understand that no one is particularly interested in us, that there is no vast conspiracy, that things are not arranged with us in mind (for good or ill)—these are the discoveries we need to make. Religion, as such, is a retreat to adolescent fantasy, the dream that there is someone who will "take us out of this. . . ." Happiness is knowing who we are, and that no one else much cares. (MR, 30–31)

Clark's response is that:

Those who argue like this cannot reasonably claim that the facts of history "require" this belief in any logical or scientific sense. Some of the suggestions that have been made about the genesis of religious feeling are indeed quite plausible, in general terms. . . . The assertion that the religious are immature because their attitudes are not unlike the paranoid depressive's could be met by the equally gratuitous assertion that the self-styled sane and irreligious are immature because they imagine that the universe makes sense. (MR, 31)

The way out of this dispute requires, at the very least, that we exhibit the intellectual humility found in the realization that our theories, including theories about the sacred, are fallible.

Clark rightly criticizes the view that the only legitimate stance for a modern mind to take is that true knowledge should be defined in opposition to religion and that the universe is a great, meaningless vacuity. Clark is correct that most defenders of this view are recognizably proselytizers, who often use the rhetorical tricks of religious apologists. The question is whether Clark can bridge the gap between sacred and natural history as easily as he thinks he can while intermittently leaning in the direction of traditional, monopolar theism. As Clark notes, an alliance has developed between proselytizing atheists and religious fundamentalists because each needs the other for continued existence. A more consistent defense, on Clark's part, of dipolar theism would make explicit the fact that he need not be drawn into this fruitless debate. As he puts the point, "Religious traditions do develop" (MR, 32–33).

The flirtation with process thought that Clark sometimes exhibits is evident when he argues for the logical impossibility of change *in the sense of* a passage from being into absolute nonbeing. Yet this Parmenidean position (defended as well by Bergson, Whitehead, and Hartshorne) is nonetheless compatible with change in the sense of passage from being into another sort of being, or from being into a relative state of nonbeing—that is, relative to the original state of being. The sense in which change is logically impossible should nonetheless make us recognize the paradoxical nature of beginnings and endings (MR, 37–38):

> It is not so much that rituals are a way of coping with the existential problem of boundary conditions, transactions and obviously opposed states of being. It is the rituals, the anomalies that create the opposition. It is because we have a ceremony called marriage that there is an opposition between being unmarried and being married. (MR, 39)

We could, for example, put the ritual markers for marriage elsewhere, just as baptism could be moved to the time of the first baby tooth to fall. The point Clark would want to make, I think, is that by being pushed headlong into dipolar theism he would be pushed too far into "rational religion." Although he views rational religion as a "noble cause," to push this cause too far is to take the "mysteries of religion" too lightly. The two poles in Clark's theism, with one receiving greater emphasis than the other, he prefers to leave in a paradoxical state, in that "the religious imagination is one that *desires* mysteries" (my emphasis). Religious believers do not

> always want to be told that the saying "This is my body" can be given intelligible sense: it is better that it be a mystery, something that both is and is not merely bread. (MR, 39)

The extent to which religious believers enjoy mystery varies. Some rituals (and religions) are almost ordinary, whereas others thrive on apparent absurdity. In many ways the sense of mystery is linked to the sense of history in a particular religion, as in seasonal rituals or rites of passage. Hence the particularities of a religious history can be abstracted away only at a great price. Clark thinks that a unified, worldwide religion is about as likely as the universal acceptance of Esperanto. As stated previously, sacred history can be conceived of as a dramatic version of, or a perspective on, some particular history. The interpenetration of the sacred and the natural in Clark can be understood best through a comparison with science. There is a notable distinction between "real life" and "real world" in Clark, with the former referring to the familiar efforts at making a living, paying a mortgage, and the like. The real world as described by the neoplatonists, however, may be entirely unfamiliar to those who are ensconced within real life. Of course, Clark does not think that subatomic particles are *really* the real world, but their distance from real life is instructive regarding the effort needed to adequately approach the religious constituents of the real world (MR, 40, 45). These constituents are far from real life, but they are no further from it than the scientific constituents of the real world.

At times Clark seems to prefer the particular sort of history found in the Abrahamic religions, where God oversees the epic drama of the cosmos; at other times he seems to prefer the Confucian sort of history wherein the universe is perpetually approximating or falling away from what is appropriate. In the latter sort of history God functions more as an immanent power than as a transcendent lord. Later we will consider Clark's controversial version of Aristotle's theism, which Clark allies with the Confucian sort of sacred history (MR, 140–41). This eclecticism is another version of Clark's own brand of dipolar theism. His eclecticism extends even as far as Aztec religion, which the first European witnesses took to be anathema because of the prevalent practice of human sacrifice. Not even this gruesome type of religiosity is a parody of religion, for Clark, however, in that it helps us to understand Christianity's more authentic version of repentance and self-sacrifice. It also helps us to understand better the divine self-giving whereby God's self-emptying takes the form of a finite being who is a fellow member of the human community (MR, 140–41, 162–64).

The *Logos* is a symbol, for Clark, of the self-finitization of the infinite and eternal, or better, of the self-immolation of the infinite. Clark is well aware of the fact that sacrifice is often a bloody business, as in the rule among the Greeks and Hebrews that no farm animal could be killed except in a "sacrifice." It may be the case that those who first killed animals on the altar assumed that the animals were being returned to the gods who gave them. The point to any sacrifice, bloody or otherwise, is not to secure favors from an egomaniacal tyrant but to share in the divine life, to enter into that divine "time" which is at least partially nonhistorical. Clark finds it noteworthy that the dogma regarding the Mass in Catholicism is that it is never a new sacrifice but a sharing in the one sacrifice of creation (MR, 165–66, 169).

This sharing in, or participation in, a wider divine identity that is self-giving will be treated in detail in the final chapter of this book. Here I want to emphasize the (largely nonrational) bridges in Clark's dipolar theism, among which are various sacrifices, including the Eucharist. This sacrifice in particular does not divide time in the way that marriage or baptism do; rather, it consists of an action performed in time that also purports to be outside of time. Clark is emphatic that nonbelievers (and some lukewarm believers) misunderstand eucharistic ritual if they see it entirely in this-worldly terms, as if religion itself were merely a matter of communal hymn singing:

> It may be as well sometimes to recall the merits of religious ritual, as an opening into a world that does not feed upon our current preoccupations. (MR, 170)

Of course, even astrology is founded on the conviction that time is not merely linear. There is something cyclic about ceremonial time, in the sense that religious ceremony, if it allows us to share in the life of God, also allows us to partially escape natural history, an "escape" that makes sense only against the background of a preference for divine eternity. If "astrology" refers to the making of predictions based on whether Jupiter is properly aligned with Mars, then it is obviously bunk. Yet, like belief in Santa Claus, astrological beliefs need not come in this debased form, as in the belief that the round of months and planetary cycles represents to us the fact that we are always walking around an eternal (or better, an everlasting, sempiternal) order. If enough qualifications are given we could even grant Marcus Aurelius's (and the author of Ecclesiastes') claim that a reasonably intelligent forty-year-old has seen the whole past and future of the universe.[13] The concept of cyclic or ceremonial time is also helpful in responding to severe antirealists, who hold that the past lasts only as long as the evidence for it does. Clark's view is that Caesar either had porridge or he did not, even if we will never know which. The past is what it is, even if past events are erratically, albeit conveniently at times, slipping out of effective reality. A divine knower, however, would not have such leakage (MR, 171–73).

Perhaps purgatory consists of the discovery of unrealized good and the memory of what is worth remembering, as is illustrated in Dante's belief that in purgatory one first drinks of forgetfulness and then of good remembrance. Or again, a link between the temporal and the eternal is established in the Eucharist when viewed as a transtemporal exchange; precise accidents matter less than the realization of the fact that we are all one body (MR, 174):

> But although the divine sacrifice gets further away in linear time, it is always just as present in the world of prayer. Religious error, correspondingly, comes in two forms: on the one hand, some devote themselves to what goes on in the world as we ordinarily conceive it, the world of linear history, and imagine that God's Kingdom is not yet established, or even that God needs our assistance [as in the writings of Nikos Kazantzakis]; on the other, some contemplate the eternal as a refuge from history. The first group gradually become indistinguishable from secular millenarians; the second are in retreat. (MR, 175)

Clark thinks it significant that medieval literature was more concerned with prayer than with social justice, with God as transcendent than with God as immanent. Clark is quite clear that he is, in this regard, a medievalist (or a defender of John of the Cross or of Buddhism), because of the emphasis placed in medieval prayer on humility and on a desire not to receive.[14] Even serious pagans, however, were convinced of the unwisdom of arrogant hubris. As before, Clark's rather conservative moral and political beliefs interpenetrate with his stance regarding dipolar theism.

By humility, however, Clark does not mean anything morbid. In fact, he notes that an individual's submission to God requires a real independence of mind and action:

Those who sacrifice themselves for others—in the popular sense—are slaves; those who sacrifice others to themselves are despots. . . . Any insistence on always being the one to "sacrifice" rather than accepting the other's service is recognizably egotistical, an arrogant assumption that the other has nothing to contribute. . . . Friendship—which is to say love purged of concupiscence (the desire to possess and dominate)—constitutes an Aristotelian middle path between slavery and despotism. It also serves as a model for genuine humility. . . . When religious tradition advises humility, it is not the sort of slavishness that cringes now in hope of gradually accumulating credit. . . . St. Francis's humility, his willingness (even his eagerness) to be "made a fool of," to be stripped of all social status and graces, was conjoined with a sense of being personally loved—not for anything he did (and might fail to do), but as a member by baptism and vocation of Christ's body. (MR, 176–77)

This divine inclusiveness, to be discussed later in conjunction with the World Soul, makes sense only if there is some integral connection between God and the world. Clarkian humility consists primarily of the realization that none of us is ultimate (MR, 178).

Becoming clear on the connection between humility and dipolar theism is important to Clark in order to reinforce his view that a traditionalist stance need not be unthinking, nor need it shy away from the possibility that it could become perverse if misused:

Religious "activists," so to call them, are often allied to atheistical reformers who desire the happiness and liberation of their chosen clientele (the oppressed masses, humankind or the natural world). Religious "ritualists" are often (accurately or not) perceived as conscious or unconscious allies of the great oppressors: if the business of religion lies elsewhere, the business of this world is left to earthly rulers. (MR, 239)

Hence, Clark is well aware of the dangers involved in religious ritualism, but in typical Clarkian fashion he is more worried about religious activism. Liberal piety does not expect an eternal God to make an end to this time, thus for this position the coming of God's kingdom is interpreted loosely to refer to an unending approximation to certain ideals. Liberal theologians or religious activists are a bit like those ancient Greek thinkers who assumed that the world would go on forever. Whereas Clark's view, which leans in the direction of divine eternality even as it admits the importance of divine infusion into the world of time, is, on this score, Hebraic, cataclysmic, or Augustinian. Just as we have a great deal of difficulty tracing back cosmic history before a certain point, Clark suggests that it should be equally difficult for us to escape the possibility that there will be a last moment beyond which there is no "afterwards" (MR, 240–41).

There is always a danger in interpreting Clark literally when he may, in fact, be pulling our legs. It may well be that he does not *really* believe in an end of time, but that he finds the concept useful in discussing how the "real world" can break in on time so as to bring about an

> end of weariness and boredom, the end of that process by which what we do becomes "past," over and done with, inaccessible and stale. . . . If this is what the end of time is to be, those who expect it may not be quite so much at odds with those who simply hope to make the best of our present world. (MR, 243–44)

These remarks help us to understand how Clark can, at times, try to reconcile his Aristotelianism with his Christianity. It takes a certain amount of time for a person to achieve *eudaimonia*; a much shorter amount of time for some other beings to achieve their respective *teloi*; and a much longer time for still others, as in certain cosmic changes.[15] What each thing is when fully developed is called its nature, although there are several routes along which an organism can grow to completion. Aristotle is not always the defender of *stasis*. For example, of Aristotle's ten categories, seven are either verb or adverb forms and only three are noun or adjective forms.[16] The importance of Aristotle for understanding Clark's conception of time becomes evident when Clark attributes the "A-theory" of time to Aristotle. McTaggart divided temporal properties into the A-series, which consists of past, present, and future, and the B-series, which consists of unchanging relationships like "earlier than" or "later than," as in the belief that the death of Socrates is timelessly before the death of Martin Luther King. The perpetually changing A-series, he thinks, is Aristotle's view and is a more fruitful series to use in the attempt to understand time; the B-series, as Clark correctly notes, is merely an abstraction from lived, temporal reality.

The question I would like to ask is whether Clark is also in favor of the A-series in the attempt to understand God. Here one can find conflicting evidence in Clark, or textual evidence that at least seems to conflict. Often Clark gives the impression that we need the B-series in order to talk about God, a series in which time is made up of "moments" timelessly "present." When Clark pushes the distinction between time and eternity he finds an unwitting ally in Bertrand Russell, who, at least at one stage in his career, viewed time as an unimportant and superficial characteristic of reality. Yet traditional assumptions still yield traditional problems. The problem Clark faces is that the B-series leads to fatalism. This problem could be avoided altogether if he offered a more careful defense of dipolar theism. As Clark notes, if X is inevitable there is nothing we can choose to do to change it (AM, 116–18). Still, at other times Clark stumbles into the trap that faces all attempts to reconcile a B-series with human freedom:

> At a more sophisticated level this fatalism may be rebutted: the mere fact that we have made *or will make* certain decisions does not mean that the decisions are fated. Where future event depends upon our will and not upon the inevitable consequences of present fact, our will is a factor in event. (AM, 118, my emphasis)

It is unclear why Clark thinks that his position here will be any more convincing than those offered by numerous other proponents of Boethian omniscience (despite Clark's sometime denial that he is a Boethian), that is, by those who are opponents to process theism.

If I understand Clark correctly, it is only when God is considered that Clark is tempted away from the A-series. His dominant view is put succinctly in these terms:

> What happens need not happen, that the difference between the expectable future and the actual future is not a function simply of our ignorance, but a real feature of reality. . . . What has been will always hereafter have been, without hope of alteration. What will be has not always been. . . . "*Fp* is true" is an inevitable truth only if *Fp* is inevitable in its own right: *Fp* cannot acquire inevitability from the ineluctability of present and past truth. . . . What matters is that past and future are asymmetrical; and not all possibilities in any given case are realized. (AM, 120)

The point I am urging is that Clark's dominant view of time (the A-series) works for God as well as for creatures. The pragmatic value of the A-series can be seen in the fact that on this view of time the problem of reconciling human freedom and divine omniscience shifts from frantic efforts to save the former to the careful effort to trim the latter. God can still be viewed as omniscient in the

A-series, but what it means to be omniscient is to know everything that is logically knowable: God can know in detail the past because it has actually happened; and God can know the present (actually the most recent past, per the demands of relativity physics) as it happens; but with respect to the future God can know only with probable assurance. A perfect knower knows past actualities as actual and future contingencies *in their contingency*. To claim that there is a being who knows a future contingency as already actualized is not to talk about an omniscient being but about a being who is ignorant of what "contingency" means. God's extraordinary memory of the past, cognizance of the "present," and awareness of the *best* probability estimates regarding the future certainly constitute a version of omniscience appropriate to the all-worshipful being.

Even if *Fp* turns out to have been true, there are some propositions that could not have been uttered until the subject had come into being. Yet there are other very abstract propositions that are universal in the sense that they never stop being true (as in the claim that something must exist because of the unintelligibility of sheer nonbeing). To admit this much, however, is not to admit to the B-theorist's "worship" of timeless truth. For Aristotle and, at times, for Clark, "the heavenly life, which contains all events in some sense, does not contain them in any Boethian *totum simul* (for not all events are simultaneous . . .)" (AM, 121–23).[17] Time as a (B-series) container is an abstraction of the human mind, according to the Aristotelian scheme of things, a scheme that pins its faith on the experience of the present world that exists as a fact with "continually realized possibilities of development" (AM, 124–25):

> The A-theory is an attempt to expound the actual structure of our lived reality, taking our judgements of irrevocability and possibility with due seriousness. The B-theory must hold that we are in practise systematically mistaken: the past is not prior to the future (except trivially). (AM, 126)

As before, however, Clark's commitment to A-theory is punctuated by flirtations with B-theory, flirtations that lead him to make the following odd distinction: although a B-theorist need not be a fatalist, he must be an (Augustinian?) determinist (AM, 128).

Although it is necessary that there be some future or other, no particular, detailed configuration of events in the future is necessary. Because past-tensed statements have been made true by the course of events, the past is in a strong sense necessary: what is done cannot be undone. For Aristotle and Clark past-tensed statements are not made true solely by the present evidence for them. Even if Aristotle at times denigrates history because it deals only with individual events rather than with universals, his denigration is not due to worries about the existence, or stability, of the past. Clark tries to reinforce Aristotle's conception of history by defending the effort to give it a philosophical (i.e., universal) element, say, by pointing out the distinction between mere chronicle and history. Not even a chronicle is a mere catalogue, however, because the beginnings of historical judgment can be found here. Consider the implicit judgments that seem to be made in these two listings: she had a baby and got married versus she got married and had a baby (AM, 130–32).[18]

Clark agrees with Aristotle that individuals, considered strictly as individuals, cannot be scientifically known, hence there is no science of individuals qua individuals.[19] If history exhibits only *some* sort of pattern or tendency short of universal law, then we cannot conclude that history is the story of unavoidable decay. Clark emphasizes this point because he is convinced by Eliade's claim that the Greeks were dominated by the myth of eternal return, a myth in which "the present age" was always seen as one of degeneration. Likewise, history was not viewed by Aristotle as necessarily progressing toward an end or consummation (AM, 133–34, 138). Again, Clark's view on this point is hard to pin down; but usually he is clear in his agreement with Aristotle that

> Political history is the story of the consolidation of desire in the midst of the unpredictable. It is not inevitable. (AM, 141)

One of the reasons why Clark takes Aristotle so seriously on time is to counteract what he sees as the Enlightenment and post-Enlightenment prejudice in favor of progress. For example, contra many zoophiles, Clark is not convinced that with the rise of the animal rights movement treatment of animals will necessarily improve. It is very possible that sympathy for animals will (say, through an economic downturn partially due to costs paid to protect the environment) revert to a moral elite. Clark is unwilling to pin his ethical concerns on fantasies regarding distant futures which cannot be seen. This reluctance is closely allied to Clark's distaste for utilitarianism, because the latter also depends, as we will see, on prophetic powers we do not have: "Our actions need some stronger root than such dull fooling with futurity" (MS, 86).

Like Plato, Clark views the present age as degenerate, although there is no necessary reason why it has to be so. In Plato's myth in the *Statesman*, the divine shepherd periodically allows things to run backward. In Clark's philosophy it is not the fact that God has withdrawn the divine hand from the world that causes the problem; rather we are in trouble because we have largely lost a sense of the world as full of love and beauty, and this largely because we have allowed religious ceremony to become stale or, what is worse, to die out altogether. Clark's citation of Plato is important because it shows that he is dealing with a perennial issue despite the particular cast of his critique of the contemporary world. In a sense, the gods have always "gone away" (CP, 27–28).

FAIRIES, OLYMPIAN DEITIES, DEMONS

Clark's imaginative symbol, which he borrows from Yeats, for the sometimes present/sometimes absent nature of God in everyday life is the "fairy." His belief is that we are entering a new age in the grip of fairies: "The collapse of ceremonial meaning, of our sense of being 'at home' in a world founded on a divine order, is itself the birth-pang of a new order" (CP, 31). Those who claim to know that fairies are fabulous do not really know what fairies are supposed to be: it is the very point of fairies to be "once upon a time," for "to believe in fairies is to think that possibility is real, and desperately attractive" (CP, 28–29). To "see" fairies is to see a sublime beauty wherein the smallness of mortal, temporal matters becomes apparent. This is a smallness to be cherished:

> Only those whose ordinary life is structured by ceremonial and human meaning, who know of their duties and their perils, their friends and children can clearly conceive that form of life which is fairy. . . . Those who have despaired of human meaning, who acknowledge no duties save their momentary whims, who pride themselves on not being charmed or enchanted by the master hypnotists of piety or affection or moral duty, whose curiosity or greed or lust is both unlimited and unimportant even to them, are living out the life of fairies. . . . Such fairies are unaware of fairyland. (CP, 30)

Skeptical readers should not assume without question that Clark is *primarily* interested in the ontology of fairies; rather, a fairy, in Clark's view, is an enchanted mood or an attitude toward the world that makes it possible for us to take intellectual constructs, like the arguments for the existence of God, seriously (CP, 32).

In the final analysis, however, Clark *is* interested in ontology. He offers us three options from which to choose: First, the God of our worship may be a hope for a future ideal that exists only in our hearts. Second, God may be a name that refers to how things work now, the worship of which forces us to abandon unreasonable hopes. Third (a position that Clark thinks has the epistemological and ethical edge), there is the option in favor of the fairylike region of enchantment: "that the right will triumph can only be a sensible expectation if the right does indeed lie at the roots of the world, if it has, as Ellul says, already triumphed" (cp, 42–43). This certainly seems to be an ontological claim on Clark's part, as is his analogous claim, regarding science, that

> we have no rational expectation that we can . . . "one day" have a complete and
> final theory of the world . . . unless there is something with which we are or may
> be in some moods united that stands at the base of things. (cp, 43)

Once again we are led back to the Clarkian commonplace that a commitment to reason itself is a matter of faith. To think that God does not exist is destructive of ethical and scientific hopes, as is the stupidly conservative assumption (which Clark rejects) that what is now is just what ought to be:

> Whatever one did or thought would automatically be the best thing possible.
> Pantheism has just the same practical disadvantages as any deterministic thesis.
> (cp, 44)

What Clark would have us do is not so much ask time to stand still or denigrate time so as to exalt eternity, but find the eternal in the temporal:

> Genuinely and firmly religious people attempt to find in their whole life some-
> thing like the unforced gaity, exaltation of spirit, creative contrition that can be
> evoked and channelled by great ritual occasions. They find the God of ritual
> even in nonritualized event. (cp, 164)

Those who do not experience this exaltation of spirit may exhibit their sour grapes in religion by blaming their condition on an ancestor who, at the "beginning," ruined the garden. It is difficult to understand, however, how Clark can make light of those who take the Garden of Eden story seriously (especially those romantics who emphasize in a Rousseau-like way primeval wholeness rather than those who emphasize the original sin part of the story) while Clark himself puts a great deal of importance on the idea of a Judgment Day at the end of history. In fact, Clark criticizes liberal theologians for not taking Judgment Day more seriously than they do:

> Those who insist that they do indeed believe in a real God . . . should either agree that God does not much mind what happens in this world, or that the days of His patience may at last run out. . . . Why should He forever leave the cosmos unreformed? . . . The Day of Judgement is no ordinary day . . . since it has to be the end of time. (CP, 172–73)

The God of any new age, including the Yeatsian age of fairies, must be destructive of the old (CP, 167, 176).

An appreciation of the coming of the age of fairies provides a vicarious experience of the coming of an ahistorical "age." In both "comings" alterity is the key:

> Only those who have lived out of water know what water is. Only those whose ordinary human life is structured by ceremonial and human meaning, who know of their duties and their perils, their friends and children, can clearly conceive that form of life which is fairy.[20]

The alterity of fairies, however, as we have noticed, can be variously interpreted. How are they other? In one (romantic) view fairies are the sweet voices of the natural world. In Clark's view they are the voices of disillusionment regarding the current world, where human endeavor is largely empty and where nature is experienced as an alien facticity, conditions that make an attachment to eternity more likely: "those who would grasp the real must at the last let go of shadows."[21] In either interpretation fairy enchantment enables us to escape from an unhistorical myopia that convinces us that our particular milieu and code of manners have existed without change for ages.[22]

An escape from this myopia makes it more likely that one could obtain what James refers to as the robust religion of healthy-mindedness: "Scientific reality is confirmed for us by technical success; 'religious reality' by the success of its techniques for preserving spiritual and physical health" (MR, 73). In addition to belief in fairies, Clark thinks it conducive to healthy-mindedness to believe in the Olympians (i.e., the gods of ancient Greek religion), as indicated previously in his remarks on Aphrodite (MR, 73). When melancholia interrupts healthy-mindedness, two questions arise: first, how is it that a new self (James's "twice-born" self) can come to be?; and second, how is it that we are not always changing, always trading in our old identity such that we never acquire a stable character? Relying on Wordsworth, Clark gives the following response to these questions:

> We are more likely to fear this breakdown, and so defend ourselves against it more fiercely and rigidly . . . if we think that our chosen identity is indeed an attempt to freeze a wave of the sea, to make solid sculptures out of butter on a warm day. We shall be less fearful of collapse if we conceive that the sea itself is the real shaper of our standing wave, that it was the former identities that were the momentarily aggregated flotsam that the waves have swept away. A stable identity, in short, is likely to be one which is believed to be the manifestation of an underlying reality . . . in touch with "something far more deeply interfused." Those who believe that their identities are maintained by their own endeavors, by their own disciplined insistence on being as they were, are very likely not to last the course. (MR, 74)

In our culture, however, we are more likely to lean toward the first pole in the following two extremes: lacking a stable character or a plan of life, on the one hand, and possessing a supreme confidence regarding who we are (à la Genghis Khan), on the other. We tend nowadays, Clark thinks, to change from moment to moment as we would a style of dress. "We are all a little like werewolves" (MR, 75). It would be better, he thinks, if we found a suitably varied life midway between these two extremes.

Three views of the relationship between temporal relations and human identity can be distinguished. One view suggests that all temporal relations are external; that is, the present self is not internally affected by "its" past self, nor is it affected by "its" future self. This "drops of experience" view (defended by Hume, Russell, and some Buddhists) in effect is a denial of a self enduring through time, and is ultimately rejected by Clark for this reason. Unfortunately Clark often runs to the other (Leibnizian) extreme, where all temporal relations are internal; that is, the present self is *substantially* the same through time, in that both past and future phases of itself are contained in it, and this largely due to an expansive belief in divine omniscience with respect to the future. The third view (of Bergson, Whitehead, and Hartshorne) is unlike the previous two symmetrical views in its asymmetricality: one is internally affected by one's past but externally related to the future. According to this view, the past provides necessary but not sufficient conditions for the precise character of the present phase of one's self. We are causally affected by our past but we can anticipate the future only through probability estimates. Clark also, at times, runs toward this third view, but because this view (accurately, I think) leaves human identity rather fragile with respect to the future, it is often implicitly criticized by Clark due to his fetish for permanence and substantiality. Clark *at times* leans toward the asymmetrical view of temporal relations, just as he *sometimes* leans towards dipolar theism, but not even his attraction to Buddhism can force him to abandon a theory of the self as internally related to the future through the agency of divine omniscience.

The modern tendency to switch identities as we do clothes has led many moralists, Clark thinks, to prefer a smorgasbord of values, a wardrobe of differing costumes. The point to be emphasized here is that Clark's dipolar theism, with a decided emphasis on divine eternity, is mirrored in his philosophical anthropology. Clark wants a balance between continuity and change, yet the latter is seen to be the greater danger. Hence he thinks it crucial to emphasize that activity of an expected kind serves as a code to others to summon up one identity or god rather than another. Nonetheless,

> the sudden emergence of a forgotten self—an emergence made easier by social ritual and the consumption of a mild drug (most usually, alcohol)—may be experienced as a joyful rediscovery or an humiliating possession by something quite at odds with waking values. . . . Religion is the collective noun for all such practices, whereby our changing selves may move in time to some unknown tidal motions, without driving us insane. (MR, 77)

These passing moods and styles of action are sometimes hostile to each other. In this contest between alien powers, each must be given due respect; this is the lesson to be learned from polytheism (MR, 76).

The view of the self as substantial in the sense that the I "has" momentary moods is rejected by Clark. The ego is more of a demand or a postulate than a plain discovery; it is something that we can see as existing *beneath* the many moods and personalities that play themselves out in everyday life. There is some truth to the familiar criticism that the ancient Greeks had no clear conception of the unity of the human subject. Yet there is also some truth in the polytheistic belief that each "individual" is a medley of competing parts and loyalties. This truth is corroborated by the fact that contemporary readers do not find Homer's heroes altogether unlike contemporary human beings. Further, the moods and styles encountered by the ego cannot be mortal, as the Greeks knew, because they are confronted again and again, not only in the life of the ego but also in the lives of other egos, and they cannot be resisted: "Those who try to proclaim their own immunity to Aphrodite find that she is raised up against them" (MR, 79). (Later we will see Clark say the same regarding Ares.) Zeus was the symbol for that order that needed preservation if human life was not to revert to fratricidal chaos, in that the service of one god at the expense of another was quintessential blasphemy in the Olympian religion (MR, 78–79).

There is something to be learned from the ancient Greek view that only the gods are single-minded, hence human life tends to be unsystematic. Even if one organizes the major deities into a pantheon, there are still *kers* (the spirits of spite and reprisal) and Furies to contend with. That is, the Abrahamic religions may be a bit premature in thinking that God is omnipotent, as we will see. Although Zeus required that gods and mortals know their respective places, and that they not rebel against Themis, or what was proper, he did not have absolute control, a fact that was symbolized best by the presence of Dionysus. The trick now is, as it was then, to discover an orderly system without resorting to force in the effort to create it. Human knowledge itself insures that this will be a difficult project:

> This "discovery," so to call it, of the possibility of an orderly world-system in which each god has a part to play, and [in] which the demands of different roles were not settled simply by resort to force . . . this "knowledge of good and evil" was what, in Greek thought, prevented human beings from becoming gods: precisely because they could look before and after, and discriminate, they could not be unselfconsciously absorbed in any single role or mood. (MR, 80)

It was part of the Greek genius at moderation to fail to conclude that Dionysus was "the natural man," human nature as it would be if the hegemony of Apollo were broken. Dionysus is not "the natural man" so much as he is a natural possibility. The temporary destruction of Zeus's or Apollo's Olympian order, a destruction symbolized by Dionysus, should be accepted as a moment in life rather than as a defeat (MR, 81).

63

Relying on W. F. Otto, Clark militates against the view of the Olympian deities as a band of brigands. In fact, echoes of Olympian religion can still be heard, as I have tried to show. Olympianism is an attempt to provide a structure for the moods and roles of social humanity and an attempt to convince us that we are vulnerable fragments of a cosmos with its own beauty. Despite the fact that Christianity is a protest against Olympian religion, it is also, as is well known, a type of Dionysian revivalism. Clark thinks it important that Dionysian enthusiasm remain a part of organized religion, so as to prevent a deleterious reification of established order. It is worth remembering that it was not only Jesus who was seen by Hellenized Jews and Christians as similar to Dionysus, but also Yahweh. Eventually, however, Yahweh and God the Father came to be seen as strictly transcendent (MR, 82–86). What I have called dipolar theism (a type of theism evidenced in Clark's writings, albeit with a preference for one pole, a preference that I think is defective) is found, according to Clark, in different ways in the Olympian religion, Christianity, and Buddhism:

> Charismatic revivalists . . . succeed only in establishing new patterns of worship and hymnody, so that bourgeois congregations sing words that take their meaning from the last revival. "Come Holy Ghost" . . . how many in the congregation really intend to speak in tongues? . . . How many Buddhists, for that matter, really test themselves upon the nonexistence of the self, and seek to realize the Unborn? . . . Like the Olympians, Christians and Buddhists have (to some extent) achieved a synthesis: their ceremonial order does contain a reference to That beyond all orders, and a vocabulary that stands ready for the next revivalist. (MR, 87)

In addition to the synthesis of enthusiastic life in religion and a ceremonial order that refers to some sort of transcendence, there is the synthesis of sequential Nous and the nonsequential One:

> Stable and continuing religious traditions neither wholly abjure nor wholly endorse "the world." . . . Zeus, Father of Gods and Men, was identified by neo-Platonic theorists—almost the last philosophers to take ordinary religious forms seriously as matter for philosophical inquiry—with *Nous*, the ordering intellect and the order it discloses. This was not the ultimately real, the One. . . . But the One and *Nous*, though distinct, were not diverse: *Nous* itself had its being only from the One, as ceremonial usage and sacred history stem, in their beginnings, from the Unnamed that lies beyond all ceremonial. (MR, 88)

There are two varieties of atheism distinguished by Clark, only one of which is really an enemy of religion. Some atheists reject existing ceremonial forms yet nonetheless, in effect, reverence the ancient god Chaos in the metephysical belief that there is something gratuitous about the existence of the world that makes it possible for human beings themselves to create meaning in their lives. The sort of atheism that Clark opposes, however, consists of a type of adolescent cynicism wherein human meaning is denied, except, perhaps, for sensual thrills. That is, the former "atheism" is actually close to the neoplatonic distrust of any attempt to close in on the One; this is an "atheism" that, in a way, transcends religion. Clark is skeptical, however, as to whether we can actually keep meaning in our lives over an extended period of time without worship, prayer, and sacrifice:

> The *truth* of a proposition lies, for us, in its having to be affirmed if we are to carry on with the life we are born to. The Olympians are real in that we recognize certain patterns in our lives. . . . The phenomenological account of religious identity that I have given can easily be transformed into anti-realist metaphysics, into the thesis that the gods are "real" only in that human life is structured as it is. But it is also compatible with a genuine theological realism that life is structured so because there are indeed such presences, such powers as gods. (MR, 89–90)[23]

The realist is willing to concede that there is some real thing with which Greeks, Christians, and even Buddhists have contact from their various perspectives. Strange as it sounds, it may be that realistic Olympianism is even further removed from polar equality than is Clark's philosophy: its gods are strictly actualities, in the sense that each is "pure," with no unrealized possibilities (MR, 91).

In any event, because Clark views religious structures as explanatory hypotheses, and *because* he is in the final analysis a realist in religion, he thinks that it is more accurate to say that birds court each other because of Aphrodite than it is to say that the obsessional desire of birds *is* Aphrodite. The danger he sees is that if we do not refer to the gods to explain phenomena, then they will too easily be viewed as poetic fictions, fictions that may well be part of a vision of how things should be; that is, they will implicitly be part of a new, antireligion religion (MR, 91–92).

Olympian religion is also very helpful in distinguishing pollution from sin. One may inadvertently be polluted, as in the case of Oedipus, when one does something that conflicts with impersonal (usually cosmic) law. By way of contrast, religions of the book tend to treat the penalties of sin as the response of a personal God. When the innocent suffer we are led to take Olympianism seriously, in that some events appear to be the case independent of any decision made by an omnipotent divine being. Pollution plays *some* role in Judaism and Christianity, as in the people with whom Jesus consorted, who had not so much committed moral errors as they had been outcasts from Israel, that is, they had incurred pollution. Hindu society, like ancient Greek society, has a stronger notion of pollution than that found in the Abrahamic religions, a notion that includes dietary practices, modes of address to superiors, and the like (MR, 103–6). Regarding sexual morality, at least, there is a strong notion of pollution in the Abrahamic religions as well:

> Christian tradition, in approving virginity for women as well as for men, made the first steps towards recognizing females as children of God in their own right, as something more than vessels of pollution to be saved by childbearing. But there is some truth in the view that popular Christian tradition has often suggested that it is chiefly by sexual irregularity that we are rendered impure. . . . Quite why sexual morality, so called, has come to loom so large in popular Christian religiosity is a puzzle. (MR, 107)

The general goal of religion is always something like Hindu *moksa*, deliverance from both pollution and sin:

> In morality no-one is to be blamed or punished who is not personally responsible for a crime. . . . Pollution, on the other hand, is only partly deserved, and may be removed by another's action. What matters in religion, one might exaggeratedly conclude, is not the moral wrongs . . . but the state of the wrongdoers' souls. . . . All those who carry that image of the loving god in their hearts are essentially pure. (MR, 112)

Yet even the goal of *moksa* can be perverted:

> In our own, partly secular, tradition the usual conjunction of "holiness" and dirt was cancelled by the aphorism that "Cleanliness is next to godliness," which has in its turn gone so far toward idealizing the ritual antisepticism of the world of white-coated doctors, plastic-wrapped meat, and vaginal deodorants as to elicit

a youthful rebellion in favour of "naturalness," a largely romantic effort to be at one with the usual processes of nature. (MR, 108–9)

It should be emphasized that it is not merely the modes of achieving *mokṣa* that differ from religion to religion. The various religions also differ regarding the guises through which God can be known. Religions of the book are often unwilling to concede that the one God can be known at all through guises. By way of contrast, Hinduism, despite the polar inequality in most varieties of pantheism, is more open regarding the possibility of many divine guises appropriate for differing religious temperaments (MR, 110).

There are indeed different religious temperaments, as is evidenced when a religious believer exhibits psychosis in the use of religious metaphors to shut out ordinary experiences like eating. In this regard we should notice that James's religion of healthy-mindedness is not as banal as it sometimes seems, because it is often the result of a concerted effort to avoid depression. It does not follow, however, from the close ties between certain religious temperaments and neurosis/psychosis that religious piety is a compensation for felt inadequacy: "That same charge, after all, could as easily be leveled at materialism" (MR, 120). Put differently, some despair inside and outside of religion is real, and sometimes it is merely a pleasing, romantic posture (MR, 118–19, 142).

One of the reasons why there is despair among human beings is that there is a feeling that the gods are indifferent to us. Clark has a hard time defending Aristotle's gods against the charge of narcissism because, as we will see, there is something super-Platonic and transcendent about his gods, an attitude that is counterintuitively *not* found in Plato's (or Clark's) World Soul. That is, the fact that Clark's dipolar theism leans toward God as unmoved is not unrelated to his Aristotelianism, although, as we will see in the last chapter, Clark himself is a neoplatonist in his adherence to the World Soul (AM, 217–20). Clark believes in both the One, on the one hand, and various gods, fairies, and demons, on the other, some of which are little "ones" in their own right, in that they do not have the possibility of changing or of receiving influence from (the sufferings of) others. Nonetheless, these gods, fairies, and demons constitute one of Clark's ways of articulating a concept of deity as relational, because these gods, fairies, and demons constantly pass through our mind's eye for us to accept or reject or ignore: "To know them is to share experience with them, to live with their life" (AJ, 192–93).

As before, Clark gives conflicting evidence as to whether he believes in divine retribution for sin. At places he suggests that one of the demons that might pass before us is the thought that we are being, or might deservedly be, punished for our wrongs, a demon that should be suppressed, he thinks. Demons, like fairies or Olympian gods, are Clarkian symbols for moods, or, better, in the case of demons, for obsessions (AJ, 196, 209). Demons are those fallen angels exhibited to us in our self-righteous indignancy, our greed, and our jealousy:

> Being thankful for things as they are, praying for one's supposed enemies as they are, rejoicing in the sense of being a unit in a wider and a happier whole—these are ways in which we can escape despair. I should add that these techniques, obviously enough, may be corrupted into sentimentalism and conceit. (AJ, 211)

Polytheism teaches us that there are angels as well as devils. Clark's very strong commitment to divine unity does not exclude an *almost* as strong commitment to divine plurality: like centripetal and centrifugal forces in equilibrium, these two tendencies provide the creative tension in Clark's theism:

> Faith in the Divine Unity amounts to faith in the intelligibility of things, that there is a single pattern, the Logos. . . . That faith was represented for Hellenes, especially the neo-Platonists, in the figure of Zeus. . . . The Logos is not now evident to us. Rational polytheists deplore the tendency of monotheists to imagine unity too soon. . . . Every mode and mood of our being, of the world's being, should be acknowledged as a fact, and as something to be "welcomed." (AJ, 212–13)

In particular Clark is bothered by the attempt to blaspheme Aphrodite, say, through alcoholism or academic infighting. Avoiding such blasphemy does not mean that we should naively preach that Aphrodite is, or even could be, ubiquitous:

> The ancients reminded us that even when kissing our child we should remember that she too is mortal. . . . That hard advice is now seen as a betrayal of "love," a refusal to be besotted, as if such love were the only real thing in an empty world. (CP, 24–25)

Nor is Apollo ubiquitous, nor could he be, if by Apollo we refer in this context to a manipulative type of science:

> What is lacking in this age of the world is the sense that there is some existing pattern in which each proper impulse finds its place. . . . Those who have lost their memory of the one comprehensive order are at the mercy of whatever passion, mood, or fairy chances to drink them up. (CP, 33–35)

According to Clark, in our age the problem is not so much that God (the One) is dead as that there has been a triumphant, hegemonic return of the ancient deities. This loss of the sense of deity as enduring has practical consequences, according to Clark, say, in the loss of the sense of marriage as enduring; or, put another way, marriage is now seen as enduring as long as there is mutual enthusiasm. Clark's qualified polytheism is nonetheless used as a device to criticize what he sees as the antiestablishment establishment:

> There is a sense, of course, in which all this talk of "God's death," and the radical desacralizing and deconstruction of any received order, is merely fashionable chatter. As Feyerabend remarks, "there is fragmentation; but there are also new and powerful uniformities. . . ." It is easy for bourgeois commentators to pretend that they do not live within an established, peaceable order. . . . Those who claim to believe that there is no such order, and that the truly modern person expects none, are usually pillars of the establishment. . . . Those who have made a comfortable living by denouncing sacredness. . . . Moral philosophers have been ready to describe morality as just the sort of rules that might be struck between brigands for their individual profit. (CP, 37–38)

Ares is certainly alive and well in the contemporary world, and a primary devotion to him is to be denigrated:

> Those who fight for killing's sake, the servants of Ares, are as dangerous to us all as the followers of Ouranian Aphrodite, the Titanic power that acknowledges no pledge of loyalty or friendship. . . . Our problem, as it has always been, is to require the gods to take their proper place. (CP, 114–15)

I take it that this is Clark's very abstract way of slipping in a defense of patriotism. Ares and Aphrodite are the most hated of the Olympians because both can ruin our lives. Yet I wonder, as a pacifist, why Ares is "unavoidably present" in our lives, as Clark contends.[24] Furthermore, why is pacifism a parallel view to virginity? We will be on the lookout in a later chapter to see if Clark can defend his Hobbesian view that war is as "natural" as sex, such that it breaks out like forest fire after a drought (CP, 111, 116). The following lines from Clark show his rhetorical brilliance, even if they do not justify violence:

> Ares . . . is not just a devil, any more than Aphrodite: our fear of him is not unlike the terror that in other ages made Aphrodite into the great Temptress; our professions of pacific virtue are as hypocritical as the double standards of past sexual morality; our good liberal contempt for fighting men is as understandable, and as damaging to all, as older contempt for women. . . . Perhaps we should ask ourselves why we are so ready to assume the worst of those who would die for us? (CP, 117)

As we will see, perhaps we are ready to make this assumption because twentieth-century warfare is integrally connected to knowingly killing innocent people, that is, to the elimination of traditional principles of *jus in bello*. It remains unclear why *these* traditional principles are so easily dropped by Clark.

It would perhaps be beneficial at this point to try to see the forest in the midst of all the trees provided by Clark in the forms of fairies, demons, and Olympians. *Pure* polytheism would consist in the radical plurality and incommensurability of value preferred by some secularists. Although Clark is in favor of organizing our lives so as to provide for the health *and diversity* of the whole earth, polytheism for him is largely propaedeutic to an appreciation of the whole. Polytheism is a prelude to an exposition of faith in a radically Abrahamic or neoplatonic One. Relying on Plato (*Laws* 903c–d), he notes that the world does not exist for our sake so much as we exist for It, as we will see in the last chapter of the book (CP, 159–60). Still, we should not get the impression that there is a radical break between polytheism and Christian faith, for Clark. A consideration of Plotinus's version of neoplatonism, for example, helps Christians to understand that the God-man or the Logos is not *sui generis* in Christianity:

> Plotinus, who was certainly as great a philosopher and spiritual leader as Hellenic civilization ever produced, remarked that Pheidias' statue of Olympian Zeus was

what Zeus would look like if He did indeed "take flesh and dwell among us" (*Enneads* 5.8.1). (CP, 178)

Secular moralists have become polytheists without realizing it in their acceptance of multiple and often contradictory ideals and in their claim that it is not always possible to do right without at the same time doing dreadful wrong (an admission that actually plays into the hands of Clark himself when he attempts to justify war). As Yeats predicted, the new polytheistic age is unconstrained by any conception of unity or due order, hence Clark's attempt to restore it both politically and religiously, an effort that, as I claim here and in the following chapter, is not without defects.[25] It is easy to understand why Clark wants to defend divine unity so energetically, in that fairyland and the shifting demands of demons and gods constitute an invisible world within which the visible world is immersed, an invisibility that makes dealing explicitly with polytheism rather difficult. Although fairies are in most respects used by Clark for the same purposes as Olympian deities, they are tied more closely to both the positive and negative features of polytheism, conceived as invisible and dreamlike. Fairies are like the gods except for the fact that they are more ethereal.[26]

However, fairies, gods, and demons are not so ethereal that they are trivial. One dominated by anger believes that he is responding to some real force out there in the world, a force that is part of a world of "moods, passions, half-glimpsed visions, apparitions, absent-minded absorptions in memory or fable."[27] Fairies, gods, and demons are symbols for what Clark believes to be real divine immanence. This real divine immanence or multiplicity is best known, he thinks, through enthusiasm, but it can also be apprehended through fairy tales that capture the sense that there really is an older life form than the human. Paradoxically, these fairy tales are stories symbolizing divine immanence, stories that, precisely because they are "once-upon-a-time," are meant to lead us outside of time to consider divine unity and transcendence.[28]

The one or a center or a stable identity is not immediately obvious in human beings because such properties require a certain degree of mental discipline; hence, we should not be surprised that some human beings exhibit, say, multiple personality disorders. Nonetheless, Clark thinks, there is a stable Being (or Truth or Substance) that we can imitate in a Chesterton-like way, a Being that makes it possible for us to elude antirationalism, nominalism, and atheism. So far, so good, I think, but instead of "Being," why not say "Supreme Being-in-Becoming?"[29]

Fairies and gods are, on Clark's quasi-Berkelean terms, as real as any other ideas, even the idea of "matter." He concludes his view of fairies and their connection to God as dipolar as follows:

> Fairies are not pygmies, nor Lilliputians, nor even biological organisms from another planet. "Fairy" is a term that has its place in an idealist metaphysic. To believe in fairies is to acknowledge, and even to make real to oneself, the intermittent presence of spirits that enter our ordinary consciousness as moods of love or alienation, wild joy or anger. They may be invoked by music, poetry, and love. . . . To doubt or disprove their existence it is necessary to do more than dredge Loch Ness. . . . The argument is a metaphysical one, about the proper description of our experience and the correct metaphysical guess about the ground of that experience . . . an appropriate metaphorical description of certain states of spiritual being. If a broadly spiritist metaphysics is ultimately found to be false, then there have never really been any fairies; but in that case there have never "really" been any human persons either. If there are persons, then there are at least some spirits weirdly mingled with the material. And if there are some, what reason is there to deny that there are also others, perhaps of a larger and more alien kind?[30]

In sum, my exploration of polytheism in this part of the chapter has consisted of the following steps: (1) The asymmetrical view of time (the past is settled but the future is not), which is a moderate view between two extremes, leaves human identity in a fragile state. (2) Yet it does not leave it in a more fragile state than it is in reality, contra the substantialist thesis. (3) Any adequate theory of human identity must account for both continuity and change. (4) To the extent that change is a necessary feature of human identity (as it is even for Clark), polytheism must be taken seriously. (5) Clark may be correct, however, that polytheism is taken *too* seriously in contemporary culture. (6) Hence, the effort to discover the underlying unity to one's life, an effort integrally connected to the effort to understand divine unity, is crucial. (7) A phenomenology of one's personal experience indicates that this unity can only be partial, in that Aphrodite and Ares, Apollo and Dionysus, the Furies, and various spirits of spite, reprisal, and memory still pull us in different directions. (8) The theodicy problem, among others, in the philosophy of religion insures that the sort of stability that would be provided by an omnipotent deity will continue to be difficult to defend. (9) Hence, we will have to rest content within the Abrahamic religions with only a partial refutation of polytheism. (Even Jesus was on several occasions tempted.) (10) This is exactly what we should expect: neither the "one" nor the "many" in the problem of the one and the many can be wished away.

CONCLUSION

In this chapter I have examined two columns of divine attributes, columns that, I have claimed, must be brought into something like polar equality in order to avoid some of the most egregious problems in traditional, Western theism. I am constantly changing, yet I retain a stable identity through these changes; God does the same, but supremely so. Clark very often gives evidence of being a dipolar theist, but even more evidence can be found in his writings that he prefers being over becoming, and the eternal over the temporal when talking about God.[31] This (over)reliance on divine timelessness has profound consequences for Clark's practical philosophy, as in his denigration of social justice issues, which hinge on a concern for God in time, and his emphasis on worship, which hinges on a concern for God as timeless. Nonetheless, much can be learned from Clark regarding how religious ceremony and sacrament, treated in chapter one as well, can put us in touch with the transtemporal. Likewise, Clark's highly original treatment of fairies, demons, and Olympian deities constitutes a serious effort to understand the relationship between divine unity and plurality, and a serious effort to alert us to the hegemony of polytheism in contemporary culture. The main criticism I have of Clark's treatment of God is that he leaves divine unity and plurality, the centripetal and centrifugal forces that energize his thought and that provide it with its fundamental tension, in a paradoxical relationship. This paradox, in effect, gives Clark a carte blanche to vent his somewhat exaggerated desire for reticulation.

CHAPTER 3

THEODICY

INTRODUCTION

In chapter one I introduced the major themes in Clark's thought, and in chapter two I examined in detail the relationship between time and eternity in that thought, a relationship best illustrated in Clark's qualified defense of dipolar theism. The criticisms I developed in chapter two dealt largely with Clark's overreliance on the traditional belief in divine eternity, an overreliance that, I claim, leads Clark into many of the traditional problems associated with the monopolar prejudice. For example, how can there be human freedom if God knows the future in minute detail? How can God be both outside of time and respond to (or even know) creatures in time? In this chapter I would like to consider one particular problem, the theodicy problem, to see how Clark's theism fares. We will see Clark's awesome originality at work, as well as his willingness to be saddled with the traditional problem of theodicy found in the Abrahamic religions, a willingness that is especially odd in that the theodicy problem is often regarded as the Achilles heel of these religions. That is, we will be frustrated by Clark's choice to pull in the reins on his amazing abilities.

CLARKIAN THEODICY

The theodicy that Clark adopts is problematic because the God he believes in is the maker and shaker of the earth, a God who "gives His creatures the mistaken sense that they are real causes, but all their doings are really His" (MR, 134). Clark admits that this is an extreme doctrine that cannot be the creed by which we live. Here we should notice something fishy because Clark, usually a pragmatist, has adopted a view that has very unpragmatic consequences. Further, this extreme doctrine confirms the claim I made in the last chapter that in certain important respects Clark rejects the A-theorist's view of time. Clark knows very well that there are grave difficulties in taking determinism as a practical creed, but as a traditional theist he feels pressured to accept belief in divine omnipotence, a belief that leads, he thinks, to either theistic predestinarianism or Mahayana enlightenment. What looks like "ours" (our experience of time in the A-series and the freedom entailed by belief in future contingencies that are really contingent) is only God's, "and there is no real volition but His":

> The enlightened burst out laughing as they understand that everything already has the Buddha-nature. Similarly, the Book-religious pray for the coming of God's Kingdom, His will to be done: the joke, for predestinarians, is that it already is. We "enter" the kingdom when we see that we never left it. (MR, 85, 135)

In effect, the tension in Clark, noted in the previous chapter, between the one and the many is mirrored here in the tension between predestinarian, pantheistic monism, on the one hand, and particularized, multiple deities among which we can choose, on the other. When we read Clark saying "there is no single cause of all that happens. The god perhaps has set the scene, but the scene is one in which many contending and co-operating spirits play" (MR, 136–37), we may easily conclude that Clark has contradicted the claim that God is the real cause of everything. A more generous interpretation, however, is that Clark prefers to leave the tension between predestinarian monism and freedom-generating multiplicity *as* a tension. Or better, the former constitutes Clark's metaphysics whereas the latter constitutes his ethics. In any event, our job as readers of Clark is to continually try to render consistency to Clark's far-flung theoretical empire.

This effort to render Clark's thought consistent regarding the theodicy problem is difficult in different ways, depending on which of three aspects of the
problem is under consideration. First, the problem of evil is one that all human
beings must confront, even the nonreligious. Clark states this aspect of the problem and gives his preferred response in the following way:

> How can we summon up the energy and courage to cope with a phenomenal
> universe that so often works against us and our ideals? . . . Robust "healthy-
> mindedness" is one response to the existential problem, but it is not one that is
> always in our gift, and those who have managed it should not boast too loudly.
> (MR, 144)

This response clearly implies that there are some things (actually a multitude
of things) that are not from God. The question to which Clark thinks we will
have to respond is this: does the existence of these things disprove the existence
of God or render God impotent? This question leads us to consider the second
aspect of the problem, which is faced only by the religious:

> Their problem is: how shall they remain loyal to a power, a principle that man-
> ifests itself in so disdainful a form? How may we serve the gods from any motive
> but ignoble fear? (MR, 145)

The third aspect of the problem is faced by the Abrahamic theist in particular.
If God is all-good, God desires an end to evil, and if God is all-powerful, God
can secure all desires. Why, then, does evil exist?

In contrast to Clark, the process theist's response to this question centers on
a critique of divine omnipotence rather than on divine omnibenevolence. It
should be noted that Clark's feminism does not extend to the One, which he
always identifies as masculine. Feminine predicates more easily apply to the
terms on the right side of the diagram in chapter two, the side disfavored by traditional theists. That is, it seems that Clark, along with other traditional theists,
has unwittingly identified God with supposedly male virtues, like being or
immobility or control, as opposed to supposedly feminine virtues, like becoming or responsiveness or reciprocity.

That Clark understands the theodicy problem as I do is evidenced in the following passage:

The simplest versions of the atheistical argument attempt to express these three axioms of Abrahamic theism as an "inconsistent triad," any two of which are incompatible with the third: (i) God is all-good; (ii) God is all-powerful; (iii) there is evil. If God wants there to be no evil, but there is, He cannot be all-powerful. If God could make an end of evil, but hasn't, He cannot be all-good. If God could and would eliminate all evil, there can be none. Critics argue that abandoning any one of the axioms must alter Abrahamic theism to destruction. (MR, 145)

Clark correctly holds that it is easy for the atheist to claim that if this form of theism is refuted then all religion can be abandoned. Yet instead of trying to improve on traditional theism by criticizing omnipotence (i.e., its fetish for a male God who controls everything), Clark is more likely to reconsider omnibenevolence as traditionally conceived. He rhetorically asks: "Does God's all-goodness really require Him to eliminate all evil?" (MR, 145). His response to this question, if I am not mistaken, leaves the problem of evil in such a confused state that one can label his theodicy only as fideistic:

There is no necessary contradiction in agreeing that many things are, in the abstract, not as God or any divinely motivated person would wish, but believing that God's purposes are good and His power infinitely adequate to bring them to completion. . . . It is the claim that even the all-powerful cannot wholly prevent all suffering, all wrong, without at the same time preventing the moral and personal growth of His creatures. . . . God's goodness and power are not incompatible with His creation and maintenance of a universe in which creatures are to be confronted with occasions of stumbling. . . . Even if we do not altogether understand just why God permits just what He does, we have no right to insist that there can be no satisfactory reason. (MR, 146–47)

This will surely not suffice *if* the theist wishes to present an intellectually responsible theodicy to the nontheist. The problem is that if one fideistically champions the belief in an omnipotent God who willingly withdraws the divine hand from the world, one unwittingly makes God into something of a sadist:

There may be some reason why the almighty Lord of love and justice lets a child perish in bewildered pain rather than revoke His gift of liberty. There may be some reason why the almighty Lord allows a cloud of lust, hatred and confusion to obscure the thought and corrupt the action of the child's killer. The child may wake to life eternal. (MR, 148)

It seems that Clark would rather run the risk that we might come to believe that God is not our friend than run the risk that God's power might not be "displayed in domination and control, but in perseverence and gradual persuasion" (MR, 148–49). This latter view, which is precisely that of Whitehead and Hartshorne, is *not* equivalent, as Clark thinks, to the view that God is a helpless victim, "subject to the whims" of creatures, that God is "entirely vulnerable to violence," or that such a God would signal "the entire absence of temporal power."

As Clark himself notes, the Christian theme of crucifixion is a reminder that God's power is not like a prince's. Jesus preaches the "power" that comes from "the soft answer, the smile, the willingness to yield and to endure" (MR, 147–50). Yet Clark sees the boy Jesus growing up into a vitriolic revenger, a view that depends on a tendentious interpretation of the cleansing of the temple texts, I think. Several criticisms of belief in divine omnipotence not yet offered are appropriate at this point.

First, a perfectly created and perfectly managed universe, to the extent that this is conceivable, cannot mean a universe that is absolutely controlled. Individuals must in *some* sense be self-managed or they are not concrete individuals living from moment to moment, but abstract, reified universals. Second, "omnipotence" tends to paralyze thinking because to believe in divine omnipotence is to think that we are what we are due to divine decree. How, then, are we to make sense of the fact that *we* apply ethical principles to action? Every humble actor seems to contribute something to the cosmic drama left undetermined by the "Playwright." Clark may try to convince us, along with John Hick, that God only gives us our character and that we make the particular choices, but even "character" makes sense only as a series of incremental deposits on past actions. Hartshorne puts the point well:

All that God can directly give us is the beauty of his ideal for us, an ideal to which we cannot simply not respond, but to which our response has to be partly self-determined, and it has to be influenced by past creaturely responses in our universe. "Persuasion" is the ultimate power; not even God can simply coerce. The contrary idea implies a false analogy with pushing puppets or passive clay about, or with hypnotism mistakenly construed, or with the use of brutal punishments, or more or less irresistable bribes, in the human management of human beings. Right action secured only by rewards and punishments, even were this conveivable, would not be genuine goodness at all, let alone perfect goodness.[1]

Worshiping God is one thing and "worshiping" a cosmic power monopoly is another. This is *not* to say that God falls short of some ideal degree and kind of power. That is, Hartshorne is not arguing for a "limited God," as Clark would perhaps allege. Rather, sheer monopoly of power, a doctrine that Clark at times supports, is a nightmare—strictly speaking an impossibility—not an ideal.

A PROCESS CRITIQUE

The greatest conceivable being could have only as much power as is compatible with omnibenevolence, in that the good and the beautiful, as opposed to "the powerful," are the key values possessed by a being worthy of worship, as Plato realized. God, for Whitehead and Hartshorne, is still more powerful than any other being, however. God, who offers a perfect model of goodness, acts *abstractly* as a *lure*; God also acts *concretely* as a *persuader*, constantly trying to convince us to take the divine model seriously. As we will see in the last chapter, God's coordinating ability, which makes it possible for the diverse elements in the world to be, in some sense, a *uni*verse, also makes it possible to limit disorder so as to avoid sheer chaos, but not to the point where sheer monotony or total rigidity is the result. God orders the world by giving free creatures an awareness, however dim, of their place in the *cosmos*. Some of us, I allege, neither desire nor worship divine powers more extensive than these.

In Clark's view, God one day will, in fact, punish the mighty, a view that, when pressed, seems to amount to the belief that ultimately there will be no evil. Clark is correct that the route to religious maturity includes a recognition of one's errors, perhaps even a radical repentance, but from this fact one need not infer, à la Kant, the need for an omnipotent paymaster to guarantee that repentance makes sense. Clark distinguishes four attitudes toward one's distress in life, attitudes that help us to understand the relationship between Clark's theodicy and his belief in the need for punishment. First, one extreme view suggests that our distress is solely due to bad luck, as if our distress were due to the entire randomness of the world or to the "hegemony" of chaos. The second view is also inadequate because it blames our distress *solely* on the indifference or malevolence of other creatures; this is bad polytheism, to say the least. The third view, which is a step closer to the truth, he thinks, is found when we acknowledge that we have a hand in our own distress. The fourth view is a continuation of the third because it posits a forgiveness for our transgressions, once we have acknowledged our own hand in our distress (MR, 151–53).

These distinctions are fine as far as they go, but if one really believes in divine omnipotence, views one, two, and three are unintelligible, and *a fortiori* view four, because it follows from view three: (1) How could there be chaos if God is omnipotent?; (2) How could there be rival, evil gods if God is omnipotent?; (3) How could we really have a hand in our distress if God is *omni*potent?; and (4) Why should God forgive us if God Himself is ultimately responsible for all that occurs? The view I am urging is that there is *some* grain of truth in all four of these views, especially view one, if the suffering of the innocent is considered. Clark, however, can give credence to these four views *only* when he is thinking as a pluralist and as a pragmatist, not as a traditional theist or as a neoplatonic monist.

Belief in reincarnation or in the devil are really extreme ways of making the universe seem just and of relieving anxiety, in that belief in the devil provides a precise locus for evil (MR, 154, 160; AJ, 56). Yet Clark's way is only slightly less extreme: "It does not seem to me . . . that there is any coherent way of avoiding a degree of dualism" (MR, 161). The dualism he speaks of is precisely the undigested dipolar theism discussed in the previous chapter, a Clarkian theism that alternates between one omnipotent God and many pragmatically convenient powers (convenient so as to solve the problems created by belief in divine omnipotence):

> If creation is to be genuine, the essentially unlimited Creator must limit himself, must become as-it-were a finite being, even if it is with a view to a re-integration of the fragmented deity, or a taming of the rebellious creation. (MR, 164)

The dualism that Clark defends is never as extreme as that in gnosticism, where evil or ugliness are blamed on matter itself. Nonetheless, this dualism is potent enough to lead Clark to say that we cannot expect to find a beauty that is without flaw, and that we will meet in this world only sweet reminders of the *Logos*:

> If we are to believe ourselves to have a reasonable hope, we must suppose that the source of beauty in Nature and in the human soul is capable of victory—

which is why the religious quest usually posits an almighty God. In doing so, of course, we create the standard difficulties for ourselves. . . . Either He is not omnipotent, or He is not benevolent. It is on this stone that most would-be believers stumble. . . . We cannot evade the challenge of evil by claiming that God's purposes and powers are quite inscrutable. . . . We need to devise some story which will make it possible to believe in a God both almighty and well-meaning. (AJ, 48–49)

As we have seen, Clark believes that all of his theories are, at bottom, likely stories. Here, however, the operative story is the one that suggests that despite the fact that there are real evils in the world, an all-powerful God can make good out of them: "We are the arena and the agents of that conflict, that would-be transformation" (AJ, 50). Clark would do well here to remember the dictum from Wordsworth that what having been, must ever be. Once Job's original children are tortured and killed (in that the natural disasters in *Job* are permitted if not actually sent by Yahweh), there is no making good on *their* lives by giving Job a new batch of kids at the end of the book.

Clark persists, however, perhaps out of a fear of a Marcus Aurelius-like *adiaphoria*:

Our pursuit of truth must rest upon the hope that the truth will prove worth knowing, the evil prove to be real evil, really conquered. A universe of evil unredeemed is not worth contemplating. (AJ, 51)

Clark's finely tuned moral sensitivity is not in question. Indeed, he is sensitive to the fact that we should not insult the victims of disaster by saying that their suffering exists in order to serve some worthy purpose. What I am calling into question is Clark's refusal to use his considerable metaphysical abilities to offer anything like a significant critique of the traditional claim that an all-powerful God will conquer evil (AJ, 55). It is clear that Clark rejects both (1) process theodicy, wherein evil is due to multiple freedoms in a world omnibenevolently cared for, but not omnipotently ruled, by God; and (2) liberal, Irenaean theodicy (as in John Hick), wherein evil is seen as permitted by God because it is necessary for the production of free moral agents. Clark's view is, however, very close to the latter stance. He believes that God has both the will and the power to make everything turn out well *in the end* (AJ, 165–66).

The theodicy that Clark offers is very much like that found in *Job*, in the sense that the mere existence of the world is infinitely superior to sheer nonbeing, hence the Creator cannot be said to *owe* us anything. God is not obligated to make free beings who will not sin, for then they would not be free. Nonetheless, I have the suspicion that if Clark's omnipotent God creates free beings, such a God has the obligation to create free beings who are at least *likely* not to sin. Clark sometimes agrees. Yet this admission on his part does not constitute a criticism of traditional theodicy. His real innovation consists in his concept of "anthropodicy," a neologism that, modelled on "theodicy," refers to the effort not to "explain the ways of God to man," but to "justify the ways of men regarding nonhuman animals." The traditional justification for killing and eating or experimenting on animals is that if it were not for us, they would not even be here. Yet, as Boswell has commented, there is a question as to whether animals would accept existence on their present terms. So also it is not sufficient to say that *any* existence is preferable to nonexistence, if some human beings would rather not be here, as in the case of a woman who has recently given birth to a deformed child:

> This point has a very general significance: if the world is not such as can be decently sustained by one who has the power to do otherwise, then we cannot decently sustain it either. We cannot decently continue to cooperate in phenomenal existence. We ought to preach sterility.[2]

Clark has here not so much offered a more plausible theodicy than that found in traditional theism as he has (legitimately) pointed out the hypocrisy of many of those who lampoon the traditional theodicy. A Gestapo officer is in no very strong position to criticize the minor human rights violations of an ineffectual bigot. Likewise, rational *human*ists should be alerted to the fact that

> flesh-foods, cosmetics, aspirins and indigestion tablets to alleviate the effects of nicotine-poisoning or over-eating are all purchased at the price of extreme suffering.[3]

That is, such humanists have no right to complain about God's ways until they change their own.

Both process theodicy[4] and Clarkian theodicy agree that the world would not necessarily be a better place if the liberty that generates evil were disallowed.

Yet the process thinker, who denies divine omnipotence, à la Plato,[5] and who as a panpsychist sees minuscule "freedom" in all concrete singulars (even in subatomic particles), can use the existence of multiple, conflicting freedoms to explain all of the evil in the world. Clark, as a defender of traditional omnipotence (or omnicompetence, as he sometimes puts it), cannot do this. In effect, physical evils not caused by human agency are inexplicable in Clark. From a pragmatic point of view Clark is correct to point out that theists and nontheists alike have no alternative but to make the best of what is offered us in the world, and when we concentrate on this practical imperative we are led to focus on the order and beauty and all that is the best in the world and on their cause:

> If the Creator is evil (what we call "evil"), and there is no escape from His world . . . we no longer have any idea what to do for the best or what that best might be.[6]

Here we can see the connection between Clark's theodicy and his qualified fideism: without a ground for belief we have no idea from where our desire to be treated justly or our desire for moral consistency come. As before, however, Clark does not believe that our cognitive situation is beyond repair; we can, in fact, legitimately try to persuade others of our moral convictions.

As I will argue in a later chapter, Clark is owed a great deal of credit for his books on animals, and these works infiltrate in a positive way his theodicy: for many individuals morality has proved to be a superstition whose foundations are immoral, *if* to be a humanist is to hate the nonhuman. Human beings, as we will see, have no right to kill animals. One wonders, however, if Clark is really glorifying God by claiming that the right (or privilege) to kill is ultimately God's, as in his positive citation of Romans 12:19 to the effect that vengeance is divine. Somehow or other, and here Clark's fideism has overstepped its bounds, what appear to be evils sent by God if God is omnipotent are claimed to make sense:

> The problem of evil is precisely that not everything that naturally happens is the sort of thing that we could bring about and still hope to be called good. . . . What good could we ever do by disobeying the Omnipotent?[7]

Clark thinks it absurd to suppose that God could ever command a rape, yet he defends the command given to Abraham to kill Isaac, and this on the ground that Abraham never did follow through on the act. Yet merely to threaten to kill an innocent person (or animal) is immoral, even in Clark's usual line of reasoning; likewise if one orders another to enact the threat. It may well be the case, as we will see, that Clark is correct that any moral obligation *ultimately* comes from God,[8] but this admission is nonetheless compatible with the belief that an action that is, from a humanly rational point of view, abhorrent would most likely be so from a divine point of view as well. God should not be an exception to moral and metaphysical principles, but their prime exemplification.

I have no quarrel with Clark's claim that we have no "independent, *authoritative* standards against which to judge God's judgements" (my emphasis), nor with his claim that

> only if we can conceive that some natural processes and impulses are divinely created, can we find any sure ground from which to pass judgement on other natural processes.[9]

The troublesome feature of Clark's theodicy, which follows quite logically from his belief in divine omnipotence, is the claim that

> If everything that happens is good, there is no charge against the Creator. But if everything that happens is bad, there can also be no charge against Him.[10]

If God is omnipotent, as Clark alleges, then there is indeed a charge to be made against God. There is thus indeed good reason to be suspect about Clark's choice to "fantasize some future felicity" when the mystery of suffering is considered in his theodicy.[11] Such fantasizing plays directly into the hands of the most intellectually sophisticated varieties of agnosticism and atheism.

DIVINE COMMAND THEORY

It is appropriate at this point to discuss in detail Clark's rather strong defense of divine command theory. Secular moralists are confident that decent people act either from sympathy or from rationally justifiable duty. Clark's view is not only that morality is compatible with religion, but that the former depends on the latter, à la the famous formulation of the question in the *Euthyphro*, albeit without Socrates' supposed response:

Is God's prohibition (or command) what makes it wrong (or right) to perform a given act, or is the act wrong (or right) independently of God's opinion? It has usually been argued that God (or the gods) cannot be the ultimate source of morality. Either He has a good reason for prohibiting X (a reason which anyone, in principle, might recognize) or He has not. If He has, then that act is wrong. (MR, 94–96)

Clark distinguishes three main views regarding the nature of the good: (1) Strict moral realism states that some acts or creatures simply have the property of goodness; that is, there are, in fact, substantive moral truths that are independent of anyone's recognition of them. (2) "Being morally good" may mean approval within a certain system of beliefs, an approval that implies a requirement that everyone who is rational will do the same in similar circumstances within the system. (3) Finally, "something is good" only expresses subjective approval of that something.

Clark has a special distaste for views 2 and 3. The problems with view 2 are closely allied to the problems with antirealism in general. These were discussed in chapter one and need not detain us here. Regarding view 3, Clark wonders why those who think that the good is nothing other than subjective preference would object to the subjective preferences of theists who prefer to believe that their moral principles come from God. It is view 1, however, that especially interests Clark: "If moral truths are facts, why should they not be facts ordained by God?" (MR, 97). As before, however, the question remains as to how Clark could possibly believe, as he does, that God could ordain as a moral fact the duty to kill, say, first-born males. Clark's skepticism regarding biblical literalism, treated in chapter one, seems to have been dispensed with here. Regarding such killing Clark asks rhetorically (and incredibly): "what could any moralist find to say against the act?" A great deal, I should think. Clark seems primarily interested in establishing that many recognizably moral acts require us to struggle with ourselves, hence the supposed hard-heartedness of killing first-born males because of a divine command is not the problem some make it out to be:

That [supposed hard-heartedness] is not enough to make such acts immoral. Or would the claim be that such acts contradicted the principle of equal respect for humanity in oneself and others? But why? By hypothesis, such sacrifice is the first-born male's route to glory, the particular task for which he is born. The Kantian principle surely does not require that everyone have exactly the same

destiny and duty. . . . Or is the thought that . . . to think it right to sacrifice all
first-born males, there could be no imaginably good reason for God to ordain
such a world? This too seems both uncertain and doubtfully relevant. (MR,
97–98)

The view that Clark is defending is that it is tautologous to suggest that the
central demand of morality is to obey *God*, if to be God is to be worshiped in
the highest degree. Rather, the central demand of morality, he thinks, is to obey
the *Lord*, which I take to be a reference to the particular view of God found in
the Abrahamic Scriptures. If the religious believer and the nonbeliever end up
in most cases doing the same things, it might be wondered if the belief that
actions are "required by the Lord" does any real work. If a believer loses her
faith she will still keep her promises, avoid theft, and so on. Clark's initial reply
is that there are some things that believers will think it proper to do that nonbelievers will eschew, as in engaging in corporate worship or in fasting, but the
gist of his reply is not that believers go to church and nonbelievers do not, such
that the rest of life is unchanged for the nonbeliever. Rather, because of Clark's
critique of behaviorism, it is not necessarily the case that nonbelievers do the
same things as believers, even if both, say, give a ten-dollar check to a famine
relief organization:

> Actions are individuated by the agent's intention. If an old woman is pushed to
> the floor on two occasions it does not follow that the same act is performed: on
> the first occasion, she is pushed down by a mugger . . . on the second, by a con-
> cerned friend to get her out of the line of fire. . . . Correspondingly, one who
> tithes his or her income solely because he or she believes it right to share wealth
> out more equitably does not do entirely the same thing as one who tithes it as a
> token and reminder that all one's wealth, all the world's wealth, is at the disposal
> of the divine. (MR, 99–100)

Well put. Yet, as before, difficulties arise when one is commanded by God not
to tithe but to kill.

The life-projects of nonbelievers, according to Clark, must be at least somewhat makeshift and something like an effort to muddle through a trying day,
in contrast to the everlasting significance of the actions of a religious believer.
Even if there is no personal immortality, a religious believer believes that his or
her actions are contributions to (i.e., they will forever be remembered and felt

by) an everlasting God. Of course the actions of a believer might not be much (if at all) better than those of a conscientious nonbeliever, a point that Clark willingly admits but that he conveniently does not weigh as heavily as he should as a sometimes pragmatist. However, even conscientious nonbelievers are, as in Clark's aforementioned distinction between real and only apparent atheists, in some sense religious believers:

> Part of the confusion in twentieth-century moral theory is that respectable moralists are constantly groping for good reasons to adopt the rules and practices we have inherited from more religious ages. Filial duty, marital affection, patriotism, keeping one's word cannot really be deduced from rationally self-evident principle. (MR, 101–2)[12]

Relying on Matthew 10:28, in a passage where the best and the most problematic features of Clark's philosophy are brought together (hence it is appropriate that the first line of the passage serves as an emblem for this book), Clark urges:

> Not a sparrow falls to the ground without our heavenly Father knowing it: nothing is too trivial for God's attention, and nothing could occur at all without God's providential will. In brief, the Creator did not establish a universe of natural forces and then absent Itself, but rather acts continually. . . . When we feel the universe to be "created," our conviction is not well expressed by the doctrine that some other thing preceded the present universe, and is "causally responsible" for it in just the same way as a human craftsman is responsible for a toy train. The point is rather that the events and conjunctions we experience seem to us like the fragments of a gigantic play, in which each event is an expression of the playwright's purpose—a play, moreover, which the author has not left entirely to others to enact. The universe has to be read as a fragmentary text, not explained as an artefact. (MR, 131)

Four comments are in order: (1) Clark's finely tuned sensitivity to the plight of animals and his commitment to connecting this sensitivity to his thoughts on religion is most apparent here. (2) By emphasizing divine concern for the minutiae, however, Clark seems to contradict his previously discussed (chapter two) opposition to what he calls "sectarianism." One must ask of Clark: Is God above the minor details? Clark's commitment to divine omnipotence seems to commit him to the idea that God is not, but his effort to defend human freedom and to get God "off the hook" regarding evil seems to commit him to the notion that God is above these details. (3) If God is omnipotent or omnicompetent, as Clark alleges, and if God cares even for the fall of a sparrow, then one must ask not only why there are suffering human beings, but also why there are suffering sparrows within the divine play of which Clark speaks, especially if sparrows are not immortal. (4) Finally, Clark's use of "entirely" creates confusion regarding who is responsible for evil—God, human beings, or chance?—and how much responsibility each is to bear.

At times Clark makes it clear that God is not *literally* the creator of all, but that God must somehow cooperate with any other local creator. This is still belief in divine omnipotence because, although God does not create every *happening*, God does create every *thing*: God makes the individual (Aristotelian) substances with powers of their own. Terms like "chaos" and "disorder" refer to the *relative* absence of God as the "all-powerful origin" of things, of the God who "holds all things in His hands." Odd as it seems at first, Clark's belief in divine omnipotence is compatible with his Aristotelianism, he thinks, as is evidenced in the following quotation, where a four-term analogy is indicated wherein *Aristotelianism: pantheism: :Newtonianism (Platonism): "conquest" theory.*

> The conquest model envisages what would happen if things were left "to themselves." . . . Whereas Aristotelian science understands "what naturally happens" as "what observably does usually happen," Newton followed a more Platonic line. In Aristotelian terms it "naturally happens" that heavy things fall. . . . In Newtonian terms everything would "naturally" either stay still or go on in a straight line forever. The fact that this is not what observably happens, leads to the hypothesis of an interfering force. . . . Correspondingly, whereas the pantheistic model understands the divine as what observably goes on, the conquest model imagines what would go on without God's mastering presence, discovers approximations to that abandoned state, and posits the interfering factor of divine agency as an explanation of why total ruin is not reached. (MR, 138–39)

Although it is clear that Clark is rejecting both the Newtonian model and the conquest model, we will have to be on the watch for clues in order to understand Clark's peculiar attachment to pantheism. If I am not mistaken, "pantheism" here refers only to the solace that comes from knowing that God is omnipresent, albeit in a noninterventionist way.

Once again Clark's belief in Judgment Day comes into play: *eventually* all of the gods and local creators will bow to God. Omnipotence consists of the promise of eventual success against evil. This is a grand promissory note when it is considered that we suffer and die in the short run, and that any possible future rewards a human being will receive cannot possibly negate past sufferings: what having been must ever be. That is, one cannot help but think that Clark's impressive rhetorical skills have somewhat gotten away from him when he urges his eschatology on us: just as the boy Jesus grows up to deliver "vitriolic attacks" on hypocrites, so also

> God's power, now manifest in human weakness, will one day cast down the mighty, and exalt the weak. . . . God is almighty, absolute sovereign. . . . The object of our worship ought to be both genuinely almighty and genuinely feeble. (MR, 149–50)

This seems to be yet another instance of Clark's undigested dipolar theism. My claim is that if Clark explicitly worked through the implications of dipolar theism he would have to discard belief in omnipotence.

The Euthyphro argument has convinced generations of students that God's commands cannot be the origin of moral duty. However, Clark is correct in noting that to be God at all is to be someone who ought to be listened to. J. L. Mackie is instructive here. He agreed with the Clarkian identity of objective morality and theism; he rejected the former because he thought he had convincing reasons against the latter. Clark's own view is that if we must choose between objective values rooted in God and merely made-up, nonauthoritative rules, it is important to notice that such made-up rules do not have much force and do not even constrain people to tell the truth. Hence, Clark draws the conclusion that "the life of reason therefore requires us to be old-fashioned theists." I do not know that we should infer that we are to be *old-fashioned* theists, but Clark's argument here for the existence of God and for divine command theory is quite careful and should not be ignored.

The difficulty with Clark's argument arises only when he arbitrarily inserts belief in an "old-fashioned" God whose original omnipotence "must" be at the mercy of the creatures. If God *must* be at the mercy of others, the creatures, a concept that makes sense if these creatures are at least partially free, then why call God omnipotent? (CP, 21, 39–40, 45).

' Even if there were no God, we would still find it necessary for practical reasons to come to some conclusions regarding our corporate practice, hence, for Clark, "being wrong" does not *only* mean "forbidden by God." Rather, Clark's view is that in any moral argument we must *in the end* rest content with appeal to *something* that carries value in itself, which for Clark (and, oddly enough, for Kant) can be only an "almighty" God. That is, nonbelievers are entitled (but not fully entitled) to use moral terms to describe the acts preferred in their own codes: "'right' fills the same role as 'true' in epistemology: sometimes this means objective truth, sometimes only pragmatic and agreed truth."[13] By making this concession to nonbelievers, however, Clark is not giving much weight to the nonbelievers' (and some believers') familiar charge that those who, like Clark, believe in divine command theory could be quite mistaken about what God tells them to do, as when Son of Sam supposedly "heard" God tell him to kill innocent bystanders. Indeed, Clark admits that we could be wrong about God's commands, but

> Morality is not exceptional in this. Epistemology suffers from a like complaint: however much evidence for the truth of a given proposition accumulates, it is still logically possible for all the evidence to be as it is said to be and yet the proposition be false. This does not worry us in *practice* [my emphasis].[14]

The ambivalence in Clark regarding pragmatic criteria surfaces here regarding divine command theory. On the one hand, nonbelievers have a (merely) pragmatic morality that functions as a rationalization for their corporate practice. On the other hand, it seems that religious believers who are divine command theorists distinguish between authentic and inauthentic divine commands primarily through historical (including biblical) practice, a practice that finds Son of Sam (but why not Abraham?) abhorrent. Pragmatic criteria are obviously not the only ones used by Clark in the evaluation of supposed commands from God. In some way or another any moral action commanded by God and then performed by human beings must ultimately be an appropriate act of praise:

> Praising God is not like praising people: we praise our children to encourage them, to give them a sense of their own worth; we praise human leaders to remind them of the virtues we hope they will go on (or even start) displaying.

The point of praising God is to acknowledge to ourselves our total dependency . . . to express our devotion.[15]

In effect, Clark's position is that by noticing that some things are *to a certain extent* valuable or true in themselves quite apart from our recognition of them, we are able to see that only God, as the necessary existent, could provide self-authenticating value.

According to Clark, theists are unlikely to believe that God would command us to kill all male children, but he holds that it is *possible* that God might issue such a command, and if God did so a theist would feel bound to obey. Because not even Clark holds that theists have a privileged access to the thoughts of God, they must rely on tradition and sound reasoning like everyone else. Yet how could sound reasoning ever reach the conclusion that killing all male children was even a remote possibility for a moral person?[16]

John Chandler is correct to call attention to the fact that the theist lacks a privileged access to the thoughts of God. To the extent that Clark sees the need for sound reasoning in order to ascertain God's commands, Chandler holds, Clark is not really a divine command theorist at all. Furthermore, if we take away the need to engage in sound reasoning then divine command theory can be true only if it is tautologous to say that what God commands is right. Finally, Chandler is not convinced that the appeal to God's loving nature saves divine command theory from the possibility of God commanding torture. Chandler puts the issue this way:

> Is love good independently of the will of God, or is it good only because God approves it? If it is held to be good independently of God, this is to abandon divine command theory. . . . If on the other hand it is good only because God approves it, all the original problems return. . . . An ethic which emphasizes love as the essential nature of God and the reason for moral action is antithetical in spirit to an ethic of commands and obedience.[17]

The response that Clark gives to Chandler is at times indirect. Regarding the criticism that on divine command theory one may be required to do things that are counterintuitive—say, to torture—Clark responds that the same criticism can be made against emotivism or subjectivism:

The theist is supposed to concede that other things might turn out to be required of her than she now supposes; the subjectivist is bound to admit that her feelings may change, that what she now thinks fine she may, with as much reason, soon think base.[18]

Clark makes sense here, but he has not really responded to the significant criticism regarding the possibility that if we adopt *his* version of divine command theory we might have to enact torture. More to the point is his attempt to show that Kant, the most influential ethicist since the eighteenth century, can only be understood as identifying each individual's idealized intelligence (and will) with God's, an identification that, as Kant admits, is asymptotic at best. That is, divine command theory is held at least implicitly by anyone who believes in objective morality:

The theist supposes that the voice which we uncover in ourselves, the voice that requires justice, mercy, and thankfulness (and which non-theistic moralists may hear as well), is that of the maker, sustainer and conquerer of all. We may mishear It. . . . If the non-theistic moralist can say, without absurdity, that she wills to do what the moral law commands . . . the theist may say that she wills to do God's will. The difference is that the theist . . . has some reason to reject the seeming possibility that quite different rules might have been made (whereas moral realists and rationalists have no plausible account of what the necessity of moral rules resides in).[19]

This is, in fact, more to the point.

I would like to reiterate that it is not, contra Chandler, divine command theory itself in Clark that is problematic, so much as it is Clark's willingness to keep alive the possibility, or even the plausibility, of God commanding us to do actions that we would otherwise consider atrocious. His "you too!" attitude is directed not only against emotivism, but also against utilitarianism, which also allows the possibility that the innocent could be tortured for the sake of some greater good:

I cannot understand why it is a charge against theists that they might, under some extraordinary but undisclosed circumstances, conclude that the Lord required of them what He has forbidden in general. Those who object to utilitarianism on the ground that utilitarian principles might require one to act unjustly at least offer some plausible scenario in which this might be taken to have happened.[20]

By "those who object to utilitarianism," I assume Clark means divine command theorists. That is, if Kantians are implicit divine command theorists, and if emotivists and utilitarians are just as open to the charge of permitting torture as divine command theorists, then Clark thinks that he is in the clear. It is not at all clear, however, that Clark has offered a better version of divine command theory than that which could be offered by a strict Kantian who was opposed in all instances to torturing or killing the innocent.

Consider the following contrast in Clark's thoughts on divine command theory. On the one hand, he makes good (Kantian) sense in opposition to any justification of torture:

> Certainly people have supposed that God required them to torture heretics and burn witches, but they have also generally come to discard this view—not because they set their "own" standard of justice against the Lord's, but because they came to see that such commands were radically incompatible with the Lord's revealed nature, and so could not really be His command. . . . Our only access to the One is through the Logos, the light that lights everyone, as it embodies itself in human reason and the church.

On the other hand, he would seem to permit torture; or better, he would seem to permit God to permit it:

> This is not to say that God might not command us to act (or to forbear) in ways that our "unaided" reason might resent. No theist could agree that God existed simply to validate or defend our own petty views.[21]

The obvious Kantian reply is that there is nothing whatsoever "petty" about the use of human reason to protect the innocent, a claim that Clark is usually, especially regarding animals, willing to admit. Yet it should be emphasized that Clark's theory is compatible with Kant's view that true autonomy lies in our recognition of duty such as would be legislated by a perfectly rational (i.e., divine) agent.[22]

DEATH

The traditional theodicy defended by Clark, along with his defense of divine command theory (including his controversial defense of some biblical commands to do things we would normally consider immoral), includes a particular view of death that is worthy of our consideration. For Clark the enlightened pagan can hope that death is a separation of the soul and body such that one can at death wake up to the real life of which this life is but a phantom (CP, 177). This is but one version of the general view in religion that, although we die, we are not meant to die eternally. Even though I know I will die, I cannot quite imagine what death will be like. The religious response to such an age of radical insecurity as ours, Clark characteristically thinks, should be to build firm structures (like cathedrals) against chaotic change that will perhaps take generations to complete, or to rebuild ancient houses. In effect, Clark thinks that to understand death we need, at the very least, to develop a more patient image of time (MR, 196–97).

The connection between Clark's divine command theory and his view regarding death lies in the fact that both views depend on the notion of intrinsic value, supremely so in the case of God, less extremely so regarding a human being's anticipation of death:

> So the good man acts "for the sake of what is noble," and does his actions "for their own sake." It does not matter what else is achieved: it is enough to find that beauty in the perfect leap, the flawless bow-shot, the act of generosity. One who is motivated in this way is quite unmoved by the news that she will die and be forgotten, that the void will "win." Immortality, of a kind, is achieved in present nobility. (MR, 199)

If actions are done for their own sake, it would seem that the atheist could be just as moral as the theist. Yet, as is often the case, Clark wants to have it both ways, a situation that is not in itself problematic as long as one works to show the compatibility of the two poles in tension. In addition to defending intrinsic value, Clark also criticizes atheism, because the atheist's defiant attitude toward evil is merely a rhetorical stance when it is considered that it makes little sense to struggle against evil if "Omnipotent Matter will inevitably crush all human projects," a stance that seems to imply that actions are not so much done for their own sake as for their effects.

There need not be a contradiction here, however. Clark's resolution of this tension seems to be, although there can be no assurance here, that the atheist cannot *really* defend the notion of intrinsic value. We cannot know what is true or valuable in itself unless there is that in us that is united with *the* truth and *the* source of value, just as we cannot really know that "human beings are mortal" without at least partially transcending mortality when we look at mortality from the outside (MR, 198–99).

Clark is well aware of the fact that his Buddhist critique of individualism, or better of the individual self, makes it difficult to argue for the immortality of that "self," as does his Aristotelian notion of the integral union of psyche and soma. Yet Clark explores several avenues that make it possible for him to argue for immortality. One is the possibility that the "soul" is an "astral body," an ethereal yet perceptible (by clairvoyants) spirit, "unfairly disregarded by philosophers." As with Santa Claus, extraterrestrials, and the Olympian gods, Clark uses astral bodies for his own purposes rather asking us to believe in them literally. His point seems to be that astral bodies point toward an understanding of immortalism that supplements theories regarding the Cartesian ego or bodily resurrection. Clark thinks it easy to conceive of his own existence without a body, however, which makes him sound more like a Cartesian than he likes to admit. Obviously the fact that "I" might imaginably exist without a body (actually I have trouble imagining this) does not prove that "I" could so exist, but Clark, in fact, thinks that there are strong reasons to be persuaded by Descartes:

> This body is this body, and I am I, but neither is the other: if "I" and "this body" referred to identically the same thing, there would be no possibility even of imagining that this thing could exist when I didn't. If I can conceive of myself as existing when this body does not, then "I" must refer to something other than this body. That ego may possibly survive this body. . . . It is certainly not the sort of argument that closes a debate, and although it is probably agreed amongst professional philosophers that Kripke's argument rules out some versions of materialism, there would be no general agreement that it established any form of spiritualism. . . . That our minds and our brains are identical cannot be that sort of simple, contingent truth. At the very least, our mental attributes (our thinking and feeling) are not the same attributes as our ordinary physical, publicly observable ones, and any connection between them must be just that—a connection. Minds and brains, mental states and physical states *may* be causally related (somehow) but they are not identical. (MR, 200–202)

The reticulative ambitions pursued by Clark typically lead to tensions in his thought, tensions that he sometimes takes great pains to render consistent, and that he sometimes leaves in paradoxical opposition. Regarding immortality it is difficult to see how he relieves the tension between his Buddhism, his Aristotelianism, and his distrust of Cartesian egoism, on the one hand, and his defense of traditional Christian belief, supplemented by Cartesian egoism, on the other. The latter tendency wins out in the following passage:

> It is at least very puzzling that some Christian writers should have been so ready to espouse the argument against bodiless persons (usually adding that ordinary immortalism was a "Greek" idea alien to the true biblical temperament) without recognizing that it presents an identical difficulty for the supreme bodiless person, God. (MR, 204)

We should also note for future reference that the view of God as bodiless is in tension with Clark's belief in the World Soul of the *body* of the world.

The Hebraic belief in the resurrection of bodies is sometimes seen as more compatible with Aristotelianism than with the dualism implied in belief in immortality. Clark again bites. He shows a favorable attitude not only toward astral bodies and immortality theory but also toward resurrection of bodies, despite the discontinuity of consciousness implied by this view. The sheer discontinuity of consciousness does not, he points out, guarantee nonidentity through time. It may be that all bodies are discontinuous at a microscopic level, just as we certainly are discontinuous at a psychic level in dreamless sleep. The identity of a person is not simply a descriptive or an evaluative notion but an explanatory one that allows us, in some sense, to identify Michael today with the Michael we saw yesterday. In this aspect of the belief in resurrection of bodies Clark has, in fact, been consistent with his Buddhist critique of too strong a sense of personal identity through time (MR, 205–7).

Further, Clark shows sympathy with Royce's belief that the demands of personal love can be satisfied only if every individual has an infinite amount of time to distinguish him- or herself. This is at least somewhat like Kant's paymaster argument, and it is very much like Plotinus's argument (3.6.6) that our present life is dreamlike such that at death we can wake up from the body (MR, 207, 210–11):

The mysterious and unfathomable thisness of every real identity is not, as Royce admitted, a solid ground for supposing that such things are immortal. But it is perhaps one of the elements that go to make up a conviction of immortality. . . . Personal love, as devotion to an individual who *ought* to be immortal. . . . (MR, 208)

An assessment of these versions of afterlife which are treated favorably by Clark (astral body, immortality theory, resurrection of bodies, infinite time to wake up) must include a thorough treatment of his otherwise firm commitment to Aristotelian principles. The *ergon* (proper functioning) of a living being consists in that activity that "makes sense" of its structure, a structure that, in the unique case of human beings, is capable of deliberative desire (*proairesis*) and hope regarding the future. Hope and real praxis (which depends on *proairesis*) are unique properties of human beings, properties that must be acknowledged in the effort to understand the human problem of theodicy. Human beings expect a great deal from life, hence they tend to be disappointed more often than members of any other species (AM, 16, 21–25):

Aristotle . . . would think that a man who made no effort to make a unity of his life, being free, was very foolish. . . . No man can wish to be a god, for such is suicide, he urges us to follow Plato's advice (*Timaeus* 89e), not Pindar's: "one ought not to follow the advice of those who tell us to think mortal thoughts, being mortal, or human thoughts being human, but ought to immortalize ourselves as far as possible" (*Nicomachean Ethics X*, 1177b). . . . If Aristotle is correct we have very far to grow. (AM, 26–27)

Human beings are certainly animals, but they are the animals who are most divine, or at least who strive most to be divine. As we will see, belief in human superiority over other animals is nonetheless compatible with Aristotle's continuity thesis, a thesis that helps to keep our anthropocentrism in check:

"Nature stretches without a break from lifeless objects to animals through things that are animated but not animals, so that there seems to be very little difference between one thing and the next, they are so close together". . . . All "adjacent" groups in a continuum share some individuals. (AM, 31)[23]

Distinctions within a continuum can be justified, Clark thinks, if we take the remark in the *Categories* (2b) seriously, to the effect that of the secondary substances the species is more of a substance than the genus, since it is nearer to the primary substance, that is, to the individual (AM, 28–29, 33, 35).

The view that Clark defends seems to be that there are contingencies unresolved in the futures of concrete individuals that are not necessarily in the futures of more abstract entities. Because these contingencies are not mapped out in advance, individuals can expect (especially rational individuals with elaborate hopes regarding the future) that things will sometimes not turn out as planned, even to the point where individuals will be recipients of extreme pain or moral evil. The distinctive way in which human beings hope for, and are often disappointed by, the outcome of future contingencies makes us realize that Aristotle's continuum is not *wholly* continuous (AM, 36, 40, 43). Aristotle pushes this point much further than Clark, however, as is evidenced in Clark's characterization of Aristotle's views:

> Beasts are committed solely to seeking some lesser end (e.g., the building of nests) whose pursuit makes sense in terms of a higher-order pursuit of which they are unaware (e.g., the procreation of the species). . . . Life's meaning, if such there be, is to be found in terms of human activities. We use everything as if it were for us (*Physics* 2.194a), and so, in a sense, it is (see *Politics* 1.1256b). (AM, 46)

THE GOOD LIFE

Recognition of, or complaints about, evil in the world implicitly contain some theory regarding what the good life is, and Clark is correct in emphasizing Aristotle's contributions regarding this issue. The good life is one that *we* must put into practice because human life is too complex for simple obedience to rules. In order to put it into practice a reasonable person orders the various goods that are desired, as is evidenced in the etymological root of *eudaemonia*: the possession of a good *daimon* or distributor. Aristotle also thinks it important, however, that we have good luck (*tyche*), a phenomenon that, if God is omnipotent, as Clark suggests, should have no place. That is, in Clark's view good or bad luck *should* be viewed as misleading ways of speaking of divine providence. In any event, the best way to avoid evil, according to Aristotle *and* Clark, is to self-consciously develop an ordering of one's desires and goals so as to avoid living from moment to moment (AM, 145, 149).

From Aristotle, Clark suggests, one can learn how to criticize the notion of the self as substantial *and* how to preserve the best in the notion of self-identity

99

and of continuity of self through time (AM, 151–57). Clark notes that the Greek language used by Aristotle makes it easy to understand the making of unity, of identity, in one's life:

> We say "I," "je," "ich," "io," and attach the action or state to this as subject. . . . Greek does not compel this isolation of the subject from the act: the subject is in the verb grammatically, and in the act semantically. . . . To think of the soul as life rather than as detachable ego . . . our languages encourage us to emphasize certain features at the expense of others. The Greek-speaker *can* employ personal pronouns to isolate the subject: he does not need to. . . . Being is doing. . . . To be single is therefore to act singly, to make one's choice coherent. Without such an effort I remain only "a heap." . . . This is not to say that other acts are good only if they serve the central act, that other ends are good only as a means to this further end. There are many things that are good independently of each other and of any one central thing. . . . One does not always seek things to subserve the central good. (AM, 149–50)

The good life for an individual-in-society consists of a balance between concern for oneself and for the community. An unbalanced concern for self, and for selfish pleasures in particular, tends to blow out of proportion how many evils there really are in the world:

> Suppose we could infallibly stimulate our own pleasure centres with a small machine [like Woody Allen's orgasmatron in *Sleeper*]: would you accept permanent and solipsistic addiction to this device? If you would not, and I suspect that only the suicidal would choose otherwise, then pleasure is not a suitable paramount end. Pleasure and life go together (*Nicomachean Ethics* 10.1175b), and all men aim at life, but "life" means many things. Aristotle is certainly not saying that all men do or should aim at their own contentment. (AM, 158)

Aristotle himself faces a tension, according to Clark, between the views of death as an intrusion and as a completion. If one adopts the former *simpliciter* one must face the objection that there are some ethical values that require our demise. The tension actually antedates Aristotle, in that the primitive division between hunters and farmers consisted largely in the former typically seeing death as an act of violence and the latter as the way of the world. That is, farmers as opposed to hunters enable us to face the theodicy problem with as much equanimity as possible because death is largely an aspect of the natural rhythm of things. Or, in Aristotelian terms, death is unnatural in respect to form (*kata to eidos*), but natural in respect to matter (*kata ten hulen*).[24] The only element of human beings that Aristotle allows as immortal has no memory at all, hence there is nothing like *personal* immortality in his thought. The divine alone lives perpetually (including perhaps the divine in each of us), while all else comes to be and perishes. Once again, these metaphysical foundations for virtue-based ethics provide the background for any adequate theodicy. One can certainly agree with Clark here without adopting his controversial defense of all of the traditional divine predicates (MR, 164–69):

> Aristotle . . . cannot allow survival by "waking-to-a-new world," for this is the only world there is. . . . It must be survival of something which can be found in the world of the four elements, the spheres, the whole complex of the natural universe. Plato argued for the immortality of the divine element in man, and apparently accepted the immortality of the whole man: Aristotle could accept no more than the former. Plato made a division between this world and reality: Aristotle denied it. . . . The discussion of death, in relation to courage, in *Nicomachean Ethics* III . . . is clear that death is an end. (AM, 170–71)

In effect, Clark has used Aristotle to illustrate how, even without a theory of personal immortality, one can view one's death with repose:

> Our awareness of the world is a value, but it is the world itself which enshrines the highest value. . . . We should place our heart not in immediate personal concerns, though they matter, but in that which is the Unborn in each of us. . . . We must live according to [the] best in us, and that best does not age (*De Anima* 408b). . . . It is because we are aware of the world as more than our own world, that we are aware of our impending death: it is because we are aware of the world as more than our own world, that we can conceive the extinction of our worlds as the possibly better alternative. (AM, 172–73)

To practice *theoria* is, in a way, to immortalize oneself by realizing the presence of the divine in the soul. This Aristotelian view, defended by Clark, is surprisingly opposed to the traditional prejudice (also sometimes defended by Clark) that immortality and God are other, if not *totaliter aliter* (totally other), from humanity.[25] Clarkian "this worldly" immortality through *theoria* is integrally connected with his belief that established practice makes it possible to actually know this world, contra the extreme skeptic:

> If my friend comes to me with a conundrum that purports to show the impossibility of knowing another's feelings, or the essential meaninglessness of life, or the impossibility of drawing any inference from past to future, I may engage her in philosophical debate. But if it is evident that she really means it, I am perhaps more likely to begin to enquire about her diet, her state of health, the progress or otherwise of her affections. (AJ, 4)

Although Clark does not think that reason can supply of itself its own ground, as we have seen, it certainly can enable us to negotiate our way through the world, so as to refute the extreme skeptic. Thoroughgoing skeptics are, however, rare, which is fortunate when it is considered that they make exasperating company. It is more likely that we will run into the less extreme skepticism entailed in relativism, a type of skepticism embedded in the contemporary culture that Clark largely distrusts. Aristotelian *theoria* and faith in objective truth and justice have not so much been refuted as people have affectively given themselves over to melancholic doubt (AJ, 5–9). Clark would have us notice, however, that such doubt or indifference is often posturing, as when those who, like the biologist Jacques Monod, deny that the universe is directed toward an objectively good end make exceptions in favor of their own bodies, friends, and careers:

> The fate of laboratory animals in the last century, treated as research tools and without serious regard for their own interests, is a warning of what life would be like if we were ruled by indifferentists. (AJ, 10)

There are certainties regarding moral evil that are as secure as ordinary factual certainties. Consider the case of one who has

> abandoned his wife and children, stolen the life-savings of a family friend, kicked his dog to death, knowingly sold poisoned food, raped a seven-year-old, given the formula of a new biological poison to a psychopathic tyrant . . . (AJ, 12)

It is cases like these that make apparent the fact that there is something comic in the pose of heroic despair found in many atheists and agnostics.

Indifferentism might seem plausible if it were not so (pragmatically) absurd. "The world cannot be wholly disdained" (AJ, 15). The question I have been pressing on Clark in this chapter, however, does not have to do with his legitimate attacks on atheism and agnosticism. Rather, I have asked whether the "new understanding" of evil that Clark promises can be anything more than a promissory note as long as his continued defense of divine omnipotence paints him into the traditional corners (AJ, 13, 16).

Clark is quite correct that philosophy should lead us in at least a vicarious Socratic way out of the cave of this world's evil:

> Our common understanding of the world is formed in us by the propaganda, which need not be malevolent, of politicians, sophists, schoolteachers. If the prisoner were to halt here she would lapse into despair or cynicism. But the way lies on: there is a path to light. . . . And by the constant friction of words and arguments and images, the fire may be kindled in us also. . . . Philosophy is the record of our explorations. It rests, however we may disguise it, on the conviction that there is a light. . . . Without that faith, it would seem better to stick with our comfortable shadows, to use such instruments of propaganda and medicine as will keep us without questions. . . . Philosophy began as the pursuit of wisdom, the care of the soul, and has not wholly lost that office. (AJ, 17–18)

He is also instructive in emphasizing that the afterlife is, perhaps, best viewed not so much as *personal* immortality as a type of waking up. He is not too much interested in debates regarding whether or not bodily continuity is an essential element in personal identity or self. Rather, we are led a step closer toward an appreciation of the afterlife when we realize in a Buddhist or St. John of the Cross-like way that there is no Cartesian "self." I die but God endures; "I" am immortal to the extent that I realize, wake up to, the divine in me: "my being Me is matter of degree."[26]

One's present experience may be structured by concepts that reflect "the true life" to which we have a chance of waking. Regarding his waking up metaphor, Clark says,

> The one who has woken up reports that even in the dream she knew or suspected that it was a dream. It is also not uncommon for people to report that they dreamed that they had woken up, and maybe woke up to many different layers of dream before at last they "really" woke (if they have woken yet).[27]

Life within the dream world (which most call wakefulness) follows the rules of Humean causality, wherein all conjunctions are matters of brute fact, equally unintelligible. *True* wakefulness, however,

> is associated with a grasp of intelligible connection, and the lack of it. It is possible for us to seem to wake up many times: each apparent waking is associated with the conviction that we now understand what is going on.[28]

Clark believes that the truth about things is not laid open to ordinary view, but, as we have seen, he also criticizes the belief that we should accept only that for which we have rational justification. It should be remembered that Clark is a pragmatist who holds that we bring theses into our program because they are likely to lead to interesting *results*, as in helping us to make sense of our lives:

> It is better to risk believing something which will do us little harm if we are mistaken, than withhold belief (or believe a preferred alternative) when error in so doing would create great harm. It is better to believe that babies are sentient individuals even if we are mistaken in so doing than to believe that they are not. . . . From which it follows that I do not need to show that the dream-model of our deaths is in itself more probable. . . . I need show only that it is an option worth exploring . . . that a mistaken belief in this would at least not do more harm than a mistaken failure to believe. . . . An experienced universe that seems to point all ways at once (so that light is both a stream of particles and a wave- formation; matter both a pile of small, hard objects and the mere intersection of probability networks; humankind both flesh and spirit) is not implausibly regarded as a dream.[29]

Even the world that science describes helps us to escape the dreamlike, as in the eye-opening properties of the discontinuous world of quantum physics:

> Maybe only in our dream-world is it necessary for an entity that moves from P_1 to P_2 to occupy successively an infinite number of locations in between. The imaginary world of sub-atomic physics does not seem to obey this inscrutable rule: why should the gods?[30]

Clark is here attempting to revitalize the medieval belief that God (and the angels) occupies several places *virtually* at once because God is an intellect, just as my attention here does not preclude your attention there. If there are genuine cases of telekinesis, it is due to some such explanation dealing with the unity of *nous* rather than to matter being converted into some sort of ethereal energy. "In our essences we are not distant from each other."[31] As before, science fiction writers often get hold of myths, like that regarding "hyperspace," which some of our theistic predecessors would easily understand. By expanding our imaginations through myth we may well be better prepared to cope with the immanent prospect of death, and more importantly, we might well be able to live more lively and delightful lives. One wonders, however, if Clark is at times a bit too sanguine in his attitude toward death, as when he claims that

> What is objectionable in murder is not the death of the victim [!], for death is no extinction of the theme that was being played in her, but the denial of our common root.[32]

CONCLUSION

In this chapter I have tried to show how Clark's "new understanding" of the theodicy problem is hampered by his attachment to the traditional belief in the Abrahamic religions that God is omnipotent. It should be noted, however, that belief in omnipotence is not necessarily a biblical notion, as in the creation *ex hyle* (rather than creation *ex nihilo*) story in Genesis. Clark's willingness to pull in the reins on his considerable talents, his willingness to defend even the possibility that God really did give Abraham a command to kill his son, conflicts with his desire to shed new light on the subject. Further, Clark's defense of divine command theory is a significant addition to literature on the topic, especially in his claim that Kantians must ultimately be divine command theorists. Yet it is not clear that Clarkian divine command theory is superior to Kantian divine command theory, when the former is connected to the possibility that God could command us to do what otherwise would be considered atrocious things. He is on much stronger ground, I claim, in his use of Aristotle to help illuminate the problem of evil from the perspective of a judicious view of what the good life really is and of what death might be. My major criticism has been that a more Greek view of the theodicy problem, a view defended on the contemporary scene by process philosophers and theologians, would have helped Clark to balance his concern for divine unity with his concern for plurality. That is, if one omnipotent God is ultimately responsible for every thing in the world, evil becomes inexplicable; but in a world of multiple freedoms persuaded—rather than dictated to—by God, partial chaos and evil are to be expected.

Clark is to be commended for trying to avoid views that are either "hellishly conservative" or "immoderately changeful," even if he leans a bit toward the former extreme. In his book on science fiction and philosophy he draws an analogy between computer networkers and shamans, in that both want radical change: they want to leave their ordinary bodies so as to commune with the powers that rule the world. This sort of immoderate change is criticized by Clark, yet the desire for such change nonetheless alerts us to a crucial element in Clark's theodicy: many human beings want to live forever because there is so much that is not noble in this life. It is important to fear death, in that those who do not do so are the most dangerous of all, but it is also important to keep alive the hope that our neoplatonic, "higher selves" will live on in some form or another.

Immortality consists, it seems, of a Clarkian "waking up" from the sleepy and at least partially evil world in which we live. This waking up does not necessarily mean that we can actually bring about progress in the world, in Clark's conservative view. Rather, "immortality" consists of a transformation of our present existence: all history is fallen history and anyone who lives in any present, where our personal grudges tend to dominate us, is in need of such transformation. Although it is unclear whether Clark really thinks we are immortal, it is clear that he feels no compulsion to believe all of the views he discusses, especially those that contain elements from science fiction. The far-fetched views he sometimes discusses, however, are both fun and necessary if we want to avoid the hegemony of the commonsensism of respectable society. That is, neither science fiction nor philosophy are necessarily more "realistic" if they mirror a fallen, rather than a spiritually transformed, world.[33]

PART II

ANIMALS

CHAPTER 4

ETHOLOGY

INTRODUCTION

The first three chapters of this book have concentrated on Clark's treatment of God-issues. In the next three chapters I will turn my attention to his treatment of animals. As the title to this book indicates, however, there are integral links between these two topics, links to which I will return repeatedly. In the present chapter I will lay the groundwork for an analysis of Clark's stance regarding the moral status of animals, to be undertaken in the following chapter. Here I will attempt to detail Clark's courageous and insightful contemporary version of Aristotelianism, a version that continues Aristotle's project of a biologized philosophy. (It should be noted that, according to Clark, Plato actually has a far more naturalistic view of human nature than Aristotle, in that Plato seems to see far less difference between human and nonhuman than does Aristotle, and this despite Plato's reputation for being the more "spiritual" writer.) In particular I will concentrate on Clark's treatment of how our animal inheritance affects our view of gender issues and our attitude toward violence. Before treating these particular topics, however, I would like to introduce Clark's approach to ethology.

A MODERATE VIEW

Clark sides with those who deny a radical division between human beings and beasts. Yet he wonders about the extent to which we can trust our own "unthinking recognition" of their fear, fidelity, and cleverness. The "almost universal" judgment of human beings has been that animals do indeed show love, devotion, anger, shame, and the like. Even the Stoics, who were no great defenders of animals, believed that human morals began with animal impulses, but they also believed that we should deny our animal roots, for animals are, after all, entirely "animal." Largely because of the theory of evolutionary transformism, we have come to be skeptical of Stoic denigration of animals. If in fact we are related to the other animals, we should expect to find analogies and homologies of behavior as well as of anatomy. As before, however, Clark wonders about the extent to which we can, say, argue from chimpanzee promiscuity to a moral suitable for human sexuality, or from the territorial behavior of butterflies to a defense of capitalism (NB, 2–4, 7).

It is obvious to Clark that human beings are freer in certain ways than other animals, but if one claims that animals are genetically programmed *simpliciter*, one has a difficulty in explaining the origins of human culture. Stipulating a "special creation" of humankind, say, by the miraculous insertion of souls into living matter, leads to such a radical discontinuity between humans and animals that Clark rejects such a stipulation as unconvincing (NB, 70). Clark's position lies between two extremes. On the one hand, there are those who think that nonhuman behavior is of an entirely different kind than human morality. On the other hand, there are those who think that human morality will eventually be absorbed into sociobiology, into the theory that suggests that human moral theories are rationalizations for those behaviors that are conducive to collective survival. Although Clark is obviously not a sociobiologist in this sense, he nonetheless, as a latter-day Aristotelian, sees a strong connection between human ethics and animal tendencies, a connection that works both for good and for ill:

> As higher mammals we are likely to find it relatively easy to form or enter into local attachments of affection and deference. We are likely to be concerned for infants, to wish to fit in with our fellows, male and female, to defer to dominants. . . . It is not unusual for those who have lived with and watched a group of beasts to conclude that they are loyal, protective and affectionate towards each

other. They show behavior that, if they were human, few would hesitate to call courageous, courteous, or motherly. . . . This is not to say that higher mammals always behave just as the higher morality would demand: we are also likely to be unconcerned for (even hostile towards) strangers, to be ready to let the weakened starve, to react to obvious disease in others by ostracising them. . . . [Animals] are also. . . . sometimes cruel. (NB, 98)

There is a defect in those sociobiological theories that imply that individuals should maximize the probability of their own genes appearing in the next generation in a higher proportion than they appear at present. What is the warrant for this use of "should," especially when it is considered that we have the values we do at present, according to sociobiologists, largely if not exclusively because it "paid" our ancestors to have them? It is true that creatures who do not notice that fire burns do not as a rule leave progeny, but it may also be true that "the whole natural system has been made in such a way that evolutionary logic will lead to creatures of a moral kind" (NB, 103). The choice between moral skepticism, theism, or some other metaethical position is a philosophical choice, according to Clark, not a matter for sociobiology. Clark's own moral stance consists of a virtue-based theory grounded in theism, rather than in a decision-making procedure (whether utilitarian or contractual), such that if we follow the rules of the procedure we will solve our moral problems. Because the overriding lesson of ethology is that living creatures are enormously variable, sociobiology does not much contribute to the debate as to how much stock we should put in the judgments of a well-informed and balanced moral character as opposed to the faith we might put in a procedure (NB, 100–6).

By making a distinction between "ethical" (from *ethos*, habit) and "moral," Clark is able to plot a middle course between the aforementioned extremes:

Beasts, let us say, are *ethical*: that is, they respond to aspects of a situation and to features of their kindred, that a good man also would respect. But they are not *moral*: for they do not, as far as we can see, have any occasion to moralize about themselves or to construct intellectual systems to accommodate their immediate responses. (NB, 107)

Kant is the great champion of the moral, the empiricists of the ethical. Clark seems to be claiming that only the virtue tradition can bring these two aspects together:

Rationalists, emphasizing the moral, are likely to find beasts wholly other than human; empiricists, like David Hume, recognize beasts as our cousins, moved by ethical concerns that move us also. The truth, no doubt, lies in between: a banal enough conclusion, maybe, but one worth emphasizing. Not even Kant could give his categorical imperative any content without appealing to the facts of natural sentiment; even those who found their morals upon sentiment will usually acknowledge that rational argument can sometimes show their sentiments to be ill-judged. We are unlike the beasts, or what we know of them, in this: that we have scope to see that we were wrong. (NB, 107)

Despite the fact that moral rules cannot be deduced from sociobiological premises, and despite the fact that animal behavior can do no more than offer us examples of what *might* be done, we can still learn things of moral importance from animals. That is, Clarkian anthropology is based both in religion and in biology. Regarding the latter we can expect that human beings will be somewhat affectionate to members of their immediate circle, especially to children, and will form groups within which they will probably not carry violence to the extreme. These and other obvious features of human life do not stem from our intellectual abilities. Our rational moral systems, according to Clark, are "rationalizations of pre-rational sentiments," a belief regarding morality that is consistent with Clark's fideism in religion. We have a very strong urge to believe that

> A mammalian group which really attempted to bring up its children to regard themselves as interchangeable components, or to hate their spouses and their children, or to suppress all sexual desire except at stated intervals, would be very unlikely to succeed. (NB, 109)

It does not follow at once, according to Clark, that we should aim for a utopian society, a belief that is consistent with his political conservativism. That is, Clark's ethology seems to grow quite smoothly out of (and partially inform) his religious and political beliefs and his reverence for Aristotle:

> If . . . our life is, or can be, good, then the ethologist and anthropologist can contribute to the study of how best to organize our lives so as to satisfy the wants and desires that have been programmed into us, which we can ignore or subvert only at our grave peril. . . . We must also remember just how easily our natural impulses may outrun prudence or a wider code of law than is provided in the family. (NB, 113)

Even if animal behavior has evolutionary consequences, such consequences tell us nothing about the animal's feelings. The act of predation allows wild cats to survive, but there is no evidence that the cat "hates" her prey; bird song helps birds to propagate, and *in addition* the birds seem to enjoy their songs.[1] It is important to distinguish evolutionary function from subjective feeling, if only because not cutting such a distinction makes it too easy to argue for "man the mighty hunter," who seethes with violent urges that help him to survive (MR, 5; MS, 35).[2] Yet it is not even clear that our closest ancestors were predators, much less that they enjoyed predation. Gorillas and chimpanzees are mostly plant-eaters, although they will, at times, eat small animals. Most modern human "hunter"-gatherers get the majority of their food from plants and eat nothing like the amount of flesh eaten in the Western world. Further, our hominid ancestors may well have been grain-eaters rather than predators:

> E. O. Wilson remarks that any Martian zoologist might well conclude that "we are among the more pacific mammals as measured by serious assaults or murders per individual unit time, even when our episodic wars are averaged in." . . . The human animal is calmer, more companionable, and less committed to a grossly predatory way of life than some have supposed.[3]

The assumption that "whatever is, is right" is a naive one, but it is still important to find out exactly "what is" with respect to the animal underpinnings to human nature. Rather than overemphasize the natural urge to be violent, we would be closer to the truth by overemphasizing the natural urge to parent, in that justice begins with parental feeling and with the evolutionary successful sort of altruism found in family life.

Clark's ethology (understood generally as the consideration of the influence our animal inheritance has on us as human beings) and flirtation with sociobiology (understood as a particular sort of ethology whereby human ethics is seen as a rationalization for those behaviors that are conducive to passing on one's genes or those of one's kind) prepare the way for his defense of the respect due to individual animals, as Robert Elliot notes.[4] Moral, or at least ethical, concern for members of other species can be traced back to natural sentiments studied by ethologists, just as people who cared for their animals indicate to sociobiologists that they left more descendents than those who used them carelessly. It is questionable, to say the least, whether Patricia McAuliffe is correct in her assessment that Clark leans more in the direction of human discontinuity with animals than in the direction of continuity.[5] This misinterpretation, as is the case regarding many misinterpretations of Clark's work in general, is due to an inability to come to terms with Clark's imaginative and sometimes hyperbolic way of putting his points as he bounces back and forth between extremes so as to eventually carefully calibrate his own position as an Aristotelian mean. Clark's *initial* hyperbole of the extremes he wishes to avoid is often a device used to challenge prevailing orthodoxies (agnostic, anthropocentric, or liberal, as the case may be). Regarding the issue of continuity versus discontinuity with animals, Clark often lumps any version of discontinuity with the "Cartesian" view that animals are mere machines. However, the careful reader will be attentive to the fact that Clark himself defends in *some* senses a discontinuity view without becoming a Cartesian in any consistent way and without letting his *partial* discontinuity thesis outweigh his dominant theme regarding continuity.[6]

Peter Miller is convinced that Clark, whose philosophical appropriation of ethology does not exhibit the sustained argumentation found in Peter Singer's *The Expanding Circle,* nonetheless shows a greater familiarity with the relevant scientific literature than Singer. Further, Miller believes that if we take Clark's distinction between rationalist-leaning morality and empiricist-leaning ethics, as noted previously, then the following attributions can be made: First, Clark is more of an empiricist than Singer because he is more deeply entangled with animal life, especially as regards familial urges, as we will see in the following discussion. Second, Tom Regan, whose acerbic critique of Clark will be considered later, is very much the rationalist, despite his strong defense of animal rights, because his position rests on a neo-Kantian belief in inherent value. That is, Miller contradicts McAuliffe's stance that Clark's views lean toward the discontinuity thesis more than toward continuity.[7]

One might assume that Clark's strong desire to root human nature in animal tendencies would be a corollary to his belief in some version of the theory of human evolution. Yet Clark, the conservative religious believer, does not believe the standard account of human evolution, for several reasons, although he admits that *some* version of the evolutionary story may be true. That is, he does not believe in the "standard" (materialist and agnostic) account of human evolution, but he is not a fundamentalist creationist, either. His criticisms are as follows:

> Firstly: the existence of consciousness is incomprehensible if we are merely complex, self-replacing kinetic systems selected for their inclusive genetic fitness over

some four thousand million years. Consciousness, the subjectivity of being, can play no part in the evolutionary story. It is enough that creatures "behave" in certain ways, as programmed automata might do. . . . Secondly: even if neo-Darwinian evolution had thrown up conscious beings, it could not be expected to produce creatures with a capacity for understanding the workings of the universe. . . . It is not enough to reply that surprising things do happen, that evolution has thrown up a world-spanning intelligence as a by-product of the practical cleverness. . . . The neo-Darwinian account of our history is not one that we can coherently believe: if we attempt to follow through its implications we find that it gives us no right to believe in the theories we form about the world, including the neo-Darwinian story itself. It must also lead to doubts about the consciousness of our fellow creatures, and even (absurdly) our own. (AJ, 28–30)

Clark's first point seems more of an allusion to panpsychism, to be discussed later, than a criticism of evolution per se. Or, better, Clark seems to be objecting only to the belief that there could be evolution from mindless matter into minded matter, *not* to the belief that minded or besouled matter could evolve into more sophisticated forms. The second criticism relies on the Peircian "neglected" argument for God and seems to be primarily directed against the theory of evolution when it is joined to agnosticism.

If we are to follow the path of rational inquiry at all, we need to begin where we are *now*. We know we are higher animals whose ancestors developed models that allowed them and us to survive and reproduce; we also know that we are mammals, tool-users, and social. In order to progress we have to take this animal framework as a secure home from which to journey, even if we must always return. Clark thinks that the slogan that one cannot deduce an "ought" from an "is" is dreadful: how else could we deduce an ought? If we deduce it from another ought we should notice that this prior ought is (AJ, 61). As before, Clark's ethology is laced with his fideism (as implied by Robert Gay[8]):

We ought to accept naturally-arising beliefs until there is sound reason to reject them (they form inconsistent triads, or engender regularly disappointed expectations, or strike us as sufficiently inelegant as to be at odds with our inmost theories even if not strictly incompatible with them). (AJ, 104–5)

The attachment Clark has to our animality is not so strong, however, that he resorts to the recalcitrance of certain sociobiologists or members of the British

Israel sect. The former agree to certain ethical conclusions (as in the claim that women are bound to stay at home) in order to further the survival of our genes, just as the latter hold that human history is directed to the multiplication of Abraham's descendents (genes). Both schools of thought show a severe lack of sympathy for, or even tolerance of, any possible alternatives. Clark disagrees with this intolerance: "We ought not to believe claims that make it impossible to recall the existence of alternative accounts" (AJ, 118–19). Even intelligent sectarians miss the sense of a community that transcends a particular race, dogmatic formula, or authority. Odd as it sounds, the possibility of taking the world in many ways, a possibility enhanced because of ethology, is both the root of relativism and "itself our clue to the right intellectual attitude" (AJ, 120).

Later I will consider in detail Clark's political views. Here it is important to emphasize the fact that, despite his critique of liberalism, he pleads for tolerance. His disagreements with the standard view of human evolution are not meant to crowd out this view, but to underscore one's right not only to impute consciousness to members of our own species, but also to allow consciousness an explanatory role regarding members of other species. There is a worthwhile distinction between self-consciousness and consciousness (or between what James designates as consciousness and "sciousness"; between contemplation and enjoyment, respectively). Awareness of self can arise only within a prior awareness; one can enjoy one's being without contemplating what this enjoyment is all about. Both "minds" and "bodies" are theoretical entities, such that one cannot simply read off the latter to the exclusion of the former in animals. As Berkeley noted, there is no mind without *perception*, at the very least, a function or property found in abundance in animals. The total refusal (say in Claude Bernard) to consider the "inner being" or consciousness of animals is itself a piece of dogmatism, lately given support, often enough, through an appeal to a computer model for thinking. However "thinking" can refer to sciousness as well as to calculation, with computers exhibiting only the latter. In short, there is no "gap" between natural (supposedly unthinking) animals and ideal rationality, but a graded continuity (AJ, 122–26, 171).

It is odd that some people try to trace the Cartesian discontinuity thesis back to the Greeks. The oddness lies in the fact that the very Greek philosophers (including Aristotle) who identified the rational human being as the primary moral object *also* emphasized that our ethical sensibility develops out of the friendly and familial concerns of other animals. We are moral at the very least because we are ethical, and we are ethical because we are mammalian.[9] Gerard

Hughes is correct to alert us to Clark's extremely wide (and controversial) use of Aristotle's biological works to interpret that thinker's philosophical writings; analogously, Clark uses the study of animals to do philosophy well today.[10] The moral result of such a study is, in fact, a move from is to ought, but no adoption of an ought follows "naturally" without justification from an is. This is precisely Clark's gripe with sociobiology:

> Such moral philosophers, including myself, as have attended to the wilder claims of socio-biologists to derive ethics from evolutionary calculation, have usually observed that this is to confuse explanation and justification. Even if it were demonstrably the case that we had the moral qualms or principles we do because having such qualms or principles had given our ancestors an evolutionary edge over those who did not, it would not follow that those principles were justified as tactical devices for propagating our own genes, as if that were our primary goal. (PS, 128)

Rather, Clark notices in a Spinozistic way that nothing that is is completely alien to me. This allows me to see my own very real complicity with dogs and whales and bees, even if Spinoza himself did not quite draw this conclusion (PS, 129).[11]

There would be something arbitrary in rationality if to be rational was to decide in a flippant way what virtue was, in independence of "our evolutionary heritage" (note Clark's willingness to subscribe to some version or other of evolutionary theory). Love is much more than chemical activity in one's gonads, but very often it is at least this. Clark thinks it is perfectly obvious that our morality is founded on our ethics, that is, on our biological and historical experience.[12] Clark sometimes puts the point this way: human beings are somewhat reptilian in their ancient ways and in their resistance to new learning, such that there is always *something* threatening about Socratic reasoning, even if such reasoning itself is in some sense natural to human beings. Radical reconstruction of this reptilian side to human nature, say, through biotechnology or through the behaviorist's techniques, is extremely unlikely, not to say dangerous, from a religious point of view:

> Absurdism nestles in the very heart of technetronic civilization. In the absence of a reasoned conviction that there is a Way away from local prejudice to the Real World, what reason can we have to believe those technocrats who claim to know the truth and to be able to manipulate us all? . . . From that absurdity I see good

reason to withdraw: those who say there is no truth, admit that they are lying; those who deny that truth can be attained, admit that they have no right to say as much. . . . The world is not so alien.[13]

That is, it is secular theory, especially when tied to technocracy, that ends in absurdity. Cuddly toys are *made* things, pets and people are *born* and sacred:

> The central motive of technetronic life is a refusal of "the natural." . . . As Chief Seattle put it long ago: "those who spit on the web of life, spit on themselves." Technetronic civilization sees nothing sacred, nothing "normative," in what arises in nature. . . . Modern moral philosophers have grown so used to criticizing "naturalistic fallacies" that the thought that Nature might have immanent *moral* laws must seem grotesque. . . . How then can Nature be the proper baseline? In the past, no doubt, our lack of power to transform required us to be practical, to bear with much that we would not have chosen. If we can choose, and change, and fashion things more to our hearts' desire, why halt? Is not the objection not another tired effort to resist the building of bridges over rivers, or of medical help in childbirth? The reply has strength. But it is the sort of reply that must be treated sceptically. If bridges and medicaments are welcome aids in *changing* nature, it is because there are natural passions we do *not* change.[14]

The devil of technocracy, as opposed to somewhat angelic nature, promises to give us the whole world, "but at the expense of what would enable us to appreciate it."[15]

GENDER AND FAMILY

Clark's ethology is perhaps best illustrated in his treatment of gender issues and in a consideration of how such issues help us to better understand politics and the cosmos. I will start this treatment of Clark's attitude toward gender issues in ethology with a return to Aristotle, who was, as is well known, a sexist. Aristotle clearly thinks that the gap between male and female is not merely a cultural datum but a biological one. Aristotle thinks that women, in contrast to slaves and children, are capable of *eudaimonia*, but women are not capable of sharing in civic virtue. Put another way, women for Aristotle are not capable of the sort of theoretic *eudaimonia* found in political life or in the space where men philosophize. Their attenuated *eudaimonia* consists in the household life. There are at least two projects that Clark implies are important at this point: first, one needs to show that Aristotle was wrong in his claim that women are incapable of "the political life"; and second, one needs to ask why the (male) political life should take precedence over the (female) familial life. Whereas Plato often gets credit for being a feminist in Book Five of the *Republic*, Clark thinks that Plato pays quite a price: the destruction of the household, a destruction that Aristotle avoided. That is, Clark, as a contemporary Aristotelian, wishes to preserve family life because the city can be only "half-eudaimon" if traditionally female virtues are not included.[16]

Aristotle at least anticipated the view, defended by Clark, that citizens should be household representatives and should not join themselves entirely to the male cohort as the Spartans did. There is no need to prove one's feminism, Clark thinks, by denying the biological roots of human nature. While Clark admits that we know too little to run a straight line from apes to humans, in that ethology should be used primarily to pose the options to us, we do know some things about mammals in particular that should cause us to pause before exorcising biology altogether when considering gender issues. In mammalian species the problem is not the female but the male:

> Popular ethology still tends to represent males as the really significant individuals, the leaders and the masters. More careful study suggests otherwise. The relationship of male to female is not of mastery. We misperceive a lion if we think he has a harem; contrariwise, the stable pride of lionesses adopts one or two lions for short periods. Male cubs are evicted early . . . and must find their own way back into the pride, where they are "kept males" until replaced. . . . In social primate species the general pattern is that males are flung out to the rim of the group, from which a few may eventually return.[17]

What to do with the males? Politics (and the theoretical life) is one particular effort by the male cohort, isolated from female lineage, to provide its members with a sense of belonging:

> Man is a political animal, but need not devote himself to male politics: he might rather seek to participate in the child-rearing, food-gathering, society-maintaining activities of the women. Hierarchical politics, dominance routines, insistence on territorial position are games that male-oriented males play. . . . It might . . . be worth considering that the form of civil life to which women have been

confined contains a truer and better sociality, to which males may also hope to be admitted. . . . The point is . . . that dominance relationships of the kind embodied either in patriarchal or matriarchal culture can be seen as peripheral to the central concerns of human society. . . . A new Aristotelianism, taking account of modern ethological knowledge, can find the human, fully human, in both male and female kinds. One error would be to seek a return to patriarchalist ways; another to encourage women to take higher places in society defined solely by the purposes of the male cohort.[18]

This is strong, thought-provoking stuff.

It must be admitted, however, that Clark travels a bit too far down the road of apologizing for Aristotle's sexism (say, by noting that Aristotle did not think that women were slaves), and of denigrating Plato's alleged feminism. That is, Aristotle does, in fact, as Clark holds, offer a serious attempt to think through male-female differences, but he also exhibits, contra Clark, a bit of unthinking prejudice. Clark's own view seems to be an improved Aristotelianism whereby *someone* must perform those aspects of life that Aristotle labels "male" and "female," even if men and women respectively are not expected to perform them (AM, 206–11).

Not only the political, but also the religious understanding of the cosmos is closely related to the construction of the household. Clark admits that both sides have a point in the following debate: some "older" thinkers hold that the social order was founded on a recognition of the cosmic, whereas many modern thinkers hold that the way we view the cosmos is founded on the social order, a social order that may well seem "natural," especially to ideologues, who tend to take their way to be *the* way. For example, there is no reason to assume that human beings "naturally" establish patriarchal families. When patriarchy is assumed to be natural it makes sense to learn that when patriarchy is in decay there is a rise in Oedipal atheism. The two relationships that no society can entirely escape if it wants to continue and flourish are sexual intercourse and motherhood, whereas all other contact between males and females is variable. Male and female are most notably related as lovers or as parents, but parentage in particular is a social concept more than a biological one. Even a brother or a sister can raise a child (MR, 180–82, 185).

We have come to think of political community as emerging from, or being imposed on, families or similar associations like clans. In fact, we have come to think of the state as being composed of individuals. Clark does not share these beliefs. He thinks that philosophers should spend more time considering those middle-sized communities within which we chiefly live, especially families. One problem with the view that suggests that the origin of the state lies in an implied contract among rational individuals is that children and other noncontracting members of the family (the very old, the retarded, and, traditionally, almost all women) are not properly parts of the community. There are social forms of life between the supposedly self-sufficient individual and the state that have largely been ignored or misunderstood by philosophers.[19] Contra some "traditionalists" (who tend to favor discontinuity with animals), Clark is not ashamed of the fact that humans share with animals the enchantments brought on by sexuality. Animals generally mate as the culmination of a *shared* ritual, although there are some exceptions, as when a mallard forces himself on a female. Yet only human beings can rape, only they can be immoral. Clark is willing to admit that the mallard who forces himself on a female is "deranged," and he might well be willing to say "unethical." If animals can be ethical (if not moral), then why not unethical? (NB, 5, 67).

The stance Clark defends regarding mating ritual and human choice exhibits the balanced view to which he aspires, and eventually reaches:

> The mating of non-human animals is governed by "ritual," in the technical sense of stereotyped behavior patterns . . . which are themselves innate: that is, in many cases, individual animals do not need to have seen the mating ritual to carry it out themselves. . . . Human mating customs, on the other hand, are enormously diverse and are internalized by example and precept. Even the mating position is . . . culturally approved. . . . Beasts must normally mate with members of the other sex, but they may also be attracted into sexual responses by orchids, human beings, members of the same sex, or mere objects. . . . Beauty . . . is a releasing mechanism. . . . People do "fall for" inappropriate things—inappropriate in that they are sterile. A species whose members did this too often would not long survive. (NB, 70–71)

Perversion occurs only when a human being's imagination supplements the occasional misapplication of animal instinct. *Emphasis* on the personal choices made by human beings, however, leads to a Kantianism that Clark eschews. The primary revolt against nature that fuels this Kantian emphasis is the ban on incest, a practice that is thought to be common in the natural world, as when our domestic animals have son-mother, sibling-sibling, or father-daughter unions without hesitation. However, the ethological evidence, it should be noted, is that inbreeding is rather rare in the wild. Chimpanzees even seem to have a ban on son-mother or sibling incest; father-daughter incest cannot be banned when no father is known as such (NB, 72–73). The implication Clark draws is as follows:

> It is worth considering . . . evolutionary forces that constrain us all. On the one hand, we must find creatures of our own kind sexually attractive (how else is a species to survive?); on the other, we must prefer creatures of a slightly unfamiliar sort, for outbreeding offers the genetic "advantage" of increased variety. This latter impulse, to lust after the (relatively) alien, is the genetic or social imperative that has kept our various and dispersed species as one species. (NB, 73)

Clark is well aware that his treatment of gender issues will be controversial. Merely to cite the following fact, as Clark does, arouses suspicion:

> The mating arrangements of mammals vary, but practically all mammals share one feature: the females are the primary parents, and the mother-child bond is the primary bond. Solitary mammals, such as hamsters or lemurs or (at least in our society) cats, mate without permanent attachment and leave all parenting to the mother. (NB, 74)

Gibbons, it is true, have a monogamous system, and among wolves only the dominant pair breeds. Yet in almost all mammal species the problem remains: what to do with the males? Consider lions:

> All male cubs are driven out, and either live solitary or stay loyal to their brothers till they are old enough to drive an old male from his haven in a pride and take his place, for a year or two, till they in their turn are driven out. . . . Human females are unusual in being "permanently receptive to sexual advance," not merely at a monthly oestrus or at rutting time. One explanation has been that this is how they trap the males into staying with them to care for their young. It is unclear why it is assumed so quickly that males, if given half a chance, would hurry off. . . . Suppose that males very much want to be part of the continuing family group, but are thrown out into the world. How shall they get back again? . . . There need be no denial that this form of life has persisted in the human species, that many males (perforce, or by choice) have made a life among

males. But there has always been this other option of finding one's way back into a family. (NB, 74–75)

There is nothing in nature to justify the trope that women are monogamous whereas men are polygamous, although some human males may well have more offspring than they should if they do not have to occupy themselves with child rearing.

Yet they *should* occupy themselves with offspring. This is precisely Clark's point. Sex is quite natural, and even chastity is natural *if* what is meant by chastity is the disposition not to be perverse, not to waste sexual energy on practices that threaten the community. Males need not be deserters or possessors. This is the possibility, even the likely possibility, made apparent through a study of ethology. Patriarchy is also a possibility, but not one that is firmly rooted in our primate and mammal heritage. Nor is it firmly rooted in nature that only parents care for children, as when ostriches lay eggs in other ostriches' nests; nor is monogamy the rule in nature, in general, or in mammals, in particular. We grow out of a background of caring groups or extended families rather than nuclear families (NB, 76–81).

There is something defective, according to Clark, about the assumption that when males are incorporated in the family group as adults it is in order to obtain sexual satisfaction. Perhaps what is at issue is their desire to become "mothers," that is, parents. Only in human beings is marriage institutionalized. It must be admitted that there may be some biological basis for the tension created when children are seen as rivals for the wives' affections, but there is no necessary conflict here (NB, 83–86). In any event, although patterns of sexual and parental behavior are not innate in either apes or human beings, these patterns may nonetheless rest on dispositions that can be readily acquired. It is natural both for parents to care for their children and to eventually have this bond severed:

The unspoken belief that mothers are somehow naturally equipped to dedicate themselves whole-heartedly to the care and nurture of small, demanding animals has been a prolific source of ill: if mother-love comes automatically, and is infinite, then mothers can do it all themselves, and if they can't, it must be that they are unwomanly. If we can remember that we are animals, though versatile and culturally creative, we may step a little closer to humane society. We are evolved to live in relatively open groups. . . . Ethological analysis of the human animal does not lead to a defence of modern Western marriage. If anything can be concluded from all this it must be that the (relatively) open group is where we are meant to be. (NB, 87)

As before, total celibacy would be a cul-de-sac. So the task for humanity is to arrange families such that "surplus" males can be productive domestic partners, not only for the sake of lovemaking and parenting, but also for the sake of domesticating and dwelling with nonhuman animals:

> For many millennia human beings have had to behave as if they were concerned about the welfare of certain animals, notably dogs, cattle, sheep, horses. The easiest way for "nature" to achieve this is for us really to be concerned. Even before we had domesticated animals, our hunting ancestors needed to feel some concern for the prey animals. (NB, 110–11)

Human beings did not evolve as anonymous individuals or as an amorphous herd, but in various familial groups, with men and women and children and animals together (NB, 99, 112).

A mean is Clark's goal regarding the pliability of the marriage relationship. Liberals tend to assume that any agreement between consenting adults is appropriate in this regard, whereas "traditionalists" tend to identify the family with its bourgeois, patriarchal variety. Clark is willing to consider the legitimacy of group marriages, on the analogy of certain primate relationships, which consist "of three or more partners, each of whom considers himself or herself to be married or committed in a functionally analogous way to more than one of the other partners."[20] Obviously these marriages are not recognized by law, hence they must exist in the minds of the partners. No doubt Clark the conservative is shocking to his conservative admirers at this point, but Clark cites the following safe example to approximate what he has in mind:

> Any network of baby-care, child-care, mutual assistance and shared endeavor may well generate special relationships of affection and commitment between the participants. . . . The almost inevitable sexual interest which such friends may begin to feel for each other is deflated, sublimated, relegated to fantasy.[21]

Clark is quick to point out that members of group marriages can be as moralistic about infidelity as any monogamist. Clark's point is that as the nuclear family disintegrates (the average length of a marriage in the United States is seven years) and as an increasing number of single parents, usually women, raise children in isolation from other adults, it would be wise to create more solid structures to care for the young, as well as for the old and the lonely. In effect, Clark is suggesting that if the patriarchal bourgeois family is on the wane, we need not assume that self-reliant individualism is our only recourse.[22]

Clark's alternative in no way trivializes the sexual intimacy that would occur among the different parties in a group marriage. Nor is he offering a carte blanche for an orgy:

> This mutual infection may afflict any people who live together, but sexual enjoyment of each other changes or accelerates the process. Here, after all, we may quite literally "get inside of each other," and only strict Cartesians can think that what they do with their bodies has nothing to do with what they do. There are, of course, occasions when we do feel detached from our bodies, but sexual congress should not be one of them. Where it is, where one or more of the partners are merely "going through the motions," there is no meeting.[23]

The emotional intensity of these relationships is not diminished by the fact that they are multilateral. What *is* lost is the sense that one is totally alone with one's sexual partner, in that one could easily imagine a third party imagining the two original partners together. However, Clark reminds us that our predecessors were never wholly private in the act, in that they would have believed God or some angel to be present. The *really* distant ancestor of such relationships may well be the system of mutual grooming and cuddling that cements a primate horde. Here we see Clark's genius at bringing the divine, the human, and the animal together as interdependent heuristic devices.[24]

There is nothing startlingly good about the success rate of monogamy, as the long history of adultery, with its attendant deception, indicates. Honesty might be more easily maintained in the type of marriage Clark has in mind, an honesty that would make these relationships indeed marriages rather than clubs formed by self-interested individuals. Yet here I am not so much concerned with the moral implications of group marriages as with their ethological basis. *Some* animals, at most, are monogamous; the dominant pattern among primates, at least regarding the arduous task of parenting, is the group or clan or group marriage:

It may be that, as it were, nature never "meant" us to live as couples (still less as patriarchal couples), that for us, as for other primates, it is the small group, of both sexes, many ages, that is our proper home. . . . But as marriages continue to break down under strains imposed by a rapidly changing society, a rapidly changing view of what women in particular should be prepared to put up with, the group marriage, considered as an attempt to provide support for mothers, and a chance for males too to practice parenting, should be taken seriously. The group marriage, in short, may be considered not as a decadent attempt to provide sexual variety, but as a realistic proposal to help with the problems faced by parents and children in a changing world.[25]

It may be that those of us who continue to maintain nuclear families could learn something both from gibbons and from those human beings in group marriages, something about parenting and something about *eros*. Regarding the latter, it seems that some people are content to reserve themselves for one partner and some are never content with such sexual exclusivity (traditionally applied more with respect to women than to men, as in the proverbial "double standard"):

> The choice before us . . . is whether our descendants shall be reared to live as liberal individualists (making and breaking temporary contracts), as members of a sexually open group, or as partners in a Christian (traditional Christian) marriage that is sustained by the care and affection of a wider group (some of whom will be celibate). . . . There are other options to traditional patriarchy . . . than liberal individualism.[26]

The fact that Clark does not go too far in taking clues from animals can be seen when he treats incest, which, as we have seen, occurs often among domesticated animals like dogs. Relying on Hume, Clark points out the inconsistency in believing all three of the following claims: (1) canine inbreeding is the same act as human incest; (2) canine inbreeding is not intrinsically evil; and (3) human incest is intrinsically evil. Cynics may well reject (3) on the grounds that incest is wrong only by convention, not by nature, but, in a way, incest is unnatural, as in its general nonoccurrence in the wild. To reject (3) is dangerously close to rejecting the objectivity of morals altogether, which Clark has no interest in doing. Not even Clark would reject (2), a rejection that would mean that dogs who committed inbreeding would be immoral; however, as we have seen, animals can be neither moral nor immoral. The rejection of (2), however, is familiar to vegetarians, who often hear it argued that if we have no duty to prevent predation then we have no duty to prevent human beings from killing other animals. This defective argument assumes, however, that predators like wild cats are immoral, an assumption that not even defenders of this argument really believe.[27]

The resolution to this problem that Clark prefers consists of a rejection of (1), and his desire for moderation can be seen here as well. One way of rejecting (1) is through a strong version of the discontinuity thesis, a thesis especially popular in Hume's day, whereby canine inbreeding is seen as different from human incest because animals are pure egoists who do not let anything stand in the way of their desires. To "live like an animal" (or like a savage) is often assumed to mean living without restraint of one's desires. Clark is correct in claiming that this is a projection onto animals of our own cultural forms. Even the obvious example of mother-love, as an innate propensity triggered by the sucking reflex, carries us beyond the simplistic model of animal egoism. Other examples lend support to Clark's less extreme rejection of (1):

> Members of the same species are natural rivals, for food and territory and mates. But it does not follow that arrogant individualists will be most successful in propagating their kind. Nature encountered her Hobbesian crisis long ago. . . . Creatures that always fight to the finish . . . may win an occasional battle, but must devote so much time to forcing their way on others that any submissive mutant will be able to leave more progeny.[28]

As we saw in chapter one, Clark is an opponent to behaviorism, an opposition that has implications not only for religion but for ethology as well. Canine inbreeding is no more the same act as human incest as a hurrying child who accidentally knocks over an elderly person is the same as a mugger doing so:

> For a human being to commit incest of the commonest kind (a father's or stepfather's seduction of his daughter) is to use another creature for his momentary pleasure, to rob a child of her childhood and to betray a spouse. . . . Only beings with experience of parental and filial affection can get outside themselves enough to take account of what other creatures value.[29]

Hume argued that moral distinctions were not based on matters of fact, because, if they were, the inbreeding of animals would be incest.[30] Clark argues that it does not follow from this argument that there are no natural goods or evils. Incest *is* a natural evil, as is inbreeding; the latter is, as it were, forced on domesticated animals who would otherwise in the wild indicate a disinclination to have sex with their close relatives: "The objectivity of morals can thus survive Hume's attack."[31]

In Clark's ethologized Aristotelianism, our primary moral loyalties lie with our children, our family, and our domestic companions, rather than with a rational intuition of "Humanity." This claim is evidenced in the fact that children and other dependents are the ones most protected by law in almost every human community, and it is not mere sentimentalism to protect them.[32] This Aristotelianism does not necessarily include the belief that there is something particularly rational in males and something particularly passionate in females, but the conservativism that works its way in a major fashion into Clark's philosophy of religion and his politics is not entirely absent in his ethology. He claims that we are in no position to know from experience how male and female children would grow up in an ideal environment, where socially determined gender roles were not at work. If I understand him correctly, Clark is leaving open the possibility, but not the probability, that Aristotle is correct about rational males and passionate females, and that it is unlikely that there is a transcendental, asexual self. In any event, Clark chides those contemporary liberal feminists who are also agnostics: it is odd, he thinks, that the "revolt against nature" is welcomed by people who should think that they are just biological organisms (CP, 46–49).

This "revolt against nature" includes technological interference in the reproductive process, interference that seems to serve the interests of women, in Clark's view, but it does not really serve them because women have often been used as ill-informed experimental subjects in the development of such technology. When joined with Clark's critique of the supposed "careless and unfettered freedom" entailed in individualism, one gets the impression that Clark is opposed to women trying to achieve for themselves the sort of freedom usually associated with the "flattering self-portrait of the rich, adolescent human male" (CP, 50). "Real feminism" starts within families:

> If there are to be free and independent individuals happily about their self-chosen business, it is necessary that someone look after those same individuals before they are free and independent. . . . The assumption is readily made that there will be someone whose nature and satisfaction it is to care for children, facilitate

the wild adventures of the individualist . . . even though the dominant rhetoric of liberal individualism suggests that all such care and duty is a burden on the free spirit, such that no one of a proud temper could be bound to it. . . . The core of human society is not, except in the most outlandish circumstances, an accidental crowd of unfamiliar and competing individuals. . . . As Aristotle said (*Politics I,* 1252a), we are the sort of animal that forms couples and family groupings, that makes friends, and is faced by duties not of our own contrivance. (CP, 52–53)

One wonders, however, if it is fair of Clark to claim that the individual autonomy defended by liberalism is equivalent to the unfettered life of the rich male adolescent, and one wonders if it is fair of him to saddle liberalism with the assumption that true freedom consists of being liberated from all obligations. Both Kant's and Mill's versions of liberalism not only postulate but *emphasize* our obligations to others.

It is somewhat understandable, according to Clark, that *adolescents* want the freedom promised by liberalism, in that if one's elders are not shining examples of virtue then convention can lean on one with a crushing weight. However, once one grows up, he seems to be saying, one learns that freedom consists of the recognition of necessity, in the finding out of what one should do. It must be admitted that this is one sort of freedom, but it is doubtful if it is the only sort. If individuals have any rights whatsoever, then there is also the need for at least some freedom from external constraint, including what are normally called civil liberties, precisely the liberties that Clark trivializes as adolescent. Nonetheless, Clark may well be correct that if families are among the real building blocks of society then political life is not entirely a matter of voluntarily contracting strangers. As before, the basis for these nonvoluntary familial ties lies in the common form of primate society: a group of females with their young existing in some delicate relationship with a throng of males (CP, 54–56).

Relying on Epictetus, Clark asks the following question: how could we be social creatures at all if affection for our children were not natural? Even hardened criminals denigrate child-abusers, such that from a practical point of view children have more rights (in the sense of laying more duties on the rest of us) than rational contract-signers. Perhaps there is still something to be learned from Wordsworth's dictum that heaven lies about us in our infancy, and that we should retain our capacity for play as if in a familial context, as do the great poets and scientists (CP, 59–60).

One of the continually interesting features of Clark's thought is the unique blend of this romantic freethinking and free play of the imagination, on the one hand, and his tight-lipped defense of tradition, on the other. He is well aware of the fact that some will say the former is a ruse for the latter. By extolling the virtues of the family Clark runs the risk of reasserting a woman's traditional role of wife and mother, especially when it is realized that the mainstream churches, which Clark likes, are now the chief proponents of gender inequality. Clark at least *says* that he is opposed to the "male-invented aspects of ancient misogyny" that are with us still. Yet he also worries that the charge of sexism is thrown around a bit too loosely these days, such that to be accused of it is a bit like being accused in the seventeenth century of witchcraft. Clark's strongest defense against the charge of implicit sexism is the placement of his views regarding gender issues within the larger political context to which he wishes to call attention, specifically to the inadequacies of enlightenment political ideals, to be discussed again later. His own Aristotelian context is one that allows him to say the following:

> I am indeed suggesting that the "pre-political" life of human society, the network of families, baby-sitting circles, residents' associations, parents' associations, children's gangs, church guilds, business and informal friendships, colleges and choirs and grocers' shops and pubs, is the most important part of human society. It is this network of "voluntary associations" . . . which continues to provide us all with a sense of who and what we are. This pre-political level, in almost all its septs, is structured and maintained by women and by children. . . . It matters less that women should join the "ruling classes" than that men and women together should learn that friendship matters more than rank or symbol. (CP, 67–68)

That is, not all political life is statist; for example, a *polis* is or should be more like an association of clubs and families than like a state. States and governments may be replaced, but after the changes families, friends, and clubs continue to exist.

The "natural base" of human existence, it is true, is elastic, or better, it is like a system of elastic nets:

> When the nets of which we are elements are highly congruent, so that the very same people are related to us in many different ways, our self-concept is relatively rigid. When the nets are more diverse . . . our self-concept is itself at once more confused and likely to be more "individualistic." . . . Because this network

constantly reforms, all assertions that we live in a radically desacralized world are bound to be exaggerated: order is not lost. (CP, 69)

VIOLENCE

It is Clark's view that ethologists and animal psychologists could benefit from a more carefully philosophical approach, and that philosophers could benefit from the investigations of these scientists. This latter benefit could be felt not only in regard to gender issues, but also in regard to issues relating to the use of violence, which will be my topic for the remainder of this chapter. We still find our vision of wicked violence among the beasts: to be violent is to "live like an animal." Unfortunately, according to Clark, it is difficult to study the biological roots of human violence because the issue is often complicated by political bias. Those who have made the most of animal analogies to violent human behavior have been "recognizably right-wing." To counteract this bias it is instructive to note that a fight between two wolves can be terminated abruptly if one submits; the victor will snarl but he will not bite. That is, his violent desire is "inhibited," a term that is at least somewhat analogous to moral conscience in humans. Contrariwise, and quite ironically, doves are not inhibited from pecking a rival to death. One may debate the question as to whether human beings are sufficiently inhibited, but in either case a human being's capacity for violence has been artificially, albeit substantially, increased by technological sophistication, which now makes it possible for humans to kill millions. It is very difficult for one unarmed person to kill another with his (the male pronoun seems appropriate here) bare hands; murder most likely began with the invention of clubs. Human beings can be hurt easily through violence because they have no natural armor, but only fleshy tissue protected by skin (NB, v, 5, 34).

Some animals, like rats, will kill conspecifics, but this is rare (NB, 35). Most animals are inhibited, as are human beings, according to Clark and most ethologists. Not many of us really want to kill people even if we are angry with them. In this regard we are more like wolves than doves, contra the popular stereotypes of these two sorts of animal. Dogs, not implausibly because of their ancestry as wolves, are inhibited to the point where they show signs of shame and appeasement when they have done some wrong. It must be admitted, however, that Clark gives at least some support to the discontinuity thesis and to the thesis that human freedom prevents inhibitions against deadly use of violence from being absolute. Wars, murders, and massacres occur so often in human history not so much because human beings are natural predators as because they can convince themselves that some human beings are not really human, but heretics, savages, gooks, or something not quite like us in a morally relevant sense. The true psychopath, the one who *likes* to kill, is not a natural or usual human being (NB, 35–37, 42–43).

Human beings obviously have a greater sense of self than that in animals, hence they can have a developed moral conscience. Yet the difference between human beings and animals in this regard is not absolute. Cats may pounce on their own tails in *play*, but in general animals distinguish quite sharply between self and world. To treat one's own self differently from the world is a necessary if not sufficient condition for having a self at all. Yet having too strong a view of self is as defective as having too little, as is illustrated in the case of a solipsist. Animals are not solipsists, in that they show a grasp of how to move through a relatively stable world, they can recognize something more than once, and very few of them wander aimlessly through the world. Some, like salmon, even travel hundreds of miles to return to the spot of their birth. The point Clark wishes to make here is that to be aware of oneself, even in a rudimentary way, forces one into a social nexus, a nexus that at times is undifferentiated among individual conspecifics, as in rats, and, according to Clark, as in universalizing Kantian morality. Some species, including primates, however, are highly concerned with differences in individual members. Once an animal has a rudimentary sense of self, it makes sense for it to lay claim to certain goods or territory, a claim that is integrally connected with its willingness to be violent (NB, 48–49).

Contrary to popular opinion, neither chimpanzees nor gorillas maintain strict territorial defenses between individuals or groups, and those mammals who do defend territory do not so much defend frontiers as chosen paths. That is, Clark thinks that it is easy to exaggerate the importance of territoriality in the effort to understand human violence. Likewise, it is easy to exaggerate the importance of having a sense of a stable self. (The most striking case of acknowledgment of past action by a nonhuman is the Ameslan gorilla, Koko, who expressed regret for having bit her teacher three days before.) In general, however, to lay down a claim to possess a certain part of the world entails a certain stability of self, a stability that is greater in human beings than in animals, but even here there are limitations. To view a photograph of oneself at eighteen years old is very often to be more impressed with discontinuity than with continuity; it is difficult, at times, to connect with our pasts. A very limited temporal gaze leaves one in a subhuman condition, but no human can view the whole of his or her life *sub specie aeternitatis*. Hence it is important to be able to adapt to contingencies one has not foreseen. Long-term plans for the future are not easily detected in animals, and in this sense they do not have a strong sense of self. Human beings do make such long-term plans, and it is when these plans are disrupted, as they inevitably will be, that violence becomes more likely. It is a constant theme in religion, after all, that we should not plan too far ahead. Hunter-gatherers heeded this advice, but with the advent of agriculture, and with the need to conserve seed for another season, plans for the future became necessary. This seems to be more of a "seed" for violence than territoriality is (NB, 50–52).

It should be emphasized that it is *long-term* plans for the future that the beasts do not exhibit. They will flee immediate situations in which they might be hurt or killed, and they will protect their young in these situations. If death occurs, it is sheer dogmatism to assert that animals are not bothered by it. Primate mothers may carry their dead young around with them, displaying great distress. Elephants actually bury dead bodies. The point is that human selfhood, including the desire to preserve that self and the selves of those close to it, comes into the world as part of a social tradition going back further than human history, although not every contemporary society has reinforced what biological and cultural tradition has given to us (NB, 53–54):

> Once creatures do have some sense of their own identity through time, their standings vis-a-vis others of their kind, it becomes possible for them to differentiate things that are bad for them and what is bad for others. I only say that it is possible, and therefore possible that they be egoists or altruists. Ants who advance into a fire, with the result that in the end their fellows may be able to cross upon a bridge of dead bodies, are only with difficulty imagined as performing an act of heroic self-sacrifice. Surely (we think) they did not intend that consequence. . . . If ants were truly rational and courageous creatures at least some of them would come to the opposite conclusion, and either hang back or quietly desert or go another way. (NB, 55)

For example, some human animals cope with war in precisely these ways. Yet the above allusion to altruism needs to be spelled out. Biologists define the term in light of consequences: an act is altruistic if it leads to a diminution of the agent's genetic fitness. The problem with this definition is that it makes altruism seem rarer than it is; for example, under most circumstances not even parental care is altruistic according to this definition. The supposed rarity of altruism leads to cynicism, such that if I sacrifice myself for my son then it must be because I ultimately want to gain something from the act (NB, 56–57).

It should now be obvious that for Clark the evolutionary aspects of our lives are worth considering, both in their morphological and in their behavioral dimensions. Altruism is a behavioral pattern that can be inherited, as in a mother bird who runs a risk when she diverts a predator away from her brood. However, Clark departs from many biologists when he claims that although this behavior results in the probability that her genes will be represented in the next generation—in that parents who desert their young too readily leave few descendants—this was not the mother's *intention*. It cannot be her intention, because she knows nothing of population genetics, Yet it can be her intention to help her young if, in fact, she *cares* for them. Perhaps it is because some human beings' escape from selfish adolescence is so difficult that they are inclined to think that animals could not make such a transition. However, it is questionable if animals even need to make the transition away from selfishness. Once again, ethological considerations make it unlikely that those political theorists are correct who assume that a social order must be constructed out of selfish, violent human beings, although it must be admitted that human beings will, under conditions largely created through certain cultural configurations, fight, especially if such fighting is in defense of family or friends (NB, 58–61).[33]

Clark will have no part of the standard right-wing explanation of why there are wars: because human beings have a natural tendency to be violent, or at least to be selfish. Yet it may well be that Clark's explanation as to why there are wars nonetheless plays into the hands of certain right-wing ideologues: it is not natural egoism that is our problem, but altruism, which sometimes can be misguided.

> It is our genuine, heartbroken love for others that engenders war (amongst other causes): we are prepared to die, as well as to kill, for cause. Our ancestors, to leave us here at all, had to be concerned for their immediate family and friends. . . . When faced by creatures of another tribe, behaving in unfamiliar ways, we are not blocked so readily from following through our rage. We do not recognize their "appeasement gestures." . . . They are enough to ensure that until we have learnt each other's ways we will be less altruistic about aliens, and seize the upper hand more often than our own good would require. (NB, 63)

This is an attempt to explain wars among less technologically sophisticated peoples, whereas contemporary wars are due to an even more destructive sort of other-directedness: blind obedience to ideologically driven rulers. On the one hand, Clark has here offered a slap against nationalism and, on the other, he has prepared the way for a defense of patriotism as an admirable and ethologically based altruism.

It should now be clear that Clark's thoughts on violence are connected to his thoughts on the family: "Both we and other animals are more willing to hurt those unfamiliar to us than our dear familiars" (NB, 64). In effect, altruism is genuine enough among family and friends, but seldom—either in animals or in human beings—extends much beyond those limits. No doubt some will cite the examples of Mother Teresa or Albert Schweitzer, but, Clark would probably say, these exceptions prove the rule. It takes a great deal of self-congratulation to compare oneself to Mother Teresa. Birds, however, are a bit like Mother Teresa in their unconscious way when they give warning cries when predators are about, cries that benefit all prey in hearing distance. Even though these examples of altruism beyond the bounds of family and friends are rare, they are nonetheless sufficient to refute those who would claim that distant miseries should not matter to us at all (NB, 65–66).

Altruism is not always the case within families, however. When child abuse occurs we should not assume that an ingrained predisposition to violence is without remainder the cause. We would be better served by looking for environmental factors:

> If inexperienced parents are to care for infants in deprived environments, expected to sleep intermittently and be on call all day, the only surprise is that more babies are not beaten. . . . But the most earnestly liberal parent in the most comfortable environment, with partners and friends to call upon, may sometimes feel pure rage and be within an inch of violence. But how is it that we aren't well-equipped to care for infants all the time, if that is what we do? Perhaps it is that we are now required to care for them much longer than we are equipped to bear. Or perhaps it would have been the whole community that cared for them, even though there was a special tie between the mother and her child (a tie that lasts into adult life at least among chimpanzees). (NB, 82)

Here we can see both that Clark thinks that there is something like an aggressive impulse that human beings inherit *and* that this impulse has been given a bad press:

> Ethologists have been interpreted as saying . . . that war, murder, rape are unavoidable, that we want to hurt each other, that only a police-state can control the war of all against all, that we had better arrange for gladiatorial bouts to relieve aggressive fury. This does not seem to be to the point. "Aggression," in ethological jargon, covers any display or threat or carefully inhibited contest. Injuries occur, and even deaths, but the impulse to "aggression" is no more than the impulse to make a good show before one's fellows, to try one's weight. Such contests do not, most often, employ the animal's most dangerous weapons nor in the most dangerous way. Such competition rests on the unformulated principle that the winner of the contest gets some other good. . . . What there is reason to suppose is that animals do not fight only to obtain such other goods as food or mates or shelter, but also for the sake of the display. . . . We do not always fight because we are frustrated in other areas—though we may then fight harder; we are frustrated, sometimes, because we have no "fight" on hand. Tomcats fight to establish a rank-order which does not match the preferences of females: dominance does not give any sexual monopoly. Birds fight in musical displays, and humans in verbal, elaborating their conceits beyond what is needed for a victory: academics know this well. . . . But the point of these displays is not to hurt or maim one's rival, but rather to establish one's own life within a social context. Robins need rivals just as they need mates. (NB, 82–83)

Clark is opposed both to those who see human beings as seething caldrons and those who have too pacific a view. What he considers to be a moderate position between these two extremes allows him, on the one hand, to defend just war theory, as we will see, as well as, on the other hand, to suggest that human cooperativeness might even be so great as to raise one's hopes regarding a (non-Marxist) socialist community: "Animals are all like werewolves; they have different parts to play at different times" (NB, 89). Not even the dominant males among animal groups have a dominance like that found in human despots:

> They do not give orders to their subordinates, but only exclude them from favoured places, prevent their performing certain acts. Most members of the group will continue about their business without being troubled by the dominant. (NB, 90)

In general, a dominant male's status rests on his ability to gain the respect or cooperation of others. A genuinely social group does have dominance as one dimension, but this dimension must be understood within the context of other dimensions: the parent-child bond, the sexual relationship, and so on. Further, social roles among animals change with the seasons and over the course of time. Among the more intelligent animals it is also the case that subordinates are likely to manipulate those higher than themselves in the hierarchy. On Clark's account, human ethics emerges from the changing patterns of these relationships among animals (NB, 92–94). In fact, Clark thinks that this emergence occurs in three specific ways:

> There are three kinds of moralist: first, those who acknowledge ties of friendship and submit to dominants, but do not reckon any rule requires a universal charity or self-restraint; second, those whose obedience to abstract order results in something like a territorial respect for every individual's claims; thirdly, those who owe obedience to an abstract and invisible super-dominant who enjoins good order upon all creatures. (NB, 97)

The first morality seems to be the Aristotelian one, with its emphasis on friendship and its belief that our moral lives grow out of particular biological relationships and duties. The second seems to be what Clark criticizes as liberalism (whether utilitarian or contractual), with its concern for universality and abstraction. The third seems to refer to theistic ethics. Clark's own view seems to be a liaison between the first and the third views; but here he rejects the joint acceptance of all three views.

Clark is well aware of the fact that Aristotelian particularism can lead to racism, imperialism, ethnocentrism, and the like. He does not approve of these phenomena, even if he is quick to point out that there is *some* biological basis for them (and even if he likes to quote Kipling):

> One disturbing report says that Washoe (the earliest of the Ameslan apes), on being introduced to chimpanzees who had not learnt American Sign Language, referred to them (with apparent hostility) as "black bugs": xenophobia, as it also seems from reports of the Gombe chimpanzees' "wars," is a habit we share with our cousins. Contempt is a mammalian pattern too. (NB, 110)

Yet we are so used to deploring violence as due to our "animal nature" that it is hard for some people to accept the idea that the analogies between animals protecting themselves and human war are somewhat thin:

> There is doubtless some truth in the notion that evolutionary forces make it likely that we shall seek to promote the interests of our kin over those of strangers, resist incursions into land we call our own. . . . But our wars are not the relatively casual, episodic squabbles of competing males, competing clans. It is not true that we only fight wars in order to protect ourselves and our material interests. Human beings frequently organize their societies around the sacred duty of military violence, and rejoice in slaughter. . . . War is an essential element in the demonstration of moral purpose. (MR, 156)

The origin of the *cult* of military violence, as opposed to spontaneous animal violence, is a peculiarly human phenomenon, but even this cult is an understandable outgrowth of the problem of surplus males, who can easily be organized into gangs, packs, or armies. The cult of violence can become so firmly embedded in a culture that to refuse to fight amounts to a religious revolution (MR, 156–57).[34]

These nonviolent resisters to evil (although Clark conveniently does not mention that Jesus is among their ranks) often fail to take account of the terrible fact that war is exciting both for the warriors and for the noncombatants. Clark moves from this terrible fact to the condemnation of liberals, whose attacks on warmongers, he thinks, are a bit like sermons against fornication. He urges:

> Really to preach against war is no less a tour-de-force. Contrariwise, those conservatives who allege that human beings are "naturally" and irredeemably warlike all too often sound like those who preach against all modifications of pure patriarchy. . . . Worship of the war-god is not the only possible religious form, though those who would renounce him must understand the costs, and the trials. The long religious effort to tame or exorcise the god of war . . . has issued, most notably, in Just War Theory. . . . Life is at its richest when it is most at risk. . . . Without [war] we would only sink down into complacent dullness, cringing from the minor pains of life. (MR, 158)

Clark compares himself here with William James, but I cannot help but notice the differences between Clark and James on this point. The latter was a pacifist who inferred from the terrible fact that war was exciting that we should devise moral equivalents to war, as in athletic events or challenges with nature. However Clark does not so much turn to pacifism as to an apologia for war:

> God, the good, "might" have made only worlds where things go easily, but has instead realized other worlds. . . . What we do not need to suppose is that a child's murder is somehow a good. . . . It is an evil, but the divine life will—we may believe—bring good from it, for parents, child and fuddled murderer. . . . Our joy must be in fighting what is incompatible with joy. (MR, 159)

As was the case regarding gender issues, Clark's conservative attachments (including his aforementioned attachment to belief in divine omnipotence) have a very strong effect on which of several ethological possibilities he thinks should be chosen.

If it is a natural sentiment that lies at the root of morality, as Clark thinks, just as faith lies at the root of reason, then the predatory and territorial aspects of nature cannot be denounced, even if such aspects are mitigated by other factors. For example, what is fascinating to Clark is not the fact that butterflies have a territorial instinct, but that others acknowledge their claims, as when the occupant of a patch of sunlight is given more favorable treatment than an intruder. Some might try to explain away this and other examples of concern animals have for each other by saying they are due to instinct. Yet even if animals lack our sophisticated types of rationality and freedom, they are certainly not automatons:

> The form of life natural to a creature helps to define what happiness is for that creature's kind, what capacities are there to be filled, what occasions are needed for it wholly to be itself. This Aristotelian concept helps us to see what is wrong in imprisoning and frustrating, say, a veal calf or in declawing a cat: not that they suffer pain sensations, but that their lives are systematically prevented from being full lives according to their kind. . . . Similarly, not every sentiment is natural; some are pathological manifestations of glandular imbalance or social corruption. Sentiment is the root of morality, as sense experience is of science; neither sentiment nor sense experience can be wholly condemned without destroying the systems grown from them, but equally they are not unquestionable.[35]

What is "natural," in this Aristotelian view, is not what usually happens, but what would happen in the best of circumstances. As is often the case, Clark steers a middle course along the narrow path between Manichean rejection of the natural world and a pantheistic adoration of all that happens. This middle course follows quite smoothly from Clark's occasional dipolar theism and from what we will see to be his panentheism, even if Clark's versions of these positions are often presented by him as "traditional theism." That is, Clark is not always as traditional as he alleges.

This middle course makes it difficult to agree totally with Lorenz's view that the wolf is inhibited from killing his rival whereas a human victor is not. Among wolves and other animals,

> It is usually better for the dominants to allow their subordinates lives of their own, sometimes even to assist them, and not to press home their attacks lest their victim turn upon them with "the courage of despair" and cost them more than they care to pay.[36]

A problem arises, however, when we suggest that human beings are radically different from wolves in this regard: "There is good reason to think that human beings too are well able to kill each other, but usually do not."[37] Just as a cannibalistic pair of chimpanzees are feared and resented by their fellows, so also gratuitous violence by human beings is feared and resented by most human beings, although it must be admitted that in time of war nationalistic ebullience must die down before many people notice their fear, disgust, or resentment. "To live like the animals may not be so revolting nor so revolutionary a policy as moralizing judges and romantic drop-outs have supposed."[38] In effect, even Lorenz's version of the discontinuity thesis is a bit Manichean.

This middle course delineated by Clark also entails that animals, although they cannot be immoral, can, in fact, be unethical. Clark seems to be willing to hold this view even when it is considered that evil does not so much reside in the physical relations among the agents as in their motives or in their broken/unbroken obligations. Regarding Jane Goodall, Clark notes the following:

> Goodall does not condemn the hyena: she feels very differently when confronted by chimpanzees who spurn and bully one of their own company who is partly paralyzed. Their behavior evinces callousness and cruelty because they do know what they are doing. One chimpanzee, indeed, did overcome his own distaste

enough to assist his sick companion. Even this is perhaps not true moral action, not a determination to do the right thing, but simply a kindliness. Nonetheless, that chimpanzee's heart was in the right place, and his acts (broadly so called) were commendable.[39]

This claim that the chimpanzees are unethical, to the point where they approximate immorality, might be challenged by those who would say that there is no escape from species relativism. It might be alleged that nothing is "really" evil any more than anything could be "really" green. Acts are evil and leaves are green, in this view, relative to a given kind's perception. Clark's response echoes that which we have seen previously regarding the dangers of extreme skepticism. "Rationality itself is constituted by obedience to certain moral codes: to seek the truth, for example, and not to contradict oneself."[40] The species relativist is indeed a relativist, hence, given the arguments against relativism in the previous chapters, there must be *some* set of interspecific or trans-specific standards presupposed by the species relativist when he or she compares and contrasts the actions of members of different species.

The rejection of species relativism, however, does not commit Clark to the other extreme whereby there is an unobstructed conduit from animal behavior to human morality. For example, if there are devices among animals for reducing the population of surplus males, then some (like Garrett Hardin) seem to assume that war can be understood in an evolutionary framework: it is a device for disposing of surplus human males. This position, which Clark finds anathema, is also compatible with the Malthusian claim that interference with poverty will do more harm than good (AJ, 66). Nonetheless, one should always keep in mind that Clark's theoretical mean between conceptual extremes is not to be confused with middle-of-the-road politics: he remains decidedly conservative. Although he lies between too little and too much linkage between animal inheritance and human morality, he uses this moderation to defend contemporary war, to condemn pacifistic arguments as "propaganda," and to accuse some pacifists of destroying the rules of war on the ground that the pacifist thinks that all war is vile, hence all actions in war are equally blameworthy (MS, 81). This, however, is to ignore the fact that there is no logical incompatibility in claiming both that "all war is immoral," on the one hand, and "war *X* is more immoral than war *Y*," on the other.

Most intraspecies aggression is carefully controlled, in that it seldom ends in death. Human conflicts sometimes end in war, but even when they result in peace it is Clark's view that the path to peace itself consists of ritualized aggression, a view that makes Clark seem more in the "red tooth and claw" camp than he would desire. Consider this:

> It is absurd to suppose—as Lorenz and his imitators seem to do—that there would be no murders, no intra-specific killings, if there were no weapons. . . . That we sometimes kill each other requires no special explanation; that we have invented war perhaps does. War is a social institution. (CP, 110)

Clark is not exactly or usually in the red tooth and claw camp, but in order to defend the *institution* of war he does refuse to give any strong critique of traditional institutions, say, the cult of the military, which may be responsible for war. Instead he is content to say that

> Human infatuation with war, or with danger in general, can be given an evolutionary explanation, and a biochemical. . . . Young males in particular, who must serve as the tribe's first defense against marauding predators, will actively enjoy banding together to see off the raiders. Doubtless the release of adrenalin is linked with a sudden brightness in the air, by comparison with which one's ordinary life is dull. (CP, 112)

Once again, this *seems* like William James's view, but the following certainly does not sound like James:

> Merely negative propaganda against war is likely to be worse than useless. . . . I have certainly no wish to suggest that pacifism in its strict sense is either logically absurd or ethically null. But the usual propaganda for peace is insulting, in so far as the propagandists assume that nothing matters more to any of us than our own comfortable life, and that those prepared to fight and die can only be crazed dupes. . . . To preach against war is to seek to tame an Olympian, just as surely as to preach against sexual indulgence. (CP, 112–13)

To claim that moral protest against war is "pontificating" and self-righteous without concomitantly claiming something negative about militarism is, I am suggesting, to deliver an apologia for the status quo (CP, 113–14).

Clark is very much interested in setting down rules of war, but he is skeptical as to whether these will ever be reached if we start out from the absolute rights of states. War has never involved a total collapse of ethical judgment, he thinks. Contemporary pacifists would be quick to point out to Clark that twentieth-century warfare, in which massive numbers of innocent people are killed on both sides (and often killed with equanimity), signals that we have come dangerously close to such a total collapse. According to Clark himself, the basis of the rule against killing noncombatants, say, is not due to utilitarian calculation, whereby the killing of some noncombatants is allowed if it prevents a greater number of deaths later. What, then, is the justification for killing innocent people in war? Clark thinks that moral rules regarding how war is to be waged (*jus in bello*) arise in the tacit bargaining of mercenary soldiers. This is a questionable view, to say the least. Such rules, contra Clark, may well be due to the sentiment that it is wrong to kill an innocent person or to the rational conviction that if justice refers to rendering to each its due, then innocent people are not receiving their due when they are killed, very often intentionally, in war (CP, 117–19).

At times Clark indicates that we should not use weaponry that kills innocent bystanders and we should not hold children hostage. At other times, however, he says that

> Sometimes, when it is clear that the police cannot capture some very dangerous wrongdoer except by methods that involve the death of innocents—a technical term that means no more than non-combatants—we allow this practice, so long as the police did not intend those innocent deaths, and did their utmost to avoid them. We are prepared to say that we would not complain at our death on such occasions, so long as this is the only and an effective way of preventing further wrongdoing of a serious kind. (CP, 120)

Clark's agreement with the killing of innocent people in war is admittedly very limited because of the conviction that human beings have what are normally called "rights." Despite Clark's desire not to be dragged into debates between utilitarians and Kantians, it is important to note that even he seems to be forced to use the language of rights when he must protect the innocent, and that he must claim, in order to justify contemporary war, that these rights must be "overridden" in "special circumstances." It is Clark's belief that he could have avoided the Kantian and utilitarian language altogether, say, by claiming that we ought not to kill children in war because God commanded us not to do so. However, this alternative language is unconvincing, both because it is not based on reason and because it is unclear how Clark receives this divine command. At several places in the Bible, for example, God encourages (or at least permits) the killing of children. Nor does Clark get off the hook by saying that we can, in certain circumstances, kill the innocent if it is the only way of halting a dreaded enemy. In the above quotation Clark implies that the police (not soldiers) must sometimes kill the innocent in order to capture a wrongdoer, but it is unclear whether this is "the only way" for the police (!) or soldiers to behave.

When we read from Clark that "Only such force is to be used as is necessary to halt and disarm the enemy, and certain weapons whose effects are long-lasting, widespread, and dangerous to non-combatants may not be used at all" (CP, 121), we could just as well be reading Henry Sidgewick. That is, as a pacifist I can at least understand why a utilitarian would try to justify the killing of the innocent in war, even if I disagree with this view. Yet it is hard to understand how Clark can hold such a view on a nonutilitarian basis. *How* does killing in war, in general, and the killing of the innocent, in particular, lead to virtue? Clark is not forthcoming here. Perhaps he thinks it part of the life of virtue to fight if one is preventing immoralities that are "outrageous." No examples are cited by Clark, which is perhaps convenient when it is realized that the Western countries whose traditional values Clark defends, and some of whose wars may well be permissible in Clark's view, have themselves done outrageous things. All of them have. "They may in the end commit as many deliberate injustices as their enemy" (CP, 124). Clark admits that this is one of the pacifist's strongest "arguments" (not pontifications). Does Clark get off the hook of this argument by claiming that "*Most* of the time the rules of war apply" (my emphasis)? I think not.

The only significant addition Clark makes to the traditional just war theory is the comment that there is no way to justify on the criteria of that theory nuclear, chemical, or biological weapons; even this is not so much an addition to the theory as an application of it in an obvious way. However, Clark fudges even here. The use of nuclear weapons is "incredibly wicked," but not necessarily the threatened use of them, say, a threat as articulated by Ronald Reagan (CP, 125–27). I agree that threatening to kill millions of people is not as bad as actually killing them, but it is incredibly bad, is it not? Or again, on the one hand:

> If we must sometimes fight for the welfare of strangers, of the widows and
> orphans, we do so as God's agents in the world and under His rulings. If we

cannot now fight without breaking the rules, then we must not fight, and must instead rely upon His promises. (CP, 128)

On the other:

If we fight, and *it must be conceded that we will*, it must be in obedience to that God, not any national demon or Titanic power. (my emphasis; CP, 128)

Here there are definite tensions in Clark's thought, if not contradictions, and here there is antediluvian optimism regarding the ease with which nationalism and patriotism (which are otherwise Clarkian virtues) can be swept away. Finally, notice that Clark holds both that governments who kill civilians cannot really claim "the higher moral ground" *and* that a government's civil peace is not to be disturbed even if the government's civil peace is achieved by force. My question: why should this government be respected if it cannot claim *moral* legitimacy? (CP, 130–31). Clark's response would seem to be that such a government should not be respected, though the civil peace should be.

By moral legitimacy Clark sometimes seems to mean the rational principles (like noncombatant immunity) of the just war theory and sometimes seems to mean "God's mandate." Yet even the latter is sometimes reduced by Clark to rational components, as when such a mandate is defined in terms of some evidence that there is a real wrong to be righted. The presence of a wrong, noticed as such by a rational agent, is not enough to justify violence, however. Those in present power have no *absolute* moral edge over those they rule, but they do always have the moral edge. Clark calls his conservativism here "methodological" (his detractors will call it pathological) because he thinks it a safe and sane procedure or method to give the nod to those in power (until they commit atrocities?) because the opposition is so far untried (CP, 132–33).

Clark has come a long way from his initial ethological point regarding violence: the popular view that humanity's violent tendencies are rooted in our animal background is false. He eventually permits nuclear deterrence, the killing of at least some innocent people in war, and he justifies even unjust governments (principally because they are there) that use illicit violence. (Or at least Clark doubts the credibility of rebels who want to overthrow unjust governments.) All of this can easily hide his initial point. As human beings we do struggle with our animality. It is those who do not struggle who are somewhat defective, as in Blake's line that "those who restrain desire do so because theirs is weak enough to be restrained" (PS, 73–74). The "beast within" is not necessarily, or even usually, unsocial. That is, if a man rapes his daughter or breaks his son's arm to teach his wife a lesson, he cannot legitimately claim that it was his animal nature that forced him to do so. It is unfortunate for our understanding of ourselves and of animals to allow animals to enter into our conception of ourselves as symbols for that which we wish to "exclude, idealize, or tame." As Aristotle noted, bad men are worse than beasts not only in what they do, but also because they chose their "bestiality" (PS, 75–76).[41] We go to war not so much to fill our bellies (*this* is what an animal-like war would be like) as to fulfill other desires. "We are warring and contentious animals not because we are like other animals, but because we are rather unlike them" (PS, 77–79).

Political philosophy is all too often predicated on the assumption that laws are needed to control our "animal passions," but neither animals nor the "uncivilized" are as bad as ideologues suppose, as Clark admits, such that civil war is not a state of nature but a decay of "statism" itself. That is, Clark thinks that his political philosophy has more in common with that of anarchists or traditional liberals than with that of fascists or state socialists, hence it is surprising that he travels as far as he does down the road of accommodation to military power in the hands of the *state*. Clark's defense against this criticism goes something like this:

> We want to be told that somewhere or other there are people who are not at odds with themselves, that there is a culture which does not create interpersonal or intrapersonal tensions, that the "natural human" is as simple and straightforward as even Plato would wish. Why else did people accept Mead's fantasies of Samoa so uncritically? (PS, 81)

Yet this utopian condition is no more ethologically based, Clark thinks, than the view of human beings as vicious beasts. We are born as open-minded apes whose biological evolution has been partially displaced by cultural evolution and its ideals. Put another way, "Human experience is of the contest between Beast and Angel" (PS, 85–86). Liberals are muddled, he thinks, in denouncing *every* effort to control our impulses, impulses that make some version of dualism a serious option for consideration.

CONCLUSION

In sum, in this chapter I have detailed Clark's moderate view of ethology, a moderation that leans very much in the direction of human continuity with animals when compared with the relative discontinuity favored by most thinkers in the history of the discipline and by most contemporary philosophers. Clark's theory that animals can be ethical but not moral provides him with the basis for this continuity thesis, a thesis that has several ramifications for how we ought to view human gender issues and human violence. Regarding the former, Clark characteristically shows both his imaginative boldness (for example, regarding group marriages) and his traditionalism (as in his leaving the suspicion that he would reassert in new dress traditional roles for women and as in his critique of the sort of freedom encouraged by liberalism). Regarding violence, Clark attacks the belief that human violence is due to the violent beast within each of us, in that beasts are not nearly as violent as many suppose, or at least they are not violent for the reasons many suppose. Yet Clark also gives the impression that the attenuated version of biologically based human violence that he defends is nonetheless strong enough to give support to contemporary military institutions so as to keep them going, a state of affairs that does not seem to bother Clark very much. In any event, anyone seriously interested in keeping alive the Aristotelian project of a biologized philosophy cannot ignore Clark's arguments regarding the philosophical significance of contemporary studies by ethologists. We have also seen in this chapter that Clark's moderation is nonetheless compatible with his use of hyperbole, and that his belief that morality grows out of ethics is analogous to his belief that rationality grows out of religious faith.

CHAPTER 5

SENTIENCY

INTRODUCTION

In this chapter I would like to make a transition from Clark's ethology (his view of animals as ethical agents and human beings as ethical/moral agents) to his view of animals as moral patients. In this effort I will start with some final considerations regarding his ethology (his logos for ethos) and his view of animals as free in a limited way, and then move to two arguments that are evidenced in his writings in favor of animal "rights" (the scare quotes are essential for Clark). Further, I will defend Clark against those critics who think that he does not so much argue for animals as moral patients as assert that they are such. Between these final considerations of Clark's ethology and the two arguments in favor of animal "rights," I will treat Clark's Aristotelianism, to the extent that it bears on these issues.

ANIMAL AGENCY

It should be clear from the previous chapter that for Clark the opposition between instinct and intelligence is misplaced. Instinctual patterns need not be unintelligent. Both Stoics and Thomists have assumed that animals might behave "as if" they had intelligence, but they are ultimately moved only by "nature": *non agit, sed agitur* (does not act, but is acted upon).[1] The key to responding to this belief, for Clark, is to avoid the assumption that "intelligence" refers to a single variable that is testable in relatively simple ways. Practical intelligence in the Aristotelian sense is perhaps largely instinctual, as when an animal tries one solution to a problem, fails, and then tries again and again in a somewhat confused,somewhat planned fashion until a solution is found. Theoretical intelligence, the sort possessed only by human beings, shows an ability to transcend all past solutions in the invention of a new technique:

> Animals, unfortunately, cannot win. If they maintain some hypothesis despite initial failure, they are stupid; if they strike out at random in hopes of doing something right, they are still stupid. (NB, 21)

The latter "stupidity" is due to the instinctiveness that allegedly determines all of their actions. It is true that we humans do not always operate by trial and error, but also by an intuitive grasp (*nous*) of what things must be like. Clark is concerned with showing that this grasp can be given an evolutionary account: "we are descended from a host of creatures who, by and large, guessed right" (NB, 21). For example, consider the macaque,

> who found out how to separate wheat from sand by throwing handfuls of the two combined into the sea. . . . This involved an extension of established ways as impressive, in its setting, as most scientific advances. . . . It looks as if some animals do dream up new solutions, even if the range from which they choose is determined by the patterns familiar to their kind. (NB, 22)

In ordinary life we do not doubt that dogs believe that their master is at the door, even if we do doubt that they believe their master will be back in ten days when he leaves for a vacation (though the latter, thinks Clark, is not impossible) (NB, 19–20, 23).

Anger is more than clenching fists. It also involves an element of belief that one has been wronged; that is, it also involves intelligence of *some* sort, in human beings as well as in animals. Anthropocentrists are quick to point out that animals cannot believe in "propositions," but if belief consists of an attitude of commitment to the contents of beliefs, it makes sense to say that an animal's intelligence is exhibited in its beliefs. Or again, if one assumes that all beliefs are *de dictu* (about statements or propositions) then neither animals nor infants have beliefs, but if there are beliefs *de re*, such that the proposition that the cat is on the mat is in fact about the cat, then animals can certainly have beliefs. Human infants really believe that there is a face behind the cloth when they play peek-aboo, just as a fish really believes there is another fish around the corner when it waits to attack. Clark finds it incredible that some believe that when chimpanzees try to entrap their prey there is an instantaneous appearance of intelligence and belief, yet negate these properties in the fish, simply because the chimpanzees *communicate* with each other and the fish do not. It should be noted that when *we* are living most intensely, "our language is all 'Um' and 'Yum' and 'Ah'" (NB, 27). Most animals, Clark seems to be saying, do not take a sideways, metaview of life as some of us do, nor do they have language about such a view, but it is unclear how these inabilities affect the attribution of beliefs to them or, as we will see, the attribution of moral patiency (NB, 24–26, 29).

If even human signs take their meaning from their concrete context, as the later Wittgenstein and many others have urged, then we should not be surprised by the general inability of animals to understand signs in the abstract. When we walk into the kitchen, give a piece of advice to children for the tenth time, or drive a car we are carried along by our bodies, and we cannot achieve the same results with theoretical intelligence or abstract language. From the general inability of animals to abstract, however, Clark does not infer that they cannot do so at all. Frogs snap at the class of moving inedibles, and laboratory animals can be brought to generalize their expectation of reward or punishment at the sight of a horizontal row of dots or squares. Some animals can even develop a rudimentary sense of analogy, as in showing awareness that a banana peel is to a banana as an orange peel is to an orange (NB, 31–33). These examples of animal abstraction, limited as they are, should cause us to pause before we become convinced of our transcendental, Kantian freedom. Regarding the capabilities to abstract, to be aware of death, to believe, and so on, we should be very cautious in drawing a fixed line between human beings and beasts. Regarding such divisions Clark says:

> It is not easy to imagine observations which would decide . . . and in most cases we should be agnostic. We certainly should not conclude, as too many positivists have done, from the (supposed) scientific undecidability of a question to the scientific ineluctability of one particular answer. (NB, 44)

A full grasp of self, involving grammatical transformations and the like, is not clearly established in animals, but Ameslan apes do appear to recognize pictures of themselves and can report what they want and are doing:

> Why should they not be able to distinguish self and other, self and world, or acknowledge things or acts as theirs, before they find the words to speak of this? . . . The concept that infants must have, and beasts surely may have, is not of a self separable from all public involvement, but of a being in the world. Those who attempt the Cartesian *epoche* (disconnecting our primitive belief that the world outside us really exists) will find that in eliminating world and friends and body they have also lost themselves. . . . If beasts have no conception of Cartesian selves that is to their credit. I can see no reason why they, and human infants, may not have a pre-verbal concept of the beings that they are, distinct from others and from the environment. . . . Having a concept and being able to consider it are different things. I may have the concept of redness long before I can talk about redness. . . . Thus Socrates characteristically argued that because all definitions of, say, justice that his victims gave conflicted with their intuitions of what act was just, they therefore did not know what justice was—but in another sense they knew quite well what acts were just, and Socrates counted on that knowledge to disprove the definitions. The normal state of most of us is this: to know quite well what we do not understand. Beasts, maybe, are in no worse state than we. (NB, 46–47)

In fact, it may well be that human beings could learn from animals regarding the relative merits of a close tie between self and world, even if self is partially distinguished from world:

> Some have held that our goal should be to advance again to an unselfconscious involvement in the world and action, that the necessary detour through self-awareness is, in the end, delusory. Before enlightenment, cutting wood and drawing water; after enlightenment, cutting wood and drawing water. (NB, 47)

Nor does the limited freedom that animals possess lead Clark to disparage them. The equation of freedom with unlimited possibility, as we have seen, is ill-conceived, according to Clark. There are different sorts of freedom, he thinks. First, there is liberty of spontaneity, which consists of doing what one wants, a type of freedom that free-ranging animals (and adolescents) have in abundance when they can go where they want to go or do what they want to do. However, only dominants have this abundance. Second, there is liberty of indifference, which requires that one be able to do otherwise than one has done. Genuine obligation or morality, as opposed to ethics, presupposes this sort of liberty. Clark seems to agree with Kant at least in this: that our sense of being obliged has its locus in this sort of freedom in our transcendental selves, not in our phenomenal selves; hence wolves, lacking transcendental selves, are not obliged or free in this second sense of the term. The third type of freedom, a type possessed by animals, is more noble than the first, even if it falls short of Kantian freedom. One is free if one realizes what is determining one at a certain time, as when one is enraged with one's child until one realizes that one is more irritable than usual today, or, Clark seems to be saying, as when a wolf's desire to harm evaporates (or is inhibited) (NB, 38–41).

Clark gives conflicting evidence regarding whether there can be one sufficient cause of what occurs, but his preferred view seems to be that there are individual causes that are necessary or compelling but not sufficient (PS, 53–55). This issue is important because, on the one hand, Clark wishes to defend the view that human beings, at least, have a hand in the determination of their fate, yet, on the other, he likes to flirt with theological determinism. The "laws of destiny" are not only natural but also moral. That is, we often have a hand in bringing about that which we "must and ought" bring about in any case. As we have seen, Clark thinks that we have very little control over the whirlwind of our thoughts, even if we can choose which to value highly and to really believe. Clark has indeed learned from James that determinism is a creed that we as appetitive and thoughtful creatures cannot live by, but he wonders if a human being should really be held as more blameworthy than "a madman or a monkey or a tidal wave." In the final analysis, however, Clark's flirtations with determinism give way to his (conservative) belief that wrongdoers *should* be blamed (and punished):

> Blaming is a dirty word in left-liberal circles, except when there is a question of criticizing the police, Americans, or moralists. I am not myself convinced that those who use such arguments as I have just been sketching to undermine the practice have themselves shaken loose of it. Nor am I convinced that "blaming" is out of place if actions are to be analyzed and explained in belief/desire terms. . . . The dog or monkey is not, properly speaking, "blamed" . . . but that is because we do not suppose that dogs or monkeys are likely to be moved by any thought that they have done a wrong. (PS, 60–61)

This conservative defense of free will, however, may well be at odds with Clark's equally conservative belief in divine omnipotence and divine omniscience (in the sense of God's having present knowledge of what are, from a human point of view, future contingencies): "I must confess myself not sure what doctrine of the Will makes sense" (PS, 63). Yet Clark, the pragmatist, is not bothered by this apparent contradiction. So much the less for reason, he seems to be saying, if two rationally conflicting propositions must, from a practical point of view, both be believed (PS, 56–59, 62, 64).

Human beings are free agents, but in a world we did not make; what occurs, even if it is not required by divine law, is at least allowed by it, and the object of the religious life is to submerge our will to God's. Clark cites Vernon White's *The Fall of a Sparrow*[2] positively to the effect that when a wicked act is done, say, if a sparrow is killed unnecessarily, there seems to be no escape from the conclusion that in some sense God wills it to occur, contra Clark's aforementioned argument *against* "sectarianism." It is God's job, Clark thinks, to take the plurality of plans, values, and discrepant strategies in the world (symbolized by polytheism) into a unified worldview:

> I do not seriously wish to advocate polytheism: on the contrary, I want to point people on past those modernist imaginings that amount to polytheism to a renewed, monotheistic commitment. . . . How can a happening be simultaneously the effect of my volition . . . and also the effect of the One God's volition? (PS, 68)

There is nothing impossible about collaborative enterprises, Clark thinks, as is evidenced in the plots of many murder mysteries. A single action can have multiple significance, he thinks. Yet Clark's refusal to engage in the "fantastical revolt" against omnipotence (I would call it a reflective attempt to initiate progress in religion) leads one to wonder if, in order to grant human beings (not animals) freedom of choice, he must at some point soften his defense of omnipotence (PS, 65–67, 69–70).

By not denigrating the freedom, intelligence, or beliefs of animals Clark is able to appreciate Wordsworth's dictum that "we murder to dissect." Animal freedom, intelligence, and belief are sophisticated enough that we are rewarded when we study them in the wild. The paradox is that in order to find out *how* free or intelligent they are, scientists tend to dope, maim, frustrate, or pain them. By employing the results of these studies Clark in no way wants to be interpreted as endorsing the ethics that produced them. We have seen that Clark recognizes a telos in individual animals such that their final causes need not be equated with occult entities, on the one hand, or with functions, on the other. People, chimpanzees, and bees have purposes or goals, he thinks, not merely certain functions:

> Those who actually deal with animals (zookeepers or farmers or laboratory technicians) rely in practice on our common resources of empathy and understanding. It is simply more helpful to be told that a given creature is sulky or irritable or playful than to be offered a computer printout of the behaviour patterns. (NB, 11)

Even Clark pleads guilty to speaking of "the wolf" or "the chimpanzee" without emphasizing the diversity and nonrepeatability of living, individual animals. The abstractions used in the methodology of modern science have been applied extensively only for the last three hundred years. Before this time human beings saw individual animals through intuitive or animistic methods for hundreds of thousands of years. Is it plausible that these methods were entirely defective? Clark thinks not. To break a thing to find out what it is is far too paradoxical a procedure to be adopted wholesale without incorporating the best in traditional approaches to animals (NB, 8, 10, 12–13).

The purpose of this chapter is to develop Clark's arguments in favor of animals as moral patients, arguments that are in direct opposition to the view that animals (or human beings!) can be adequately described without reference to an inner life because, it is assumed, such a reference is unscientific, at least, if not meaningless. Clark finds it significant that ethologists, who generally study animals in the wild, may use behaviorism as a methodological device, but hardly ever as an ontological dogma. They may describe animals without too much empathy, but hardly ever in such a way that an animal's inner life is ruled out entirely. Surely it is not enough, ethologists seem to be saying, to claim that an animal bristles, cowers, and crouches but it does not get angry or afraid or have purposes. It should be noted, however, that Clark is quite willing to admit that it is not always easy to know when an animal is angry, nor is he defending an "inner life" in the sense that such a life is radically divorced from an animal's publicly perceived physical life. Clark sometimes, when he is careless, speaks as if he is a Cartesian who holds that the proper route to knowledge is to cut oneself off from all ordinary belief and natural engagement with the world. Yet such speech is an example of his hyperbole, in this case to point out the importance of an inner life that is part of an (Aristotelian) whole. Behaviorism would, in fact, be an amazing sort of intellectual parsimony *if* it worked well in the description of nature; unfortunately, it does not quite have the accuracy sometimes alleged in its favor (NB, 14–18).

ARISTOTELIANISM

Before moving to an explicit consideration of Clark's arguments in favor of animals as moral patients, I would like to link his treatment of this issue to other facets of his philosophy and to his Aristotelianism. By describing a human being's or an animal's situation from within, Clark is offering a phenomenological account, not a transcendental one in terms of what gives rise to its experience. This phenomenological account, which agrees with most ancient psychology, supplements the work of ethologists and cannot be refuted through Wittgensteinian aphorisms. It must be admitted that there are some ancient texts that see "the body" as the enemy of "the soul" or as its tomb. However, the body of our experience, the one that we inhabit, is one that hungers, thirsts, and feels as an animal's does. The "parliament of the soul" is composed of many thoughts, purposes, and appetites. These interests are especially competitive in human beings, but even a young chimpanzee can be diverted between a bunch of bananas and a female chimp in heat. The points Clark wishes to draw here are that (1) this phenomenological distinction between spirit and flesh does not support a metaphysical distinction; and (2) animals are, albeit in a diminished way in comparison to human beings, "polytheists" in need of "monotheism." "Even the beast within is groping for immortal beauty" (PS, 92). To be a pure "monotheist" would require that one be a disembodied *cogito* bereft of bodily distractions altogether, in that "we experience ourselves as plural entities, negotiating bargains" (PS, 92). These plural entities are precisely those *daimones* traditionally symbolized as beasts. Yet, "rather than enlisting angels to repress the beast, we may occasionally ask ourselves if the beast is not an angel" (PS, 94). We should in no way be ashamed of our animality. Rather, through a controlled imagination we may come into contact with powers deeper than the everyday, powers that reveal themselves in the shape of animals. This is the lesson, Clark thinks, of religious traditions as diverse as those of the Amerindians, the Celts, and that founded by Teresa of Avila (PS, 86–91, 93, 95).

The view of animality that Clark is defending, the view whereby neither matter nor form alone can be identified with the individual, is thoroughly Aristotelian or, given Clark's reading of the ancient texts, thoroughly neoplatonic. We may be afraid that there is no real psychic continuity in store for us, but we can be assured that materially we are continuous with the constituent elements of the exploding stars that existed geologic epochs ago. The gods are also everlasting, with "gods" referring to moods or possibilities that we can represent to ourselves. Who we are is constituted by the complex configuration we assemble from among these possibilities (as in Whitehead). The cosmos is composed of "colonies of colonies of colonies," wherein each organism is a segment of the whole, but each segment that is conscious, as we will see, has a certain value that is irreplaceable. Philosophy can be seen as a Penelope-like endeavor wherein one comes to realize that individuals, with their irreplaceable value, can become unstitched, say, through death. Likewise, the value of philosophy itself largely consists in being willing to have even one's best arguments undone, hence one must be prepared in philosophy to offer several arguments in favor of the conclusion one wishes to defend, arguments that may, because of their multiplicity, sometimes be at odds:

> Any sensible theorist, of whatever tradition, tolerates an indefinable amount of dissonance, even while hoping for, but not now enjoying, a unitary theory. Indeed, the very moment when it becomes clear that there is no one identifiable fault to be found with a popular theory is that at which, being completed, that theory must be transcended. (PS, 137)

As before, Clark receives inspiration from (dissonant) Chalcedonian orthodoxy in favor of the God-man, or, in the context of human or animal nature, in favor of the spirit-body (PS, 130–36).

As Aristotle emphasized,[3] it is the whole person (or, Clark would add, the whole animal) who raves in anger, not one thing fearful and the other thing moving its hands or paws. The materialist (monophysite) position is opposed not only by the spirit-body of the Hebrews but also by the view held by most of the Greeks; that is, by all of those Greeks not influenced heavily by Pythagorean or Orphic dualism. Neither human beings nor animals have corpses untidily united with a living spirit:

> The person is both physical and mental, accurately describable in both physicalist and mentalist modes. It is sometimes suggested that the former mode involves description from the "outside" (or objectively), and the latter description from the "inside" (or empathetically). . . . This is no more than an evasion.

> Single-subject theories always seem to end up as materialist one. . . . "Getting the
> old adrenalin going" can easily enter folk psychology as a synonym for those
> processes that our predecessors knew as invocation of a patron spirit. (PS, 141)

Clark fails to notice here that "single-subject theories" can be panpsychistic as
well as materialistic. If what it means to explain a human being or an animal is
to account for both mental terms and predicates and bodily ones, then it is
important to notice that there are at least three (not two) options: (1) mind and
body are separate substances; (2) mind is reducible to body; and (3) body can be
explained in terms of mind, or at least in terms of partially self-moved, spontaneous, active microscopic singulars that can feel. Clark's view is either (3)—see
his claim that body is part of soul (PS, 140)—or (4), Aristotelian hylomorphism,
a view that seems to be compatible with (3) and perhaps is similar to it in many
ways (PS, 138–39).

One of the problems with view (2) is that it would seem to imply that an ache
that a sentient being experiences is a state of the brain or blood or muscle, a state
that does not, for all we can tell, experience something as essentially painful.
According to Clark, the muscle does not *experience* the pain, although panpsychists who hold view (3) would defend the claim that muscle cells may well be
agitated, even pained, when pain is experienced by the person or animal as a
whole, say, when their cell walls have been ripped apart under stress:

> These very familiar arguments—well known to William James—leave us with
> several imaginable theories: first, that pains and other such compellingly real
> events are sheerly epiphenomenal. . . . Second, that they are to be thought away,
> illusions of folk psychology; third, that "being painful" and the like will eventu-
> ally prove to be strictly deducible from the known physical natures of the things
> concerned; fourth, they are what they indefeasibly seem, real events to be under-
> stood only "from within," as elements of a mentalistic world. (PS, 144)

Clark thinks that the third theory mentioned in this quotation is closest to
panpsychism. It is doubtful if Clark has thought through this view as carefully
as Hartshorne or Whitehead. He is correct that blood does not literally boil, but
individual blood, nerve, or muscle cells do, in fact, have their walls ripped open
through intense heat, for example; they are, in fact, agitated (pained?) by intrud-
ers. It seems that because of Clark's very sharp criticisms of materialism, he
should take panpsychism more seriously: "Modernists who criticize 'occultists'

for confusing metaphor and literal truth can sometimes be astonishingly credulous of the metaphors deployed by modern materialists" (PS, 145). The panpsychist would grant that many aggregates (e.g., a rock), lacking a central nervous
system, cannot collect together on a macro-level the protosentient activity found
at the micro-level. Human beings and animals have precisely this ability; not so
with plants, whose growth is explained by botanists at the level of cells and not
systems. In any event, Clark's hylomorphism and his occasional enticements by
panpsychism or dualism are all in agreement on the point that "we cannot avoid
a reference to an experiencing subject" (PS, 146). The panpsychist would go on
to claim that "experiencing subjects" include microscopic centers of feeling if
not of consciousness (PS, 140–43). It is crucial, claim panpsychists, to note that
pleasure and pain are *localized*, as in sexual pleasure or as in having the tip of
one's finger burned by a campfire.

Rather than explicitly defending panpsychism, Clark is much more intent
on defending folk psychology against, say, the materialism of the Churchlands.[4]
One of the devastating consequences of the denial of the animating presences in
natural beings found in folk psychology has been what is commonly called the
rape of nature:

> It has been important to a mobile and entrepreneurial culture that the land, the
> trees, the tools of trade, the high heavens, and even human bodies be emptied of
> their spirits—which is to say, of our empathetic engagement. (PS, 149)

Here we see that Clark's conservativism sometimes has the consequence of a critique of capitalist political economy, as in Michael Oakeshott. He speaks of

> the very emotional and political purpose that underlies the willed "disenchant-
> ment" of the world, to empty the world of anything that might resist our will,
> precisely elevates that will as something not to be thought away. (PS, 150)

Cartesians are as bad as materialists here; the former leave most of the world in
an inert, exploitable state with only a few scattered minds about who deserve
respect. Although Clark is not a panpsychist of the Hartshornian or White-
headian variety, he does move toward panpsychism when he says that he prefers
an intentional, personalistic description of nature to a merely physical, objective
description devised to disenchant the world:

I do not mean that we should not attempt such non-intentional accounts: their merit is exactly that they can be called upon when we do not know or cannot imagine what particular imagined spirits might have in mind to do. . . . If I am too inclined to think that women fancy me I would be well advised to try and empty my thoughts of them of sexual affect, to try and see them with a degree of "objectivity." . . . These worlds which materialists declare to be the real substratum of our mistaken lives . . . are better conceived as models, metaphors, partial descriptions. (PS, 153)

Likewise, it is foolish

to imagine that any of our stories can describe in any literal sense what the world looked like before there were any lives around to see it. (PS, 154)

That is, Clark is not so much a panpsychist as an oxymoronic Aristotelianized Berkeleyan, as we will see toward the end of this book.

This Berkeleyanism is compatible with Aristotelianism in the sense that the hylomorphism that Clark defends is tied to a belief in *nous* as the controlling *daimon*, a *nous* that is at the root of concern for "rights." That is, a conventionalism that elevates the idols of the theater and tribe has a hard time keeping alive some basis for the justification of rights. For the purposes of this chapter it is crucial to ask where this emphasis on *nous* leaves animals. Clark's view seems to be that animals also have a controlling *daimon*, albeit in a lesser sense than humans have one. Many of the techniques and rules of practical, if not of theoretical, reason are found in animals for various productive or destructive purposes. As was noted in the previous chapter, animals can be ethical if not moral. We will see that Clark departs from Aristotle's speciesism regarding the respect that animals deserve from us, but it is worthwhile to state here that Theophrastus, a vegetarian, noted that his master might not have been true to his own principles in this regard.[5] It may be stretching things a bit to call the controlling *daimon* in animals *nous*, in that *nous* implies a godlike element making possible intellectual intuition and conscience. These latter phenomena are what give rise to morality in humanity in addition to ethics: beings with *nous* can see the whole of which this organism is a part—that is, they can take a critical stance on themselves:

True choice arises only from that distanced, balanced look. . . . In these moments of noetic insight we are allowed a glimpse through eyes that are not quite our own. (PS, 163)[6]

Clark is interested in determining exactly what it is in our animal inheritance that enables us to awaken to this wider vision of things. Here again he relies on Aristotle:

> *Nous* comes from outside the animal (Aristotle, *De Generatione Animalium* 736b), and its exercise is not a bodily function even if the bodily being that receives it must have some natural capacity to receive it. (PS, 168)

It is not the heart or brain or any particular organ but the whole body functioning as one that predisposes us to understand God's presence in us as *nous*: "that is the abiding reality of which our worlds are the stained reflections" (PS, 176).

Although Clark is willing to supply an Aristotelian basis for respect for both human beings and animals, he is skittish, as we will see, regarding rights. The Greek city was, by modern liberal standards, he thinks, totalitarian, yet it is precisely the Greek polis, built on the model of a family, that offers us some idea what a "form of society" is, now that we have lost such an idea. On the one hand, Clark wants to criticize liberalism, on the other, he wants to extend many of the "rights" granted to human beings in liberal society to animals:

> Aristotelian political theory, suitably informed by ethological data concerning the likely bases of ethical sentiment, may offer us a route between the advocates of State power in its modern form and individualistic libertarians. The social form that best fulfils our natures will be a relatively small community in which many ages, types and species are represented and in which everyone is encouraged to participate in serious decision-making. It is unlikely that any such community would long accept the favourite liberal dogma, that all rational adults are entitled to do what they please so long as they directly harm no one else. (NB, 115–16)

Clark also has harsh remarks for "conservatives" who favor decentralized government yet who simultaneously multiply state power to commit mass murder. (Ronald Reagan is the prime example of this contradiction, as is evidenced in the enormous budget deficit created by him, yet Clark, as we have seen previously, paradoxically seems to praise Reagan's militarism.) These conservatives also fuel the engines of destruction regarding animals. Yet Clark, in response to liberals and conservatives, tends to lean in the direction of conservative (and, he would say, Aristotelian) concentration on the attachment to family and friends, including pets, first, and strangers later, if at all (NB, 117).

This attachment to kin is not initiated by *nous*, hence an overemphasis on reason as *daimon* can be regarded as demonic. To be *eudaimon* we must, in a sense, identify ourselves with *nous*, but a critical attitude toward the *nous*-"self" is prompted by various ethical factors, including the status of animals. We will see, however, that a proper understanding of *nous*, for Clark, consists of the realization that our metaphysical center is *the* center, it is *Nous*, to which we can awaken. Such an awakening includes further realization that the distance between a human being and an animal is not nearly as great as the distance between any transitory creature and *Nous*, which is, in some sense, divine: "The fault of moderns is that we have, unaccountably, forgotten the undying Self without ever quite admitting to ourselves what it is really like to live in a world without it."[7] A mechanistic or a nominalistic view of the self is defective not only for biological but also for metaphysical reasons. "We may believe that the real world is one of discrete, non-recurring particulars and that all universals are mind-dependent, but that is not what we find in our experience."[8] Real universals and real divine presences can be experienced again and again:

> Where common sense suggests that all universals are merely abstract, mind-dependent conveniences, I shall suggest that some are real, spiritual presences. Where common sense would have us all believe that the only reliable explanations are ones that refer to the mechanical connection between discrete, material elements (a notion which is itself highly metaphorical), I hold that reality is a realm of communicating intelligences. . . . Our ordinary experience and language are full of non-particular presences.[9]

Historians of science have testified to the role of heightened consciousness or flashes of genius without turning to an ontological account of these experiences:

> Being possessed, or inspired, or dedicated, is a matter of allowing some one particular god-vision to dominate our lives. In Neo-Platonic terms this is not only a psychological, but an ontological claim.[10]

The point to the (monotheistic) effort to bring together these (polytheistic) impersonations is to be in a position to comprehend all of the lesser centers of value, including animals.

DUTIES TO ANIMALS

How much value do animals possess? At this point I would like to examine two specific arguments in favor of duties human beings have toward animals, duties grounded in the moral patiency of the animals themselves. The first is usually called the argument from sentiency. In abbreviated form, the argument from sentiency goes something like this:

1. Any being that can experience pain or suffer has at the very least the right not to be forced to experience pain or suffer unnecessarily.
2. It is not necessary that we inflict pain or suffering on animals so that we can eat, because eating vegetables can be perfectly healthy.
3. Therefore, to inflict unnecessary pain or suffering on an animal in order to eat it is morally reprehensible or cruel.

Modifications to this argument can be added to apply it to the clothes and cosmetics we wear, to the illegitimacy of animal experimentation, to the products we use, and so on. There have been many criticisms made of this argument in the last twenty-five years or so, many of which Clark himself has anticipated or responded to explicitly.[11] For example:

What is the evidence that they feel less distress than we do or that their desires are "of another sort" than ours? Doubtless there are all sorts of distresses, at the way the country is going to the dogs, or at Jones's new car, or the like, which beasts are fortunately spared—though the fact that they most probably do not appreciate our idiosyncratic problems might raise the question as to whether *they* have idiosyncratic problems too. It does not follow, however, from their lack of these distresses that calves cannot be acutely distressed at the absence of their mothers, nor that chickens are not distressed when unable to stretch their wings. . . . Animals, maybe, take as little thought for the morrow . . . unless, perhaps, they're squirrels. But this can hardly excuse our inflicting present distress on them, merely because they cannot foresee a future *end* of such distress. . . . We do not, emotionally, at least, have much understanding of death: my absence from the world is strictly unimaginable to me. . . . Cattle taken to the slaughter are similarly terrified. (MS, 40–41)

It is odd, to say the least, that human beings who are, say, from a domesticated cat's point of view, half-blind, half-deaf, and without a sense of smell, should think themselves more sensitive than animals. All pains are painful, and a cat whose eyes burn is as agonized as a baby whose eyes burn:

> It has been urged, in a last desperate throw, that animals, who lack any consciousness of themselves, must find each pang of agony a new thing without past or future, so that they do not seem to themselves to suffer any long pain. Even if we grant the premises—which I do not—yet even pangs of agony are ill to be borne. (MS, 42)

In response to these (Clarkian) claims many have reacted by paying at least lip service to the thesis that it is wrong to cause unnecessary suffering to an animal, but also by defining "necessity" in terms of human activities that cause death to animals, activities that are never seriously questioned. That is, the argument from sentiency shows a minimal respect for animals, in that it does not go so far as to argue for an animal's right to life, a "right" that Clark defends. Yet even without a right to life an animal has a right not to be tortured, especially if such torture is connected to the desire to demonstrate human superiority: "It is of little use claiming that it is wrong to inflict unnecessary suffering if anything at all will do as a context for calculating necessity" (MS, 44).

In addition to it being unfair to eat animals when it is not necessary to do so, in that eating them creates the demand for factory-farming practices whereby animals are imprisoned and tortured before they are killed, it is also inefficient in the "laborious transformation" of plant proteins into animal ones. There is something disingenuous in the efforts of those who frantically commiserate with the aboriginal Eskimos, who had to eat animals in order to survive, in an effort to justify their own abuse of animals: "if we are to mean what we say in outlawing the unnecessary suffering of animals, we must become, at the least, vegetarians" (MS, 45). No one can tell which animals have been "decently reared" before they are killed, as if killing them for the sake of human pleasure could be decent. Just as the existence of concentration camps acclimatizes us to slums, so also the most brutal treatment of animals has given some the incredible impression that by killing animals "painlessly" we are not denying them anything. Animal pain (or better, suffering, according to Clark) includes their missing what they ought to have: sunlight, room to move, a chance to meet their kind, and so on. Existence is, other things being equal, better than nonexistence, but this in no way should be construed as a carte blanche to make the existence of individual animals miserable: "suppose I would not have begotten my son without the intention of selling him into slavery—do I now have a *right* to sell him?" (MS, 48). Even if it seems to be true that the lives of individual animals are of little consequence in the ultimate scheme of things, the same could be said of the lives of individual human beings, were it not for the fact that an omnibenevolent God cares for all individuals, human or animal, as in the biblical assurance regarding sparrows (MS, 45–49).

Clark is willing to admit that all sentient life involves *some* pain, as we have seen in the chapter on his theodicy. Hence there is something futile in trying to avoid all destruction of sentient life, or of life in general, as when Jain monks tred on a path only after another person, of a lesser caste, has swept it clean of insects:

> I do not urge, as an immediately practical policy, that all distress be eliminated from the world: in the present dispensation that could only be achieved by eliminating all sentient life. I do insist that acceptance of the principle that we should not cause distress beyond our necessities must, if this principle is to have any meaning, require us to abstain from all flesh-foods. (MS, 53–54)

Although pains may involve sensations, they are not to be identified with sensations. Rather, pain is an abstraction from one's experience of distress or of seeking to avoid something. Clark wonders how civilized we really are if we can tolerate such distress in animals with the rationalization that a goose's suffering, say, is necessary for the purpose of eating pâté de foie gras. He also wonders whether pigs would be much happier than they are now if they were treated, as the cozy picture down on the farm has it, as family pets until the winter, at which time they would be killed reluctantly so that the rest could see another spring (MS, 55, 57):

> In that situation perhaps pigs would, as it were, accept the bargain, or perhaps not. I am not myself in danger of starving, nor do I know anyone with a family pig. Nor would I think very highly of a family that found it easy to kill and eat such a pig. (MS, 60)

The argument from sentiency refers to individuals, to entities who deserve a singular rather than a universal term to refer to them: "A cow *might* be compensated for her distress by the charming thought that there would always, by man's gracious care, be cows" (MS, 62). Clark obviously does not think that this possibility is too likely, however. By concentrating on the respect due to individual animals, Clark brings to light the difference between (democratic) individual plants and stones, say, which can be cut in half and still be plants and stones, on the one hand, and (monarchical) animals, on the other, who act and feel as one and cannot be cut in half and still be animals, except in the case of Siamese twins. One frog's pain is not another's, except vicariously through the care one has for the other, and a cat, although unable to use the pronoun "I," does not mistake itself for someone else. As we have seen, the ethological evidence from Williams, Goodall, Maxwell, and Howard indicates that if we try we can communicate with individual monkeys, chimpanzees, birds, and even fish (MS, 63, 66). Regarding the "pogrom" against animals, Clark says,

> We speak of the Cow, the Pig, the Fox, and somehow persuade ourselves thereby that we do no damage when we kill a cow, a pig, a fox. Of animals we are superstitiously Platonic: it is the Idea that is real to us, not the individual, suffering entities. We want there to be pigs, because we want to be able to go on seeing the Pig, or because we think the Pig bizarrely likes to be instantiated. Most of the orthodox would of course fervently deny that they are Platonists. . . . As an occasional Neo-Platonist I would not deny that there may be some truth in this, though not a truth that the orthodox should so willingly accept: that the phenomenal universe is in some way the expression of a spiritual reality. . . . But as an occasional Aristotelian I insist that we must not forget the dear particulars in the name of the universal. The idea that one can show love for the Cow by subjecting actual cows to continual pregnancies, taking away their children, rearing them in darkness and solitude, killing and consuming them, is really quite astonishing. (MS, 64–65)

It is extremely paradoxical, Clark thinks, that death should not be recognized as the "greatest of single hurts." Not to have such a recognition makes it possible to have a cat "put down" with equanimity if the cat does not match the new drapes, just so long as it is killed "painlessly." It is true that *sometimes* it is the lesser evil to euthanize an animal or a human being, but this in no way helps to establish the claim that death is not an evil:

166

I think little of a murderer who comforts his proposed victim with the information that it won't hurt. . . . Yet because killing is thought no evil, in comparison
with pains which in other contexts liberals are eager to minimize, laboratory animals are killed in the thousands rather than suffer any temporary pain on the road
to recovery. Better that such victims *should* recover consciousness, even with some
pain, and be delivered into freedom as some honest recompense for their ill-treat-
ment. . . . Certainly it is worse to kill slowly than quickly. (MS, 76–77)

Clark is not trying to offer a blanket approval of euthanasia, in that even elderly animals enjoy life in their own way:

If we must kill to live, let us kill cleanly, and let us not forget that sometimes we
have no need at all to kill. In short, humane killing is better than careless, but
worse than no killing at all; the foreseen, but unintended death (as those of
insects on a car's windscreen) weighs less heavily than a deliberate killing; killing
for food is one thing, killing for fun another. . . . That even vegans thus require
death in no way licences still further death, of cows and sheep and birds. (MS, 82)

There are stages on the road to hell, but it is better to be returning on that road
than to be traveling toward the absolute nadir, toward that point at which we
deny animals consciousness and forget that they are sentient (the two are, for
Clark, inseparable), and at which point we reverence them only in their Form
and not in their individuality, and finally at that irreligious point where we
think that *we* are the masters of the world (MS, 80–83, 102, 118).

Part of the problem regarding most people's views of animals lies in our fantasy that cows are placid and incurious hunks of flesh. We do not *see* the individuals, such that it is easy to convince ourselves that these creatures somehow
actually cooperate with their would-be killers. We tend to see animals as symbols for our own potentialities, especially those we wish to suppress (MS, 121).
Clark is not so much offering a theory for demarcating reality from fantasy
as he is asking us to be skeptical of any supposed fantasy-free description of
animals:

It is difficult, if not impossible, to give any formal account of the difference
between a realistic outlook and a fantasy: I am myself quite prepared to believe
that even the most carefully realistic picture of the world is essentially a fantasy,
and it certainly may *operate* as one. (MS, 133)

Even talk of "rights" can be affected by the fantasy of a social contract that we can *imagine* to have taken place at some historical moment. Clark is not so much bothered by the rights theorists' claim that more matters than "mere" pain and pleasure, but rather by the abstractness of such claims:

> Rights play no large part in my political philosophy, and I do not care to express my own concern for animals in terms of their putative "natural rights." . . . What concerns me most are not abstract natural rights but concrete historical ones. . . . I do not share Regan's apparent conviction that our only important duties in these matters rest upon the sort of rights that he imputes to subjects-of-a-life.[12]

Here we can see a tension in Clark's thought between the argument from sentiency, which seems to be precisely an abstract, philosophical, liberal argument (albeit about concrete pain) that applies universally to sentient beings, on the one hand, and Clark's concern for historical communities, in this case only British beasts, on the other.

This tension is usually relieved by Clark's (surprisingly) liberal tendency to legislate in favor of all beasts. An electric light that goes on when a switch is pressed is hardly alert, awake, sentient, or conscious, nor does it operate as a goal-seeking system within a changing environment. Animals, even non-British ones, possess these abilities. Clark also argues on behalf of all animals against functionalist or behaviorist approaches, which avoid the supposed privacy of animal consciousness altogether, an effort that fails because it does not account for the massive amount of evidence in favor of the belief that sentience or consciousness is both an introspective reality and inferable from others, given certain classic sorts of evidence supplied both by human beings and animals (as in writhing, twitching, groaning, staring, etc.). Animals have never been *observed* to be nonsentient; rather, on ill-conceived materialist, Cartesian, or Thomistic metaphysical grounds they have been required to be so. As before, it is individual animals who are sentient (AJ, 128–29, 161, 163):

> To say that all human beings, whatever their appearance, have a certain nature is to rely upon a form of essentialist typology which is no longer widely approved of in biological circles. On the older view, to be a given sort of creature was to have one-and-the-same nature as all others of that sort. . . . The problem with this view always was that difference and variety were defects. Perfect people

would be identical—but in that case it was difficult to see why individual idiosyncrasy should be respected. (AJ, 162)

Likewise, modern biologists reject "the essential idea of Dog." Rather, a species is a set of interbreeding populations. Individuals do have essences, Clark thinks; that is, they have "properties that they could not lose without ceasing to be the very individuals they are" (AJ, 164). Yet individual cows are not to be regarded as more or less defective specimens of cowhood:

> This is not to say there are no such things as species. Creatures are not, as it were, scattered randomly over conceptual space. They cluster in genealogically related groups whose members do bear a family resemblance. . . . But there is, none the less, nothing like the metaphysical division between humans and non-humans that the older typology required. . . . With the collapse of typological explanation as a respectable scientific theory comes the realization that other animals than us may have such individual souls (as Plato, of course, already believed), even if they are not so far awake to their own being. (AJ, 164, 177)

The claim that individual animals deserve respect even if they are not as self-conscious as most adult human beings is supported not only by the argument from sentiency, but also by the argument from marginal cases, the second argument in Clark that I will examine. This argument, like that from sentiency, has received several criticisms anticipated, or responded to explicitly, by Clark himself. Simply stated, the argument goes something like this, according to Peter Singer:

> The catch is that any such characteristic that is possessed by *all* human beings will not be possessed *only* by human beings. For example all humans, but not only humans, are capable of feeling pain; and while only humans are capable of solving complex mathematical problems, not all humans can do this. So it turns out that in the only sense in which we can truly say, as an assertion of fact, that all humans are equal, at least some members of other species are also "equal"— equal, that is, to some humans.[13]

Theological statements of a human being's privileged status cannot be philosophically justified. The statement, however, that we can legitimately eat animals because human beings are rational, or autonomous, or religious believers, or language users, or the like, does not in fact refer to all human beings. These "marginal cases" include infants, the mentally feeble, and the like. If we "lower" our standard to that of sentiency (for example, the ability to experience pain) so as to protect these people, in order to be consistent we must also protect many animals, including those that we eat. Or, as Tom Regan puts it, if an animal has characteristics *a, b, c . . . n*, but lacks autonomy (or reason, and so on), and if a human being has characteristics *a, b, c . . . n*, but lacks autonomy (or reason, and so on), then we have just as much reason to believe that the animal has rights as the human. These rights would include the right not to be forced to suffer or be killed unnecessarily. Clark clearly agrees with this argument, even if he does not like to call it from "marginal cases," as we will see.

Clark makes it clear that, *in a crisis*, if he had to choose between saving his wife's life and saving his cat's, he would save his wife. Then again, however, on Clark's grounds, if he had to choose in a crisis between his wife's life and his neighbor's he would still save his wife's. Universalizing Kantians and utilitarians would in fact make the same choice, he thinks, although in theory they should be as willing to save the neighbor as the wife:

> But what if the choice lies between, say, a chimpanzee and an incurably comatose human? Is the choice *so* easy? And how comatose must the human be, or how close to human the animal before we can defend the less racist [speciesist] choice? (MS, 87)

Again, consider that if a man is forced in a crisis to choose between saving his mother or saving his girlfriend, he really is in a dilemma. Suppose we say that he should save his mother. Would this make it legitimate for him to *kill* his girlfriend to obtain something that would save his mother's life? Hardly. Analogously, *even if* human beings are more worthy of moral respect than animals, it does not follow that animals exist solely for us. Most zoophiles, including Clark, are willing to distinguish morally between human beings and animals. The question is whether speciesists (modeled after "racists" and "sexists") can distinguish between cats and cabbages. Hierarchical order is not to be confused with licensed tyranny, according to Clark, with "hierarchical order" diminishing in importance the further we get from household and friends (MS, 89).

Zoophiles might not be bothered so much by Clark's defense of the argument from marginal cases as by his, to use a pejorative term, nepotism. For example, he admits that he is fonder of most cats than most dogs (even though the former are more likely to bring decapitated mice into the house). Clark's claim is that there is a certain insincerity in claiming to be completely impartial in this regard, especially on the part of speciesists who have an obvious favorite: humanity. Along with William James, Clark thinks that the claim of strict impartiality is a boast of "scientific" moderns that will be the greatest surprise to our descendants. A hierarchy between human beings and most animals on the criterion of rationality is fair enough, *as long as* such rationality does not attempt to take on a life of its own apart from the heart's affections, affections that are the highest expressions of many members of our own species (the marginal cases) as well as of most animals. Some animals are (ridiculously) treated better than some children, but these pampered pets should not occlude our vision of the fact that to be an unowned animal is still largely a capital crime, as Henry Salt also noticed a century ago. If rationality is the criterion of value, then even pets could be tortured along with "food animals," psychopaths, and idiots (MS, 90–94). However, Clark's fideism may be overextended when he flirts with the idea that we sometimes ought to try out alternatives to the ideal of rational consistency (MS, 106). This sort of language only gets him into trouble with his critics without advancing his own claims regarding animals.

Plutarch notes in his *Moralia* (965b) that boys will throw rocks at frogs in play but that the frogs die in earnest. Should we exonerate the boys by noting that the frogs did not exhibit (perfect) rationality? What are the consequences of such an exoneration? Clark's apparent answer: the consequences dictated by the argument from marginal cases. "We are absolutely better than the animals because we are able to give their interests some consideration: so we won't" (MS, 108). Only Clark, however, could link this defense of the argument from marginal cases with his conservativism-patriotism-militarism (which is, perhaps, a double redundancy):

> It is probably evident that I have little sympathy with the claim that we should always and only act as would the generalized One of rationalist myth: I fear that such advice seems no more than an uneasy extrapolation from the demands of social class and professional role. It seems to me that there is more to normal ethical concern than such rational obedience: a readiness, for example, to think something worth dying for, as animals at least appear to do. (MS, 108)

Adherence to the rationalist myth, as before, has as its consequence a willingness to put the sick and feebleminded beyond the moral law. How much more fruitful and humane, Clark thinks, to adopt as a myth the lure of "irrational affection, artistic imagination, loyalty":

> The attempt to transform our various social hierarchies into a single, rationally defensible morality that will license all and only acts of affection and justice to creatures of our species, seems to me to be a failure. The real springs of our action lie elsewhere. (MS, 109)

There are sentient beings all around us, and to assume that the intelligence of some of them, however intelligence may be defined, licenses abuse of animals also makes it possible for any intellectual elite (God, the angels, extraterrestrials, or the Nazis by self-proclamation) "to treat the rest of us like trash" (MS, 182). The argument from marginal cases makes it apparent that if we are willing to mistreat animals we should also be willing to mistreat imbeciles. R. G. Frey comes close to adopting this view when he claims that the marginal cases do not really have rights, but we act as if they do because we are squeamish about abusing them. Clark notes, however, that some of us are reminded of our own condition by animals and are squeamish about abusing them as well:

> But suppose we did not feel squeamish about tormenting, say, microcephalics or brain-damaged orphans? A good many people, indeed, probably do not. And many more, if they thought that some advantage could safely be won for the rest of us by torturing such defective humans. . . . I see no reason to suppose that squeamishness on its own is much of a barrier against the exploitation of the human weak. . . . Secretly, I suggest, we know that we *ought* to care for the subnormal precisely because they are subnormal: they are weak, defenceless, at our mercy. They can be hurt, injured, frustrated. We ought to consider their wishes and feelings, not because we will be hurt if we don't, but because they will be hurt. And the same goes for those creatures like them who are of our kind though not of our species. . . . The *descent* of our potential victims has nothing directly to do with their susceptibility to injury.[14]

Clark, contra Frey, wishes both to defend the argument from marginal cases and to forthrightly defend Mongoloid children:

> A mongol child is not an imperfectly embodied Human, but a genotypic variation within the boundaries of the human population that does not seem to be

capable of separate, sustained existence. . . . [They are] not defective embodiments of an Ideal Essence: they are simply what they are. . . . We no longer have
the metaphysical assurance that imbeciles are really rational souls and chimpanzees are not. (AJ, 165)

Thus far we have seen that if it takes possession of *nous* to enter the community of moral concern, then some human beings are not in the community,
and to state that it takes membership in a species (the human one) to enter the
community of moral concern is to defend a position (speciesism) that is very
close to racism or sexism:[15]

> The evils of sexism are that females are denied the opportunity to live authentic
> lives. . . . A nonsexist society is one in which people are not oppressed, exploited,
> and manipulated to fit sexual stereotypes. The evils of speciesism, similarly, are
> that creatures are robbed, assaulted, and killed, not simply that they are distin-
> guished from members of our own species. It is right so to distinguish them. . . .
> What is wrong is to use them with cruelty and disrespect.[16]

It should be emphasized that Clark does not think that mentally defective
human beings are really "marginal" human beings, hence he prefers not to refer
to the argument under consideration as that from marginal cases. In fact, he
finds the designation somewhat offensive, a view that is consistent with what we
have seen to be his ethology:

> Children, imbeciles, lunatics and the senile are not marginal to society, any more
> than the domestic animals. Society does not exist to serve the purposes of self-
> seeking rational adult individuals but to maintain the households within which
> we all grow up.[17]

Each human being is an individual organism having largely unpredictable
similarities with others. This unpredictability should not be surprising when it
is realized that scientific taxa are not the same as folk taxa, as in "weeds" or
"fish" (including whales). There is no set of properties such that all weeds and
only weeds have them, nor is there such a set of properties for "trees." By way
of contrast, scientific taxa consist of genealogically related individuals rather
than of a "Platonic" or perfect type that individuals imitate. Folk taxa are not
foolish inventions, however, in that for landscaping purposes it makes sense to

talk of trees and weeds, but these taxa should not be allowed to do our work in morality for us, say, by *stipulating* that "humans" have rights and "animals" do not, and then by resting content with the assumption that a real or a metaphysical distinction has been made. The folk taxon "human beings" embodies an a priori concept of normality that acts as a contrast to those who are less than normal. In this regard folk taxonomy ends up in contradiction: human beings universally are the sorts of beings who deserve respect, but human beings are essentially or normally rational. Opponents of the argument from marginal cases are saddled with precisely this contradiction. Yet in scientific taxonomy every being in a given taxon is as much a member of the taxon as any other, no matter how atypical or "marginal" it is. That is, Clark thinks that we can learn a moral lesson from scientific taxa, even if, for pragmatic purposes, we cannot do without folk taxa. It is, in fact, true that all human beings belong to the same species in the sense that there are no barriers (social, geographical, or physiological) to interbreeding among human groups. Yet it is also a fact, Clark notes, that there are biological grounds for claiming some sort of unity among all mammals, primates, and so on, in that they belong to the same class, order, or super-family. An awareness of these unities militates against the prejudice that says that human persons should think that any conspecific is worth more than any individual from another species.[18]

The unity of humankind, from a biological point of view, does not rest in the possession of a common, essentialist "nature," but in being a common breeding population, and *this* sort of unity does not support the case for speciesism. For example, it does not support the case for the Kantian variety of speciesism wherein only rational agents are of moral worth, a view that has as one consequence that "some creatures of another species might turn out to be 'human' in the morally significant sense; many of our species might turn out to be 'subhuman.'"[19] Clark does think that Kantian liberalism is laudable in the sense that it focuses on one morally relevant feature of many human beings. Only one, however:

> The price of this laudable insistence on moral humanism is a profound unease . . . about any attempt to treat the characters and talents of human populations as explicable in something like the way that we might explain the behaviour of baboons or horses. It is asserted, in advance of any evidence worth mentioning, that our species has somehow escaped from the nexus of evolutionary selection, and become pure mind, governed only by the laws of reason.[20]

These Clarkian considerations regarding the differences between folk and scientific taxa, and regarding the inconsistencies found in the former, are meant to drive home the importance of what is commonly called the argument from marginal cases, an argument that Clark defends without naming it:

> The problem, notoriously, is that the harder we make it to meet the qualifications of "real humanity" (so as to exclude dolphins, chimpanzees, squids and honey-bees), the more creatures of clearly human descent we also push beyond the pale. In the end either only the Wise are worth troubling about (and they, so far, are found only among the biologically human) or any individual with feelings and purposes of its own is a proper moral object. Either most human beings may rightly be treated "like animals," when we deal with them at a practical level, and when we try to explain their behaviour, or a good many animals should not be treated like that either.[21]

Clark is urging us to judge certain categories, traditional within Judaism, Christianity, and Islam, but not within the Greek world, as merely artificial:

> Once we have acknowledged that a species is not a natural kind—not a set of individuals who share a common, underlying and causative nature—we can afford to allow that other linguistic communities have other views on who are "people" (i.e., respected members of their community). . . . The question is . . . why do we make so much of any differences there are?[22]

Clark's frustration with Western anthropocentrism is in evidence when he criticizes the (surprisingly) still prevalent Cartesian view. It is an

> oddity that those moderns who regularly seek to dissociate themselves from these older doctrines of the soul (which they characterize as dualist or Cartesian) . . . still wish to maintain the moral divisions that only made sense upon the assumption of a distinctively human soul. If there is no such soul . . . then there is no reason to distinguish sharply and generally between domestication and slavery, flesh-eating and cannibalism, the killing of an ox and the slaying of a man. Liberal humanists need to believe in the myth of a common human nature, but have abandoned belief in the human soul, and so equate that imagined natural kind with the human species. They should think again.[23]

That is, Clark's defense of the argument from marginal cases is a part of his conservative critique of modern liberalism, a conservativism that, on this score, reaches back at least as far as Porphyry, who also defended this argument.[24] In fact, it reaches back to Aristotle, who, although not a great defender of respect for animals, nonetheless thought that humans were characterized not by some one essential property, but by complexes of resemblances and homologous structures:

> As we advance upon the Aristotelian road . . . we have steadily less excuse for believing that the presence of our biological species can be detected simply by discovering instances of tool-making, food-sharing, exogamic structures or verbal activity.[25]

The moral Clark draws from this Aristotelian lesson is that drawn by Aristotle's pupil Theophrastus, which is given the following sort of contemporary articulation by Clark:

> We live in a world of mutually dependent and competitive organisms, such that there are relatively enclosed gene-pools, and relatively stable species-forms. . . . We cannot assume that all "human" communities should be explained one way, and all "non-human" communities another, as if chimpanzees and whales were more like worms or amoebae than they were like humans, and all human groups more like each other than any of them are like baboons or chimpanzees. . . . We should not assume that slavery or cannibalism needs some special explanation, different from the sort of explanation we give for domestication or flesh-eating.[26]

Other creatures than the biologically human might be persons, if by "persons" we mean those who wear the mask of moral patiency.

CRITICS

I am now in a position to respond to the critics of Clark's views regarding animals as moral patients, critics who very often are not speciesists but animal rightists who have difficulties with the way in which Clark goes about the business of defending animals. The critics seem to have ignored Clark's warning in the preface to MS that his work is "a *consciously* outrageous publication" (my emphasis) in the aforementioned sense that he hyperbolizes extremes so as to calibrate his own position in the middle, a position that is, in many ways, a minimalist one:

> This at least cannot be true, that it is proper to be the cause of avoidable ill. There may be other moral principles than this, but this at least is dogma. And if this minimal principle be accepted, there is no other honest course than the immediate rejection of all flesh-foods and most bio-medical research. The point, whatever its later complications, is a simple one, and the attempts of our hypocrisy to evade the issue provide a fascinating case-history of the corruption of our moral and philosophical sense. (MS, preface)

Clark's views are also "outrageous" in the sense that he refuses to take his convictions lightly, because, as Peirce noticed as well, if one takes them lightly then other, and perhaps less scrupulous, debaters with vested interests will set their own limits to the argument. This point will not necessarily win over those who have a more sober conception of the intellectual life than Clark's partly Dionysian one, but at least Clark is honest (sober scholars can, in fact, be deceptive in their sobriety): "I am a committed crank and zoophile, and my hope is to convert my audience" (MS, 2–3).

Another reason for some critics' misunderstanding of Clark's views on animals is that *MS,* if read alone, gives one only a fragmentary grasp of his views on animals, a fragment that needs to be supplemented by a consideration of his views on God, ethology, and politics. The present book is meant to provide such a synoptic vision. Clark is quite clear in *MS* that he is not presenting a consistent moral system there, even if it is open to question as to whether he offers such a system anywhere else. Actually it is doubtful if Clark's thoughts can ever be laid out in terms of a deductive system, in that he is skeptical of the sort of reason that would have to be used in such a deduction. He actually views systems as "lethal," as in the system of rationalistic scientism that has encouraged our worst behavior toward animals. Nonetheless, there are numerous reflections that each facet of Clark's philosophy casts on all the others, as I am trying to demonstrate in this book (MS, 186).

The best part of moral philosophy, according to Clark, lies in the elimination of prejudice or bias in the pejorative senses of these terms, but if the extreme skeptic is correct, then such an elimination is a mere fantasy. Clark avoids such a skepticism precisely in the two arguments I have presented above, arguments that presuppose that there can be a very real difference between right and wrong. That is, Clark's stance is both zoophilist and realist, and he is confident enough in his zoophilist, realist arguments that he openly asks his critics to refute him, with the only proviso being that in the end what matters is not what we say, but what we do and do not do (MS, 189–90, 198). Have Clark's critics refuted his zoophilist arguments?

Tom Regan admits that one can learn much from Clark regarding the classical and contemporary literature relating to the moral status of animals and how *not* to argue for a cause. Regan sees little humility in Clark's writing, especially when he claims that those who still eat flesh when they could do otherwise have no claim to be serious moralists (MS, 183). Regan puts his point in these terms:

> I should have thought that it is just this sort of breathtaking claim, dismissing in a single stroke the greater part of the best thinkers in the Anglo-American world, that is most counterproductive to the vegetarian cause for which Clark labours.[27]

Regan is correct that Clark has a tendency to make "breathtaking" claims (as in my preceding treatments of Clark's preliminary use of hyperbole so as to reach a mean), but he is premature in asserting that Clark does not offer detailed arguments in favor of his theses. Clark's arguments are explicitly there, as the preceding citations indicate, but they are interspersed with rapid-fire quotations and invectives. Nor is Regan convincing when he says that Clark is really obscure when he tries to be profound. There is nothing obscure in claiming that there are stages on the road to hell, but what matters is which direction we are going (MS, 83). If "hell" refers to the absolute nadir, to the Cartesian view of animals as machines, then it makes a big difference, according to Clark, whether we tend toward Cartesianism or are at least trying to escape from it. Fergus Kerr not only points out Clark's arguments, but also notices that one of the major premises of the argument from sentiency is the principle familiar to many moral philosophers that it is intrinsically wrong to be the cause of avoidable ill. Further, Kerr emphasizes the fact, which Regan does not, that Clark's view of animals as moral patients is rooted in his Christian Aristotelianism and in his ethology. MS is best understood, Kerr seems to be saying, along with *NB*, *AJ*, *MR*, and so on.[28]

Regan is not alone in his criticisms, however, a fact that does not necessarily point out a defect in Clark's philosophy, even if it does make Clark's admirers (including myself) wish that he would sometimes make more concessions to those who might read only one of his books. One might also wish that Clark would make more concessions to those who do not have the time or patience to reread him so as to sift through the elements that are not essential to logical rigor (elements that admittedly constitute half of the edification and three-fourths of the fun that come from reading Clark) to find the logical structure buried beneath. Consider Dale Jamieson, who finds Clark's *MS* disappointing from a philosophical point of view. Jamieson thinks that the argument from marginal cases is

> the strongest philosophical challenge yet mounted against our ordinary views concerning the treatment of nonhumans. For this reason it deserves the closest scrutiny. It is a shortcoming of *The Moral Status of Animals* that it fails to engage with this argument.[29]

This is just not true, as the preceding treatment of Clark's repeated engagements with this argument indicates.[30] Clark's writing is not quite the "hodge-podge" that Jamieson alleges, but it must be admitted that the demands Clark places on his readers to find the logical structure to his work make it understandable why Jamieson adopts the attitude he does.

Consider L. W. Sumner's frustration:

> Regrettably, the central issue of Clark's discourse is lost in the tangle of a hundred codicils. If you are seeking an argument which is plain and direct, which begins by announcing its presuppositions and premises, which sets out the relevant facts as fully and fairly as possible . . . if these are your demands then you are well advised to leave this book alone and to read Peter Singer's *Animal Liberation* instead. . . . Stephen Clark seems constitutionally incapable of carrying out such an enterprise.[31]

Sumner is not especially fond of Clark's policy of "dialectical defoliation," nor of his "cartpath through a wood rather than a Roman road," yet he is, like Jamieson, in agreement with many of Clark's conclusions. Sumner, unlike Regan and Jamieson, comments not only on Clark's style, for lack of a better word, but also on the substance of his arguments. He is specifically worried about Clark's strategy of moving from the minimalist philosophical basis of an opposition to causing avoidable ill to some rather far-reaching conclusions:

As a dialectical device the minimalist strategy is undoubtedly attractive. If it can be made to work then what appears to be a strong and uncompromising practical consequence will be somehow manufactured out of the commonest and most innocent materials. . . . It is a great flaw in Clark's exposition that he nowhere acknowledges the existence of developed moral theories (of which contract theories are the best example) which provide a *reason* for thinking that animals merit no moral consideration in their own right.[32]

This is surely incorrect, however, if we look at Clark's corpus. As we have already and will see again regarding his political views, Clark is quite explicit in his criticisms of (ahistorical) contract theories. Furthermore, there are also problems with Sumner's confusion as to what Clark's own theories are. He knows that they are not utilitarian, but he has no idea how to adjudicate among Clark's attachments to Aristotelianism, skepticism, neoplatonism, and Christianity, attachments that I am trying to sort out in this book. Perhaps because Clark's theories seem murky to Sumner, he wishes Clark were a utilitarian and, we are to assume, safely within the bounds of acceptable theorizing. Nonetheless there may be some justice in the following swipe by Sumner, but not enough justice to avoid criticizing him for failing to come to terms with Clark's theoretical underpinnings:

"Conversation has convinced me that utilitarianism, whatever its origin, is now merely a final, and entirely vacuous, pretext for doing whatever the speaker himself fancies" (MS, 74). I should like Stephen Clark to know that this remark has given considerable offense to one of his readers who is both a vegetarian and a utilitarian, and who became a vegetarian *because* he was a utilitarian.[33]

The belief that Clark only *claims* to give arguments, including arguments against utilitarianism,[34] is rejected by Mary Midgley, one of Clark's most favorable reviewers.[35] She notes that moral philosophers have tended in this century to make the odd claim of neutrality on most or all practical questions, a claim that has largely reduced moral philosophy to triviality. Clark, in rejecting this tradition, sometimes self-consciously takes the other dialectical extreme for the purpose of setting up the limits within which a reasonable mean can be located: "I suggest that he is in no way wrong to be so much in earnest, but that books of this kind (*MS*) may call for a special sort of discipline which, for lack of practice, philosophers have largely forgotten." Midgley makes a distinction between Clark

R (for reasonable) and Clark E (for extreme), with the former referring to that part of Clark not noticed or emphasized by some commentators. She admits that Clark E can be somewhat frustrating, as when Clark lumps all speciesists together as "the orthodox," when, in point of fact, they are, according to Midgley, a "mixed bunch." Like Peter Singer's *Animal Liberation*, Clark's *MS* "begins the spring-cleaning of our wildly confused ideas about animals." The cleaning is badly needed precisely because of the intellectual currents that Clark criticizes: anthropocentric Christianity; an overconfidence in (human) reason (say, as found among utilitarians or contract theorists); and, as Midgley emphasizes, the dogma that rights are correlated with duties, such that without the latter a being cannot have the former.

Rational argumentation does not have to be pedantic or boring, such that even some critics who have negative things to say about Clark's thought are willing to admit that he is always "stimulating and intelligent,"[36] and that even the analytic philosopher who has a preference for the kind of argumentation (and mode of presentation for one's argumentation) in contemporary analytic philosophy can nonetheless learn a great deal about what is defective in Kantianism, scientism, and the like in a careful reading of Clark.[37] Perhaps one of the reasons why analytic philosophers have a difficult time in reading Clark is that they are still affected, however implicitly, by the reductionistic materialism out of which analytic philosophy grew and concerning which it still must contend. That is, from the perspective of some of Clark's critics his oddity has to do not only with his style but also with the substance of his remarks.

Despite the efforts of eliminative materialists and Wittgensteinians, most human beings and most philosophers still think that introspection does reveal *something* of a region closed off from public commentary. This closed off region does confront a common world, but this common world is not as easily accessible as analytic philosophers under the spell of naive empiricism have assumed. Berkeley's spell on Clark is not so strong that Clark would claim that one's percepts are self-sustaining (if, in fact, this is Berkeley's view). Our access to the common world is not direct, in that one must go through one's bodily parts. As before, Clark does not intend to reify mind and body into separate substances, but he does intend to call into question dogmatic materialistic monism, the insistence that there is only one sort of real thing, an insistence that Clark thinks is as metaphysically wild as any ancient creed. As James also noted, some types of soft dualism are pragmatically useful, as when one notices the difference between one's own perceptual universe and another human being's or another animal's. Part of any defensible code of conduct regarding the treatment of human beings or animals includes an acknowledgment of the fact that "I here" am different from things as they are on the far side of my veil of subjectivity, but also that I have the strongest possible evidence that on the other side of the veil are sentient beings who each have their own "I here." Clark uses the following example regarding sexual passion to illustrate this point, but he could just as well have chosen one regarding a human being's desire, say, to kill or eat an animal:

> If what I immediately, and prejudicially, observe is—let us suppose—an amorous young woman who is only pretending to refuse, it is clear that my perceptual universe, and the image of that woman, is erotically suffused. . . . One does not transcend the immediate illusion of supposing that one's erotic fancy is identical with a someone out there in the world by making believe that women are impersonal mechanisms! (PS, 29, 35)

Defenders of animals among analytic philosophers do not make explicit that there is something defective in believing that the truth can be approached by cutting out all that is personal, a belief integral to positivism and to positivism's legacy:

> The weird assumption that only those with a "scientific" training can actually think is as obvious a piece of self-serving ideology as that of any ancient priesthood. . . . Misplaced animism may be an intellectual sin, but so is misplaced mathematization. (PS, 31)

Clark's own antipositivism is close to Popper's concept of objective knowledge as consisting of bold hypotheses *and* severe attempts at refutation: "The process by which we chiefly find out what is, or what could sensibly be thought to be, is a combination of more or less inspired guesswork, combined with rigorous testing" (PS, 32), although in philosophy this testing is obviously not done in the laboratory. The "scientific method" is not necessarily tied to any impersonalist method, a method that has disastrous consequences for animals because in it animals tend to be viewed as machines or as fodder for research or as locomotor meals. "To rule out intentional explanation, or empathetic identification, as routes to knowledge amounts to a process of self-blinding for which there is historical explanation but very little philosophical justification" (PS, 32). A rigorously impersonal world is one in which there are, by definition, no odds in favor of the emergence of experiencing animals or human beings. Yet there are such beings in the world, hence Clark thinks that the hypothesis of an essentially personal world has the edge over the alternative. Understanding other intending and experiencing beings in this personal world is accomplished not only by analogy with our known selves, but also by the shock of coming into contact with animal others who enlarge our knowledge of who we are. Clark agrees with Einstein that having a "feeling" for the order lying behind the appearances, and having a powerful "intuition" regarding the ways of nature, are crucial, for without them we remain like the prisoners in Plato's cave (PS, 26–39). Hence, "to perfect our understanding we should seek to found ourselves more securely on what lies 'within'" (PS, 37), on our powers of feeling and intuition:

> The impersonal universe constructed, for whatever reason, by objectivizing scientists—and one reason among many has undoubtedly been the wish to leave "nature" and natural creatures free to serve our purposes—is a thing that we have made. (PS, 38)

If one of the consequences of "objective" science, or of philosophy done in imitation of such science, is that it makes no difference to the results if the researcher or scholar is honest or courageous (i.e., if doing science or philosophy has nothing to do with morality), then we can expect abuse of animals to continue. For without such virtues scientists may well *say* that they welcome reasoned criticism even if they do not in fact welcome it: "Scientists emphatically do not welcome criticism" (PS, 46), as is evidenced, say, in the animal research boards found in research institutions in American universities, the vast majority of which are obviously stacked decks in favor of the (often reductionistic) researchers themselves. (I have taught at a university where the "ethics and animals" committee was the only university-wide committee whose members were not selected through democratic elections.) Clark's views on the inadequacies of dogmatic scientific materialism and the fact that such materialism causes an inadequate understanding of animals can be seen in the following:

> Two things, then, need to be remembered: on the one hand, I feel no necessity to understand the human mind only in such terms as might prove acceptable to learned primatologists infected by materialist prejudice; on the other hand, I do

believe that any adequate account of the human mind must rest upon, and help towards, an adequate account of mind as it manifests itself in other primates, mammals, chordates. (PS, 52)

Although Clark sometimes gives support to Feyerabend's attack on fixed methodologies, and sometimes approves the elaboration of maverick hypotheses, it does not follow that he rejects reason. He does reject the sort of "reason" that is identified with the thought of "currently fashionable sages" who end up defending a materialistic reductionism that has disastrous consequences for animals: "reason involves a difficult ascesis, a humble readiness to transcend past limits" (PS, 53).

Clark not only thinks that it is possible for us to sympathize with the feelings of animals, in some cases he feels that it is easier to sympathize with and understand them than it is to sympathize with and understand fellow human beings, in that the latter may be more likely to have hidden motives than animals. For example, he thinks it easier as a male to sympathize with and understand a horny bull than it is to sympathize with and understand a fellow (female) human being with menstrual pains; and it may be easier to know what one's domestic cat requires than what Brazilian Indians require (AT, 118). Wittgenstein's too often quoted remark that if the lion could talk we would not understand him does not get us as close to the truth as another one of his remarks to the effect that if we want to understand the natural expression of an intention we should look at a cat stalking or at the activities of other animals who are not human (AT, 145–46).

CONCLUSION

In this chapter a transition was made from Clark's ethology to his view of animals as moral patients. Two arguments—from sentiency and marginal cases—have been considered and defended. Clark's use of these arguments differs from that of other zoophiles in that: (1) more than Singer, Regan, Jamieson, and others, he is interested in placing moral duties toward animals against the background of a *philosophia perennis* going back to the Greeks; (2) he locates his views within a theistic metaphysics; and (3) he bases his concern for animals on an ethologized version of the polis. That is, if Clark's views on animals as moral patients are distinctive among contemporary philosophers, it is because he has, more than any other defender of animals, tried to avoid what he takes to be free-floating, abstract argumentation about morality and has tried to place his own argumentation within a historical, metaphysical, and ethological context.[38]

Further, Clark's view of animals is distinctive because of the precise character of his critique of humanism. Just as a folk taxon like "fish" does not name a well-defined biological kind any more than does "weeds," so also "humanity" is not a mysterious rational essence or a natural kind (as Aristotle realized, but not the Stoics, according to Clark). Rather, a species, in contemporary terms, is a set of interbreeding populations united by genealogical relationships rather than phenomenal or logical ones. This view requires us, nonetheless, to respect all human beings—the great virtue of humanism is thus preserved—but not at the expense of other beings that possess morally considerable properties like sentience or consciousness.[39]

CHAPTER 6

FROM SENTIENCY TO THE ENVIRONMENT

INTRODUCTION

In the previous chapter it was noted that there is a conflict in Clark between his abstract (liberal) arguments in favor of respect due to all animals and his concrete (conservative) concern for historical, tradition-bound communities, a concern that might require him to respect British beasts or people only. One device that Clark uses to resolve this conflict is to explore the way in which larger wholes are, in fact, communities or unities, even if they do not at first seem so. The purpose of the present chapter is to complete a consideration of Clark's approach to individual animals and then to move to a consideration of one such larger whole within which human and nonhuman beings are found: the watershed or ecosystem. This move will be good preparation for later chapters, where we will consider the extent to which other wholes like the state or the cosmos are communities. Before considering Clark's environmental ethics at the end of the present chapter, however, I will examine: (1) the historical background for Clark's views on animals; and (2) some of the consequences of a concern for animals, specifically regarding vegetarianism, antivivisection, and pet "ownership."

ANIMAL RIGHTS AND VEGETARIANISM

It should now be obvious that Clark is very much opposed to the Cartesian view (anticipated in antiquity by Strato of Lampascus) that without human intelligence animals cannot even perceive. Claude Bernard is one recent defender of this Cartesian view that the living organism is nothing other than a "wonderful machine." Yet we know "by a route enormously shorter than any scientist's that *we* are conscious" (MS, 38), and the aforementioned arguments in favor of respect for animals indicate that there is sufficient evidence to infer that animals are conscious as well. At the very least, the burden of proof is on Bernard to show why animals are not conscious, a view that traditional folk psychology, at least, sees as inane. To be exact, Clark is not so much bothered by the Cartesian view itself, which because of its inanity is not too convincing, but by the effect it has had, say, on Christianity in terms of the perversion it has brought about of Pauline "dualism" (MS, 37, 94, 197). Clark worries, however, that merely by saying that we can *infer* the existence of animal pain already is to play too much into the hands of those influenced by Descartes:

> I emphasize that our ability to recognize patterns of behavior, to sympathize with other creatures, is indeed a cognitive function, part of the way we know the world. It is unfortunate that professional biologists and animal psychologists seem, on this point, to be several decades behind the philosophical times. Few philosophers would now describe "mental states" as things uneasily inferred from purely impersonal descriptions, as though we could only *see* a creature twisting about, sweating, emitting high-pitched noises (and so on) and must thence *infer* that there is a mental cause of these motions, namely pain. . . . I can recognize the latter directly. I cannot infer the existence of fire from the sight of smoke unless fire and smoke are at least sometimes observed together.[1]

It should also be obvious by now that Clark is very much opposed to Stoic, Thomistic, and Kantian views of animals. For example, the author of one of the most influential Thomistic textbooks, Joseph Rickaby, claims that animals are effectively things that are owed no more duties of justice than are "stocks and stones."[2] Rickaby *even* holds that we should not be bothered to take any care to make animal pain as minimal as possible when we experiment on them. It is doubtful if either Aristotle or St. Thomas would have gone this far. That is,

Rickaby shows the deleterious influence of Cartesianism in his views of animals, views that live on in the minds of many devout Christians:

> The Thomist tradition has helped to harden men's hearts and to substitute an enormous mass of casuistical gallimaufry for the word of God, and for the common sense of Aristotle. (MS, 5)

Laws that protect animals are not merely expressions of good manners; they are embodiments of the thought that animals can indeed be injured and that by respecting them we at least indirectly show reverence for their creator. St. Thomas, like Maimonides, sometimes, but only sometimes, exhibits a cognizance of the respect due to animals, as in the injunction against killing a calf in the presence of its mother, which shows at least an inkling of respect for the cow, if not for the calf. Likewise, Thomists have generally followed Pius XII's dictum that no human being has a right to run a serious risk to himself in a medical experiment, but they have done so without thinking through carefully the argument from marginal cases so as to justify the risks animals face in experiments whose numbers are biblical: even pithing frogs is usually done with great pain inflicted on the frogs (MS, 15–16, 24, 72).

In antiquity there were clear cases of philosophers who showed respect for animals (Pythagoras, Theophrastus, Plutarch, Plotinus, Porphyry), clear cases of disrespect (the Stoics), and mixed cases (Plato—although he leans decidedly toward respect for animals, I allege—and Aristotle).[3] It is a defect in many contemporary thinkers that they have unquestioningly followed the Stoic view that all that is not human is mere flesh, that all cats are "grey" (in the dark of our own blindness to animal individuals), or that animals are, in contemporary terms, so much protoplasmic stuff (MS, 59). Clark admits that the pathological alienation from the body that Stoicism produces sometimes has its uses, but generally it errs by disregarding altogether the nonrational impulses we share with animals. A more satisfactory moral system would not assume that only pleasure and pain are of significance to our nonhuman kin and it would not assume that pleasure and pain are of little moral significance to us.[4] The axis that runs from the Stoics to St. Thomas also runs through Kant, whose followers engage in

> rationalistic attempts to find an absolute stability in the moral domain . . . implausible in themselves and ineffective to produce any absolute dichotomy between

man and beast. They are really no more than desperate and often unintelligible reconstructions of the Stoic ethic. (MS, 110)

Thomists and Kantians are "forced to dissimulate: for them, animals are a superior sort of toy, to be cared for only as practice for caring for people."[5]

One of the reasons why Clark's own defense of animals cannot be called a defense of animal *rights* is that rights are too closely identified for his liking with "humanism." An adoration of humankind, as exhibited, say, by Passmore, exacts a price for its lessening of human persecution of other humans: it substitutes "yet more innocent and defenceless victims" (MS, 8). These victims may be animals, or human beings who are accused of being animals, as when the Nazis referred to Jews, Poles, and Gypsies as vermin. Talk of animal rights is appropriate, Clark thinks, if by "rights" one means to claim that treating animals well is a matter of justice rather than of charity or supererogation. In *this* sense animals have rights because they have interests that deserve their due, because they can be *wronged* (MS, 7, 14, 17, 20, 29, 59). Anthropodicies are very often as unconvincing in justifying the ways of human beings regarding animals as theodicies have been regarding the ways of God:

> We have no rights against animals unless they have duties to us. . . . Rights and duties *are* to this extent correlative (though not in the Thomists' sense). But I suspect that guard dogs and the like do have duties, and understand themselves to have such. . . . Correspondingly, we have certain limited rights against them (though insofar as it is *we* who have imposed this restriction on their natural ways, these rights *are* extremely limited). . . . We . . . have taken the place of the dog's pack-leader and doomed it to permanent adolescence. . . . Even Kant urged that to shoot a faithful dog was, at least, to damage one's humanity. . . . In general, we have *no* rights against animals: no right of punishment, no expectation of "good" behaviour, no right to command. Man's dominion, if he has such, is not of that sort. As with babies in our care, so with animals: we may not consent to operations that will benefit us only, but only operations that will benefit the child, or the animal. . . . We have, in some sense, rights *over* the child or the animal: but such rights amount to no more than a general or special responsibility to *defend* the child or the animal. . . . No-one has a right to experiment on an animal . . . unless (at most) he imposes it for the *animal's* own sake. (MS, 72–73)

Clark is, at times, willing to speak of animals and even of plants having a right to our *consideration*, at the very least, because we are so utterly dependent on the natural world, as we will see. However, Clark's use of "rights" is almost always negative, in the sense that he is more than willing to use rights as tools to stop the "war" against the beasts (MS, 107, 168, 186, 191).

It will become clear in later chapters why I am not convinced by Clark's critique of liberalism and of rights, but it must be admitted that he is correct in claiming that the concern for human rights has not exactly been a boon to animals. As long as talk about rights is taken as a legal metaphor for the ways in which we ought to act, or as a reminder that some beings are not merely means to a generally desired conclusion, then Clark can himself talk in the language of rights. However, he does not think that it is obvious that all human beings *just as such* are equal members of the kingdom of ends. Put another way, Clark does not seem to be bothered by talk of rights, if what is meant is the idea that all human beings are contributors to the divine life. What bothers him is the idea fostered by "liberal humanists" that we are to be valued (i.e., that we have rights) because of our contributions as avatars of the "goddess reason." As before, imbeciles and the senile can be productive contributors to God even if they are valueless to the goddess reason. Perhaps Frey is correct in claiming that *if* reason is the basis for rights then infants and imbeciles have them due to an irrational sentiment on our part. The anthropocentrism that underlies many defenses of rights certainly cannot be defended on biological grounds (AJ, 158–60):

> We have no more assurance in empirical history of our own continuance than of any other kind's. So how can we any longer pretend to believe that the Creator is concerned only or even chiefly with the production of such agents as ourselves? . . . That God aims only at us, and that only we are destined for His companionship seems no longer sound. (AJ, 166–67)

A convenient summary of Clark's position on rights is found in the following, where the connections between this position and Clark's conservativism-theism are apparent:

> Those who believe that other creatures than the human "have rights," that there is a way of justice in which all obtain their due, can adopt at least two stances. According to the first, we ought to act by the principles of conservative justice, allowing the world to continue and acknowledging the limits that are placed on

us. Hubris and cruelty and *pleonexia* (i.e., always wanting to have more) are sins, are the very essence of sin. Such a conservative may refuse to participate in the careless practices of our corrupt and superstitious age, but will not hold it right always to refrain from killing fellow creatures, in such honesty and regard as possible. The more radical view reminds us that each of us is more than the creature, or the world, with which we at first identify ourselves. Our life is to live out the implications of that higher vision, offering the promise of a world from which this realm is a temporary aberration. . . . Catholic Christianity has been loath (with good reason) to admit that there may be two ways, the more and the less perfect. Other traditions (with good reason) have insisted that there are. (AJ, 178–79)

What is important, according to Clark, is to know that we ought not to disregard the suffering of fellow animals; the question of whether animals *really* have rights is secondary, and the question as to whether these rights are positive or negative (Clark thinks of them as negative) is tertiary. It is not true that Clark disparages rights altogether; rather, he thinks of them as secondary or tertiary. For example, suppose we say that a cat who, while being hurt, will struggle, scratch, and try to bite, is in effect claiming its rights, and this is due to a type of "self-owning" on its part. This ethics of self-ownership, which is close to Regan's concept of "subjects of a life," has considerable strengths, Clark thinks, but it cannot stand alone:

What rights can all self-owners have, once the class is extended to include blackbirds and foxes?. . . It is then mockingly deduced, or uncomfortably accepted, that moral agents ought to protect blackbirds against foxes, even if not worms against blackbirds. . . . It is not enough to reply . . . that foxes commit no injustice because they do not know what they are doing: if their victims genuinely have rights . . . if a criminal psychopath attacks my neighbor, and I do nothing to assist her . . . it is I (not the psychopath) that have violated her right of defence. . . . It seems better to abandon abstract argument, in favour of historical. . . . The self-owning individual is a relatively late social invention. . . . We have to do with historical claims and protections, not with the pre-social rights of self-owners.[6]

Thus far in this chapter we have seen Clark's disagreements with Stoics, Thomists, Cartesians, and Kantians regarding the status of animals. We have also seen that Clark's own defense of animals does not necessarily lie in a very strong conception of rights. Understanding his attenuated view of rights is crucial when Clark's positions regarding environmental issues are considered: rights possessed by self-owners cannot include any right of immunity to disease, famine, or predation. Ecology is organized around the fact of predation, a fact that is then exploited in the rationalizations of meat-eaters. Clark holds that

> the cats who share my household have no "right," in the abstract, to my special care and attention, but once received into the household and contributing their particular value to it, they do have such a right. . . . Historical rights, as defined by the law of nations, and not the law of nature, are what animals, and humans, chiefly need. . . . The rights of "British beasts," for example . . . are more extensive than the natural rights of animals.[7]

At this point, however, one might wonder about the extent to which Clark could construct an environmental ethics that included principles covering animals other than domesticated ones. Clark's response to this worry consists of the claim that gradually we can gain solidarity with the terrestrial biosphere, as in our recent capacity to sympathize with the great whales. That is, Clark's environmental ethics is built on the belief that we can develop a familial sense for nature in general, a sense of kinship with all of creation under the divine parent. (Yet why not also with humanity in general, as in liberalism?) Clark characteristically and peculiarly finds this sense of kinship in Aristotle, specifically in Aristotle's belief that humankind is just one animal species among many, rather than in Plato's much stronger notion of an inclusive (Great Mother-like) World Soul for the body of the world.[8] I will treat explicitly later in the chapter Clark's environmental ethics; here I am still concerned with the transition from concern for individual animals to concern for the environment as a whole. Some might fear that Clark, by failing to give primacy to animal rights because of the environmental impossibility of preventing the victims of predation from being killed, makes it possible to permit severe abuse of animals, just as a failure to give primacy to human rights makes it possible to permit slavery. R. M. Hare is like Clark in believing that slavery is wrong not just because it violates "fundamental human rights."[9] However Clark departs both from Hare's utilitarian position and from Hare's exclusive concern for humans: Clark sees a strong analogy between slavery and the history of domestication of animals.

The problem with utilitarian opposition to slavery (or domestication) in terms of the long-range misery it causes is that it does not confront forthrightly the fact that when human beings attempt to weigh costs and benefits they tend to count their own concerns "as of more moment." The utilitarian calculations of the masters will automatically discount the interests of the slaves or farm animals. Note in the following Clark's use of scare-quotes around "rights" and his opposition to slavery (or domestication) in terms of its defective conception of "family" and "friend":

> Slavery is wrong because it violates the right of self-determination, and that "right" is the projection, whatever else it may be, of our recognition that here is another creature with whom there are more profitable modes of companionship. . . . The point of these remarks is simply to suggest that the institution of slavery is not, in the first instance, to be rejected . . . because it increases misery (as Hare alleges). . . . Our rejection of the master-slave relationship rests more securely on our understanding that this is an inappropriate or disrespectful one. To enslave others is to violate their rights, even if only in the sense that it violates the natural relationship between creatures capable of companionship.[10]

Regarding slavery Clark is only partly an Aristotelian:

> Aristotle's conviction that there were natural slaves is not well supported by appeals to ethological data. But we should not dismiss them so abruptly as custom dictates, with bland declarations that "of course there are no natural slaves in the world." A natural slave, by Aristotle's account, is a person who cannot live her life in accordance with a rational plan. . . . It is not obvious to me that there are no people like that, though I would be more hesitant than Aristotle . . . in expecting any usable criteria for picking them out from the mass of the population.[11]

Slaves generally are bothered by the abuse they receive, as are exploited animals, women, and men who cannot control themselves. Even though Clark is skeptical as to whether there are genuinely natural slaves, he does think that as a psychological or cultural form slavery is still worth thinking about, especially when it is considered that all citizens in modern states are something like slaves, in that they do not really participate in the polis if the state approximates a monopoly of force within a given region. That is, Clark reacts against slavery and abuse of animals by tending toward anarchism.

The last thing that Clark would want to do would be to slip in a defense of the petty bourgeoise aversion to discipline through his explicit defense of anarchism. Yet by "anarchism" Clark refers to minimal state rule. The greater part of order among human beings and animals is *not* due to the effect of government, he thinks. Rather, it is due to those forms of social life that arise "naturally" from the communion of free agents ("free" in the sense of an absence of slavery). This antistatist, ethologized, Aristotelianism can in fact develop into a type of despotism, as Clark admits. He thinks it more likely, however, that when we see the modern state as composed of partly reformed brigands we will be willing to make decisions in small communities in an "intensive and time-taking consultative process," decisions that have as their aim a consensus not in the adversarial mode to which we have become accustomed.[12] It should now be clear that in the effort to move beyond the "rights" of individual human beings or animals it is likely that Clark will find meaningful wholes in families, small communities, ecosystems, and in the cosmos as a whole, this last leapfrogging over the pseudounity of the state, which Clark largely disparages.

As we have seen, individual human beings as well as individual animals might be seen as uniquely suited to the broiler by a race of space-travelling anthropophages, a point made by Clark under the inspiration of Aristotle's biological works, which he uses as helpful addenda to Aristotle's works that deal directly with ethics. Clark's objections to the analogous abuse of animals by human beings largely rest on the belief that our perceptions of how animals really are are more likely to be true than our fantasies about them. We perceive them to be perceptive, and what has perception also has desire and an awareness of pleasure and pain, as Aristotle noted (AM, 16, 69, 70, 74, 77).[13] It is because of this desire and awareness that Clark holds vegetarianism to be a moral duty. Eating flesh, he thinks, is a practice continued by human beings out of habit, in that our palates are conditioned to an ample supply of animal corpses. That is, the distinction between killing for food and killing for fun is not too sharp when meat is seen as a luxury rather than as a necessity. True carnivores kill quickly and only what they must. With Thoreau, Clark notes that there would be far fewer meat-eaters if people had to kill with their bare hands and then had to butcher their kill themselves (MS, 52, 138).[14] The bad habit of meat-eating, Clark thinks, is also due to at least three corruptions of our ethical sense:

> The first, our readiness to discount all such "emotional" reactions as cannot, we think, be backed by any general principle; usually indeed the only admitted principles are those determined by a naive calculation of immediate utility. The progressive weakening of our sensibility is a danger far more real than

over-squeamishness. The second, our readiness to believe ourselves the masters. . . . The third, our readiness to think that those unlike ourselves, the poor,
the weak, the stupid, have no title to their lives. (MS, 140)

The third corruption is counteracted by the argument from marginal cases; the
second by any sort of commitment to theism; and the first by the argument from
sentiency. As before, it is by no means clear that the pathetic fallacy is more dangerous than the a-pathetic one.

Clark's defense of vegetarianism is thoroughly consistent with his traditionalism, in that he thinks that meat-eating has always been, or at least has been
since the Greeks, a corrupt application of symbolic processes, as Porphyry suggests in his *De abstinentia*. "Perhaps in the beginning flesh-eating was only a
metaphor, and then a sacrament, and at last a secular feast" (MS, 177). Christians,
at least, should notice that those who take the Eucharist seriously have offered
an implicit criticism of meat-eating as a sacrament, in that the Eucharist is a
bloodless sacrifice: neither grapes nor wheat experience pain when harvested.
Christianity is by no means unequivocally opposed to blood sacrifices, but notice
how Clark treats the Christ-like symbol of the lamb and, once again, how he
inches toward an environmental ethic:

> Perhaps in nature the lamb might die, by wolf or weather or sickness, before its
> prime. And all die in the end. Is that a reason for our not helping it to live? Or
> for killing it? We have chosen to take control, to some extent, of fate insofar as
> it touches our kin. . . . Acceptance of the tides of life and death is better shown
> in bearing *our* death than in drowning others. . . . Let us at least acknowledge as
> an ideal a community not merely of many races, many cultures, but one of many
> species. . . . We have examples, on a small scale, in "primitive tribes" and com-
> munes of the ecomystical—in whom, despite their manifold absurdities, I see the
> only hope that has yet been lit. (MS, 178–79)

Clark goes so far as to elevate vegetarianism into a devotional practice. It is the
following passage that led Regan to accuse Clark of hubris, but perhaps only
because Regan does not quote the last sentence:[15]

> Vegetarianism is now as necessary a pledge of moral devotion as was the refusal
> of emperor-worship in the early Church. Those who have not made that pledge
> have no authority to speak against the most inanely conceived experiments, nor

against hunting, nor against fur-trapping, nor bear-baiting, nor bullfights, nor pulling the wings off flies. . . . Those who still eat flesh when they could do otherwise have no claim to be serious moralists. This judgment is perhaps unfair: though those who say so should remember that I make it also against my own past self. (MS, 183)

Vegetarianism is not supererogatory, even if veganism is, in that we may, in fact, be able to take *some* milk from animals without pain and without injustice (MS, 185). Clark's concept of religion, which takes ritual as crucial, enables him to emphasize a point that few other zoophiles could even notice: that "flesh-eating itself is for most of the West of largely ritual significance, bearing very little relation even to real gastronomic pleasure" (MS, 188).

The careful reader of Clark begins to see that his zoophily is thoroughly integrated within his theism and his conservativism, and that his (liberal, universalizing) arguments for animal "rights" or environmental ethics are not meant to stand on their own apart from these commitments:

Correspondingly zebras as such have no rights against people (nor people against tigers), though people are perhaps capable of a more sympathetic response to a zebra's plight than dogs may be. Conservatives, accordingly, stop short of advocating an ideal vegetarianism, though they may well (and rightly) boycott the denatured products of present-day farming practice, that treats the world and our fellow creatures merely as material, rather than as the companions of a more respectful day. If individuals do not matter all that much, then their deaths do not matter all that much either. Liberal tenderness about inflicting or allowing death (whether of farm animals or of moribund humans) is, on this view, the product of a superstitious regard for individual existence in the world. But there is an alternative route to ideal vegetarianism, to which Barth bears unwilling witness. To live without offering direct harm to God's creation is to anticipate the Kingdom. (AJ, 176)

Clark is candid about the autobiographical details that surrounded the publication of *The Moral Status of Animals*, and about his "sins" against contemporary culture and modes of philosophizing:

Our wedding celebration was very nearly the last time that either of us ate dead animals with any pleasure. . . . Those lectures became *MS*. . . . I was astonished, and hurt, by the offence they caused: not hurt by any offence caused to the uncaring and unthinking, of course, but by the reactions of those who might have been thought allies. Apparently people could not see when I was joking, or when I was advancing a thesis only to change or controvert it by a necessary antithesis. . . . I had sinned against the light by offering no single system within which to work, by suggesting that utilitarian principle could not, by itself, give any substantive result, that "rights theorists" could not finally or usefully close all exits. . . . What I aimed to produce was the possibility of a gestalt switch, a transformation of world-view, a genuinely realistic vision of the way things are for God, for the one abiding pattern to which all things move. . . . Since then I have come to realize how tightly rights are tied to a particular "liberal" politics which are not mine. My early, and familial, socialism has gradually been transformed into a vision of "shalom," a traditional and even conservative understanding of human and other duty. I am by now a kind of anarcho-conservative. . . . Peter Singer and Raymond Frey agreed on almost every theoretical issue: why did they disagree in practice?. . . Could even Tom Regan's wish to give all "subjects-of-a-life" the very rights that American liberals have wished for human beings—a theory with which I had a lot more sympathy than he with mine—avoid scholasticism?[16]

Singer and Frey, it should be noted, are both utilitarians. One gets the impression here that Clark feels that he has been treated unfairly not only because of his heterodox philosophical style, but also because of his defense of orthodox religious beliefs and conservative political beliefs. As a Catholic I am at least somewhat sympathetic to Clark's claim that those agnostics who profess toleration the most very often find it quite easy to make disparaging remarks about religious believers. He is rightly indignant when it is implied that his religious orthodoxy makes him unthinking. Even with respect to his theodicy, which I have previously criticized, Clark is willing to make some alterations to the orthodox view, especially if they lead to a better understanding of animals. For example, traditional theodicy includes the belief that the suffering of sentient beings is necessary for the production of free (human) beings, which conceals, according to Clark, a rather vicious version of anthropocentrism (MR, 146).

ANIMAL EXPERIMENTATION

Clark is well aware that if animals deserve the respect that he alleges they do, there will be consequences not only for the way we eat, but also for scientific-educational-commercial experimentation on animals, experimentation that is often (and sometimes misleadingly) called "vivisection." Clark uses his jeweler's eye for ritual to locate those rituals in contemporary science where living animals are experimented on so as to (supposedly) advance knowledge or train novices. The experimenters no doubt "love" their pets at home, but in the laboratory an artificial, fantasy world is established wherein all sorts of stories and theories are judged as true only within their own context. Clark describes the process by which scientists are made:

> The novice's first incision into living flesh, or her first attempt to see how irritable starved, shocked, blinded rats can be, are events as traumatic in their psychological effect as subincision or clitoridectomy. What went before was childishness: the new world is born in pain. (MR, 47–48)

Clark trusts vivisectors even less than did William James (who seems to have distrusted them a great deal), even if he is still willing to hear their side of the story:

> Science is an activity of men, and is as subject as any other activity to moral debate: the substitution of expert, technical debate for moral debate is one of the most vicious of rhetorical fallacies. Experimentalists have a right, perhaps, to a fair hearing: they have no more right than other and more public figures first to conspire in concealing the evidence and then to denounce their critics for ignorance and injustice. (MS, 6–7)

As we have seen, Clark's traditionalism forces him to defend the *argumentum ad verecundiam* (appeal to authority), but the sort of appeal to authority he has in mind is not the supposed authority of scientists.

To cut a rat's eyes in an experiment rather than to blindfold them is, quite simply, sadism, according to Clark, as is causing distress or suffering unnecessary to the success of the experiment. Clark finds it peculiar to claim that any medical experiment performed on a human without informed consent is an assault, yet to also claim without perturbation that we have lawful authority over the beasts to decide what they should or should not mind us doing to them. Why should animals pay for our irresponsibility when we fail, as we usually do, to explore first those experiments that involve human tissue cultures or computer simulations? Clark tries to keep alive the ancient notion (see Plato's

Gorgias, 465) that the surest way to health, to the extent that there is a sure way, is through a disciplined (athletic) way of life, not by (medicinal) prescription. Vivisection is tolerated because we assume we will profit from it in terms of better health. This assumption needs to be called into question (MS, 43, 55, 67–68). Yet *even if* it is true that we are better off in the present cycle we are in (e.g., undisciplined, cancer- or heart disease–producing habits yielding animal exploitation yielding more profligate habits), it is not necessarily the case that vivisection is legitimate. Relying on Dubos, Clark states:

> "The tide of infectious and nutritional diseases was rapidly receding when the laboratory scientist moved into action at the end of the past century.". . . It is *possible*, after all, that medical science profited from the Nazis' treatment of the Jews. Nor is it easy to balance material profit against spiritual harm to our sensibility. (MS, 69)

If it is true, as the vast majority of zoophiles, including many scientists, allege, that biomedical experimentation has created enormously more "anti-hedones" than it has eliminated, then the justification of vivisection lies not so much in utilitarian calculation as in the "simple declaration that those higher in the hierarchy may do what they like to those lower" (MS, 71). Nor is it obvious that the lower being would willingly sacrifice itself for the higher:

> Perhaps, if I am heroic, I would accept some distress to benefit another: it does not follow that I am justified in imposing that distress upon a third party without the latter's informed consent. (MS, 72)

Or again, is it the case that human pains are justified by animal benefits? Clark might even tolerate such utilitarian calculations regarding animal (or human) experimentation, if these were carried out carefully, as they usually are not:

> Only those pleasures that are "necessary," whose absence is itself a distress, are relevant to the calculus. We may legitimately pain one creature if the alternative is to pain several . . . by taking account of the probability of that relief. The pain we inflict is certain: our hopes are almost always uncertain. . . . Many human ills can be avoided or alleviated by the herbal remedies of our ancestors or by changing our diet and way of life. More would be saved from death by cancer by a simple ban on cigarettes than are ever likely to be saved by the millions spent on

giving malign tumours to the non-human. . . . Antivivisectionists have recently limited their attack to such atrocities as the testing of cosmetics. . . . But even the "medical" experiment is open to question, even upon utilitarian grounds. (MS, 78–79)

If one takes duties to animals seriously, one may very well narrow the gap between duty and supererogation, say, by rejecting any remedies for one's ills based on animal suffering, as did Plotinus or George Bernard Shaw. What virtuous person would buy extra years at the cost of drugs distilled from the livers of tortured, retarded babies (MS, 88, 116)? This question is not asked for the purpose of histrionic show, in that torture is a very real possibility:

> The terrifying thing about Nazi Germany is that its agents were often ordinarily decent husbands, fathers, citizens. . . . As Plato knew long ago, the "honest citizen" would often be a tyrant if he had the chance. . . . Decent men will readily torture other men if that is what they think is expected of them. . . . An analogy between science and religion. I think we should take very seriously the tendency of devoted religious and scientists to commit enormous evil. (MS, 142–43)

Laboratory habits instilled into young scientists merely formalize the abandonment of "deeply rooted repugnancies and sympathies." For example, folk psychology would find abhorrent what many scientists have come to think of as an unmeaning physical event demonstrating the laws of matter: whirling a cat in a centrifuge so as to take a sample of its spinal fluid: "Objectivity requires that we strip our vision of all emotive difference, all 'participation mystique'; but objectivity itself reveals that our bodies, our dear selves are entirely part of the world" (MS, 148–49). Vivisection, Clark thinks, is the logical outcome of stripping from our vision of the world all sacred significance and emotional attachment:

> A certain cultural ideal, that of the objective scientist, is effectively responsible for corrupting and denying certain human sensibilities. True objectivity, applied also to the self and to its professional context, drives remorselessly towards the mysteries of Buddhist enlightenment. . . . Who is it but the psychopath, after all, who sees the world without emotional effect? . . . "The dream of reason produces monsters": it is one of the gravest charges against modern moral philosophers that they have permitted this to pass, without qualms or comment. (MS, 150–51)

Consider Clark's use of an analogy from Aristotle in the attempt to criticize contemporary science:

> Science originates in this love of Being: a love that transcends the dictates of immediate, practical profit. As long as it is this, no scientist could even think of tormenting the creature he loves. . . . But our emotional interest is readily diverted from the *thing* to our own activity. . . . Science ceases to be the love and worship of created Being, and becomes the pursuit of personal satisfaction. . . . By ceasing to care for and enjoy the thing itself, we transform the quality of the activity. We cease to esteem the thing we paint, and come to admire our own brush-strokes: it is a familiar fallacy, and its results in art, and social life, and science speak for themselves. . . . As Aristotle also remarked, the intemperate man desires not food but eating (*Nicomachean Ethics III*, 1118a): he is willing to vomit up his food so that he can start again. This perhaps casts a new light on the occasional philosophical allegation that it is not knowing the answer that matters, but the process of getting there. (MS, 152)

Science itself has become something of a religion, hence it should, at least in part, be evaluated on criteria other than the standard ones:

> My charge against science, or rather scientism, is that it would destroy our personal lives in the name of a god whom only the pseudo-psychopath could love. Does "science" say that all the world is an unmeaning mechanism? (MS, 154–55)

Many scientists say exactly that. However it is precisely reason, Clark thinks, that can take us to a more appropriate appreciation of nonhuman emotion, an appreciation that most scientists currently lack:

> To be truly objective we must *have* no purposes . . . a strange enlightenment. . . . If reason has an office, it is this: that we give some slight attention to what is more distant from us, whether that distance be spatial or emotional. . . . Ethical reason likewise must allow, and strengthen all our personal attachments. A rationality that tells us not to cherish those we love, not to believe our senses, is surely self-refuted. What such reasoning should do is to remind us that there are creatures out of sight of us, and sentient beings whom we do not like who suffer nonetheless. Let us cherish our immediate friends, whatever their ancestry, and let us also

remember that there are other things who might have been our friends and whom it is our weakness to ignore. (MS, 156–57)

Previously we saw a surprising sort of admiration on the part of Clark for Noam Chomsky, and here regarding the depersonalizing tendencies of contemporary science he shows the same sort of admiration for Theodore Roszak and Louis Mumford:

> My belief is that there is a constant impulse in at least some men to construct models, or more compendious descriptions of events which may license certain predictions or draw events a little closer to the intrinsically intelligible. Such men wish physical events to be as obvious, as self-explanatory as the theorems of mathematics. Whether such an end is possible I do not know, but I say nothing against the effort. Such "science" dispels mysteries only in the sense that it subsumes them in larger mysteries. In the end we are still faced by the brute fact, the pure glory of what *is*. . . . "We are training, in the name of experimental science, a race of young exterminators.". . . Attempts to revive a traditional respect for natural being . . . will not destroy true science. . . . What is not worth respecting is not worth understanding either. (MS, 158)

Clark finds it understandable that scientists should react against sentimentalism, and that it is essential for serious investigators to be "objective" in the sense that their claims should refer to qualities that exist independently of our attitude toward them. Yet Clark doubts if such claims are "objective" in the sense of being unbiased or lacking in emotive force, "when the facts described are such as to move any normal person."[17] If we *really* believe that the world should be seen without emotional effect, then we should not even identify with our own bodies. By eliminating subjective discriminations we not only take away the basis for ethics but for science itself, in that we would no longer have the ability to pick out any particular aspect of the phenomena, to *seek* the truth.

Scientific method owes a great deal more to normative analysis than is usually admitted. For example, physicists have been known to hypothesize the existence of unnoticed particles because they "ought" to exist for the sake of elegance or harmony. Scientists should be much more like members of a jury, according to Clark. They should not let themselves be corrupted by an *idée fixe*, but this is quite different from vowing never to make moral judgments, as Aristotle noted: "People who are puzzled to know whether one ought to honour the gods and

love one's parents or not need punishment" (*Topics,* 2.105a). Likewise, the knowledge and wisdom that is really worth pursuing in science is not compatible with the violation of creaturely integrity (CP, 22–23). Clark, like the ancients, believes that "the truth is made known to those who approach the world with a kind of love, love purged of concupiscence, and who are moved to admire the real form of things" (CP, 24). The result of scientific indifferentism is that

> researchers exalt their own selves and purposes over the purposes and beings of the things they study. Objective research comes to mean the habit of treating living beings merely as material for our own purposes. (AJ, 113)

Once one gives up on the attempt to gain angelic understanding and sympathetic penetration of things as they are, one is left with an accumulation of external facts, the practical consequence of which is that animals (with no inner being or consciousness) can be vivisected with no second thoughts (AJ, 114–15, 127).

A thorough acquaintance with our own condition enables us to imagine the condition of others, and hence to describe their condition more accurately. Further, it is not perfectly obvious that all animals lack these abilities:

> There is in fact evidence to suggest that non-human animals may attribute beliefs to others, that they can predict the behaviour of others in very much the same way as we do. Witness the young chimpanzee described by Goodall, who deliberately walks away from a luxury he has spotted, and surreptitiously returns only when the rest of his troop have thus been lured away. (AJ, 134–35)

At the very least Clark wishes to prevent the hegemony of scientific thinking in its behaviorist-mechanist mode, in that other realities are logically possible than those permitted in this mode. Clark's opposition to this attempted hegemony leads him once again to be tempted by panpsychism or by an animist ontology:

> If the wholes are conscious then the parts have properties that, within a well-worked-out system, entail the property of being conscious. In short, as Nagel very convincingly argues, consciousness can only be the property of physical wholes if the parts of those wholes have psychic or mentalistic properties themselves. (AJ, 143)

However, Clark is only tempted by this view. His overall stance is that there are subjects in the world, including animal subjects, who are just as much a part of the objective world (i.e., one that exists independently of our will and perception) as everyday objects are. We have a remarkable

> capacity for "getting under the skin" of the most unlikely objects. Empathizing with other creatures, whether they be wasps or trees or quarks, is indeed one of the most significant of our exploratory techniques. We so readily interpret things in an "intentional" way. (AJ, 150)

The prospects for those human beings who do not exercise this capacity are not too bright, unless they are dealing with (i.e., abusing) animals:

> Those who genuinely doubt the existence of other human minds end up in asylums; those who genuinely doubt the real existence of animal minds are confirmed in their doubts by the approval of their scientific peers and the needs of laboratories. (AJ, 154; also see 136–42, 147, 155)

PETS

The third issue in applied ethics to be treated in this chapter, now that we have considered vegetarianism and animal experimentation, concerns Clark's attitude toward pets. It should be kept in mind that these topics in applied ethics are both interesting in their own right and propaedeutic to a consideration of the synoptic vision needed to treat issues in environmental ethics. Regarding pets, Clark's concern that our ethics grow out of domestic and communal relationships is taken quite literally: he lives with wife and children and cats.[18] Just as Clark demurs from the opinion held by some animal liberationists that all experimentation on animals is wrong, so also he is opposed to the view that all domestication is tyrannical: animals are not outside the community of which we are a part. Once animals are domesticated (or affiliated), it does not necessarily follow that all other animals are outside our moral concern, just as moral obligation does not necessarily stop (even if it begins) with the polis with which we cooperate. Pets are important if for no other reason than the fact that they remind us that we do not have to go out of our way to invent a concern for animals if the very households in which we live already include nonhumans, and also because "the whole earth that it is our duty and our joy to serve requires that all kinds and conditions of living creature have their own lives and territories."[19] Nonetheless, Clark thinks that environmentalists can be just as megalomaniac as engineers in their dedication to remake the world and human nature; in addition to an aggressive Faustian strand in Western culture there is also a much neglected Magian (or Platonic) strand that acknowledges that there is a real natural world to which we have access. The world "apart" from value is a postulation on the part of some scientists and philosophers; the real natural world is actually made of beauty.

Yet this concern for pets, although more prominent than that for "food animals," is not so great in the general population that people are bothered by the tens of thousands (in Great Britain) or hundreds of thousands (in the United States) of dogs killed each year due to carelessness on the part of human beings (MS, 116). This despite the fact that a dog is a man's best friend:

> A dog is a man's best friend, though this has not stopped us employing the creatures in biomedical research and killing them by the thousands when their presence is minimally inconvenient to us. . . . We call dogs friends: we mean they are our slaves. When we hear of other cultures that consider dogs to be meat animals, or feral abominations, we are righteously outraged. . . . Our suspicion that the flesh of carnivores is hardly wholesome perhaps marks a certain guiltiness about our own dietary habits. (MS, 125)

Cats are symbols for different realities, in that they "figure largely in the fantasies of the psychotic, presumably as being unsocialized, self-sufficient, beautiful, pitiless and strong" (MS, 124). Dogs, who for thousands of years followed leaders in packs, perform quite well in their socially defined role of giving a sense of superiority to their human masters, whom they now follow. (See the extraordinary French film *Baxter* in this regard.) By way of contrast,

> The repugnance often felt against cats deserves anthropological attention more than psychological or medical. In the cat, perhaps, we are aware of Nature as an alongside world, without guiltiness or need of us. . . . The common thesis that there are cat-people and dog-people perhaps marks an awareness that there is a way of relating to Nature alternative to the orthodox. (MS, 126)

That is,

our curious relationship with the dog is indicative and symbolic of our attitude to Nature. . . . We are kind to animals, all too often, because it makes us feel superior. (MS, 127)

As before, however, we are still willing to experiment on, mistreat by over-breeding, or kill massive numbers of dogs, even if they are more domesticated than cats, who act as a bridge to the consideration of wild animals.

Pets make us aware of the extent to which human beings can indeed communicate with animals, very often in terms of nonverbal abilities and judgments (MS, 25). Human language is a great ability, such that without it our young children lag behind chimpanzees in intellectual ability. Hence,

> it is difficult to see how language could even get started without an appeal to the common, tacit appreciation of our situation which we share with the animal creation and which is most probably the basis for our capacity for ethical discrimination. . . . What is lacking in them is any capacity to act on principle, any capacity to call something their own or another's on the basis of agreed codes of conduct. I do not believe that this can be true in any clear sense—the very songs of birds are, in a sense, declarations of an agreed property. (MS, 26–27)

The obvious communications (sometimes even threats) that we give to and receive from pets enable us to more easily notice the communications of which nondomesticated animals are capable:

> I see that animals are in distress, and the notional addition of a language would not assist my perception. "I am in pain," after all, only "replaces" a cry of anguish, which must be recognized as such before the words may be taught or learned. "I am in pain" does not explicate, identify or prove the existence of that anguish. . . . It may be that animals feel less distress, or fewer distresses, than we do, though we might remember that the same has been said of the human poor, and of the racially distinct. (MS, 39)

Human linguistic creativity may be infinite in potential, but not in practice when it is considered that we usually speak in cliches; and animal communication and behavior is far more inventive than animals have been given credit for. That is, our communication is less, and animal communication is more, sophisticated than is normally supposed. Animals very often hear our voices not as mere sounds, but as conveying meaning (MS, 64, 95):

> It is not that we have *discovered* them to lack a language but rather that we define, and redefine, what Language is by discovering what beasts do not have. If they should turn out to have the very thing we have hitherto supposed language to be, we will simply conclude that language is something else again. (MS, 96)

If it is true that animals do not recognize different sets of phonemes as semantically equivalent, it is also true that we are "not properly equipped to internalize the grammar of any other species" (MS, 97–98).

Clark has no problem with calling communication among birds "personal,"[20] but even if it is stipulated that animals have no language, it would be premature to assume that they are only stimulus-response machines. For example, most who have known a cat attest to the fact that animals can pretend (e.g., that a ball is a mouse) or anticipate in ways that indicate a certain sort of rationality:

> It is surprising that *theists* should ever think otherwise: if only those entities with language are rational, then God is either unreasoning or has vocal cords (or some equally physical equivalent), for only those with bodies can exercise the gift of language. . . . Perhaps He just *sees* and understands, or is Himself that sight. Nothing could be more likely: but in that case it is in our unreasoning intuitions, not our painstaking rationality, that we are most God-like, as Aristotle knew. (MS, 100–1)

An animal's world is not meaningless just because it does not see *our* meanings: the eye of the hawk is not to be equated with the eye of a camera, because what the hawk sees makes an internal difference to it; the demonstration and advice that cats and mice give to their young are not to be totally divorced from the human concept of tradition; and so on. Once again, Clark thinks that we often distance ourselves from the beast without for fear of the beast within, hence my preceding efforts to understand the influential Cartesian link between speciesism and dualism (MS, 104, 112, 120). It is a commonplace to attribute to animals the ferocity and promiscuity we fear in ourselves. An indirect indication of this fear can be found in the shortage of good poems about animals, which is not merely a function of the general shortage of good poems. Most poems on the subject are really only about the author's feelings. . . . Our choice then seems to be to regard animals sentimentally, moralistically, or with terror of the unmeaning void. (MS, 123)

In short, the human war against animals, in particular, and against nature, in general, which has been raging at least since the industrial revolution, is largely due to an anthropocentrism that is itself based on a peculiar mixture of ignorance and willful perversity. Clark states, relying on Thorpe:

"Forty or more years ago . . . it was said (1) animals cannot learn; (2) animals cannot plan ahead; (3) animals cannot conceptualise; (4) animals cannot use, much less make, tools. (5) It was said they have no language; (6) they cannot count; (7) they lack artistic sense; (8) they lack all ethical sense." Every one of these disparities has lapsed. . . . In the real world of encountered fact we are not the masters. We are as subject now as we ever were, or as any species is, to the changes and chances of this mortal life. All our culture is designed to conceal this from us. (MS, 134–35; also see 128–29)

Perhaps because pets are generally viewed as individuals, and this perhaps because we give each a personalized name, laws have been enacted that prohibit one person from being unkind to one animal, but if a great number of people are cruel to a great number of animals who are not pets, then the law permits the cruelty. Clark rightly notes that this is a puzzle (MS, 11–12). As we will see regarding Clark's political views, he is somewhat skeptical of the likelihood of ethical or moral progress being brought about through civil law. *If* such progress is possible, it would come through a rediscovery of, and amplification of, honored tradition. Earlier in this chapter we saw that Clark thinks that the historical axis from the Stoics to Thomas Aquinas to Descartes to Kant should not be as honored as it is regarding animals. Rather, our historical roots more properly lie (or should lie) in religion and in certain philosophers such as Aristotle (properly read) or Plutarch. The tradition Clark has in mind is part of the same covenant community described in the Bible, a covenant tradition within which human beings and beasts were created on the same day (Genesis 1:24 ff.). It is not Clark's intent, when placing animal "rights" issues within a religious context, to worship animals, in that this is an almost certain way to have them sacrificed for others. It is also not his intent, as we saw earlier in this book, to interpret Scripture literally: when Peter is commanded to forget the division between clean and unclean beasts (Acts 10:9 ff.) he is not receiving a command to eat everything, but rather to accept Gentiles into the faith; when Jesus says that it is what comes out of a man that matters, rather than what goes in, he is not disparaging vegetarianism but emphasizing the praxic implications of the religious life (MS, 31, 103, 124, 178).

The grave damage done to Christianity by Manichean "vegetarianism" has prevented some from appreciating certain biblical passages (e.g., Romans 8:21 ff.) where it is clear that the *whole* created universe groans. Affection for animals can be found in the Bible even if it does not always contain "specific injunctions of a kind to appeal to zoophiles" (CP, 148), say, in the common practice mentioned above of returning animals to God through sacrifice. The dogma that animals are machines or are meant solely (or primarily) for human benefit is not a biblical idea but a Greek one *as it was perverted* by Descartes and the like (MS, 197; CP, 149).[21] Clark is quite clear regarding Matthew 10:29 that "The Lord who preached, in opposition to the Rabbinic tradition of His day, that God's care extended even to sparrows . . . has been ill served by His disciples" (MS, 10). The most convincing saints, Clark thinks (perhaps he has Francis of Assisi, John of the Cross, or Therese of Lisieux in mind), actually welcome the nonhuman into their lives because they see the fulfillment of the lark's God-given nature as an example of what could happen to all of creation (AJ, 168–69). We should not misinterpret the passage regarding God and sparrows, even if Clark admits that it can be variously interpreted, as in his own aforementioned use of it against the belief that God arranges all of the minute details of our lives (a belief that he calls "sectarianism"):

> Christ's own sardonic instruction to rely upon the Lord who is with the falling sparrow, who clothes the anemones and finds the ravens their food, is usually quoted to "prove" that he thought people—or at least his followers—more valuable than sparrows, and so licensed to take unfair advantage of sparrows, anemones, and ravens. Such saints live within the promised covenant, "with the beasts of the field." (CP, 146)

An omnibenevolent being no doubt would forgive us our necessities but would not, could not, forgive us our luxuries without first noting that a wrong had been done if the luxury was acquired at the price of animal pain (MS, 28).

The Aristotelian roots to Clark's view of animals, which supplement the religious roots, are not immediately clear when it is considered that the Stoics, for whom animals were defined by extrinsic teleology (plants were for animals and animals were for humans), loosely based their view on Aristotle (*Politics* 1256b). The link between Aristotle's and Clark's views becomes understandable, however, when we concentrate on ethological concerns, on the Aristotelian claim that justice is based on friendship (broadly understood), and on Aristotle's belief that animals can act according to reason (*kata logon*) even if they cannot do so with reason (*meta logou*) (MS, 15, 23, 36). Clark expands on Aristotle when he emphasizes the fact that the claim that animals are intellectually defective is largely a self-fulfilling prophesy:

> We think them stupid, finally, because we have bred them so that they may confirm our secret wish, and keep them in confinement that they may stay that way: sullen, stupid, incurious, irresponsible, profligate, and dumb. (MS, 37)

Animals have (Aristotelian) natural wants and needs, Clark thinks, and these wants and needs are *partially* peculiar to their kind (MS, 55):

> Though some beastly activities are entirely instinctive (as are some of ours—such as smiling), other activities, or the detailed application of the beasts' capacities, are learned: a cat *learns* to use a cat door. . . . It is part of *civilized* living, which we require by unalterable decree, to eat pâté de foie gras: so the goose's suffering is a necessity. . . . Aristotle, in his search for the good life for man, employs an argument from the fact of man's distinctive nature as a practical creature with the gift of language. . . . The argument has often been misunderstood. (MS, 56–57)

Aristotle's texts sometimes indicate that animals are instruments, but they also indicate (e.g., *Nicomachean Ethics* 3.1111b) that animals have wishes and that they have the possibility of a decent life within their kind. Such a life can be minimally defined as the absence of painful sensations, but also depends on achieving those pleasures that enable it to flourish. Clark cites the following remarkable passage from Aristotle's *De Partibus Animalium* (1.645a) (MS, 58, 141):

> We must avoid a childish distaste for examining the less valued animals. For in all natural things there is something wonderful. And just as Heraclitus is said to have spoken to the visitors who were wanting to see him but stopped when they

saw him "warming himself at the oven"—he kept telling them to come in and not worry, "for there are gods here too"—so we should approach the inquiry about each animal without aversion, knowing that in all of them there is something natural and beautiful.

It may well be true of monkeys, as Aristotle thinks of men, that they desire to know, as when they can be bribed to solve puzzles, even if their reward is nothing other than another puzzle to solve. Yet even if animals are not intellectually curious, they do display parental care, they pity the weak, and sometimes they even give up their lives for their fellows. As we have seen, it is because we are warm-blooded and mammalian that we can do these *ethical* things as well; only a few of us are *truly moral* beings (see *Nicomachean Ethics* 8.1159b). So few of us are saints or bodhisattvas that we should be skittish about claiming to be moral authorities, even if we can at least try to be ethical. The decent person, the sound one, the reasonable one does what he or she must, finding meaning in natural bonds and friendships and in the shared worship of natural beauty. Herein lies the Aristotelian basis for Clark's defense of animal "rights" and environmental ethics. Only the person with *phronesis* (practical wisdom) is really in accord with nature; there is something unnatural about willful perversity. The good life consists of sharing with others (for prosperity is not much good if there is no one to share it with—*Nicomachean Ethics* 8.1155a), just as most animals share their love with others. Ethical experience is so rich that no set of rules or system can do justice to its biological vagaries and sensitivities (MS, 151, 155, 183–84, 186, 192).

There are impulses to the noble in animals (*Magna Moralia* 1206b), and even more of these in humans, which means that greater responsibilities regarding the care of animals and nature rest on our shoulders, responsibilities that ought to be guided, Clark thinks, by the law of moderation.[22] Clark also relies on Plutarch in the development of his hierarchy of ethical/moral concern: it makes no sense to speak of a tree's being more intelligent than a bush, whereas similar judgments regarding animals are quite intelligible (MS, 18). In theory, at least, if not in practice, Darwinism should similarly encourage not only finely tuned judgments regarding the different levels of sentience and intelligence in animals, but also different degrees of fellow-feeling and kindliness. We should

surely be expected to think of our cousins as cousins and not as trash. Unfortunately, the symbolic use to which Darwinism has been put is to exalt

Man as heir of the ages, and depress the non-human animals as errors, or back-slidings, or material. (MS, 30)

Clark is insistent that his *concepts about* natural sentiment and fellow-feeling are not open to the charge of "sentimentality." His concepts are: (1) formalized within the arguments presented in the previous chapter; (2) historically grounded in a tradition that includes some of the most important philosophers in the history of the discipline; and (3) open to various tests of practical application and consistency, say, with respect to the issues of vegetarianism, animal experimentation, pet ownership, and a defensible version of environmental ethics. Points (2) and (3) are the key ones advanced in the present chapter:

Certainly, sentimentality is our enemy: the inability to see the real, suffering animal for a haze of aestheticism, misplaced piety and emotional projections. . . . If, on the other hand, "sentimentality" means merely a concern for the well-being of my fellow- creatures and an unwillingness to torture them for my own satisfaction . . . then I willingly subscribe to it. (MS, 8–10)

ENVIRONMENTALISM

Thus far in this chapter I have concentrated on the historical roots to Clark's views of animals and on some of the practical applications of these views. Yet I have also been gradually moving toward Clark's view of the natural environment in general, a view that I will now examine explicitly. He is quite clear that "the land is a community to which we belong" (MS, 114), a solidarity that the reigning conception of scientific "objectivity" would disallow. This sense of belonging obviously works against the view of nature as violent to the core. Even predators exhibit "cooperation" with nature, in that if they are too successful in the short run they may be extinct in the long run. Likewise, Clark thinks that we need to learn self-control before we utterly perish: "Our long term interests, as a species, will be best served by a present tenderness" (MS, 161). Long before the word "ecology" was known there were those who enlarged the normal boundaries of community to include soil, water, plants, and animals. These wealthy "preservationists," however, very often cared for nature because they wished to have their game (e.g., the fox in Great Britain) preserved. Clark characteristically does not emphasize that this expansive notion of natural community was often at the expense of members of their own species, as in

213

Wordsworth's poem "Goody Blake." Alternatively, these preservationists were the middle class, who wanted landscapes preserved so they could have interesting country walks (MS, 145–46, 164–65, 169, 171). Clark's environmental ethics, along with his defense of animals, bears his political stamp.

Lacking sentience, or at least lacking sentience of a sophisticated enough level that it could experience acute pain, a plant is not the sort of being concerning which we could, as with an animal, clearly say that it has "rights." Yet we already think of some arboricide as culpable, and we may in time think so even more. The culpability lies both in the aesthetic diminishment for sentient beings in general when trees are killed and in the weakening of an ecosystem that sustains those sentient beings. What bothers Clark, however, is mourning the death of a tree because it will make it less likely to sustain a bird population that we wish to hunt. That is, Clark's ecoholism is not extreme (nor is his defense of individualism), in that he remains cognizant of both the value that individuals possess intrinsically and that they then contribute to the whole. Like Regan, Clark is opposed to "environmental fascism." Plants are not quite as much the individuals worthy of respect as animals are, but Clark's respect for individual plants and their intrinsic value is not altogether nonexistent, as when he commends the (panpsychistic or animistic) attitudes of those in the Findhorn settlement. Yet even on utilitarian grounds we should be more careful in our treatment of plants and of the rest of nature:

> Our use of DDT is a convenient symbol of our practice. Certainly, we have saved lives with it, but at the price of fouling the whole biosphere and polluting even human mothers' milk. Certainly we have saved lives with it, but at the price of strengthening our "foe." (MS, 172)

Clark is advocating a more quietistic (something of a Taoist) approach to nature, where we learn to live with our "foe" rather than try to destroy it: "Our medical ideal should not be the anti-septic, anti-human hospital" (MS, 173). He hopes for a world in which we cooperate with the others in it, even the non- or slightly sentient ones. Although obviously not a Jain himself, Clark thinks that the extreme efforts of the Jains to avoid killing even insects constitute a standing reminder to the rest of us against wanton killing (MS, 174). Put another way, if we accept that atoms themselves are not aware, then the awareness of a complex creature is a strictly emergent property. It just so happens, it seems, that when atoms are put together, consciousness emerges! Clark points out that we usually are inclined to seek something more than a mere conjunction in nature: we want the newly apparent property to be explicable in terms of the old. Panpsychism, he thinks, is a real option (AT, 36–37).

Many hunters claim they are nature and animal lovers, but it is unclear to Clark how one can love the thing one is destroying, especially if one has a choice not to destroy it (MS, 175–76). As we have seen, the respect that animals, in particular, and nature, in general, deserve is not best described in terms of rights, according to Clark. If a mouse, strictly speaking, has a right not to be tormented, then a cat ought not to torment him and hence *we* ought to restrain the cat. If this were the case then we would be putting on our shoulders responsibility for almost the whole of the natural world. Clark responds to this problem by claiming that mice no more have rights against cats than they do against earthquakes, just as our "rights" are not infringed upon by epidemics. "One can have rights only against those capable of acknowledging them."[23] In order to develop a plausible environmental ethics, in addition to a defense of animal "rights," it is essential to emphasize that it is only moral and not physical evil that is to be denounced, and cats (perhaps not chimpanzees) are exempt from doing moral evil. Or better, physical evil in the natural environment is surely evil *in its own right*, in that cruelty or callousness can only be bothersome, as they are, if suffering itself is an evil. One of the key problems to be dealt with in an environmental ethics, according to Clark, is that regarding the extent to which we should be susceptible to distress caused by physical evil. *This* distress, unlike that which human beings themselves inflict on animals, can make sense only within the context of a carefully thought through theodicy, a topic that I have treated at length above, and a topic concerning which Clark is not always convincing.

It seems that "even if the cat has no duties towards the mouse, and the mouse therefore no rights against the cat, it may still be that the mouse has rights against *us*, to safeguard his life and liberty."[24] However, Clark is not convinced by this view. He thinks that we violate the rights of animals when we hunt them, but not in allowing them to suffer at the hands (or better, claws) of predators. His reasons are twofold. First, animal suffering is an evil, but not all such evils can be eliminated without introducing worse ones. A familiar example with many variations can be found around the world: if we spare caribou, say, the pain of wolves, there may be a population explosion among the caribou that will lead to overgrazing, disease, famine, and then a population crash. Second, although we have a moral responsibility regarding whom *we* kill, we are not masters of the earth. That is, Clark's environmental ethics is integrally connected to his theism (and to his theodicy), whereby we show our wisdom as much in accommodating ourselves to physical evil as we do in trying to lessen or eliminate it, *if* in fact we can lessen or eliminate it. Clark is well aware of the fact that this stance (which is similar to Hellenistic repose, Ignatian indifference, or Buddhist "passivity") may, at times, appear callous. Yet he thinks that, at least at this stage in the history of our involvement with nature, with Nature, callousness is not as big a danger as hubris. The following analogy with politics may be helpful, even if Clark himself would not approve of my pacifistic leanings: just as the Allies, in avenging the deaths of fewer than 5,000 Kuwaitis, in turn killed approximately 250,000 Iraqis (many of these were civilians), so also our supposed humane management of nature can turn out to be quite inhumane.

Clark himself adopts Robert Nozick's suggestion that rights are side-constraints regarding what *we* ought not to do, and we ought not to torment mice even if it is not our job to prevent cats from doing so (but perhaps no danger would be done to the ecosystem and perhaps there would be no danger in committing hubris by putting a bell on the cat). *Usually* the pains of predation cannot be alleviated without making matters worse: "On a side-constraint view we ought not to violate animal rights, but are under no obligation always to prevent such violations."[25] There are some things that we just should not do, even if it is often difficult to determine what we should do:

> There is a limit to the positive action any of us can take. Merely to abstain from flesh-foods, cosmetics, unnecessary medicaments is not generally an enterprise that diverts energy from other goals. Veganism, in the present state of society, perhaps does. . . . Few of us can wholeheartedly devote ourselves to the defense of mice. . . . We have an obligation to let the *cat* live a natural life after her kind. If mice have a right to life, so do cats. . . . Prima facie rights conflict.[26]

The ecological community is not a moral community in the sense of there being agreed upon procedures regarding how natural beings should treat each other. Rather, there are manifold sympathies in nature, sympathies that very often are affected more by unusual dangers than by the usual ones, and more by sufferings felt by our clients than by those felt by nonclients. For the most part we should leave well enough alone: "We have done enough remaking."[27] An example of an "unusual" danger to animals would be floods, with predation providing the "usual" danger.[28]

Because of the inevitability of predation there is no imaginable perfect peace in the natural world. Our best hope is to avoid changing our techniques of land use too often or too radically (note the effect of Clark's politics here): "conservation is, inevitably, conservative" (AJ, 173). Very rapid changes give an advantage to opportunistic species who perhaps do not "deserve" such an advantage. Further, land conservation and political conservativism encourage us to keep in mind our dependence on Nature in general (on God) and our interrelatedness with various facets of nature (with creation) (AJ, 170, 174, 178). Very few of the natural areas that we admire are truly wild, Clark thinks, a claim that perhaps is more true in Great Britain than in, say, the North American West. What we are often preserving in nature is our interrelation with it. We are preserving

> a great mnemonic, the externalized history of our tribe. The sense of history, the way in which we can read our real or imagined past from the landscape we inhabit is a vital ingredient in the ethic of conservation, and of patriotism itself. . . . The value such things represent is more than aesthetic. . . . (CP, 86–87)

In the following remarkable quotation we can find the clearest link between Clark's environmental ethics and his politics:

> If there is a government anywhere that really deserves our loyalty it will be one that seeks to preserve the land we live by, and that encapsulates the very historical tradition that has made us a people. When we no longer find that land worth living by, that royalty worth honouring, we shall be condemned to live by transitory bargains among deracinated strangers. (CP, 88)

The terms "conservationist" and "environmentalist" are synonyms for Clark, terms that can refer to the desire to preserve the rain forests of the Amazon or antique lampposts. Even in the United States there is usually no strict division between pure wilderness areas and human history. By "historicizing" ecology Clark knows that he runs the danger of elitism: "Conservation . . . has been used to protect privilege—to keep the peasants out of the forests, the campers off the private beaches, the lower class out of the suburbs."[29] However, Clark's stated intention is to preserve old churches or forests for the benefit of all, an effort that some have tried to link with the attribution of rights to buildings or trees:

Some commentators would probably be willing to accord or recognise rights in buildings or works of art. . . . My own view is that this can only be a subterfuge, and in the end a dangerous one. There are real differences between animals and paintings, even between trees and buildings, that are not well considered if we say they all "have rights." We may, of course, choose to give them all rights (i.e., to give them a certain sort of legal standing), but it cannot be because they already have them.[30]

A better solution is the traditionalist one, he thinks: rather than give things worth preserving rights, we would be better served by convincing present "owners" that they are really custodians who must pass on their trust:

> Conservationists do not need to relapse upon totalitarian socialism nor yet to claim that buildings themselves have rights. . . . We have a shared interest in the buildings. . . . The point about a patrimony is not only that the heirs have a right to deal with it, but that they ought to do so with due respect for those who come after. . . . What we inherit we ought to pass on in such shape as shall not give us cause to feel ashamed, whether that be the "natural environment" or the "built" one (remembering that the distinction is not a clear one).[31]

However, Clark does not notice that Aldo Leopold (whom Clark often cites) tried, and largely failed, along these same lines in the attempt to preserve American wilderness areas in the hands of wealthy hunters, who very often sold the land to the highest bidder. That is, it is questionable, to say the least, whether preservation efforts can avoid the preservation apparati made possible by government.

The land is as great a mnemonic as a cathedral, which is itself built upon a rocklike permanence that, as was seen regarding Clark's problematic version of dipolar theism, is of greater significance in Clark's view than changeability or responsiveness. The ancient land and ancient cathedrals anchor us in a meaningful world.[32] The moral sensibility born in our household, city, and church should be extended to the whole earth, once we see the earth as a whole as an *oikos* (a household) for which we can offer a logos, hence a literal ecology.[33] In later chapters I will treat the fear many liberals have of the idea that we owe allegiance to the earth as a whole. That is, liberals tend to equate deep ecology with environmental fascism, and despite Clark's claim that he is opposed to environmental fascism, some will continue to fear the possibility that there will be an elevation of the good of the whole over the suffering individuals who make up that whole:

> Deep environmentalists, libertarians and zoophiles, in short, are constantly at each other's throats. It is my object to suggest that they need not be. We can place the arguments of zoophiles and libertarians within the deep environmentalists' account of our situation, rather than remain content with bare intuitions about the intrinsic value of creatures that are "subjects-of-a-life" (Regan).[34]

Stable ecosystems are those in which an indefinite number of individuals work together. "Even egoists and utilitarians . . . may come to understand that there are rules of mutual aid and non-interference which bring more profit in the end than simple-mindedly exploitative attitudes."[35] There is no doubt a tension in Clark's thought between his conservativism in its libertarian mode and his conservativism in its traditionalist mode, the latter of which seems to be much more compatible with an environmental ethic. Clark tries to resolve this tension as follows:

> The first begetters of libertarian doctrine did not appeal to absolute rights of self-ownership (restricted by the equal rights of others). Private property was defended as the likeliest way of enabling a society of freemen to subsist in mutual harmony, and cultivate their virtues: if we each had some portion of the land to tend we would be less likely to fall prey to tyrants. . . . What we owned, however, was not the land itself, but the lawfully acquired fruits, and we owned these only for their lawful use.[36]

Relying on McCloskey, Clark responds directly to the three main criticisms that could be made of his version of deep (i.e., nonanthropocentric) environmentalism:

> The main theoretical objections usually made to "deep environmentalism" are as follows. Firstly, it denies to individuals any absolute or inherent value. Secondly, it allows inherent value to things other than the merely sentient [or rational], whereas it has been a moral commonplace for most of this century that states of mind and experience are all that can be "really" good or bad. Thirdly, "the practical implications . . . are reminiscent of the morally objectionable views and attitudes of primitive moralities."[37]

That is, the objections come from individualists, "mentalists," and nonegalitar-ians. Clark's simple answer to the individualists is that there are no individuals *in the sense of* self-sufficient, eternal substances, although there are people, frogs, and trees. We have already seen Clark's critiques of the claim that rationality is the necessary condition for moral patiency. The nonegalitarian objection that entities of our (civilized) class should be valued more than those of any (primi-tive) other begins to lose its force when it is realized that *some* sort of deep ecol-ogy (or "primitivism," if in fact nonanthropocentrism is primitive) is needed in order to assure the continued existence, health, and beauty of the natural world and of our place in it. Clark urges that one can be both an individualist, in the best sense of that term, and an ecologist as long as one recognizes that

> Modern zoophiles, knowing well that dogmatic humanists will readily charge them with pet-loving sentimentality, have been chary of founding their case on such domestic affections, and preferred utilitarian calculations or abstract notions of egalitarian justice. But it is because we have experienced the possibilities of interspecific affection and communication that we can envisage a new, radical possibility. We can moderate the merely libertarian ethic by the ethic of solidar-ity. . . . This would be a "fascist" vision only if it implied that there was some elite group entitled to inflict upon an ignorant world the legislation they thought justified. . . . The "natural" rights of self-owners are more limited than human rights are generally supposed to be. By "the law of nature" none of us may justly demand more than our "fair share of life and liberty."[38]

Clark is by no means consistent, however, in the language he uses regarding the environment. At one point he refers to a "cosmic democracy," whereas at sev-eral other points where he discusses the World Soul he implies that the cosmos is ultimately a (divine) monarchy.[39]

CONCLUSION

In this chapter the biblical and especially the Aristotelian roots to Clark's views on animals have been explored, views that are sharply different from those held by Stoics, Thomists, Cartesians, and Kantians, as well as by the contemporary (often unwitting) epigoni of these movements. Further, I have shown that Clark has done a remarkable job of putting his views of animals to use, even though he does not have a strong notion of animal *rights*. The most prominent areas where Clark's concern for animals receive application are vegetarianism, animal experimentation (where he defends a position just short of the abolitionist one), and care for pets. Clark's concern for nature does not stop short at animals, however, in that the respect due to individuals—whether human or nonhuman—is not absolute. He considers himself a "conservationist," a "conservative," and an "environmentalist," with these three terms functioning as rough equivalents. That is, Clark's defense of animals and his environmental ethics are integrally linked to his political conservativism, his theism (where the intrinsic value of individuals is matched by the value they contribute to the divine whole), and his critique of the hegemony of contemporary notions of scientific objectivity. The next task is to examine in greater detail the tension in Clark between his libertarianism and his traditionalism, and the reasons why he thinks we should leapfrog from concern for individuals to concern for Nature as a whole, a leap that places relatively little importance on the state.

Clark is not convinced that our current environmental crisis is due to the Judeo-Christian tradition, as some allege. Gardens, the woods, and the stars used to be "polluted" by the "perversions" of late paganism; only when centuries of ascetic practice had purified the imagination could the natural world be rededicated (as in St. Francis), such that we can now say with Chesterton that true thinking about nature is thanking.[40]

POLITICS

COMMUNITY

INTRODUCTION

In this chapter I will begin to examine explicitly and in detail what I have been treating at least implicitly throughout the book: Clark's political views. Because the major topics treated in this book (God, animals, and politics) are in various ways interrelated in Clark's thought, there is no clean way of isolating any one of these topics from the others. It is thus perhaps best to say that in this part of the book I will focus on Clark's political views to the extent that it is possible to do so. Such a focus will allow us to see a crucial distinction in Clark between community and society (he is primarily interested in the former), the importance he places on ritual in the maintenance of community, his communitarian distaste for—yet partial submission to—liberalism, the attachment he has to particularism rather than to universalism, his critique of political abstractions, and his partial defense of anarchism. All of these themes are elaborated on the basis of his familiar theocratic and Aristotelian commitments. Regarding the latter I will emphasize Clark's similarities to and differences from Alasdair MacIntyre.

COMMUNITY AND SOCIETY

Although he does not treat Tonnies directly, Clark very often implies the distinction made famous by him between real community (*gemeinschaft*) and society (*geschellschaft*), with modern states usually exhibiting the latter rather than the former.[1] Yet Clark thinks that our goal in politics should be the flourishing of community, especially the flourishing of a *lebensgemeinschaft*, or a life-community held together by blood or shared living space, as opposed to a *geistesgemeinschaft*, where the bond is spiritual or abstract. Clark's fear is that if the "community" is too abstract it will degenerate into a mere society, where utilitarian principle reigns supreme. Communities are usually marked by certain rituals that mark the passing of time, as in seasonal festivals, inaugurals, and celebrations of birth, death, or marriage. These are the great occasions of life, sacred moments that no just political order can ignore. These rituals are easily placed within a conservative political order, but Clark is not at all opposed to new rites being introduced, especially if these rites are efforts to get back to an earlier "original" event. Politics and history become perverted if they imply only one thing after another. Very often great occasions (and the proper narrative form describing them) are created by ritual rather than the other way around. Festivals, ceremonials, or rituals have the Orphic quality of bringing certain human phenomena to life: we do not so much "observe" conception or burial as the first and last of life as we name and create them as such through our rituals (MR, 35–37).

The greatest example of this Orphic quality in orthodox Christianity is the eucharistic ritual whereby bread and wine are transubstantiated into the body and blood of Christ.[2] "If the words are pronounced by any but a priest, it is not the Body" (MR, 42). Likewise, an actor, as it were, brings King Lear to life, such that those who have never been to the theater may be tempted to leap upon the stage to prevent a "murder" from occurring:

> Ritual utterance, likewise, is not intended to reach out to "ordinary life" in quite the way that literalists (atheistical or religous) imagine. . . . Religious rituals are games or dramas. . . . "The sacrifice of the Mass" . . . many performances, one play. (MR, 42)

A good religious (or political) service or ritual is one that raises up appropriate emotion. In order for a play to be an effective drama, however, it should not remind us too often that it is indeed a play; the same applies to religious rituals or political conventions (MR, 43–44).

This concentration on Clark's part on ritual affects his treatment of the constant theme in religious tradition regarding the tension between the contemplative life and the active. Political security is important to Clark, but because the spiritual welfare of humanity is more important than even political security, a much more plausible case can be made than many suspect for the claim that the contemplative life is the superior one. Even noble and wise political leaders have no truly great influence on the populace. Clark doubts if we can think of three who are, in fact, noble and wise and who have had such influence. Although I do have three in mind (Mohandas Gandhi, Martin Luther King, and Lech Walesa), I admit that I would have a hard time expanding the list, and not even all of these three were really rulers. I admire (the somewhat apolitical) Mother Teresa more than I admire any other recent human being, and I am not alone in this regard. No human being, however, is the most worshipful being in the world. The being who is most worshipful is just as well served by worship, of course, as by political action: "But even monks are not as eager as once they were to contend that praying for one's neighbor is a better help than merely visiting or feeding her" (MR, 167–68).

Clark admits that the case for the active life can also plausibly be made. This case is fine, as far as it goes, but what Clark the communitarian would object to is building this active life on an individualistic foundation, a foundation that is a relic of three movements: (1) the notion of an inner (Quaker-like) light sent by God; (2) the notion of political authority emanating from below, from the consent of the governed; and (3) the tendency on the part of intellectual elites to use individualistic explanations, as opposed to tradition-bound, functionalistic explanations of morality in order to deal with a mobile populace with members from many backgrounds and localities. Regarding (1) we can see Clark moving in two directions at once. He encourages the interiority integral to the contemplative life, yet this inner life, if I understand Clark correctly, he sees as not so much an intrinsic good as an instrumental one in the effort to produce inspired believers who fervently desire community with others in shared ritual (MR, 183–84). Notions (2) and (3) are Clarkian commonplaces that we have treated before.

At times Clark's own version of "individualism" approximates classical liberalism. He believes that it is best to allow the maximum liberty of conscience to each that is compatible with an equal liberty for all, and this because there is a field of debatable opinion within all but the narrowest sorts of sectarianism.

Yet the fact that he is not always willing to grant such individual liberties and that he is still willing to call some positions heretical does not distinguish him, he thinks, from scientists, who are often thought to be more open-minded:

> The common view that it is typical of science to be willing to question all theories without exception, of religion to adopt an unquestioning credulity, is clearly exaggerated. Most specialists are in fact very unwilling to take radical criticism seriously. . . . However often scientists claim to trust nothing but their senses and experiments, science of any kind would be quite impossible without a general acceptance of testimony. . . . If it is wrong to accept the received opinion, it would also be wrong to rely on one's own memory and records. Every experimental result would have to be "re-confirmed" each day. (MR, 251–52)

Tradition and innovation work together in any human enterprise, including religion, politics, and science, such that those who *say* they are in favor of a radically open society, where one is encouraged to question everything because nothing is sacred, rarely intend that their own theories be on trial permanently. If "questioning everything" is impossible, we must rest content with operating within the context of received opinion:

> None of this, to state what should be obvious, in any way supports the cruel and conceited measures that have been taken against innovators in the past. If intellectuals have a duty to submit in the end to the common judgement, the judges have a duty not to close their ears entirely, and not to kill, torture, insult or ostracise the questioners. (MR, 253)

The parallel lines drawn by Clark, lines that represent science, religion, and politics, are intended to subvert a current orthodoxy. It is not the case that one can move easily from the concept that authorities or received views may be mistaken to the concept that believing on authority is, as rationalists would have it, an intellectual sin.

Following Plato's lead in the *Statesman*, Clark believes that there are three sorts of authority in politics: the democratic, the oligarchic, and the monarchical. On a democratic view, where all members have a part to play in defining doctrine, one can expect a diversity of opinion, whereas on an oligarchic view, where bishops, theologians, or their structural equivalents rule, one can expect some version of scholasticism. In neither scientific, religious, nor political scholasticism does an oligarchy remain on top forever, but in the religious world the gradual surrender of authority is less marked. The contrast between science and politics as innovative and religion as traditional is an inexact one indeed, even if there is *some* truth to the claim that religions are especially traditional, as is evidenced in the fact that they cannot be governed solely by the scholarly, in that they must bring the believing masses along with them or be brought along by them. In effect, there are three sorts of error that Clark thinks are destructive of the sort of (oligarchic-leaning, if I understand Clark correctly) political authority conducive to community: taking "science" as the final author-ity in contemporary culture, giving absolute authority to the momentary wills of individuals, or refusing to give *any* sort of authority to religion in the estab-lishment of community (MR, 254–57).

As with many other topics, Clark's conception of community is both reli-gious and Aristotelian (or "biological"). Just as health, for Aristotle, consists of the ability to maintain a precarious balance, the best form of government, he feels, lies between democracy and oligarchy, precisely because in this balance the conflicting claims of the rich and poor can be reconciled (*Politics* 4.1294a, 1296a). (Clark's view seems to be that contraries can be reconciled, but not contradicto-ries such as good-evil or proportion-disproportion; Clark relies here on *Nico-machean Ethics* 2.1107a; AM, 88.) Most actions cannot be declared right or wrong in the abstract, but only in terms of what the good person would do in a response appropriate to the demands of a particular environment. *Sophrosyne* (modera-tion) is seldom self-referential; usually it has communal implications, as in the *mesotes* (mean) between "total good-friendship" and being thoroughly disagree-able (AM, 84–85, 87, 89, 90–92, 94–96). "Equilibrium is the foundation of the world, and harmony its universal path" (AM, 97). It is not surprising, therefore, that Clark agrees with Aristotle regarding both the gregarious and the solitary dimensions of human nature (*History of Animals* 488a), the partial reconciliation of which constitutes the task for each individual-in-community. Despite his strong critique of individual*ism*, Clark admits that no person's identity can be exhausted by his or her social role (AM, 98, 100–1):

> A citizen is one who can share in the city's life, the city's civic activities, judici-ary, and rule (*Politics III*, 1275a), but the human being who is the citizen does not exist for the sake of the city (unless perhaps the ideal city). The city is for its members, a *koinonia* or companionship of free men (*Politics III*, 1279a). (AM, 102)

In a true community, where freedom and sociality are reconciled, there is a need for a middle class large enough to prevent the domination of the state by either mob rule or great individuals (*Politics* 4.1296a). However, it is not only the middle class that should rule, even if it is members of this class who are most likely to obey the logos (AM, 103–5). Further, a large middle class signals the demise of master-slave relationships and the rise of friendship, broadly conceived: "This companionship is what the state exists for" (AM, 106), not the other way around and not merely to allow the economic system to survive. Clark is aware of the fact that each thinker tends to think of his own homeland as the mean, a problem that goes back at least as far as Aristotle. He despised barbarians, Clark thinks, not simply because they were non-Greek, but because they failed to meet certain criteria of value that Aristotle considered important. Clark, like Aristotle, thinks that slavery *as an institution* is an evil, but for those (known to any social worker) who cannot rule themselves it is an expedient worth considering, as is indicated by our current practice of incarcerating criminals (AM, 107).

The highest sort of friendship, the sort most conducive to community, is possible only among good human beings, among those whose friendship lies more in loving than in being loved, and in loving because the beloved is worthy of esteem without ulterior purpose (AM, 108–9).[3] Clark uses Hartshorne to defend the claim that selfhood is social or friendly or it is nothing at all (AM, 110).[4] We make ourselves by accepting such responsibilities as are constituted by our relationships with relatives and friends who surround us. This active life in community with relatives and friends, although it is never the purely theoretic life enjoyed by the gods, should never be wholly disconnected from the theoretical life. Human beings naturally reach out for knowledge, especially for knowledge of the Whole, which is superior to any of the knowledge requisite to participate in civic life (AM, 111–13, 159). Yet, "a supposed *theoretikos* who is thus antisocial . . . is no true contemplative" (AM, 160). *Theoria* is theo-ria, a continual approximation of the service of god (AM, 161–62).

LIBERALISM

It should now be clear that Clark's thesis is that current political preoccupations and vocabulary are best challenged not so much from the left or right but from below, from the long tradition of premodern thought. He agrees with Marxists that current philosophers of mind and state are really political ideologues in disguise, but he thinks that Marxists challenge these ideologies incorrectly.

Clark realizes that it would be contradictory for him to think that he could, through argument alone, *refute* current political ideologies, in that the kind of gestalt shift he has in mind also includes a change of heart and, perhaps, a change in the way we live from day to day. Clark's pragmatism commits him to the belief that we should not second-guess ourselves too often, but it is periodically helpful to be shaken out of our (modern or postmodern) complacency by a "showman" like himself (this is Clark's own designation). He speaks as an "Anglican philosopher" to the effect that absolute and eternal values are the most real, as we have seen previously regarding his dipolar theism, in which there is an obvious penchant for the eternal. Relying on R. C. Morgan, he puts the point as follows: only a Catholic can be a good Protestant, in that *constructive* criticism of tradition entails a respect for that tradition.[5] Clark's antipathy is directed not so much toward religious and political reformers as to those who have had an "extraordinary attack of amnesia" (cp, viii, 1–3).

The theocentric traditionalism that Clark sees as the one true rival to modernist and postmodernist error is very much unlike Heidegger's attempt to return to the presocratics so as to sidestep the supposed errors committed in Western thinking from the time of Socrates on. It is also unlike (but less so) Whitehead's attempt to revert to pre-seventeenth-century thought so as to avoid the materialistic, mechanistic worldview that has been the legacy of that century, as has been dualism, where most of the world is assumed to be mechanistic, with a few minds scattered about as the exceptions to the general mechanistic rule. As before, however, Clark does not follow Whitehead or Hartshorne all the way toward process theism or panpsychism, even if he does at times flirt with these views. Clark's thought, even more than Whitehead's or Hartshorne's, receives sustenance from Aristotle's, although it might be suggested that he receives as much sustenance from Plato's thought as do Whitehead and Hartshorne.[6] Further, Clark takes more seriously than most philosophers biblical and poetic tradition (although Whitehead's debt to Wordsworth, as is well known, is profound[7]) (cp, 4).

It is crucial for Clark to show that he has not turned "liberal modernism" into a strawman. The following doctrines are among those that he sees as definitive of the position:

No one ought to believe or ask others to believe anything more than she can herself demonstrate on the basis of her own personal knowledge. . . . No one ought to believe any positive doctrine that cannot be verified by "the scientific method."

... Long-established beliefs and practices have no greater claim on our practical and theoretical allegiance than newly minted ones. . . . No one ought to believe that there are any obligations "laid down from above.". . . All modern persons must acknowledge that the body of genuinely true propositions is entirely value-free. (CP, 5–6)

As we have seen, Clark's oxymoronic pragmatism-traditionalism dictates that we cannot even come close to reconstructing the body of information by which we live on the basis of either self-evident principle or personal knowledge, as liberal modernism alleges; we live in a sea of testimony through which we must negotiate our way by trusting the most reliable sources: "too many of those who have criticized modernist dogma have done so by adopting a limply contrived relativism" (CP, 10). Clark agrees that each of us is to be master or mistress of our own soul and that heteronomy is an enemy, but

Self-command emphatically did not mean doing what one chose to do from within one's normal cloudy and concupiscent individuality: it meant seeking to live in accordance with a higher principle even when one had almost forgotten why. . . . Kantian "autonomy" is not to be identified with egoistic self-determination. (CP, 17)

He asks us to imagine what it would be like to hire self-styled electricians who, in an "experimental" turn of mind, did not believe in traditional wiring practices. Yet these are precisely the sorts of people some are willing to "hire" in their politics and religion, according to Clark (CP, 19).

Further, it is by no means clear to Clark that moral nonobjectivism lends support to liberal values, for if there are no objective moral truths then the moral views that dominate any particular community may or may not be liberal, in that they would largely be a matter of historical accident. Why *should* liberals allow as much liberty to every individual as is compatible with an equal liberty for all? Clark (like Martin Luther King) thinks that this use of "should" is in fact metaphysically grounded in theistic personalism, hence in a peculiar sort of way he is more liberal than the liberals, in that they cannot account for their "should." The solidarity of mankind is problematic, according to Clark, both because it usually conceals some type of speciesism and because it very often cannot be explained in terms other than those associated with relativism or individual preference. When "solidarity of mankind" *can* be explained, it is not likely to be part of liberal propaganda. It should be noted, however, that Clark's attempt to criticize liberalism's inability to deal adequately with the solidarity of mankind is at least somewhat tongue-in-cheek, in that Clark himself is only marginally committed to such solidarity. Regarding the protection of mentally defective infants, for example, he is committed to such solidarity, but regarding family and personal friends, colleagues and neighbors he is more than willing to confer preferred status, in contrast to, say, starving people in Sudan. To deny such a preferred status, he thinks, is thereby to deny that one really has any (true Aristotelian) friends (CP, 20, 57–58, 60).

> Universal love of humankind, however praiseworthy, is not obviously what we wish to see in those around us, nor do we unfailingly praise those who give their money to the desperately poor at the expense of their own family, friends, and fellow-citizens. . . . Jesus himself had one disciple whom especially he loved. (CP, 61)

Defenders of undifferentiated love (or undifferentiated duties) unwittingly support dualism by implying that morality has no special application to proximate relations, to those materially close to us, as embodied human beings who can be in only one place at a time.[8] Undifferentiated love presupposes that my psyche could be as morally close to an unknown, distant person as to any other. There can be no doubt that unknown, distant human persons and whales face many dangers, but Clark thinks that charity or justice toward such beings "rests first upon the perception that they are someone's friends" (CP, 62). It is also possible, Clark admits (albeit reluctantly), for one to go too far in the direction of particularity by stating not only that ethics starts with, but that it, along with morality, *ends* with kith and kin. Christians before Constantine were often accused of this error, and politicians today sometimes wish that Christians would commit it again when contemporary believers express moral judgments on global issues. In the end, however, Clark's view seems to be that when a country ceases to be a community and is, at best, a society, then the smaller circles of friendship become the true community and the "true country." We can "unchoose" our countrymen, but not our relatives and friends. Our countrymen are brought within our sphere of moral concern only to the extent that we have a civil relationship to them analogous to a kind of friendship (CP, 63).

Tramps and unattached itinerant workers, who have few obligations to others, do not have the sort of liberty we usually desire. Clark uses these examples to show that true liberty should be defined, as the ancients realized, in terms of acknowledged duties (CP, 65–66, 71). In fact, *natural* law is given to us "by the constantly renewed experience of friendly and familial confrontation, where individuals find their dignity in the fulfillment of particular and local duty" (CP, 72). Clark's right-wing anarchism can be seen when he argues that *civil* law has its origin in the desire of the ruling class to give permanence to its own customs, a belief that has strong similarities to left-wing anarchism (CP, 73).[9] However, most right-wing anarchists like Clark are different from most left-wing anarchists regarding the greater attachment the former have to natural law:

> The genuine welfare of the governed would be best served by getting off their backs, not by taxing, conscripting, and regulating their doings in accordance with some vision of a higher good which they had not themselves endorsed. Governments are protection rackets. The suggestion—still to be found in some political theorists—[is] that real consent can be inferred from the victim's participation in some political processes (like casting a vote, or even campaigning). . . . But what right has the state to require of me new duties, ones I would not have in nature, even when that "nature" is understood to include the pre-political network of family and friends? (CP, 74–75)

Clark's right-wing anarchism, it should be noted, dovetails with his critique of scientism, because state power and civil law in the modern era rest significantly on what Clark thinks is an unfounded trust in scientific "experts" who are very often hired or funded by the state (CP, 76).

The right-wing anarchism that Clark defends can legitimately be described as a version of classical (as opposed to contemporary, interventionist, or redistributive) liberalism. It was entirely reasonable, he thinks, for the early liberals to restrict the power of *princes* and to insist that the power of princes came only from the consent of the governed. It is unclear, however, what Clark's approach to nationalism is. His intellectual defense of parochialism and traditionalism, as we have seen, as well as his defense of a version of the just war theory, tend to push him toward nationalism. Yet his anarchism (including his resistance to conscription) tends to make him as opposed to state funding of weapons of mass destruction as he is to state funding of gay rights groups. The familial and natural obligations (or the *gessa*, as in the ancient Irish restrictions placed on chieftains) that make it possible for us to be free also make it possible, according to Clark, for us to be individuals (CP, 77–78):

As in epistemology, so in politics: our actual historical and personal experience is not one in which authority is accorded to our rulers or our dogmas after lengthy thought and by indefeasible argument. Things work the other way: we find ourselves believing, and reverencing, all manner of things, and then slowly find reasons (internal to the system in which we live) for abandoning or modifying some constraints upon belief or action. The self-owning individual does not stand at the beginning of political society, but—as MacIntyre has it—near its end. (CP, 79)

Clark's nationalism, it seems, can be rendered consistent with his anarchism *only if* national heroes are presented as *natural* authorities or as outgrowths of organic, natural (as opposed to civil) law. At one time in human history, before the rise of self-owning individuals, rulers did indeed appear to be authoritative by nature.

Clark, however, is not too convincing here. Even if we grant that our natural condition was never an "accidental congress of unobligated strangers," it is still hard to see current political leaders as anything but cultural artifacts. We started out living in, and in a sense we still do live in, families, alliances, and clans. Yet there is a tenuous connection, at best, between natural community and current political institutions. This tenuousness allows one to either attempt to justify the existence of the state regardless of whether its basis lies in nature or attempt to defend anarchism. Clark often takes the latter course, but never in a consistent enough way to convince one that this is his true position. The states that he criticizes are those that are not rooted either in nature or in theocracy. Hardly any contemporary states, and no Western ones, are so rooted (CP, 80). In effect, Clark leaves us with a choice between "anarcho-capitalism" and "the sort of polity that we in the West identify with Islamic fundamentalism or the Bible Belt": "Either the state can have no authority beyond that of a simple police force (if it has that much), or else it must be supposed to embody a sacred, moral purpose" (CP, 82). If "we are not to live and die for such an embodied, or partly embodied, vision, then the role of the state can only be what minimalists or anarchists propose" (CP, 83).

One of the problems with liberalism, Clark thinks, is that it gives us nothing to die for, hence it cannot command obedience. It is unclear, however, what the connection is between having something to die for and political legitimacy, and it is unclear whether the long history of (supposedly) just war theory—that is, something to die for—has been a boon for human beings, in particular, or the natural environment, in general. Nonetheless, there is something to be learned from Clark's view, even if it is not immediately apparent what sort of political philosophy and *praxis* he is urging on us:

> Either the state is to be no more than the guardian of existing property rights and common law institutions or it is to embody a high purpose that takes precedence over local rights and duties. . . . If it is to be a minimal watchman-state, it can claim no right to regulate its clients' lives except to insist that they forego violent expropriation as a tool of policy. . . . When it no longer acknowledges any transcendent authority, it must become our servant, providing protection and certain amenities—a kind of glorified Water and Sewerage Authority . . . and who would die for the Water Board? (cp, 84–85)

Clark, however, is not always humorous when he is in his anarchist mode, as when he refers to state officials as "barely civilized brigands" who, at their best, protect us against still worse brigands, and who have a right to our obedience only within this narrow province. These state officials certainly have no right to force us to finance weapons of mass destruction, as Clark admits on the grounds of traditional just war theory. Clark's fear is the Platonic one that if more than minimal power is given to the state then we will find that state officials are "profoundly ill-qualified to be moral educators" (cp, 88–89).

The state arbitrarily, he thinks, decides which actions are prohibited and which are duties or are supererogatory. The lines dividing these categories are more clearly drawn in the para-political familial order dominated by women and children, an order often threatened by the contemporary state (a male conspiracy). Ancient Athens, which sought to represent the goddess Athena, forged a unity out of families, craft associations, and clubs. In this sense it is a model for us today:

> Only a state that can convince its subjects that it speaks for a god they know, or will come to know, can hope to claim authority beyond the minimal. The question then is: what god can we locate and represent in something like the forms we have inherited? If there is none, then the choice will indeed in the end lie between anarchism and the consciously theocratic politics of Islam or the Marxist. (cp, 90)

Clark's traditionalism, as we have seen, is not synonymous with patriarchalism, in that the latter consists either in the hegemony of some male god or in the perversion of mammalian biology. Proper state authority acknowledges natural and sacred boundaries, especially the sacred ones:

> A sacred centre . . . arises to challenge the complacent properties of familial and friendly association . . . where the institutions of the "natural" level all too easily imagine that the land they farm, the animals they hunt or train, the servants whom they patronize are "theirs." (CP, 90)

Clark is well aware of the fact that "a sacred centre" can also be perverted, as when the words of human beings are substituted for "the word of the High God" (CP, 91). It should be noted, however, that Clark is here in danger of contradicting his claim (in MR) that biblical literalism is (for various reasons) a mistake.

Here and there, he thinks, there exist states that serve to focus the moral aspirations and the piety of a people, and only these rare sacred centers really deserve our obedience:

> Anything less than that had best be replaced by the minimal night-watchman state, or by the familiar net of friendly association. Either there is a moral or religious demand that transcends our own individual wills or there is not. If there is not, and individual consent alone is the root of any authority another may exercise over us, then no existing state government has any such authority. But even if there is, it cannot easily be identified with just any state, or any state at all. . . . There is no social or political order, present or to come upon this earth, which can be unequivocally and eternally endorsed. (CP, 91–92)

Because the state, even the theocratic state, is a suspect organization, the best state is one where priest and king are separate, Clark thinks. If Clark is correct here regarding the separation of religious and secular power, however, then one wonders about the legitimacy of any claim to a sacred center, and hence one is forced to conclude that Clark is really an anarchist. Back and forth we go from anarchy to theocracy, with few clues (or better, with too many clues) as to which view is the "real" Clarkian one. Perhaps his point is that *any* state should be treated with irony and should not be taken too seriously, a view that would constitute an indirect or bastardized anarchism, if not a forthright or consistent one. Evidence in favor of this interpretation of Clark is found when we see him criticize Ayatollah Khomeyni: "Better a minimal or 'convenient state' than rulers who think they have the Mandate of Heaven to flog, stone, mutilate, and kill"

(CP, 94); we should remember that Clark in other places seems to praise Islamic fundamentalism (CP, 82). He is consistent in at least this much: that the corruption of religious leaders is no worse than the corruption of political leaders in an expansive state. It is odd, he thinks, that a government that had abandoned any claim to a divine mandate, because no government official could ever have the requisite knowledge, could simultaneously be the sort of government that could claim to have the requisite knowledge

> to take all manner of decisions about the education and medical treatment of children, the deployment of resources, the availability of this drug or that, the proper mode of interpersonal relationship, and so on (CP, 93–94).[10]

The defense of anarchism (or perhaps better, of the minimal state) that Clark offers is not to be confused with a carte blanche for revolutionaries: "Government is illegitimate, maybe: but so, in that case, is organized rebellion, and for just the same reason" (CP, 95). The key practical issue in politics is to find that (religious) order which can claim the loyalties of a sufficient number, as Christianity once did convincingly for Western peoples. Because attempts to replace Christianity have failed (those of socialism, Marxism, and market capitalism among them), Clark thinks that it is more appropriate to reconsider Christianity than to rebel against it without having any idea for how to replace it (CP, 96–97). National symbols and monuments are great mnemonics, hence those who think of such things as mere commodities are to be pitied, but there is a higher loyalty than that owed to the nation-state, in Clark's view. As we will see in the following chapter, Clark's political philosophy lends itself to a certain sort of internationalism. He obviously does not defend that sort of internationalism whereby the effort is made to bring about the unity of mankind, an effort that Clark thinks is fruitless.[11] Rather, Clark's internationalism consists of the preservation of the rights and splendors of each little tribe or community against those sophisticated tourists, missionaries, or businessmen whose tactics are corrosive of particularity. A sound internationalism, he thinks, respects the gods of each place, if only because each god is a reflection of God (CP, 100–1).

Clark is well aware of the Hobbesian and Kantian argument in favor of a world state on the grounds that only such a state could insure international tranquillity or a true approximation of the kingdom of ends. By way of contrast, Clark fears that the larger the state the greater the distance between the government and the people, and thus the greater the danger of despotism. Only a federation of independently existing communities can secure the necessary conditions for a worldwide "community" and for international peace. Clark is correct in noting the defects in many varieties of universalism or internationalism, but he seems to be too generous to particularism. Consider both the strengths and weaknesses of particularism in the most distinctive region in the United States: the South. Much can be said in its favor: people there have a strong sense of place and of tradition, they "know who they are," they have a distinctive and proud culture (say, in music, as the birthplace of the blues, jazz, and rock and roll, perhaps the greatest achievements worldwide in twentieth-century popular culture), and they have generally maintained traditional religious values (very often in the form of Bible Belt fundamentalism, which Clark alternately praises and damns). Yet this is also the region, perhaps partially because of its parochial pride, that is the most xenophobic and racist in America, even if xenophobia and racism themselves are near ubiquitous phenomena around the world. That is, even if one grants Clark's criticisms of universalism, as I am willing to do, it does not necessarily follow that particularism is faultless. It may well be that Clark's typical ability to balance a way between extremes is especially needed here.

"International order," for Clark, does not mean noninterference in the internal affairs of another state, for this would be an analogue to the liberal belief in merely private morality: "it cannot be a matter of indifference to us that people with whom we are inextricably involved at economic and personal levels are practising iniquity" (CP, 102). I suspect, however, that this is thinner ice than Clark admits. He agrees with Marxists at least to the extent that they criticize individualistic liberalism: "It is the whole community, existing through time, that has interests" (CP, 103). It should be remembered that regarding animal "rights" Clark emphasizes that it is individual cows who suffer (or who have interests), not cowhood. Likewise, this black here and that woman there can be harmed (i.e., have their interests ignored or violated), and the health of the whole community is little consolation to these harmed individuals qua their individuality. Once again, Clark's usual moderation is not in evidence here. Clark admits that a world state would be an asset *if* it were a genuinely just one, and a just state is one, on good Platonic grounds, where *each* receives its due. We condemn the Pol Pot regime not merely because it upset the Cambodian communities existing through time, but also because *individuals* (albeit massive numbers of them) were tortured and killed. Clark is on firmer ground when he emphasizes the fact that one of the common ways in which harm can be done to people in other states is by neglecting their gods. For example,

One complex way of neglecting the gods of the country is by importing inappropriate agricultural techniques and ignoring the pre-political network—very often of female agriculturalists—in favour of an ersatz and soon-to-be-slavish system of cash-crops planted by men in order to get foreign exchange to buy consumer non-durables. (CP, 104–5)

There are types of sacred power, Clark thinks, which could help to prevent these egregious abuses of political power:

> What I am after . . . is an account of *Sacerdotium*, as a check on *Regnum*. The long medieval dispute between the spiritual and temporal authority ended, in effect, with a victory for state power. The right of the Church to excommunicate and so depose a king had rested upon a general perception that kings had their authority from God. . . . Popular history suggests quite falsely that the West has moved smoothly away from tyranny into the well-lit uplands of liberal democracy. The fact is that even the most liberal of modern states claim a degree of authority over their subjects that past kings never envisaged. (CP, 106)

The sort of sacred power Clark has in mind rests with the community of the faithful and in the lines of connection between "local synod and the general council." By "community of the faithful" Clark refers at least to the attenuated Christendom of the West, resurgent Islam, or any other religous core that, as before, is "worth dying for" and that forces us to respond to the sufferings of others. More specifically, by "community of the faithful" Clark refers to Israel and its offspring: Christianity, Islam, and Communism (CP, 107, 109, 129).

In a previous chapter we saw that one form of Clark's critique of reason consists of a defense of charismatic revivalism, a defense that is also part of his critique of political, ecclesiastical, and academic hierarchy. However, Clark is unwilling to so accentuate the importance of private religious experience that the structure of belief as a social phenomenon breaks down altogether. Even mystical experiences must somehow be harmonized with the beliefs of others in a shared form of life. That is, Clark's religious epistemology is somewhat libertarian, but it is not as extreme as Feyerabend's, where all believers or investigators stake their fortunes on the gratuitous preference for some project or other. The problem with Feyerabend's extreme libertarianism is that it ultimately does not so much permit any belief whatsoever as it undercuts the very possibility of belief (AJ, 77, 85, 106):

There is a pleasing irony about this proposal, whereby the notion of "facts" or "scientific facts" that has been employed in deliberate contrast to the supposedly fluid and inarguable realm of "values" itself dissolves into the sea of dreams. If . . . there are no good grounds for preferring one research programme or one theory to another . . . what is to be believed is a matter of private decision—and so nothing is strictly to be believed at all. (AJ, 107)

Individual autonomy is not so much in opposition to theological realism as it is its outgrowth: "It is because God speaks in each of us that no one of us should claim despotic power" (AJ, 203), a view that is very close to the Quaker-like inner light which Clark has elsewhere criticized.

MACINTYRE

The moral basis of Clark's political views is similar to that found in the thought of Alasdair MacIntyre, especially with regard to the claims that moral debate only makes sense within a tradition, that virtues are needed that are appropriate to the roles performed in a given community, and that we are living through a new dark ages. Yet there are also differences between Clark and MacIntyre. Clark's traditionalism makes him skeptical of those who think that moral and political problems can be solved by creating ersatz communities, especially because there are already many local forms of community that have resisted erosion: "People of my acquaintance do not live as pleasure-seeking atomies."[12] We do not have to wait for a new St. Benedict to come along, as MacIntyre implies, because we "still live in historical communities, whose strength is forgotten both by romantic individualists and by romantic conservatives." The job of political philosophers is to develop the proper rationalization for those existing forms of community that are currently undervalued and that must persist "to avoid sheer barbarism."[13] Modern society is not quite yet a collection of strangers, even if it has been moving in this direction for the last few centuries, a degeneration mirrored in a severe philosophical skepticism regarding the foundation of morals.

Both Clark and MacIntyre are at odds with John Rawls's alleged attempt to find out which principles of justice would be agreed to everywhere and at all times by all reasonable persons. To take one example, traditional communities encourage their members to admire loyalty to the groups of which they are a part, whereas in liberal society moralists would regard such loyalty to contingently organized groups as defective or jejune, according to Clark. (Rawls's view is actually more complex: traditional communities should be encouraged *as long as* they are reasonable in the sense that they do not trample on the rights of others.) The difference between Clark and MacIntyre is apparent in the following:

> Is it conceivable that there be a society in which there are no received duties, nothing to serve for honour, nothing sacred? And could morality continue there? MacIntyre's reply, I take it, would be that, in a sense, there could (for this "society" of ours is it), and morality could not survive therein, except as propaganda.[14]

Pride in craftsmanship and love of ancient things are not dead, according to Clark, hence he thinks there is more hope for us in the West than MacIntyre is willing to admit:

> Consolingly, we can remember that every age has thought ill of its successor, that it is the standing temptation of conservative thinkers to mistake new covenants for mere betrayals—as it is of radical thinkers to mistake mere betrayals for revolutionary insights.[15]

This is Clarkian moderation at its best.

Communities that know no other way than their own tend to change slowly, and do so very often under the impetus of persecuted geniuses or heretics. When traditional societies meet, however, the pace of change accelerates, a pace that makes it extremely difficult for some to take tradition seriously. Clark understands this difficulty, in fact he understands it so well that he is skeptical of Hume's own skeptical (foot-dragging) conventionalism:

> Once we have realized how far traditions differ, it is difficult to retain an un-self-conscious devotion to our own. We must do so in the knowledge that we would have been as devoted to the alien values were it not for historical accident.[16]

This is not relativism on Clark's part, in that he is not defending the claim that each tradition has its own validity or truth that cannot be improved on, nor is it liberalism, in that he is not claiming that the truth is best explored by variant cultures and a diversity of morals. Rather, by realizing that different societies contain different roles, we are better able, on neo-Aristotelian grounds, to appreciate the distinctive contribution we can make to our own community by performing our own roles well. It is precisely this appreciation that gives Clark hope:

> If we are to retrieve anything like the pre-modern understanding of life, it must be through the revitalization of local communities within which human beings may find authentic social lives. In the society of strangers and the war of all against all we shall soon find that morality no longer even has a propaganda value—the secret is out.[17]

The project of the enlightenment, he thinks, of establishing morality on the dictates of universal reason, has failed, as might be thought by some conservatives to be indicated in the thought of, say, G. E. Moore. Yet Moore is not necessarily Clark's enemy in his attempt to elucidate the moral basis of politics. Moore is more like Aristotle than many suppose, because the latter, like the former, held that both ethical and logical truisms must be simply seen to be true, they exist for their own sakes. Or better, whereas Moore's naturalistic fallacy might initially seem to be a significant challenge to the sort of ethologized politics Clark is defending, it is really an example of a contemporary Platonism that in some ways Clark finds compatible:

> When Plato's Socrates inquires what knowledge, justice, piety, courage or the like may be, his interlocutor often retorts by offering examples of acts or persons that have these properties. . . . To know what it is to be *X* is different from knowing what things are *X* or display the property of being *X*. Being *X* and "having" or "participating in" *X* are not the same. Plato's (or Socrates') discovery was that whenever there is something intelligible to be said of the form "*a* is *X* and *b* is *X* and *a* is not *b*," there is something (*X*) which neither *a* nor *b* strictly and identically *is*. . . . It was with the nature of the things named by the terms for which "*X*" is a dummy that he was concerned. . . . But most of the forms with which Plato was concerned could be defined. . . . Justice, for example . . . but what Good itself may be cannot be resolved into any more primitive ideas. Good lies even beyond Being. . . . We cannot understand what it is to be Good by resolving it into other ideas, for we could not understand those ideas without a prior grasp of (or at least a gesture towards) Good.[18]

Those things that are manifestly impediments to ordinary human lives are bad, and the reverse (like food) are good. However, an intuitional view of *the* good does not commit Moore (or Clark) to the view that there are self-evident principles regarding what *actions* ought to be performed. In fact, Clark thinks that Bloomsbury itself was an example of a (countercultural) civil community meant to save its members from the barbarians.[19]

In order to inspire confidence in current civic life, which Clark thinks MacIntyre fails to do, one must avoid at least one understandable response to deracination: Humean abandonment of any expectation to find truth or justice. This abandonment is defective largely because it is a self-fulfilling prophecy. MacIntyre is closer to Hume than he thinks he is, for merely *waiting* for a new St. Benedict furthers the process of deracination such that it may well be that instead of a new St. Benedict a new Hitler will turn up instead. For whom does MacIntyre write, if not some group of people other than a mere society of strangers? Clark sees around him, as did the American pragmatists, widespread concern for truth and decent argument, even if it is a mark of high moral seriousness in some quarters to "denounce contemporary society for its lack of high moral seriousness."[20] That is, Clark's political views are integrally connected to his moral realism (i.e., to his Platonism or Aristotelianism): "Obligations that are wholly self-created do not oblige: 'meanings to life' that are arbitrary imaginings do not shield us from the thought that nothing matters in the end."[21] It is deracinated (one of Clark's favorite words; note the organic metaphor at work here) intellectuals who are part of the problem in contemporary society because they are *professional* strangers. These intellectuals are correct that any society with a rightful claim to our allegiance must allow us scope to see beyond the norms it sets for us, but they fail to see that the best efforts at detachment from particularity are accomplished by those who have a glimpse of eternity, by those who have some sense of how time-bound, parochial (in the pejorative sense of the term), and merely analogical our moral and political concepts are.[22]

One of Clark's (not MacIntyre's) criticisms of liberalism of the Rawlsian variety is that it leads to a denigration of animals because members of animal species cannot sign contracts; but neither can children or the mentally defective (MS, 16). In effect, when Clark talks of "community" he is not assuming that these beings are inferior members:

> The need for language as a medium for effective compact-making has been much exaggerated: common sympathies and purposes, mutual attractions and puzzlements are quite enough to provide a mutual sense of fair dealing at least with our most immediate, mammalian kin. . . . Just-so stories about the once-

upon-a-time contract between man and beast are doubtless merely stories; but so
are stories about primitive contracts between man and man. . . . We were social
before we were human, and each of us is born into a pre-existent society. (MS, 34)

(In order to be consistent I think Clark should say we were *communal* before we
were human.) Moral rationalists, Clark thinks, are mistaken both in methodological principle and in practical detail: "That man is a political animal is a
truth that goes deeper than rationalists imagine: political society is not a distortion of our underlying nature, but that very nature itself."[23] This truth goes so
deep that it touches even the animals. Despite disclaimers made by social contract theorists, Rawlsian theory is a fiction, according to Clark, bad fiction at
that because behind the veil of ignorance, with only a "thin theory" of good to
work on, Rawlsian individuals lack the depth and complexity that may be found
in characters in good fiction.[24] (Rawls himself, however, is willing to admit that
the original position is a device of representation not completely unlike a play.)

Clark is like Vico in thinking that philosophers have been deluded into
thinking that there is something complete in the geometric method, say, as
applied to morality and politics. Or better, he is like Aristotle in thinking that
future citizens are best trained not through a geometric method but through
imitation of good models and through habituation. Yet the Aristotelian view,
lacking any close connection to the geometric method, is assumed by some to be
therefore anti-intellectual:

This view of moral and practical judgment is so far unfamiliar to mainstream
moral philosophers that they often mistake its expression for a mere lack of principle. There is a seductive charm about the idea that we could solve our moral
crises by arguing from first principles, whether they be utilitarian or Kantian.[25]

The false completeness found in arguing from moral first principles is evidenced in the smugness of dominant groups who each think that *their* system of
law is transvaluational:

Thus: Albert, an honest mink-farmer, believes himself entitled under the law to
keep and slaughter minks, while Belle, a radical zoophile, believes herself entitled to rescue her imprisoned kin. . . . None but Albert (and not even he on every
issue) is likely to view the High Courts of Parliament as spokesmen for their
moral community. . . . Respect for individual liberties under the rule of law is

not the product of abstract argument (for no such arguments work), but of a historically grounded sense of mutual respect.[26]

Rationalist politics is thus (and here Clark agrees with MacIntyre) incorrect in assuming that we can easily distinguish between "natural" and "conventional" political ideas, that this distinction will be Newtonian in its supposed absoluteness, and that we need this axiomatizable distinction in order to be able to criticize various conventions: "A rationally acceptable moral *gestalt* . . . need not be an axiomatizable set of moral rules."[27]

A critique of political abstractions is crucial, according to Clark, if only because political atrocities, as well as atrocities in animal laboratories, depend on treating the "enemy" as an abstraction, rather than as a concrete, sentient individual.[28] Or again, abstraction in logic or mathematics is a good thing because what follows from true premises must itself be true. Regarding political questions, however, it is not necessarily the case that what follows from true premises must be true. It is true, for example, that an increase in learning is a good thing, and it is also true that experimenting destructively on orphan children will increase learning, but it is *not* true that performing such experiments would be a good thing. At times Clark is even willing to claim that it is easier to swing one's opinions on great abstract metaphysical questions than it is to do so on questions regarding concrete values, as in the values found in the aforementioned orphan children. There are prodigies in mathematics precisely because this discipline is, in some respects, extraordinarily simple (because abstract) in comparison with political philosophy. The difficulty in political matters is to make sure that at the concrete level of decision making and acting, where the issues are likely to be most difficult and where emotions are likely to run most high, we do not abandon rationality for the sake of the *argumentum ad hominem* or for the sake of sheer power-play.[29]

TRADITION, AGAIN

Tradition is Clark's usual guide in politics: the tradition of our animality, of our religion, and of our own personal lives. Regarding the latter, Clark allows ontogeny to recapitulate phylogeny in the sense that younger individuals, who have yet done little with their lives, do not have identities or opinions as secure as older ones. Clark's conservatism on this point is visceral, in contrast, say, to Thoreau's instinctive romantic sense, evidenced in *Walden*, that the "experience" of the mature is a ruse for worn out ideals, such that wisdom is more likely to be found in the freshness of youth. That is, Clark does not seem to be convinced that the child is, as Wordsworth has it, the "best philosopher." Nonetheless, Clark is aware of the fact that the stories that we tell, or those that are told to us, over the years may be accepted unquestioningly without our noticing contradictions setting in. Why do we generally think that terrorists who kill children are evil whereas targeting civilian neighborhoods with bombs is permissible, if not commendable?[30] Sometimes youthful minds (of any age) are needed to point out such contradictions. Perhaps this was Wordsworth's or Thoreau's point.

In any event, the intellectual life is only marginally connected with the acquisition of wisdom, according to Clark. The usefulness of intellectual systems, he thinks, lies in their being machines that generate imaginable strategies *to supplement*, rather than generate, practical wisdom. For example, Clark thinks that both Kantianism (which he sometimes refers to as libertarianism, a misleading designation when it is considered that he refers to his own view as libertarianism) and utilitarianism are useful systems, *as long as* they are seen as ancillary:

> Historically libertarians have restricted the class of rights-holders to the human species, and utilitarians have generally allowed much greater weight to the moral claims of sentients. But there seems no good reason why libertarian principle could not be extended; and it is unfortunately true that utilitarians need not, in practice, allow sentients so much moral weight as to stand in the way of anything we want to do.[31]

When used not as tools, however, any abstract intellectual apparatus (say, the "duty to universal happiness") can be destructive of our primary duties to family, friends, and fellow citizens (to the extent that the latter are friends).

It is debatable whether Clark has really faced up to the hard cases that confront his view of politics. For example, it has historically been the universal rights of man or the universal brotherhood-sisterhood of humanity (i.e., Enlightenment ideals) that have liberated blacks and women from slavery and near slavery, respectively. Could blacks and women have been treated fairly relying solely on Clark's traditionalist grounds, say, by invoking Book Five of Plato's *Republic* so as to show that the equality of women is compatible both with natural inclination and time-honored tradition? We cannot know if such a method *could* have worked without Enlightenment notions of individuality and of rights. What can be certain is that traditionalist methods did not, in fact, liberate blacks, women, and others from mistreatment. However Clark at least sometimes faces squarely some rather difficult challenges to his theory. Consider the following example: how should we react when two British girls are sent back to Yemen against their wills for forced marriages? Clark's response to this question is coy because he *almost* follows through, however counterintuitively, on what a consistent application of his antiuniversalism would dictate. He says that

it is only the deracinated West that ever imagined that mere individuals were sovereign over "their" own lives. . . . Is it not more reasonable, or as reasonable, to think of family lines, or tribes, as sovereign over the short lives that compose them? . . . It is necessary no doubt to emphasize that this is not my view. My point is merely that neither utilitarian nor libertarian doctrine, as long as they attempt to be genuinely abstract, unhistorical or value-free, can really answer the case. . . . Asking what abstract individuals "behind a veil of ignorance" would have chosen, is vacuous: such intelligences could actually choose nothing.[32]

Clark thinks that neither liberal universalism nor antiliberalism can offer a sound answer to the question as to how we should react to the Yemeni case, but this case does help us to understand the presuppositions behind these two different responses: liberal indignation at the treatment of these girls and the traditionalist claim that this is a family matter. If I understand Clark correctly, he wavers between these two views, a wavering that at least indicates that Clark is willing to associate with liberal views when it becomes extremely embarrassing not to do so.[33]

It is odd that Clark's inability to deliver a clear message regarding the Yemeni case does not bother him as a pragmatist, but his retort would seem to be the Aristotelian one that anyone who really needs an argument to act morally cannot be too moral in the first place. People habituated to lead good lives do the best possible in difficult situations such as this one. That is, theoretical inadequacy does not always bother Clark:

But the truth is that this is simply a feature of the human intellectual condition. The principles that explain why simple mathematical or physical facts are as they are will themselves be less immediately convincing than those facts. . . . It is very rare to find in any area of life, that there are simple, incontrovertible principles from which we could systematically deduce all lesser truths. It does not follow that it is pointless to try to systematize our knowledge, check our observations and our theories against each other. . . . The aim is to explore the might-have-beens, the yet-might-bes, of human life. Those who seriously attempt the task must end by being fiercer with themselves, gentler with others. . . . The Forms, the patterns of ideal activity and character, are the lineaments of the divine intellect, and true philosophy is the inevitably incomplete attempt to think like God, or (better) to submit our thought and action to the rigours of objective truth.[34]

The critique of abstract reasoning in "morality and politics" (something of a redundancy in Clark) that Clark offers is not really a denigration of reason in general. Rather, there is a Vico-like strain in Clark such that even in science we believe realism to be correct because *we participate in* scientific practices. The very diversity of human goals makes it necessary to devise ways of settling disputes—through the use of *practical* reason—and assigning responsibilities so that the community can survive.[35]

CONCLUSION

In conclusion, in this chapter one can see both the considerable strengths and some of the weaknesses in Clark's political philosophy. The strengths include his ethological, Aristotelian reminder that we were communal before we were human, such that there is no need to construct a social contract out of supposedly self-interested or selfish human nature. As he aptly puts the point, people with whom we are acquainted are generally not purely pleasure-seeking atomies. Clark is correct to encourage philosophers to try to offer rational defenses of *existing* communities and to try to revitalize local communities and families (in their various forms) when they start to crumble. These encouragements are part of Clark's quite legitimate critique of universalism and they are connected to his claim that the state exists for the sake of family and friendship and not the other way around. That is, Clark's political philosophy attacks current dogma in politics not from the left or right (hence it is only with qualification that one can call Clark a conservative) but from below (or better, from above), from the perspectives of premodern, theistic wisdom and from modern ethology. In effect, Clark is claiming, rightly I think, that from the historically conditioned nature of particular religions one cannot infer that there are no transhistorical goals higher than political ones.

Clark's view is that ethics starts, but neither it nor morality ends, with friends and relations. There is also a sense in which our rituals have an Orphic quality through which religious and political reality is brought into being, but *in the end* he is correct in suggesting that there has to be some sort of objective ground for moral values for even liberalism to make sense, for without such objectivity liberals could always be wrong about liberalism. Further, without some sort of objective basis for moral values it is unclear how contemporary liberals (as opposed to noninterventionist, classical ones) can justify the power they wish rulers to have over educational practices and regarding life-and-death issues. By focusing our attention on the ultimate goals of political activity, Clark provides a service for our frenetic age by calling into question the widely shared assumption that the active life is superior to the contemplative (or at least theoretical) one. There needs to be *some* sort of reintroduction of religion into politics, Clark thinks, or else we will likely decline and fall as a civilization, for no civilization can long last with only a thin theory of the good at its core. At the very least, no civilization has been able to do so thus far, as Toynbee attests.

There are also problems, however, with Clark's political views. For example, even if we grant that we cannot do moral philosophy well by determining in the abstract how we should behave on the advice of some "geometrized" formula, but rather should look at what a truly good person would do in a particular and concrete situation, still we must have some theoretical principles to guide us in the effort to keep our religious, political, and scientific traditions alive. Nowhere is the need for consistent theorizing more evident than in Clark's approach to market capitalism. As we have seen, he wavers between anarchocapitalism and theocracy. Yet capitalism has historically been built on a self-interested, philosophical anthropology, if not a selfish one, as can be seen in Adam Smith,[36] an anthropology that is in direct opposition, it seems, to Clark's communitarianism. Which force at work in the Western world, if not capitalism, is the most destructive of tradition? Perhaps we are to assume that Clark, along with Smith and the Stoics, thinks that an invisible hand is at work in the universe whereby self-interested individuals unwittingly constitute community without intending to do so. If so, Clark should make this view explicit.

There is a similar tension found in Clark's view of interiority. On the one hand, he encourages interiority for various reasons: it is often associated with either the contemplative life or charismatic religion; it helps to combat behaviorism; and it is compatible with—even if it is different from—capitalist self-interest. On the other hand, there is a tendency in Clark (say, in his response to

Feyerabend) to discourage interiority and individuality, or at least to value them only to the extent that they are conducive to community. Perhaps interiority is in fact conducive to community, but without theoretical explication it seems that the transition from interiority to community is performed, once again, by an inchoate invisible hand.

It is also somewhat unclear what, in the final analysis, Clark's attitude toward liberalism is. Usually he criticizes contemporary liberalism either from the perspective of his premodernism or from the perspective of his own classical (anarcho-capitalist) liberalism. In addition to the problem of reconciling Clark's Aristotelianism with his classical liberalism, there is also the problem of reconciling Clark's criticisms of contemporary liberalism with his own capitulations to this position, as in his defense of a maximal liberty of conscience compatible with the liberty of all, and as in his ambivalence regarding the case of the Yemeni girls. One is tempted to say that even Clark, along with the rest of us, is a contemporary liberal when he needs to be one. Further, when Clark wavers between liberal democracy and some sort of scholastic oligarchy, he leaves us wondering whether he really leans toward the former (in which case his criticisms of liberalism in all its forms are watered down) or, what is more likely, toward the latter (in which case one wonders about the precise nature of the new scholasticism he has in mind and about the ways in which it will be different from the neomonasticism for which MacIntyre hopes under a new St. Benedict).

Or again, there is an unresolved tension in Clark between his anarchism, which would seem to militate against nationalism, and his patriotic defense of the just war theory and of something to die for. Clark's attempt to bridge the gap between his anarchism and his nationalism by floating the hypothesis that national leaders can be obeyed if they are seen not so much as political officers as *natural* authorities is not likely to be found convincing by most readers.

In short, there are many questions left in Clark's political philosophy, some of which we will explore in the final two chapters of this book regarding the relative strengths *and* weaknesses of particularism and regarding the weight to be placed on individuals (especially the sufferings of individuals, including animal individuals) as opposed to the state or the World Soul.

The *tenor* of Clark's writings on politics, however, is decidedly traditionalist, such that he supports Kipling's principled opposition to democracy and to participation in government through what both of them see as a merely symbolic vote. (At times he also, like Kipling, supports political empires—at least the British one—and at other times he denigrates supranationalism or imperialism. In this latter mode he thinks that peace comes about through a network of—admittedly accidental—nation states.) Both Clark and Kipling believe that, although good education is more important than good breeding, the latter nonetheless counts for something as a criterion for political leadership. That is, those with both good breeding and education know that there are some practices that just *are* wrong, regardless of what most people think, just as there are some sorts of arguments that are fallacious, regardless of how most think or vote about them. Logic, and not only bias—Clark often admits in a Newman-like way his biases—lends support to his traditionalism or conservatism.[37]

CHAPTER 8

SOCIAL CONTRACT AND UTILITARIANISM

INTRODUCTION

In the previous chapter a distinction was made between classical and contemporary liberalism. We saw that Clark sometimes, but not always, agrees with the former, for example at those points when he treats favorably anarcho-capitalism, as opposed to those points when he treats favorably theocracy. However he is almost always critical of contemporary liberalism, whether it appears in the guise of social contract theory (as in Rawls) or in the guise of utilitarianism (as in Singer or Frey). In this chapter I will examine in detail Clark's criticisms of both social contract theory and utilitarianism, and I will prepare the way for the final chapter of the book by examining what the implications for human politics are, to believe, as Clark does, that this is God's world.

FANTASY

There never were any truly solitary hominids in our ancestral stock, and this because we are animals. Even among *theria*, or carnivorous wild beasts, mothers die for their young:

> Hardly anyone could ever seriously have thought that human beings were ever
> rootless solitaries, strangers who must make external, heavily policed agreements

if they sought "friends" or allies. Modern society, or modern society as seen by the most influential political theorists, may be, as MacIntyre suggests, a "society of strangers," but that is not where we started.[1]

As we have seen, however, Clark does not move too quickly from the natural desire for community to a justification of the state, in that such a justification usually is offered as some type of antidote to the supposed nasty, brutish, and short character of "natural" human existence. For Clark, the polis as a communal form is best seen as a peaceful network of clubs and fraternities, friends and acquaintances. This peace is not at all derived from a struggle against what some political theorists take to be our primitive animality. There are some critics, however, who think that whereas Clark does serious damage to current political orthodoxies, his own political thought is suspect at least partially because it sweeps across the whole spectrum from ethological realism to utopian fantasy.[2] Wishing for either the dismantling of the state or the rise of theocracy is a bit like "wishing there were unicorns," as the title to one of Clark's essays has it.

Clark is not bothered by the charge that he fantasizes: "It is the non-existent that we wish were real, but real, if that were possible, in its very non-existence."[3] A ghost that really existed would be yet another pest to deal with. The whole point to postulating possible worlds is to capture the sense that things *could* be different from the way they are now; we need not have a state that has hegemony over para-political community and we need not totally divorce religion from politics. The "real being" of unicorns consists in their intangibility. That is, there is an extreme type of political realism (more extreme, say, than Clark's modified ethologized realism) that deserves rebuke because it tries to make the world far more boring than it really is. Clark wonders why we would think that automobiles are more alive than centaurs, fairies, or political utopias:

> Or in Chesterton's words: "folk-lore means that the soul is sane, but that the universe is wild and full of marvels. Realism means that the world is dull and full of routine, but that the soul is sick and screaming."[4]

It nonetheless seems as if Clark has gone too far in defending the world of fantasy. Does even he *really* believe (on the most telling pragmatic criteria) that the world of fantasy is no more "made-up" than the world of science, as he sometimes alleges? For example, if Clark's child were terribly sick would he seriously consider taking the child to a witch or a warlock rather than to a physician? I think not. His real target is not so much "science" as "scientism," for, as he admits, "Scientific theory is our best bet yet for an account of how things work." Put another way, Clark's attack is not so much on science as it is on the commodification often associated with contemporary science:

> The merely "objective universe" is as fictional a world as any, a way of emptying the world of its once-given significance in order to possess it more perfectly. The trees that once housed dryads are now ripe for felling; the lands that embodied stories are to be remade; living animals are but "matter in motion," and even human flesh has lost its sacredness.[5]

One of the reasons why Clark thinks it legitimate to balance his ethologized political realism with at least a certain degree of political fantasy is that even the practical (realistic) world we live in day to day is at least partially fictional:

> It is not that we first see horses and then invent unicorns: the things we see are *horses* from the same stable as the unicorn. Our children do not learn to speak of "bears" by encountering them: they learn of bears by playing bears.[6]

Literalism in language, in general, and in political language, in particular, is a historical achievement rather than an original condition. It must be admitted that the magician's or the demagogue's dream of altering reality by playing with words remains a dream, yet it is nonetheless true that the world we inhabit is far wider than materialists or positivistic political scientists suppose. For example, the very possibility of telling the truth in politics is parasitic on the possibility of lies, fictions, or fantasies. The fact that human beings have for so long (although perhaps without sufficient evidence) denied animals speech is largely due to the fact that animals cannot lie or fantasize (although it is clear that they can pretend). Yet not even fantasy is wholly made up, in that there is, as fantasy writers such as Tolkien have attested, even in the fantasy-writer's craft an element of recording what was already there.

SOCIAL CONTRACT

It should be remembered that Clark's criticism of social contract theory is not so much that it is a piece of fiction as that it is bad fiction, because the relevant parties are but shadows of real historical, tradition-laden human beings. Further, he thinks, the individuals fantasized in social contract theory are assumed to be rational, hence there is a tendency not only to see animals but also children as marginal on the basis of this theory. If one beats the baby, he alleges, one is not *necessarily* violating the interests of anyone in the Rawlsian original position. Perhaps Rawls and others would, even as mutually disinterested persons in the original position, *choose* to protect marginal people and animals, but there is no reason why they would have to do so. We can at least imagine a group of rational (mutually disinterested) individuals who would not protect the marginal cases:

> We may have a real, voluntary compact to be nice to the "marginal people," but we cannot complain if others do not make this bargain any more than we can complain if others do not share our sentimental attachment to wildflowers. We would not hire such people as our baby-sitters, no doubt, any more than we would hire someone who hated flowers as a florist or a park-keeper.[7]

It is by no means clear that all rational human beings would, in the original position, choose a hedonic rather than an agonistic mode of control over animals and over marginal cases of humanity. In fact, Clark thinks that the Stoics may well have been more consistent than most contemporary defenders of social contract theory, because they did in fact deny respect to animals and to marginal cases:

> I am therefore within an ancient tradition in suggesting that we might profitably turn current political theory on its head. The relationship with children is not a marginal one, and children are not marginal cases. They are what the civil community is for, and the bond of parental care is the beginning of society.[8]

(Again, for the sake of consistency, Clark should say "community" rather than "society" at the end of this quotation.) Civil law is only a reminder that we should not murder family members or friends; it is not *because* of civil law that we should so restrain ourselves. For example, the bond between mother and child, as we have seen, is so thoroughly natural that some neglect to give moral credit to the unfortunate woman who must raise her children alone. This natural bond forces us to consider seriously the Clarkian claim that: "Instead of thinking of our young as marginal to the real interests and concerns and habitual practices of adult society, it is worth noticing the extent to which the rest of our society is centred on the needs and delights of the young."[9] Civil communities are really extensions of the relationships we have with the young, the old, and the marginal. That is, political community, if there is such, arises out of the (Aristotelian) habits of care and affection. There is nothing intrinsically rational about adult self-interest, nor anything intrinsically irrational about altruism. Or, more precisely, according to Clark, social contract theory is not so much modeled on adult self-interest as it is on that of young adults or adolescents who have not yet assumed responsibility for other members of their respective families. Clark's view is that it is these adolescents who are the truly marginal members of a particular human community, just as the young male baboons are on the fringes of a baboon troop.

It is odd that the view of children as having rights only in a marginal way ever became popular: child murderers are hated even by violent criminals. Parental (and eventually political) authority derives from parental duty, not the other way around, hence the good community is not one that rational beings could have chosen from ahistorical, uncultured ignorance, in that it is a community that has been in the refining process for thousands or millions of years. The following extended quotation sums up well Clark's view, with his reference to "over all the world" providing a clue as to how he would try to combat the charge of being a naive particularist or nativist:

> By making the adult-child relationship the central social form, and relegating the supposedly free adolescent to the outskirts, I may seem to be committing the same error of taste and manners as some marriage counsellors, who make it appear that the unmarried are the unsaved. . . . But responsibility . . . comes in many forms. What is central to my claim is the notion that we have the rights we need to meet our responsibilities, and that those responsibilities include securing those same rights for others. . . . Even the wholly childless can and often do occupy important slots in society. . . . Children . . . freedom . . . for them is not the adolescent departure to the edge of things, but the promise that their hopes and fears will play a part in determining social order. . . . Eminently sane people, after all, can make the real, self-moving, and attentive child their pattern. . . . There are no abstract individuals to "contract in.". . . What there is is the network of familial and friendly relationships over all the world, from which irresponsible adolescents may on occasion temporarily "contract out." The risk we presently run is that too many such adolescents and their functional equivalents will fail to regain responsibilities. . . . In denying them the right of responsible

authority, we make them outlaws or untimely dependents. In paradoxically insisting that such deracinated unfortunates are the "real" human beings, we neglect our real situation, as well as the innovatory, conciliatory, maddening, and controlling presences of our children.[10]

At times Clark plays fast and loose with the problem of the one and the many. His view seems to be that there is but one human nature that we inherit from the animals, yet there are various cultures, political systems, and religions that Clark doubts can be reduced to a single culture, political system, or religion. For example, he compares each religion to a ship on the sea of chaos:

> Perhaps the very attempts to throw away unnecessary trimmings, or to tack on the jetsam of another ship, will be what brings the failed ships down. If that be so, and we have reason to suspect it, no amount of flattery or abuse should make us fiddle with our seaworthy ship. Such an insistent conservativism would rather be neither elitist nor inhuman, but our one security.[11]

When it is considered that for Clark our religion largely determines our politics, we can see that the question as to whether there is, or ought to be, one world religion is not a small matter in politics. A religious order differs from a merely military or political one because membership in it comes by way of self-identification, such that a world state without a world religion would be imperial rule only. The appeal to a universal core of human reason made by some in the West is much like an appeal to a universal religion. Likewise, in politics,

> Post-Christian humanists suppose that we would all agree (if only we were sensible) that every human being is a uniquely valuable individual to be accorded liberty and welfare-rights so as to cooperate in the progressive enterprise of deifying Humanity. . . . Oddly enough the "essential core" of all religions, and the core of such modern cults as have been contrived as candidates for global acceptance, always turn out to be cautiously expressed versions of the speaker's own personal or ancestral creed.[12]

According to Clark, liberalism does not necessarily protect cultural diversity; in fact, it is often destructive of such diversity.

It is doubtful, according to Clark, if we can identify an essential core for all religions or political states. One reason for such doubt is that Christians,

Marxists, liberals, and fascists alike are extremely unimaginative in assessing what other people might think:

> In some societies vultures count far more than visiting anthropologists; in others the important individuals are families; in very many wisdom comes through pain. We help no-one by pretending that the UN Declaration [of rights] was anything but a piece of middle-class Western ideology adopted for want of anything better by people who openly interpret it in ways its authors disavowed. . . . So can we turn aside from the Kantian or quasi-Kantian dream of a rationally ordered vessel that could suit us all?[13]

(It seems that Clark answers this question in the affirmative.) It is possible to have a religion or a state which is *available* to all, to have a literally catholic religion or state (*kat'holou*) at least in aspiration. However *this* sort of universalism usually is cut short when it is realized that Bible Belt fundamentalists (to pick one example among many) are not interested in "Catholicism," just as Catholics are not interested in them. As Clark puts the point,

> Everyone can be ethnic except rednecks. Everyone is right except those on the right.[14]

Might there be, however, good reason to suspect "redneck" ethnicity or any other right-wing nativism, especially because it is likely to lead to (or at least tolerate) racism, at a minimum, if not fascism? Is it not the case that there is something more than bad manners in even the most abstract defense of a political philosophy that arises from the soil when such a philosophy is by its nature divisive? Think of Heidegger's rather ethereal and deceptive version of Nazism or of Gadamer's rather conservative surprise that anyone could be bothered by Heidegger's Nazism.[15] That is, some of the most appalling events in human history have been done in the name of ethnicity and local pride, hence Clark would do well to distance himself as much as possible from those events.

I am decidedly not trying to slip in the suggestion that Clark leans in the direction of fascism, but I am claiming that because there are some notable philosophers who have either been outright fascists or fascist sympathizers/apologists he would do well to be a bit more careful when claiming that liberal universalism offers only a pretense of toleration and that the gains of the Enlightenment ought to be called into question. Clark sometimes exhibits the sort of distancing from right-wing extremities that I have in mind. For exam-ple, in the effort to rhetorically defend some particular religion or national faith, one is likely to find a sharp distinction made between faith-oriented and reason-oriented creeds, so as to glorify the former, a distinction that Clark quite rightly calls into question.[16] Clark's synthesis of faith and reason is one that entails a (Gadamerian) critique of the prejudice against prejudice (or against faith). That is, attachment to one's native place or religion is never a matter where one can entirely avoid certain intellectual commitments that are at least initially accepted without rational justification; they are accepted on faith.

Like Aristotle, Clark believes that a society founded on continual revolution should not be expected to survive. A universal religion or state, he thinks, is nec-essarily tied to a sort of neophilia, if not continual revolution, in that the pasts of particular religions or peoples would have to be forgotten in order to pledge one's allegiance to the universal. Although Clark does not think that there is a single axiomatizable system to encapsulate necessary religious truth, if there were it is not immediately clear that it would be a Christian one (contra Toynbee), even if Clark does think that it eventually would have to be Christian:

> There is certainly a case for saying that Buddhism is better suited to global authority than Abrahamic religions, which are crucially and indissolubly linked to the actual histories of Abraham, Israel, Jesus, and Mohammed. . . . Abrahamic scriptures are a closed canon; originative experience is normative.[17]

If there is a possibility of a global Abrahamic religion, it lies in the belief that the recitation of the Koran or the celebration of the Eucharist are expressions of the *logos*. In something of a credal statement, Clark states:

> My own preference, as may already be obvious, is for a global religion that is parapolitical, decentralized, faith-holding, non-humanist, eternalist, Platonic and historically particular. . . . My own commitment, over and above anything I can devise by way of rational argument, is to the body of Christ. The world and human kind are already unified—eternally—in that particular being, but we shall not be unified in time until there is a global acknowledgment of our single derivation and devotion. . . . Much that pagan naturists, Hindus and Buddhists say is true, holy and of good report. In the absence of a particular incarnation and revelation in the flesh and speech of Israel they would together be the best that humankind could offer. Often enough they can justly rebuke Abrahamists

(of whatever sect) for insincerity, stupidity and sin. But in the last resort there is one ship alone that comes in safe to harbour.[18]

Having his cake and eating it, too, is a familiar practice of Clark's, a practice in evidence here in his concessions to universalism, but concessions rooted in his own prejudice (not in the pejorative sense of the term, he thinks) in favor of Western Christianity.

Thus far in this chapter we have seen Clark's skepticism regarding the likelihood that transcommunity principles can be established on the basis of social contract theory. His principal criticism of this theory, as well as his principal criticism of utilitarianism, is that no such social contract debate is strictly conceivable, because there is no such thing as an abstract individual. We are bound to work within a conservative framework, even if such workings often issue in liberal action: "Indeed my object was to suggest that if we want liberal action at all, we have to rely upon conservative thought" (PS, 1). In a rare turn of speech, Clark defends "a free society" on such a conservative basis, but with the proviso that a free society could never be constituted by a concatenation of strangers because political freedom rests upon *shared* values. If abstract values turn out to be determined by the *weltanschauung* of the dominant group (as in Hume's standpoint of "universal" human nature, which reflects the assumptions of the Hanoverian ruling elite), then (Rawlsian) impartiality is "either a cloak for unconscious prejudice or a condition in which no decisions can any longer be taken" (PS, 5). However, this is where Clark needs to place considerable distance between himself and other critics of the Enlightenment, such as Heidegger. If there are no neutral principles on which Nazis and liberals can agree, then what is to prevent the Nazi (Heidegger) from implying that the Holocaust was no worse than mechanized agriculture and no worse than Allied treatment of East Germans after World War Two?[19] Clark's attempt to establish such a distance is not as strong as I, at least, would like it to be, but it must be admitted that the attempt is in fact there:

Respect for individual liberties under the rule of law is not the product of abstract argument . . . but of a historically grounded sense of mutual respect. . . . Someone who pleads that he is "conscience-bound" to beat children to death or betray his neighbors to the Gestapo is defying what has been unequivocally revealed to the abiding tradition within which our talk of conscience makes sense. (PS, 5–6, 8)

If the idea of "pure intelligences behind a veil of ignorance" is just as much a piece of mythology as the morality by which Antigone acted, as Clark sometimes indicates, then one wonders how human reason could be powerful enough to determine which elements in the Western tradition are "abiding" and which are the perversions. At other times Clark's view seems to be that Western reason, popularly understood, has the upper hand in disputes among ethical systems, because it is more inclusive. Returning to the case of the Yemeni girls treated in the previous chapter, Clark claims that to ask whether they should be loyal Muslim daughters or independent citizens is *already* to identify them as the latter (PS, 9–10). Yet the greater inclusiveness of Western rationality, in contrast to less synoptic points of view, only partially resolves the difficulty:

> Our problem is that we seem to be faced by two alternatives: either we must be able to identify a Newtonian or Archimedean point from which all parties can be judged, or else we are thrown back upon the mere confrontation of ideas and ideals, to be settled by war or by such quieter versions of military confrontation as go under the guise of modern politics. (PS, 11)

That is, although Clark denies that there are any such Archimedean points in our possession, he nonetheless believes, if I understand him correctly, that we can asymptotically approach such points through what I have called in the preface the Popperian method of bold hypothesis and severe criticism (even if Clark himself is not a fan of Popper). This is a method that tries to keep in check our inescapably historical and shifting horizons:

> Not all truths are of our making, nor all conventions either. . . . I recognize a class of truths that are *made* true, "true by convention.". . . I retain the older vision, that there is a real world which can yet enter in to our conscious experience: *nous*, which is the intelligible universe, comes "from outside" into the inquiring mind. (PS, 15–16)

Here Clark the skeptic or anarchist gives way to Clark the neoplatonist.

It might be argued against Clark that by reverting to neoplatonism to help resolve contemporary political issues, he has given up altogether on the preservation of individual rights, because the Greeks lacked any notion of individuality. Yet Clark thinks that the Greeks did have such a notion; in fact, he does not think that there has ever been a human being completely unaware of his or her individuality. Biology is helpful here:

> Biologists can point out that things which we habitually regard as unitary systems are better conceived as aggregations of smaller units: what looks like (and, in a sense, certainly is) a swarm of fish or flock of birds may not really be managed by any unitary purpose shared among the individuals. (PS, 18–19)

If the ancient Greeks, or other pre-Renaissance peoples, appear like a swarm of fish to us, Clark is suggesting, then perhaps we should look a little closer at individual Greeks (think of Socrates, Alcibiades, Plotinus, Cicero, Sappho, etc.). Generally speaking, the more intellectual the species, the more highly individuated the members. Herein, however, lies another Clarkian device used to approximate the logos: human beings are both individuated *and* social all around the world and in every era:

> Crudely, table manners differ—but all human kinds have table manners; marital arrangements differ—but all human kinds have marriages, and also have adulteries; even the topography of the soul may differ, but we can all recognize ourselves even in what seem to us, whoever we are, distorted mirrors. (PS, 20–21)

We cannot map the experience of another people (or species) onto our own, but we can translate from one culture (or species) to another:

> So it is not only those "we" classify as human who are overwhelmingly likely to be non-alien. No familiar animal is beyond our empathy: an aphorism which hovers between the biologistic and the a priori. If there were things that were wholly alien we could not even begin to think of what they were; if they are the products of the same sort of evolution as ourselves they could not be wholly alien. (PS, 22–23)

Really alien worlds are described not by anthropologists or ethologists, but (if at all) by science fiction writers:

> What we are groping for is a convincing picture of the Shadow, the Self that we are not, in order that we may find out what we are, or hope to be. The same

function, as Said has pointed out, was (and is) performed by Western images of the "Orient." (PS, 24)

One of the features of Clark's thought that reviewers rightly find noteworthy is his ability to articulate already existing Aristotelian friendships with supposedly alien beings like animals (or "Orientals"). Each of us has a personal hierarchy of attachment, with real concern being possible even for beings on the bottom rungs of that hierarchy. These reviewers, however, especially John Benson,[20] sometimes claim that once Clark has legitimately pointed out the possibility of true community on the basis of experiences we share he should not counter the exaggerations of defenders of other views by exaggerations of his own. Yet, this charge seems unfair. Clark is extremely careful *not* to exaggerate the importance of friendships or of communities beyond the bounds of those we have with those we live with and share space or interests with; he does not even exaggerate our friendships with animals, even if speciesists may tend to think of him as an extreme animal "rightist":

> In the absence of an agreed international law, agreed between *all* the nations of the earth, we should perhaps attend to the regulation of our own immediate households and not seek to actualize our conception of animal rights throughout the world. Just as Burke preferred the rights of Englishmen to the rights of men just as such, so we may maintain and seek to extend the rights of, as it were, British beasts. . . . In short, wild things are like Nozick's independents, who have hired no protection agency.[21]

Onora O'Neill is one of the few commentators who emphasize what is crucial in Clark's approach to animals, but not even she drives home the point that this feature of Clark's thought is just as important in his approach to politics:

> Clark takes neither reason nor sentience alone as the basis for moral concern for animals. Rather he holds that animals are our kin whom we cannot decently treat in ways that are currently practised. The claim of kinship is not merely a reference to evolutionary connections. Kinship is revealed in varied family resemblances and (the possibility of) shared lives. . . . The relationship between farmers and circus trainers and "their" animals is one of caring *and* exploitation. To find cases without any trace of exploitation we have to go either to the lives of the saints or to the situation of family pets. . . . Clark . . . believes that human

beings can become sufficiently embracing in their affections to include all living beings and perhaps even the rocks and landscapes and larger realms of the biosphere.[22]

Note that O'Neill interprets Clark as leaping from a strong kinship to friends and family members to a somewhat lesser friendship with animals to a greatly diminished friendship with the biosphere without ever trying to place our friendship with compatriot human beings into this relative hierarchy. She does notice, however, that Clark's favorite example of an appropriate relationship between humans and other animals is that of human and cat rather than that of human and dog: a relationship of mutual respect and noninterference rather than one of domination. The analogy with Clark's political philosophy should be rather straightforward: although he does not see the "human political community" as a terribly helpful phrase, he nonetheless refuses to treat other human beings "like dogs," that is, like obsequious inferiors.[23] To be precise, Clark's principle of noninterference in the affairs of others (and this based on his view that our friendship with abstractions like "fellow Americans" is attenuated, to say the least) can be stated in more positive terms: it is wrong to be the cause of avoidable ill.[24]

UTILITARIANISM

To get a stronger moral vision of politics than the minimalist one offered by Clark would take more than abstract argument, he thinks: "To change a moral vision all the world must be transformed." Or again:

> What I had hated in "modern philosophy" was the conceit that "we philosophers" could sensibly debate and settle issues that had engrossed our moral and intellectual betters, without stepping outside the narrow confines of fashionable, academic philosophy. . . . In the past I had so disliked the attitude that Stoics (and Thomists) took to non-human animals that I had neglected the real virtues of that tradition—which was, after all, the very tradition of moral and philosophical discourse in which I grounded myself. In *From Athens to Jerusalem* (1984), and now also in *Limits and Renewals* . . . I seek to draw attention to the ancient way, the perennial philosophy that always had the resources for a better and more truthful way with animals and with the biosphere.[25]

Note that Clark does not say "with our fellow citizens." Clark is especially insistent that a communal bond among all people in a state cannot be generated through a utilitarian calculation of pleasure and pain spread throughout the "community" (MS, 22, 48). Our desires and pleasures are not ineluctable facts such that utilitarian theorists can easily make the sorts of computations necessary within their theory to justify the state:

> Not only do they change: they can be changed. . . . The carnivore may feel that he would greatly miss his roasted pig: I can assure him that within a month of his turning vegetarian he will find the stench the odour of decay. . . . The utilitarian calculus is ambiguous between a comparison of abstract pains and pleasures, and a comparison of the pleased or displeasured entities. In the first case, we are asked to quantify via some common unit the pains and pleasures of distinct entities. This is plainly impossible: there can be no direct comparison of the enjoyments or distresses of different creatures even of the same species. . . . Pleasure is subjectively assessed. (MS, 67, 70)

Further, Clark finds it a defect in utilitarian thinking that it cannot, on the one hand, isolate what, exactly, is wrong with the (supposedly) painless killing of an animal or a human being, yet, on the other, it encourages us to create as many beings, human or otherwise, that will give us the highest proportion of pleasure to pain (MS, 74).

Despite the laudable practical achievements of utilitarianism connected to the abolition of slavery, the reform of prisons, and the treatment of animals, Clark thinks that utilitarianism lacks the "moral seriousness" found in the tradition of Aristotle's ethics. Even utilitarian reformers believe, contra the tenets of their own professed theory, that there are some things that we should just not do. That is, utilitarian reformers do not merely aim at a world in which there will be a better pleasure-pain balance:

> Dissatisfaction with the inadequacies of common utilitarian theory may lead us to conclude that there are some pleasures I have no right to demand, and some pains I have no right to be spared. We ought not to take pleasure in another's pain.[26]

Benson supports Clark's criticisms of utilitarianism, and of Singer's utilitarianism in particular, with the following argument, an argument that can apply not only to the need to consider the form of life for which an animal species is adapted, but also the form of political life for which human beings are adapted:

> Singer's error can be traced back to his claim that the possession of interests rests upon the capacity to suffer. If we say that the possession of interests rests also upon the capacity to fulfill autonomous purposes, or to achieve the form of active life to which the species is adapted, which does not seem less intuitively acceptable, then respect for a creature's interests will quite naturally involve refraining from killing it or subjecting it to a life of torpid unconsciousness or happy slavery. The right to life, on this view, is not just the right to be left alive but the right to a certain sort of life, a man's or a cow's. To my mind the case for not eating meat rests more securely on the consideration that your portion of steak is at the cost of some beast's portion of life, than on considerations about painful experiences it may have undergone.[27]

Obviously Benson's view here is somewhat different from Clark's, but both would agree that we care for other members of our own species and for animals not merely because they are sentient, although this is a significant part of the story for Clark, at least, but also because of the close living connections we have with other human beings and animals. The danger in the attempt to eliminate partial affections is that it may eliminate the source of all affection.

Clark would also like to know why we—collectively or individually—should adopt utilitarian arguments if the adoption of these arguments itself does not maximize our happiness (AJ, 97). Virtue, not pleasure, according to Clark's Aristotelian line of reasoning, is the *telos* of action, hence utilitarian thought over the last three centuries has (again, despite its positive practical accomplishments) played a part in the slow erosion of value systems. Utilitarians obviously did not intend to turn human beings into beasts, just as Epicurus did not intend to defend an "epicurean" way of life. Likewise, the great practical benefit of anaesthetics has played a part in our present inability to see that some pain at some times can be good for us, even if not nearly as much of it is as good as Clark's theodicy would dictate. Clark is instructive in pointing us toward the ancient commonplace that the just polis was integrally connected to the practice of moderation (or asceticism, when properly understood in terms of its athletic roots in *askesis*), not to the practice of pleasure maximization and pain minimization. One of the reasons not to despise asceticism is that it makes our political duties to others easier to bear.[28]

Utilitarians like R. G. Frey could agree with Clark's opposition to ethical egoism and with some of his criticisms of rights, whether human or animal. Yet, as before, Clark is bothered by the utilitarian's difficulty in objecting to the killing of those who do not know about their coming deaths and who have no long-term projects:

> I regret the tendency in some recent philosophical writing to eliminate the notion of the Self. Without the Self we have no final defense against an aggregative and totalitarian utilitarianism a lot more simpleminded than Frey's![29]

That is, according to Clark, Frey's utilitarian attack on animal and human rights ultimately leaves both animals and humans unprotected. One of the purposes of this part of the book is to determine the extent to which Clark's ethologized traditionalism in politics leaves human beings in better shape than in utilitarianism and less amenable to exploitation.

Utilitarianism very often leaves us in bad shape because it encourages us to abandon human individuality altogether, even if Clark's own defense of individuality is kept within strict boundaries, as we have seen:

> The ability to identify others as individuals and to recognize oneself as an object in public space is perhaps connected with the sort of upbringing animals receive. Creatures who produce a lot of young, of whom only a few will survive, are unlikely to recognize or care for them, or for anyone else, as individuals. Creatures who have few, slowly maturing offspring can be expected to care for those offspring.[30]

Likewise, in some bird species members form couples because of a lack of available space, whereas in other species

> the problem is dealt with by their ability to recognize each other as individuals and their being bound to marital fidelity. Barbary doves, for example, have been shown to be monogamous, to be faithful to their first partners even at unfamiliar nesting sites.[31]

It is true that human beings are the only truly political animals, the only animals who "so far as we can see, have taken the next step, that of trying to assess their own sentiments in the light of reason," but "Good animals of any kind (including the human) have some grasp of the physical and social worlds in which they live and prefer the paths of friendship and fidelity."[32]

ON THE "DEATH OF GOD"

Clark is convinced that any just political order requires a walking away from the sort of shadow-show described by Plato and an effort to come into contact with that truth that loves to hide itself. Two of the three main epistemological responses to the apparent death of God constitute a refusal to engage in such a walking away. "Scientism," according to Clark, is simply a relapse upon the received doctrines of our own atheistical and self-styled scientific age, whereas "anti-realism" (or "social relativism" or "social idealism") consists of an effort to question the assumptions of any sort of foundationalism. Clark's own response to the alleged death of God is to reaffirm theological utterance, specifically to say that Christian faith itself *is* a type of realist, foundationalist philosophy, such that attempts to turn to antifoundationalists (say, to Wittgenstein or Nietzsche or Heidegger) for theological wisdom are bound to fail. Like Plato, Clark wishes to do philosophy of an exploratory kind wherein one has the courage to follow an argument where it leads, even if absolute consistency must be sacrificed. Clark's argument, as we have seen, is that philosophy begins with a reflection on something with which we are already, and sometimes irretrievably, engaged, that is, the Gospels. We have lost faith not because theism has been refuted, but because an understanding of the Gospels as contributions to sound philosophy and for sound social relations have been abandoned through lack of practice: "practice comes first in any field, though this is not to imply that practice is less problematical than theory" (GW, 18). Or again:

> Those who are seriously troubled by our inability to reason our way to knowledge of "the external world" or of our friends and neighbors are generally best advised to do some household chores, or find a friend. Analogously, the cure for theological hesitation . . . is simply to get on with the religious life. (GW, 19)

With the abandonment of religious practice comes the supposed death of God, with this death comes the cessation of objective obligation, and with *this* death comes political rule that is little more than ideological control. The remedy for this decline, however, consists of more than the reestablishment of religious practice, in that intellectual reasons will be required at least in an ancillary status to "justify" the reestablished practice. As before, as long as there is nothing hegemonic intended in its use, say, in favor of an overly muscular use of reason in the religious life, a careful consideration of the ontological argument makes us aware of the dogmatic character of the Kantian denial of existential necessity.[33] For example, have contemporary unbelievers really refuted the Parmenidean claim that "something exists" is necessary (GW, 1–25)?

We have not so much "found out" that God does not exist in contemporary society as we have made it a *demand*. Likewise, we have not "discovered" political and metaphysical conclusions on the basis of scientific theory so much as we have unscientifically deduced them. It may well be that some theists (like Teilhard de Chardin) have made too many concessions to scientific opinion out of guilt for previous theistic intransigence. Clark notes, however, that it has sometimes been the theologians who have held on to the most humane and scientifically defensible results, as in the belief that humankind was one species against the insinuating belief once held by some scientists that aborigines could not be "of us." Clark is interested in restoring not merely religious architecture and music, which are hardly religion, but rather real belief in God and a real confidence that our holidays are holy days. He believes that this effort at restoration includes rational argumentation, but it is not exhausted by such argumentation if unbelief really is, as he thinks, an ideology or a political strategy rather than a truth-seeking one:

> It is not that we think nothing matters infinitely because we now have reason not
> to believe in God: we have rejected God so as to be free to think that nothing
> matters very much. . . . It is modern to feel guilt about our notional or national
> involvement in vast social evils even though it is just as modern to deny that
> there are real evils or that an individual can be held responsible for what others
> of her family, nation, or race have done. . . . Our situation is like that of a hus
> band who, wishing to betray his wife, has decided to believe that she has given
> him cause. (GW, 38–39)

Clark's hope is that by pointing out the shadowy nature of contemporary agnosticism and atheism, and of their attendant political consequences, we might point ourselves in a direction where it is likely that we will receive a "breaking inward" of truth in religion, a truth that demands that we acknowledge that the divine existence is, in a sense, in flux if only because the divine existence cares for us. If the world is *really* valueless, then so are "the intuitions and futile longings that dispose us to disvalue it" (GW, 46). Clark has hope for future religiosity, but his hope is grounded in the belief—a belief in turn bolstered by the ontological and cosmological arguments—that God already is (GW, 25–47).

The almost certainly mistaken etymology in Heidegger of *aletheia* (truth) as *Unverborgenheit* (unconcealedness) is nonetheless associated with a correct insight; and despite the fact that Heidegger, according to Clark, mistakenly thought that Plato misunderstood *aletheia* and hence tainted the history of philosophy, Heidegger nonetheless was correct to alert us to the rightful skepticism shared in science and religion, in that the truth is often not obvious: to be *alethes* is to be unforgetful, or, as Plato reminds us in the *Cratylus* (421B), to *ale theia* is to wander with the divine. One must wake up to greet the divine and the really real, as Plato, Plotinus, and Augustine have argued. Heidegger does a disservice to philosophy, however, by claiming that only the Greek language, heard by German ears, is logos: why, for example, not Hopi, which lacks reifying substantives? Philosophers can do better than to look to Heidegger for theological and political insight, Clark thinks, by humbly accepting "realism," by which Clark means the view that there are truths that we do not know, but some of which we can come to know. He is not a logocentrist in the (Wittgensteinian or Heideggerian) sense that the boundaries of language are the boundaries of the world: "If we cannot think beyond the limits of our language . . . our thoughts are no longer statements subject to correction, but party political slogans" (GW, 56). The plausibility of realism is found in the fact that we already catch a glimpse of something that lies above and beyond every passing horizon of our thought. The plausibility of theistic realism in particular is found as soon as we treat Christian or theistic doctrine generally as philosophy, contra Tertullian. If "reason" refers to its fashionable use for the last several centuries, then Clark is willing, along with Feyerabend, to bid it farewell. However if the term can refer to what was revealed in Christ as the Logos, and if this Logos is compatible with what was thought and lived before Christ in persons of good will, then Clark is a qualified rationalist. In Clark's "rationalism" we recognize the intrusion of Logos, like the intrusion of a long-lost relative; we recognize when we are literally inspired, breathed into by Logos. It is a commonplace in Plato that the standards (say, of justice or equality) to which we appeal when we (confidently) judge something are not learned straightforwardly from sense experience. There *is* such a thing as equality, but no two experienced persons or things are essentially equal (GW, 48–65).

In this regard Clark sounds more like a transcendental, Platonic realist than like an immanent, Aristotelian one. Yet both of these are in opposition to nominalism (or social relativism or antifoundationalism), which is Clark's ultimate enemy. According to Clark's intradeical interpretation of Plato, this traditional distinction between Plato and Aristotle can be ameliorated.[34] The forms are concretized, albeit in the mind of the Demiurge, who eternally contemplates them. If both God and the forms are eternal for Plato, and if the former eternally contemplates the latter, then it does not make much sense to claim strict independence for either. As Aristotle put the point (*De anima* 439b), the mind in a way becomes the object of its own thought, especially in the case of God. It is at least momentarily possible for human beings to share God's life to the extent that they know logos. In short, the whole contrast between Hellenistic and Hebraic ways of thought is ill-informed. Palestine at the time of Christ had been under Hellenistic rule for 360 years, and every literate Hebrew would have spoken at least some Greek. How could an intelligent first-century Jew not have come into contact with philosophic Platonism? W. R. Inge has even gone so far as to claim that Greek philosophy ought to include Paul and John as well as Plotinus. Plato himself was not opposed to appeals to priestly testimony and he certainly considered traditional ritual duties important. Clark is especially intent on taking Philo seriously, not because he prefers Philo's logocentrism to the Chalcedonian one, but rather to clearly indicate what the basic thought pattern (a logocentric one) was of his century, a century that included Jesus, Paul, and John. All four of these first-century thinkers expressed a Platonizing tendency, if such a tendency refers to a pursuit of *logos*; it is almost a definition of Platonism that it include dialectical tensions in pursuit of the *logos*. Further, the dynamic, linear character of Hebraic thought is not nearly so much at odds with Greek "substantivist" or "cyclic" thought as many allege.[35] No one who has read Whitehead or Hartshorne carefully can continue to make this invidious contrast between the Greek view and the Hebraic view without detailed argumentation. Or again, the saints and angels of later Catholic thought echo much that is neglected in Plato and Plotinus. The key question is how the various *logoi* (angels, saints, Moses, Jesus, Mohammed, Zeus, Socrates) are to be united into, or subordinated to, the one Logos. Christianity is different from Greek religion not because it adheres to, or shies away from, logocentrism, but because it has determined from an early stage that there is no other way to God than through the Logos, Christ. However, even the Greeks saw *something* special in Socrates' connection to logos that no one else quite reproduced (GW, 66–87).

Clark defends a pious gratitude for what exists, but he realizes that this attitude can lead to complacency, to the bourgeois conviction that God is a good fellow and all will be well, or to the "scientific" rejection of mystery. However, the modern disparagement of any trace of mystery is not necessarily connected to gratitude; it can also be connected to absorption in power politics, even in (especially in?) academe. The euphemistic way of describing this absorption is to suggest that because of Wittgenstein and others we now know that society, not self, comes first, as if the worldviews of Jesus, Paul, John, and Philo were solipsistic. Clark's own mode of appropriating the legitimate insights of Wittgenstein is to suggest that different discourses do not define or create another reality but rather another part of the one reality. Realism, as opposed to Wittgensteinian social relativism, consists, in the broadest sense, in the willed recognition of necessity (in the Greek sense of *anangke*). Once again, at the bottom of Wittgensteinian exaggeration is a political motive: "Those who would have us think that death itself can be interpreted away, that what is 'true' is only and for ever what 'we' say, usually reveal quite quickly that what they really mean is that truth is what they say, and we must gratefully revere" (GW, 97). From Clark's critique of social relativism, however, we should not conclude that he evades uncomfortable political realities in the way of Platonism, wherein one supposedly tries to escape time so as to enter eternity. Clark is correct in doubting if there is very much that is Greek in this conception of Platonism. Platonizing philosophers were surely well aware of, and concerned about, the atrocities at Melos, Titus's slaughter of the Jews, or various plagues and diseases. *Apatheia* is not best translated in English as "apathy," in that lack of *apatheia* is literally pathetic, as in the person who never really lives life again, say, by becoming an alcoholic, after a death in the family. People die, and we do not serve *them* by self-pity. For Clark (as for the Greeks, he thinks) there is one world only, a world that includes forms, sensory impressions, and so on. The Flight of the Alone to the Alone and the trek outside of the cave are not journeys for the feet but transformations of vision. Nonetheless, Clark at times holds on to the belief in personal immortality, a belief that seems to indicate a two-world thesis at odds with his reticulative desire to bring it all together in this world.[36] The most consistent version of Clark's thesis is that

> there is a real world which we ordinarily misperceive, whose causal powers do not depend on our contrivance or description, and that this world is discoverable through the use of human reason because we are at some deep level in touch or tune with its maker and design. . . . If being were wholly external to us, we could

not penetrate it by means of cognition. . . . Modern scientists show occasional signs of losing their grip on these advances: wave-particle polarities, and the uncertainty principle, are both occasionally invoked to suggest that it is "our choice" what happens. . . . Redescribing things so as to evade reality is an ancient game. (GW, 108)

We have seen previously that for Clark there is an integral connection between the evacuation of sacred meaning in the world and the political motive to see monkeys, say, as "animal preparations" or as living test tubes:

We evacuate the world of sacred meaning so as to fill it with our meanings. . . . The Platonist . . . seeks to see and be transformed by the embodied beauty of a phenomenal and physical world through which she catches sight of eternal truth. . . . Greek . . . science sought not to "make" a universe a work of God's art, but to see "God's artistry" in it, which is to say, signs of a beauty that could inform the soul. (GW, 111)

In the effort to reintroduce sacred meaning in the world Clark is intent on closing the gap between faith and reason:

According to our Platonizing predecessors, the world of our present experience is an image or shadow (on various levels) of the one true logos. . . . So although pagans regularly objected to the Christian identification of a man with God's eternal Word it was common doctrine that the Divine Reason was achievable, in our degree, by human beings. (GW, 118)

Or again,

If "the Word became flesh" means simply that a fleshly being took on the character of the Word, it is not inconceivable either to Jew or Greek. . . . If it means instead that the Word was made identical with a fleshly being . . . the problem is not—as theologians regularly suggest—that the Greeks, or even Platonists, thought "flesh" unworthy of divinity. . . . The very idea of "one thing's being or becoming identical with *another*" is deeply incoherent. (GW, 122)

Clark is obviously not claiming that any ancient Greek believed that the logos was indeed embodied in Socrates exclusively, but he does think it would not have been impossible to speak in this way; indeed, he thinks it would have been relatively easy for them to think in this way. It was also relatively easy to think in this way when Jesus arrived, even if Arianism is an easier position to understand than the Chalcedonian one. Whatever difficulties there are in *understanding* the Chalcedonian view are responded to by Clark in the following lines, which appear to be his chief contribution in the philosophical effort to treat belief in Jesus as the Word:

> It is . . . faulty practice to decide beforehand what we mean by "human" and then announce the incompatibility of that account with what Jesus must have been if "Jesus" names the Word. . . . If Jesus *is* the Word, the Man, then it is he that reveals what it *is* to be human. . . . Even without the incarnation, Philo could have seen that we are less than really human because fallen away from the archetype, the Man. (GW, 128)

Clark is also correct in pointing out that it is not necessary that God be biologically human, even if it *is* necessary that God be embodied or concretized in *some* sense in order to maintain the one-world hypothesis:

> On my account, it may be said, the Word does not "take on" humanity, for He is forever and essentially just what "human" indicates. Humanity is not a second nature for Him, but the first. Humanity, accordingly, does not need to be redeemed, or transmuted into godhead: genuine humanity always was the Lord. . . . There was no moment of time when "He became flesh" from having before been spirit. (GW, 135)

Clark's incarnational theology has as one of its corollaries—and this despite his occasional and puzzling commendatory remarks regarding life after bodily death—that we should do all of our acts as worship and not look to the future. For example, we should resist fascism now, whether violently or nonviolently, regardless of whether we can bring our utilitarian calculations to a conclusion regarding what the future would bring under fascism. As we have seen, Clark thinks that it is in the nature of utilitarian calculations that they be inconclusive (GW, 88–137).

Clark is well aware of the charge often made against the traditional conception of God (especially by process theists) that such a conception either makes God into something of a dictator (to the extent that it is believed that an omnipotent God, with a cold, reptilian intelligence, imposes his will on the world) or makes him into a distant, apathetic deity (to the extent that it is believed that God is unmoved). Further, the long history, and only recent abandonment, of the divine right of kings indicates that such theology has practical political consequences. Clark retorts that "reformist theologians" run the risk of making God into a "cosmic parasite." Surely, however, Clark has misinterpreted process theism here (he seems to rely on J. J. O'Donnell's version of the thought of Schubert Ogden[37]). The God of process theism does not need our suffering in order to grow; but if we suffer, as surely we do, the greatest conceivable being cannot remain unmoved. This process conception of God also has political consequences, as in Paul Weiss's description of it as the democrat's God.[38] Clark is on surer ground when he states that God does not suffer *in the sense that* God could be corrupted by the (vicarious) suffering received. In the following passage, however, we see the familiar Clarkian attempt to have things both ways. Here he tries to preserve both process (and biblical![39]) responsiveness and traditional impassibility. The key word here, and the bothersome one, is "essentially":

> Without incarnation God cannot appreciate what pain and disaster are; with incarnation we lose the need to suppose that God the Eternal Father suffers in His own being. Which is to say, the incarnate Word does suffer in his finitude, but is not essentially changed by suffering. (GW, 144)

From the perspective of myth there is not much need to worry about the relationship between time and eternity, in the sense that in myth both creation *and* judgment are only a moment away. Clark, when pressed, seems to think that there is something to this view, in that we "should seek eternity here-now, through contemplation, liturgy, and moral action" (GW, 148). That is, the world is "in eternity" already (GW, 138–48).

The point Clark wishes to make regarding the relationship between religion and politics is not so much that there is a need to make the victims (citizens) believe some particular doctrine or other about the world as there is a need to wake them up from the ordinary half-sleeping condition they are in. Even philosophers and theologians can be "drugged with desire, or spleen, or accidie" (GW, 150), as in their reverential treatment of Heidegger as a source for *theological* insight. Romantic nihilism is hardly the same thing, Clark thinks, as being rooted in divinity; and Heideggerian disillusionment with bourgeois truth is not

at all the same as believing in Truth and divine reason. "The belief of some theologians that we can find the Kingdom of Heaven on the far side of nihilism . . .
betrays a failure to think through the century's chief lesson" (GW, 155), which is,
as Clark sees it, that social relativism is a failure. Social relativism can even lead
to Nazi or Heideggerian ideology. Waking up consists of realizing in a Socratic
way that previously we were asleep, yet obviously Clark does not have in mind
here a recreation of philosophy from practically nothing, as in Descartes, but
rather a waking up from our most recent somnambulance so as to recover what
previous thinkers had also woken up to:

> That is the merit of the methodological conservativism I prefer. It amounts to an
> admission that we cannot, logically, prove everything, but must remain content
> with what we find ourselves supposing till we are proved wrong (or given rea
> son to modify our views). (GW, 159)

We must be awake to be good traditionalists, he thinks, to be engaged with our
ideal yet historical self, as opposed to our own idealized self-image. Our ideal
self is not the sort of thing that could fall victim, despite our parochial attachments, to an evil like racism. Hitler's hatred of the Jews in part rested on his
accurate conception that a people chosen by God could not endorse the German
national dream. The ideal selves of the religious elect are described as follows
by Clark:

> This is the thought behind those speculations about the Elect that have generally
> had a bad press in liberal circles. If we are to be redeemed, this cannot be only a
> predicted future state within a continuing temporal order. Such temporal glories
> are identified in Buddhist thought as heavens, from which the inhabitants will
> one day fall again. Buddhist, Platonist, and millennarian Abrahamist all require
> something more than this: a radical break-out from the crystal palace.
> Abrahamists have tended to emphasize that it will come for all; Platonists that it
> is There already; Buddhists have set themselves, especially in the Mahayana, to
> work for the "enlightenment" and "release" of every blade of grass, while con
> tinuing to operate with a mythology of infinite pasts and futures in the tempo
> ral sequence. (GW, 165)

The "movement" of this world into the New Jerusalem requires us to rethink
the causal structure of this world here: "If we can wake to immortality, to the

eternal world, it is because that world is already the true cause of what is happening here" (GW, 168). This view is a moderate one, Clark thinks:

> How can it be both that the pagans wrongly deified the cosmos, and that they wrongly sought to escape from it? How can it be, conversely, that Christians identify the logos with a corporeal being, embedded in a temporal universe, while denying that the world embodies the divine?. . . Two opposite errors, Manicheanism (so-called), which separates God and the world, and secularist acceptance of the world. . . . The world is best conceived as God's temple. (GW, 171)

Platonists are not Cartesian dualists precisely because they think of bodies as included in soul (especially the World Soul) and because bodies are, as it were, portions of soul perceived through the five senses.[40] Traditional theologians provided a service to theism when they purged the anthropomorphic orgies found in polytheism, but often they ran to the other extreme wherein an overly transcendent, unmoved God could not know or love on anything even remotely resembling a human model of knowledge and love. Clark, like the process theists, tries to steer a course between these extremes; or better, Clark has one foot in a moderate anthropomorphism like that of the process thinkers and one in the camp of the traditional theists (GW, 150–74).

We will see in the next chapter that Clark is aware of the political dangers in talk about wider and wider wholes, culminating in talk about Gaia or the World Soul. The fear is that one may unwittingly stumble into a totalitarianism, once one adopts such a holism. This is indeed an old concern. For example, Aristotle was worried that Plato's Republic, like a whole man writ large, destroyed the virtues associated with a communicative polis of variegated intellects. In this regard Clark's politics may show too *little* a debt to Aristotle. It is one thing to say that a whole is a *metaphysical* monarchy rather than a *metaphysical* democracy (e.g., a swarm of gnats is a metaphysical democracy), and another to disparage *political* democracy. Hartshorne is an example of a thinker who defends human beings as metaphysical monarchies (with considerable power over their cells) without disparaging political democracy, contra Clark's interpretation of Hartshorne. There are real and purposive organic wholes, hence it is foolish to adopt an extreme atomism, nominalism, or value-neutrality with respect to nature. We can find the truth only by rising above immediate prejudice and personal affections so as to fairly consider wholes:

To surrender the hope of unity is to despair of science; to suppose that what is here already is already perfect is to despair entirely. Pantheism (the latter) and nihilism (the former) are identically irreligious. (GW, 187)

Clark wonders whether "human nature" is such a real and purposive organic whole:

So is there any such thing as human nature? If there is not, then what becomes of Chalcedonian claims . . . and what becomes of all good liberal claims for a universal humanitarianism? My answer, predictably, is that there is a human nature, but that it must be conceived Platonically, not as the essence of a particular biological species. . . . Aristotle's dicta that humans are political animals, animals with language, animals capable of recognizing and acting upon general principles all amount to the same thing, a picture of the human essence that identifies human beings as something unlike all other animals. (GW, 188–89)

However, Aristotle was not really the essentialist regarding human nature that some assume him to be; nor was human nature a nominal class for him, like "weeds." His view was a moderate one and it is adopted by Clark, although he supplements it with what he takes to be the best in the modern world. One of the positive features of the tradition started by Descartes is that of refining Aristotelian descriptions of human beings such that we do not "find" human beings the way we do wildflowers; we can discover what it is to be human only by asking what it is to be "me" as a subject. Clark partially agrees with this tradition, but he balances it against the insights of the older tradition:

Chalcedonian Platonism prefers to say, remember, that Jesus is the Man, that there is indeed one individual and sometimes localized entity that identically is the Word. It seems easy to infer that those who are more like that Man are more nearly human. (GW, 192)

The Body of Christ, the Man, is communal (GW, 175–94).

In the effort to recover the tradition of "Man," as Clark uses the term, he wishes to avoid both Whiggish history, which identifies what happens with what was always going to happen (even if it is difficult to fulfill this wish if one continues to hold a strong version of divine omniscience, as Clark does), and stochastic history, which suggests that history is nothing but a drunkard's walk through possibility. Between these extremes is his preferred view: "Pious history acknowledges both that what happens happens freely, and that there may be patterns, goals, ideals that pull things inward to take up those shapes" (GW, 197). None of us can wholly internalize the Logos, so a certain amount of pluralism is required in our historical search for truth, provided that the many contending parties are beginning from what has been commonly accepted (or "authoritatively declared") in tradition; otherwise there is something chimerical about the attempt to reach truth through pluralistic means. Because our knowledge is fragmentary, we must be willing to live with a certain degree of dissonance, and every once in a while with the realization that we have contradicted ourselves. Those who are too determined, Clark seems to imply, not to contradict themselves end up believing in silly trivialities. Obviously Clark does not intend to push reason to the point where it becomes an expression of "confident insolence," to borrow a phrase from Feyerabend. Rather, we seem to be stuck with our limited, yet efficacious, ability to unite with Logos, sometimes contending with each other along the way. That is, there is no end to history, in the sense of there being a time at the far end of thesis and antithesis. This is another way for Clark to advance his conservative claim that there is little to support the myth of progress:

> That is the Charlie Brown illusion: how can we lose if we are so *sincere?* For every problem, social, medical, or scientific, that we "solve," there will be more. (GW, 213)

As usual, however, Clark is too hard on the Enlightenment here, including two of its stepchildren, utilitarianism and social contract theory. When he says that "All that descriptions of existing states and laws can do, at best, is show— after the event—that some new thing was possible" (GW, 214), he is, in effect, denying that there has been real progress because of Enlightenment insistence on rights, say, with respect to a significant degree of amelioration of racism and sexism among almost all human beings who are at least remotely reasonable. It seems that one of the reasons why Clark denigrates human progress, whether through utilitarian or social contract means, is to prepare the way for what he takes to be divinely imposed progress in the way of miraculous intervention on the part of an omnipotent God:

> A unified view of the physical [or the social] world simply does not exist. We reach towards the best that we can manage by common practice, conversation, trying out ideas of this and that until the unexpected light breaks in (see Plato, *Seventh Letter*). . . . We may not see that God as an object, any more than those ascended from their cave can see the sun: but we may grow aware of the light by which we see a new world dawning. (GW, 216–17)

As before, Clark is not encouraging a move away from the physical universe, as if "physical" were simply the opposite of "mental." Rather, the world of bodies and artifacts in which we live itself can be spiritualized and seen as having consummatory value just as it is. Yet even here there is the need to "avoid the sin and singular mistake of turning that Vision of the Presence into yet another article or piece of furniture" (GW, 222). This refusal to reify divine presence, Clark thinks, is what keeps tradition alive (GW, 196–223):

> The contemptuous misstatements of orthodox doctrine that pollute the conversation and writings of our literati deserve little intellectual credit. . . . But it is no part of my thesis that there can be no newly discovered truths, no reasonable but unfamiliar inferences. We should not be too eager to deny to our contemporaries what we concede to the Founding Fathers, the right and responsibility to explore the world and our tradition further. (GW, 222)

Indeed, Clark is a religious and political conservative, but from his point of view this is precisely what puts him, along with Chesterton, on the side of revolution against more "modern" and "progressive" ways. Furthermore, as before, his heterodox, yet convincing, view of animals makes his conservatism quite unlike that of most other thinkers who identify themselves by this label.[41]

CONCLUSION

In sum, in this chapter we have seen that Clark is certainly correct that political language is very often fictional, especially when describing the social contract, and that literalism in politics is an only partially realized historical achievement. Yet it seems that Clark goes too far in the effort to defend the deliberate use of fantasy; it does not seem that he can adequately defend his claim that political or religious fantasy is no more "made up" than science. Clark is on stronger ground when he argues that a major defect in social contract theory is its marginalizing of children who are, as Clark sees things, *central* to human community. Clark's political beliefs, and all political beliefs, he thinks, are explicitly or implicitly based on religion. Hence, our inability to establish a central core to various religions makes it doubtful that we can do so in politics. That is, the hope of the Enlightenment, in general, and of Kantians, in particular, to establish universal values is not at all likely, according to Clark, and may well be dangerous. We would do better, Clark thinks, if we admitted a prejudice—not a pejorative term here—in favor of Christianity. As he puts the point, only one ship comes into harbor. Because of his anti-Enlightenment prejudice, however, Clark is forced into the unwelcome position of having to show how different his view is from Heidegger's, whose political beliefs were disastrous. It must be admitted, however, that Clark is somewhat successful in this distancing effort. For example, regarding Heidegger's infamous comment on the identity of the death camps and contemporary agriculture, Clark thinks that Heidegger may have had a point *if* he had in mind the way contemporary factory farmers evacuate the natural world of meaning; however, if (as is more likely) his intention was to mitigate the Nazi offense, then he deserves to be viewed as a "moral monster."[42]

Clark's antipathy to democracy can be seen when he compares having opinions on contemporary political matters to children choosing which football team they will support. Why, he asks, should most people know any more about the reliability over the next thousand years of current techniques of radioactive waste disposal than they do about the ancient Assyrian copula? Clark, like Heidegger, thinks that all scientific, cultural, and political views are the working out of a single set of beliefs, although Clark and Heidegger disagree about what that set is (for Clark, as we have seen, it is explicitly or implicitly religious). By way of contrast, Rawls, the greatest defender of social contract theory, would have us rest content *in politics* if Catholics, Mormons, and agnostics could articulate the moral sensibility that enables us to be fair to people with whom we have very little in common, philosophically speaking. That is, for Rawls, as opposed to Clark, religious toleration is *paradigmatic* for a just, democratic society.[43]

In addition to criticizing Kantians, social contract theorists, or defenders of the Enlightenment, Clark also goes after utilitarians in an analogous way. There are no abstract human individuals, as utilitarians imagine there are or as they rationally stipulate there must be. Although utilitarians rely too much on a certain sort of reason, Clark's own greater reliance on tradition also requires at least some confidence in reason as the tool that deciphers which parts of tradition are abiding and which are perversions. We should not *calculate* what to do in politics; rather, he thinks, we should care for our kin and our friends and adopt a principle of noninterference with respect to everyone else. Clark's qualified commitment to reason is sufficient to make him take Plato's myth of the cave seriously, although Clark wavers between a one-world hypothesis, as is evidenced in his defense of Gaia, to be discussed in the next chapter, and the traditional interpretation of Platonism and of Christianity as entailing a two-world view, one of whose implications is a denigration of politics. The one-world view seems to have the upper hand in Clark's thought: why would Platonists deify the cosmos only to escape from it? Yet it remains unclear why, on the grounds of the one-world view wherein *this* world is already redeemable, if not redeemed, we should be as pessimistic as Clark is regarding the possibility of (enlightened) progress in politics and history.

In any event, for Clark, as for Plotinus, reason is not to be valued for its utility, as though we might intelligibly exchange it for unreason if the latter were more successful; rather, it is to be valued because it just *is* the presence of beauty in us. Reason is also not primarily a tool to avoid pain, as utilitarians imagine; in fact, in Clark's Plotinian view bodies, with their pleasures and pains, would not be the things they are if soul had not made them so. We will see in the next chapter that to reason our way to the truth presupposes the prior existence of that truth and, in Clark's view, an intellect that has already grasped that truth. This everlasting intellect is none other than that possessed by God, conceived as the soul for the entire world. By reasoning correctly we are made one with the mind who can with legitimacy be called "Reason" or "Logos." Contrary to the utilitarian view, the wise man is not a calculator, but is rather one who strives to unify with the mind of God. That is, the "other world" of reason is not apart from "here," but is rather discovered in the realization that we inhabit a besouled world that is already made.[44]

CHAPTER 9

THE WORLD SOUL

INTRODUCTION

In this chapter I am going to examine in detail Clark's theory of the World Soul and his theory that we are citizens of the cosmos as much as or more than we are citizens of the state. I will claim that these theories carry much more weight than most contemporary philosophers are ready to admit. Along the way I will also treat: (1) Clark's concept of "the city of the wise"; (2) his attempt to build his case for the World Soul on Aristotle; (3) the implications of belief in the World Soul for political issues; (4) the implications of belief in the World Soul for gender issues; and (5) the implications of belief in the World Soul for human understanding of death. In order to introduce Clark's World Soul (which is built on phenomenological, scientific, and religious grounds) it will be fruitful to discuss once again the notion of sentiency.

THE WORLD SOUL

Three sorts of sentiency (S) can be distinguished, all three of which can be found in Clark in various ways under different labels. S_1 is sentiency at the microscopic level of living cells. The nightmare of determinism has faded, as living reality in its fundamental constituents seems to have at least a partially indeterminate character of self-motion. That is, the sum total of efficient causes from the past does not supply sufficient cause to explain the behavior of the smallest units of becoming in the living world. S_2 is sentiency per se, sentiency in the sense of feeling of feeling, found in animals and human beings, whereby beings with central nervous systems or something like them can feel as wholes, just as their constituent parts show prefigurements of feeling on a local level. Feeling *is* localized; think of a knife stuck in the gut of any vertebrate, or of sexual pleasure. S_2 consists of taking these local feelings and collecting them so that an individual as a whole can feel what happens to its parts, even if the individual partially transcends the parts. Hurt my cells and you hurt *me*. S_3 is divine sentiency. If I am not mistaken, Clark shares with Plato and Hartshorne the following four-term analogy:

$$S_1 : S_2 :: S_2 : S_3$$

The universe is a community or an organism, a Platonic World Soul, of which one member (God, or the Platonic Demiurge) is preeminent, just as human beings are communities of cells of which the mental part is preeminent.

Clark would not find the following four-term analogy an adequate tool in describing the cosmos:

$$S_1 : \text{a table} :: S_2 : \text{the "uni"verse as a concatenation of parts}$$

Or, as Erazim Kohak puts it:

> Shall we conceive of the world around us and of ourselves in it as *personal*, a meaningful whole, honoring its order as continuous with the moral law of our own being and its beings as continuous with ours, bearing its goodness—or shall we conceive of it and treat it, together with ourselves, as *impersonal*, a chance aggregate of matter propelled by a blind force and exhibiting at most the ontologically random lawlike regularities of a causal order?[1]

Clark obviously opts for the former alternative.

As we will see, Clark's defense of the World Soul is primarily religious (or metaphysical), but he also relies on biological evidence supplied by defenders of the Gaia hypothesis like James Lovelock.[2] In addition to these two bases, however, he also offers a phenomenological approach, for lack of a better word, wherein one can experience oneself as part of a cooperative endeavor, an effort of fellow-feeling cosmic in scope (MS, 160, 162):

> Plants too, and every clod of earth are animate: not mystically so, but in straight-forward biological terms. The earth itself, the biosphere itself is made up of liv-ing things and their products in a single, interconnected whole. We are all members one of another, and the lowliest organism may be as vital to the whole as any Nobel prize–winner. More so, indeed. For the very fact which can imme-diately be adduced to mark the difference between man and plants, or men and micro-organisms, reveals that the latter are strictly very much more important than any one of us. . . . We too are composed of individual cells (MS, 170).

Political efforts at trying to solve the various environmental crises that face us, Clark thinks, are not likely to succeed until human society finds a goal beyond its own continuance. We will see that Clark identifies this goal with the (Aristotelian) First Cause that, if it chose anything, chose that citizens of the world should be mutually dependent. To believe in the World Soul is not to believe in the celestial spheres of the ancient world, however, but in the princi-ple of necessary diversity in unity, a principle that was metaphysical before it was ecological. Clark insists that there is nothing totalitarian in the World Soul, in that the life of the Whole is improved by the multitude of parts just as the health of the body as a whole is dependent on the health of its cells. Although Clark very often talks (misleadingly, I think) of the creature-Creator relation-ship as one of finitude-infinitude—the problem lies in the fact that a God who relates to particular beings in time must in some sense be finite—he more accu-rately refers to the relationship as one between fragmentariness and all-inclu-siveness (MS, 171, 175, 177, 184–85, 193).

The most important philosophical predecessors to modern belief in the World Soul were the neoplatonists (and St. Paul), whom Clark praises as follows:

> When any organism acts the whole world acts in that organism. We are mem-bers of each other, and all of us are joined in making the whole world with which every one of us is coextensive. Is it not time that we remembered our loyalty to the world of truth, and forgot the delusive appearance of our being pure indi-viduals in competition? . . . If we men have an office "higher" than those of other creatures it is the office of care and understanding—understanding of cosmic unity, care for the diversity of creatures. Neo-Platonists have been successful in

practice to this extent: they predicted that the universe would turn out to be mutually interdependent, that all things arise together . . . all contribute to the life of all. (MS, 194–95)

Clark wonders how we can understand either Paul (it is now not I that lives but Christ—Galatians 2:20) or the Upanishadic writers (the divine Self is in all things) without something like the World Soul to which to appeal . Further, the familiar ritual of conversion or of putting on a "new self" can more appropriately be described in terms of a coming to awareness of where (trans-human) Selfhood really lies. Even Kantian morality should be seen against the background of the World Soul, strange as that sounds:

> I am my own Lawmaker only in the Pickwickian sense that the laws that govern (or strive to govern) me are those through which there is an understanding of my being as a rational agent. On this view my being is not a being separate and individual, but universal reason. (MR, 113–15)

Clark is correct to remind those who are skeptical regarding the World Soul that belief that there are individual selves identical with the persons recognized in ordinary social life is not a metaphysical truism; in fact, eliminating such a belief is seen, in some religious thinkers (John of the Cross among them), as salvific *moksa* (Hindu release):

> Neither Buddhists, Hindus nor Abrahamists need deny that there are identifiable persons, who are born, mature, and die. What none of them need assert is that these persons are real irreducible subjects, or "selves.". . . That the Self is identical with Brahman . . . or that the Self is the spiritual substance that reincarnates . . . or that the Self is Christ, constitute alternatives to ethical individualism. . . . Repentence is a matter of acknowledging one's place; redemption is being recreated as a member of that whole which may outlast all others. Religious piety consists in that lively sense of being one of the "whole company of heaven," and impiety is pretending to a selfhood independent of that whole. (MR, 116–18)

THE CITY OF THE WISE

To see the universe as a great city is, perhaps, slightly less anthropomorphic than to see it as God's body. Yet anthropomorphisms are not entirely without intellectual content, Clark thinks, even if they do fall short of the degree of abstraction usually thought appropriate for academic discourse. To experience oneself as part of a "great city" is to say, at least implicitly, that the *telos* of humanity is not merely to preserve political harmony as political harmony is usually understood (MR, 163–64, 169). Yet Clark's particularism prevents him from making his belief in the World Soul too ethereal. One of the ways through which we experience ourselves as part of the great city, or, alternately, as fragments, is in ritual:

> A religious experience is participation in a religious ritual, or a sudden perception that some everyday event is like the ritual. Just occasionally a family meal, or a party, is suffused with the sort of gaiety, unforced affection, sweet sadness, or even worshipful terror, that a great ritual occasion is meant to evoke, to praise, to capture.... "Really religious" persons at least hope, or try, to carry those emotions over into their daily lives, but will earn the vague dislike of their compatriots if they are too obviously happy, too much inclined to uncomplaining courage and affectionate joy. The British, at any rate, do not greatly care for uttering "great shouts of joy" when asked to by their clergy, and reserve the right to pay due service to the minor deities of malicious gossip, complaint, laziness and lechery once outside the church.... They are the states of mind and practice that we are not quite prepared to abandon. (MR, 215)

Many religious and political rituals are maudlin or syrupy, and hence these do little to inspire a heroic life that contributes something worthwhile to God. If a supposedly uplifting ritual is immediately followed by ennui then the ritual was most likely defective: The real work of religion goes on in those long years of "spiritual dryness" (MR, 216). Once again, Clark is both impressed by the ability of charismatic revivalism to produce experiences conducive to awareness of the World Soul and angered by religious institutions that are more interested in controlling such experiences than in evoking them.

There is indeed solitary or subjective human experience even in public ritual, and even if such an experience is one where one feels oneself to be part of an immense whole. This experience can be felt from within as a *personal* encounter, hence Clark has in mind here the sorts of mystical experience found in John of the Cross or Julian of Norwich (experiences where the World Soul is likely to be described in terms of the mystical body of Christ) rather than the impersonal experiences of intense light, say, claimed by atheistical monists. Clark admits that it is easier to believe as credible claims regarding these non-theistic experiences, where one experiences oneself as a one among many, than it is to believe as credible a claim regarding experience of God or of the Buddha-nature just as such. Even the numerous claims to these latter, however, are credible to the individual who has personally had such experiences. It should not surprise us that many people claim to have had experiences of a personal deity when it is realized that God, as the World Soul, is alleged to be ubiquitous. Likewise, it should not surprise us that many people have not had such experiences, in that it is easy to be aware of realities that are sometimes present and sometimes absent, with the latter providing the background against which we can easily see the particular reality in question when it is in fact present. For example, it is easier to notice a dog in one's living room if one does not have a dog, as opposed to the difficulty we sometimes have in finding the cat, because it is always there somewhere in the house (MR, 217–19, 223–25).

Despite Clark's praise of religious enthusiasm, he is aware of the fact that disciplined mystics see ecstasies and visions merely as aids in the attempt to experience a more intimate union with God. These disciplined mystics (Clark once again seems to have John of the Cross in mind) not only have a less histrionic view of mystical experience than nonmystics might suppose, they are also more committed to normal sacramental and ceremonial life (MR, 226–28). That is, the mystic realizes that The One confronts a real multiplicity, or, in Clarkian terms that depend on a belief in creation *ex nihilo*, The One *wills* multiplicity. There are different ways in which one might respond to this troublesome, sometimes painful multiplicity in the effort to return to The One, but this multiplicity cannot be wished away as so much phantasmagoria. These responses include the atheistic exhortation to do the best we can with multiplicity, progressive humanism (which can tend either toward atheism or toward theism), and piety. This last is Clark's response, wherein awareness of the world as a living whole militates against the view that the world is nothing more than material for technocratic control. We need not lose hope if the days of "sentimental humanism" are numbered, and this because we have the *network* of living nature to take as our best image of the divine. At its best, ecomysticism fosters not only a respect for the earth's household but also an understanding that we human creatures are not all-important. The "cosmic city" is not, in Clark's view, a mixed metaphor (MR, 232–37).

It might be argued that Clark's attachment to the World Soul is at odds with his particularism and his Aristotelianism. It might also be argued that belief in the World Soul constitutes "Platonism" in the pejorative sense of the term. Yet Clark thinks that Aristotle, too, believed in the World Soul, even if he did not name it as such, as did Plato.[3] What makes the world one is also what makes us one; we mirror the structure to the world, in this interpretation of Aristotle. Because Aristotle did not believe in a temporal beginning to the world, he was committed, Clark thinks, to seeing it as a self-maintaining biosphere, although this reticulation is often expressed in Aristotle in contrast to the priority of a plurality of entities. The paradigmatic *ousiai* (substances) are those with an obvious principle of unity—animals, plants, natural bodies, stars (see *Meteorology* 1028b, *De anima* 412a)—as opposed to heaps like earth, air, fire, or water, or as opposed to semiunified things like cities (see *Politics* 1303a). Or better, whatever is unaffected by rearrangement may have "all" or *pan* attached to it, but not "whole" or *holon* or "real unity." Among the paradigmatic *ousiai* themselves it is living entities that deserve priority because of the tight connection between formal and final causation in such living entities (see *Metaphysics* 1044a), not in the sense that the final, adult form beckons to its past self—this is impossible—but in the sense that in living organisms the embryonic entity characteristically develops in certain ways (AM, 47–48, 50–52, 56).

In Clark's interpretation of Aristotle, the paradigmatic *ousiai* are wholes and the paradigmatic wholes are living entities that exist dynamically through time. When Aristotle says that god and nature do nothing superfluously (*De caelo* 271a, 279a, 285a, 286a), Clark interprets him to refer to a deity that is not an absolute deity outside of space and time, but a god who animates the whole of the world. The world as a whole lives, with the heavens at the world's heart. Although Aristotle only once likens the universe to an animal, and here in an *aporia* (conundrum) (*Physics* 252b), he does insist that it is a whole and an organism rather than a haphhazard aggregate (*Metaphysics* 1069a). Aristotle obviously thinks that *some* events occur by chance (*apo tyches*—*Physics* 198b–199a), but it is impossible that everything should happen by chance once one sees pervasive *teloi* (plural of *telos*) in nature. There is no such thing as a bone or a blood vessel developing in isolation, at least partially because organic development is a matter of increasing differentiation of an original whole rather than a building up of contingent and extraneous additions; this leads Clark to suggest that a highly differentiated item like a human mind is no less isolated than a blood vessel within an original whole (AM, 58–64).

It is obviously orthodoxy in the contemporary world to assume that the universe is not living or besouled, as if life, sentiency, and rationality are incidental to the world's being. This orthodoxy is not so much a triumph of reason as of superstition, specifically the Manichean or Gnostic superstition that life is alien to the world or that the universe derives its claim to life solely from its parts' lives, as if increasing organic complexity could occur in a lifeless vacuum. Animal and plant communities (biocoenoses) are not themselves organisms, even if they are not exactly aggregates, but

> it is surely plausible to maintain that the universe is much more such a biocoenosis than a mere aggregate, and perhaps a whole in the strict sense. Certainly parts of the world are unliving in themselves—but so are many parts of my body. . . . Then that world is an organism, and very probably a living one. . . . The world is not merely everything that is the case, but rather everything subsumed in a unitary whole. . . . Similarly the cells of our bodies live their own lives in a fashion not wholly unlike that of their independent cousins, but also serve to maintain the wider unity that is the human being. (AM, 65–66)

In effect, Clark is saying that for Aristotle the fundamental *ousia* is neither notional bare matter nor abstract form, but the world in its entirety:

> Precisely because the Whole is a living and perennially unfolding whole . . . there is a real indeterminacy in events. . . . The being and the intelligibility of the Whole lies in its perennial effort to reflect, to become Nous: the being of man is in the end the same. (AM, 67–68)

However, if the World Soul exists it is not so much its self-reflexiveness that is bothersome as the sort of political organicism it may engender. Yet Clark is quite clear that he does not favor an organic view of the state, because he is skeptical as to whether human rulers (selves and cells like us) can harmonize the demands of individual creatures like an all-sympathetic coordinator (AM, 103–4).

The World Soul, according to Clark's neoplatonizing Aristotelianism, is the concrete actuality of *nous*, which is the World Soul itself in abstraction. By including the orthodox interpretation of Aristotle's God (as wholly narcissistic) within a larger whole, Clark wishes to call attention to Aristotle's cosmology, in a way that is seldom done. *Everything* naturally has something of the divine in it (*Nicomachean Ethics* 1153b), specifically *nous*, which can survive each particular organism's death. In *this* sense *nous* is immovable, in that it cannot be moved into or out of existence. There is an old age for thinking (*dianoia*) but not for *nous*. Clark's view of Aristotle is not pantheistic (or Stoicized), in that *nous* (or better, *Nous*) is separable (*choristos*) not merely because it survives our death but because it is *already* in some sense separate, in that it is "puzzlingly disentangeled from our lives" (AM, 183), analogous to the way we are somewhat disentangled from cells in our hair before a haircut. *Nous* is also separate from us because it does not think intermittently even if the World Soul from which *Nous* is abstracted is, in a way, everything (*De anima* 431b). That is, just as "I" am both somewhat immanent in my body (cut my arm and you hurt *me*) and partially transcendent of it (even if I lose my arm altogether I am still a whole person), the World Soul is somewhat in each part of the world, especially human beings, and partially transcendent of the world (AM, 174, 177–78, 180–82, 184–85):

> The being of the Whole is divine. . . . To see that Being is not simply to recite Newton's laws of motion: as always, material description is not to the point. . . . To immortalize oneself, to practise *theoria*, is to realize the presence in the soul of the undying which is itself the Prime. . . . To realize the god in oneself is to discover the world . . . as an intelligible and undivided whole, such that there is no room for any grasping ego. (AM, 186–87)

For Clark it is "quite right to distinguish the godlike from the god: but what makes us godlike is our mirroring of that God" (AM, 188). Obviously my ordinary self is not divine, but that does not necessarily mean that there is no divinity in me, as Aristotle indicates: "We must not recoil with childish aversion from the examination of the humbler animals. Every realm of nature is marvellous" (*De partibus animalium* 645a):

Cosmological models, Clark thinks, are inevitably part of our personal concerns. In Clark's case the prime personal concern as it relates to cosmology is that the eternal part of him, the god in him, is part of an exocentric world such that "We are not aware of the world as it is from one point of view only, but of the world as it is for something at once in and beyond us" (AM, 193). One's degree of exocentricity may vary, however, say, with respect to those who are sociocentric or politicocentric as opposed to those, like Clark, who are theocentric, in that he thinks of the divinely animated cosmos as the true polis (AM, 191, 194):

> The very fact of exocentricity impels us to believe in a common world: the very certainty of death impels me to believe in a world wider than my own in which I die. . . . Until the self-worlds are united there is no more than a mathematical aggregate. . . . What is needed is a world that does already embrace all lesser self-worlds, from which all other worlds derive. . . . Not more universal in being more abstract, in having fewer and fewer distinct characteristics, but in being more comprehensive. (AM, 196)

Clark's hope is that belief in the World Soul will enhance our ability to see God as the center:

> There is no inference from egocentricity to the exocentric: neither is there from the exocentric to the theocentric. Theocentricity, like egocentricity, is perhaps a limiting case, but the exocentric must always hover between these poles, of self and the god. In seeing with the god, we see with our own eyes but in a certain way, and in seeing thus, momentarily, we meet *not* a self-world ordered by our pleasures and pains, but the World . . . the realized, actualized world of human living, and its core is the realization of the divine. (AM, 197)

It must be admitted that Clark does not entirely resolve the tension in Aristotle between the commonplace that soul and body are one as the stamp and the wax are one (*De anima* 412b), on the one hand, and on the other the separateness of divinity (AM, 213). In this regard one may well wonder if Clark is more of a Platonist or a Plotinian than an Aristotelian. Strange as it seems, although Plato developed a dipolar categorial scheme (where form is contrasted to matter, etc.), his cosmology is ultimately a psychical monism, where the World Soul holds the cosmos together as a *uni*verse. Aristotle, however, developed a single categorial scheme of embodied form. Paradoxically, from this emphasis on embodied form Aristotle ultimately constructed a more vicious dualism than any ever envisaged by Plato, in that Aristotle's divinities, as interpreted by almost everyone except Clark, are *completely* self-sufficient entities, unmoved, and separated from all change, multiplicity, and embodiment:

> Nor are all events associated with the stream of my life directly part of my life-world: some are aspects of the lesser worlds of my cells. My world, my life, comprehends and sympathizes with the lesser. (AM, 198–99)

So also, God sympathizes with us if God is the *Platonic* World Soul. The *telos* of Clark's Aristotelianized philosophy would thus seem to be, as it was for the Greeks, neoconfucians, and Buddhists, an opening to the world (AM, 216). My claim that Clark would be better served by basing his belief in the World Soul on Platonic or Eastern sources supports that of Martha Nussbaum, who argues that final explanation in Aristotle is restricted to plants and animals and does not extend to the universe as a whole. Nor is she convinced that Clark's "panpsychist mysticism" (Nussbaum overstates her case here regarding Clark's alleged panpsychism) can enable him to establish the thesis that Aristotle is something of a Mahayana Buddhist.[4] Clark's daring here is not without its supporters. Julia Annas thinks that his analogy between microcosm and macrocosm is "fascinating," but even she is skeptical of Clark's overly benevolent reading of Aristotle's "egalitarianism" wherein, once we have realized that we are all citizens of the cosmos as polis, we notice our commonality. Clark should reread the *Politics*, she thinks, to see what the real implications are of Aristotle's abstractions.[5]

HUMAN AND DIVINE CONSCIOUSNESS

Thus far we have seen that Clark's belief in the World Soul is loosely based on phenomenological (feeling oneself to be a part of a whole) and quasi-scientific (in terms of the Gaia hypothesis) grounds, and tenuously (or questionably) connected to Aristotelian roots. It should be noted, however, that his chief support for such belief is religious. True well being or *eudaemonia*, he thinks, resides in service and contemplation of the ultimate principles of Nature, of God. To love God is to share in the divine life, a sharing that is most often not pure, but broken or ambivalent. This ambivalent sharing in the life of God is (unfortunately) part of Clark's effort, treated in a previous chapter, to defend a theodicy based on the concept of divine omnipotence (AJ, 38, 40–41): "If the Whole is supremely worth knowing, complete with warts, then all the episodes that our local perspective finds abominable must shrink into their proper place in the universal economy" (AJ, 42). This seems to be the Stoic option of believing that all is well with the world just as it is, but at times Clark wonders how we can take delight in predation. His response to this concern seems to consist of a Buddhist or Christian way "outside the world" that, he thinks, is not apathetic in the pejorative sense of the term (AJ, 43–45):

> If we ought to do anything we surely ought to attend to the distress and futility of our fellow-creatures' lives. . . . What is needed is hope. . . . Hope is a necessity if we are to remain sane. To set out upon the road to saintliness we need to be able to hope that the evils of the world can be, will be, remedied. . . . To hope is to put our trust in something. . . . Such hope is very easily denigrated as wishful thinking. . . . We can only hope that there is a remedy which does not depend on us. (AJ, 46–47)

Here Clark has entirely abandoned the Greek (and Hartshornian) view of life as tragic and the view that it is possible to set out on the road to saintliness even if there is, in fact, and always will be for those with memory, evil in the world. The remedy that Clark has in mind comes in the form of an omnipotent deity as opposed to the (much more plausible God, as I have claimed) Platonic Demiurge/World Soul, who must confront a recalcitrant material world that is at least partially outside of divine control. That is, Clark's belief in the World Soul is at odds with his belief in God as omnipotent.

We can bear the evils of the world only if we believe that the divine pattern toward which we are drawn is not yet *fully* operative in the world: "The proper attitude to the world is not a reverent contemplation of whatever is, nor a fearful rejection of it, but willingness to be part of the solution" (AJ, 53). The solution, Clark thinks, lies in a certain sort of discipline. Although he has no interest in defending the grimmer examples of asceticism, Clark thinks that those who speak so easily of the need to say "yes!" to everything deserve rebuke, yet,

> To say "yes" to the world, if it means anything worth saying, cannot mean that we do or should accept things as they are. It must mean instead that we accept the challenge, join in the adventure. (AJ, 54)

Once again, this is fine as far as it goes, but even when we are provided with the wide-angle lens that is necessary to become awake to the World Soul we are still left with Clark's troublesome claim, which relies on the thought of D. S. Wallace-Hadrill, that

> the only solution to the problem of imperfection is that good will triumph in the end. But no ultimate moral triumph is possible in this present age. (AJ, 57)

To solve the problem of theodicy by appealing in this way to divine omnipotence does nothing, I insist, even when such an appeal is buttressed by a belief in the World Soul, to get beyond the devastating criticisms of Voltaire, Hume, and so on, of *traditional* theism, hence it makes some sense to explore what Hartshorne calls neoclassical theism, a more Platonic theism wherein divine omnipotence is criticized.

At first glance Nature is perfect simply as it is, but at second glance it is not yet perfected. In more secure ages than our own the first glance supplies a stable image. Our age is obviously less secure, an insecurity due in part to our exploitation of Nature, but Clark's conservative defense (and sometimes his defensiveness) regarding Western civilization prompts him to quickly note that (AJ, 58–59):

> Attempts to show that Westerners are uniquely aggressive towards the natural world, that "other cultures" embody a respect for it, depend too often on selective quotation from romantic poets and ignorance of what actually has been done by other cultures. Late Roman Paganism, with its gods and spirits of the sacred springs, did not prevent the Romans from making a desert of North Africa.... Japan, despite a background of Nature-worship and Buddhism, has shown little enough respect for Tokyo's air, or the world's whales. (AJ, 60)

Or again, Amerindians of the Great Plains engaged in a fire-drive hunting technique that arguably made their ecological rapacity worse per capita than that introduced by the white man, which was in its own way incredibly rapacious. In any event, to establish a strong connection, as Clark does, between Nature and God, one must admit that God is in continual change, or better, that God, as an omnibenevolent being, reacts in the best way possible to the various good and bad things that occur in the world. This preeminent ability to react well should offer at least some consolation to us in the hard, if not horrible, lives we lead in Nature. Consolation may also come from knowing that our lives, hard as they are, nonetheless constitute the cutting edge of a huge project (AJ, 64–65):

We are the one vertebrate species whose evolution has equipped it to deal empathetically with other species, to be concerned for the health of our environment over the long term, to reason about long-term and abstract possibilities. . . . It is not uncommon now to find people suggesting that in us Nature, or at any rate the terrestrial biosphere that Lovelock has called "Gaia," has grown conscious of itself, that we may turn out to be the leading edge of evolution. (AJ, 67)

On the one hand, human beings are at the cutting edge of evolutionary history; on the other, many of the most reflective humans have a penitent attitude with respect to the course of this human development thus far. This penitance can take either a Benedictine form, wherein one especially notices the desolation created by human mistakes, or a Franciscan one, wherein one takes seriously the promise of paradise restored (AJ, 68–69).

As might be suspected, Clark is somewhat skeptical of the romantic hopes that might be raised by Franciscanism, but he admits that the inwardness fostered by Franciscanism would help to shake us loose of a crudely utilitarian approach to the world that he thinks is currently hegemonic:

A "true and felt knowledge (not merely nominal knowledge)" of the inner life of other humans, other animals, of Gaia itself, may come on anyone. . . . But though the price of this awareness is a knowledge of agonies, the testimony of those who experience it does seem to be that it is also an experience joyful in itself. . . . Nature-mysticism of any kind must be some sort of regression to infantile or embryonic life. . . . To be strongly conscious of the inwardness of things is to be joined in that perpetual reaching-out for God on which Aristotle thought the world depended. It is to fall in love. (AJ, 70–71)

Perhaps there is some sense in Clark's claim that the only sure basis from which to care for the world is to love all created things, even in their weak and fallen state, *as long as* such love does not function as an *apologia* for political apathy, war, or corruption. Theists should keep Voltaire in mind here as, for example, process theologians or liberation theologians tend to do (AJ, 72).

Defending a religious belief in God as the World Soul obviously opens Clark up to the charge of "mysticism," but this charge is vague if Clark is correct that the term refers to any reliance on truths that cannot be proved by reason and of which our assurance must be immediate. By this wide definition it is not only belief in the World Soul that is mystical, as in Wordsworth's hearing the "one song" of the universe in *The Prelude* (2. 409ff.), but also the knowings of every scholar and scientist, at least in part. Even if we restrict the term to refer only to "those who seek or have achieved an experience for which they can find no *wholly* adequate verbal description" (AJ, 74; emphasis added), we still have something ill-defined, because "no experience, of eating chocolate or climbing the Grand Canyon or kissing a friend, is *wholly* conveyed to the uninitiated by any word of ours" (emphasis added). As before, however, because of the power of analogy the supposed total incommunicability of mystical experience by any definition of the term "mysticism" has been greatly exaggerated. It is perhaps a safe generalization to say that mysticism can be described by the analogy of human activity and passivity: "Enlightenment is not to be achieved by careful building up of knowledge, careful control of the mind's acts, but by a certain sort of surrender" (AJ, 78). This surrender sometimes consists of the Gnostic belief that the material world is a mistake, sometimes not, but the differences among mystics are often exaggerated because defenders of different religions often argue at cross purposes. For example, even if there is some truth in the Buddhist complaint that "God" refers to the powers whom Gautama defeated, and even if there is some truth in the Christian complaint that the Buddhist life is (paradoxically) a selfish retreat, it should be noted, Clark thinks, that mystics in both religions are attempting to deal with, or respond to, the same reality: the Unborn and Indestructible in Buddhism is not wholly unrelated to the eternal (or better, the everlasting) God of Christianity (AJ, 80–82).

The enlightened in many religions (Judaism; Christianity, for example, Origen; Hinduism; etc.) may be found describing God in terms of the World Soul for the body of the world:

> Paradoxically, the enlightened may sometimes sound like solipsists, for they may say that they see everything as their own body. They feel everything with the same immediacy as we sometimes (not always) feel the bodies we usually consider ours. . . . Metaphors of possession, embodiment, or copulation abound in the literature of enlightenment. The enlightened have a real sense of what we can all, in some sense, know: that this body here, this individual cannot be broken from the greater whole. . . . Because the enlightened have a real sense of this, what they say may *sound like* a denial of reason. (AJ, 88–89; my emphasis)

The World Soul is not even foreign to Buddhism at its best. Clark asks: "Is the One Original to be found wholly in our awakening to a sense of unity with all the world, or is there something else to which that union points?" (AJ, 90). Buddhists are commonly supposed to rest content with a monistic vision whereby they are unaware of the partial distinction between Creator and cosmos (AJ, 197):

> On the one hand, Buddhists need not be understood as denying the reality of personal existence: the new life is the life of sharing, the realization that "there is no I without a We," that the Self is not a Solid. . . . On the other hand, Christian theories of the Trinity or the Atonement must cast doubt on any attempt to make our individuality a solid thing, or to identify the LORD with a particular exis- tent. (AJ, 90–91)

Although enlightenment or mysticism are in tension with reason, they are not opposed to it. It is only when the slogans of religious believers are subject to rational analysis that we can find ourselves in a position where the various enlightenments or mysticisms in religion are available across the boundaries established by cult. In addition to slogans, another impediment to progress in religion, and specifically with respect to belief in the World Soul, is attachment to Scripture or cult as inerrant. By attempting to overcome the deficiencies of particular religions—an effort that, it should be noted, is somewhat at odds with his conservative Anglicanism—Clark hopes to show that whatever defects there are in religious morals, even at their worst, are no worse than those found in Soviet bureaucrats or biological scientists (AJ, 92–93).

To believe that the World Soul is conscious, or that individual cells exhibit at least some protoconscious properties, is to believe that the World Soul can be viewed in an intentional mode that does not necessarily compete with physico- chemical explanation. In the case of an amoeba, for example, we can see the efforts to avoid being eaten by a larger being and the trying out of various strat- agems to achieve this end: "'consciousness' does not name an entity or realm dis- tinct from the physical" (AJ, 130). Rather, the use of intentional concepts is much more successful in describing and predicting the behavior of various sentient beings than the failure to use such concepts. Or, at the very least, we cannot test the hypothesis that only physico-chemical processes are involved in the work- ings of the microstructure or the macrostructure of the universe. Certainly all of our experience has some sort of affective tone and can be described most eas- ily in *some* sort of intentional language, such that Clark wonders how *our* (obvi- ous) consciousness could have developed in a universe devoid of conscious- ness and in a universe incapable of being described in intentional terms. Clark criticizes J. C. Dennett for his attempt to analyze consciousness away while using such obvious intentional concepts like "attention." He also criticizes Thomas Nagel for positing protomental properties at the microscopic level within an overall context that is insentient (AJ, 131, 133).[6] *How* do the proto-mentalistic particles form a mongoose's psyche?: "my being conscious does not seem likely to be the sort of thing that is composed of anything" (AJ, 144). Exactly what combinations of mind-dust are needed to produce a higher mind? That is, panpsychism seems to be tolerable to Clark only if it is a part of a larger scheme that includes the World Soul. Clark thinks that S_3 is as essential as S_1 and S_2 in the formula $S_1 : S_2 :: S_2 : S_3$.

> This conjunction of properties of a radically different kind at the elementary level is as brute an unintelligibility as the supposed emergence of mentalistic properties from the sheerly physical. (AJ, 145)[7]

Clark is quite willing to admit that there is something anthropomorphic, but not anthropocentric, in belief in the World Soul. In grasping one's own consciousness, he thinks, one acquires the capacity to attribute a similar stream of thought to others (AJ, 146):

> Nothing can be described without subjective elements. If that is so, the whole problem of consciousness's "emergence" from a non-mental world of pure objects can be allowed to lapse. There never was such a purely non-mental world. . . . To explain evolution we must have recourse to such entities as do not depend for their existence on the outcome of that process. Whether it is possible even to begin to construct a theory of what such entities would be like in the absence of any conscious theorizer seems uncertain. (AJ, 148–49)

By this line of reasoning, human consciousness is a reflection of that mode of conscious being from which all things are derived and in which they dwell (AJ, 151). Or again, "if realism is to be secure we must advance some account of what sort of universe this is if creatures of our kind are to have such ready access to empirically and logically indemonstrable truth" (AJ, 156). Clark's shorthand way of putting the options is, therefore, in terms of a choice between theistic realism (including a belief in God as the soul of the world) and atheism, whether in its materialist or constructivist modes. Neither type of atheism, he thinks, can account for *any* consciousness, much less the divine one.

Contemporary appreciation of the World Soul is likely to be mediated through belief in "the balance of Nature" or through something like Lovelock's Gaia hypothesis. Yet even if a new balance is achieved no matter what is inflicted on nature, this is not necessarily consolation to any particular species or to any particular individual. Forest ecosystems can be transformed into desert ecosystems, and this not only through human intervention, but also perhaps through cosmic "accident" or evolutionary "variation," to the extent that these latter are possible under the Clarkian belief in divine omnipotence (AJ, 171–72). In a previous chapter on environmental ethics I weighed Clark's attachment to both individuals and species, a weighing that, when his strong commitment to the World Soul is considered, gives the nod to species over individuals, a preference that seems to be at odds with his individualism/anarchism in politics:

> If individuals are all that matter then it does not matter if there are no more individuals of a given kind, unless this makes some painful difference to surviving individuals of another kind. A better understanding of what it is to be suggests that individuals (so called) exist as elements or nodes or slices through a wider whole. . . . It is, accordingly, not the individual zebra (human), nor yet zebrakind (humankind), that has "rights" in any ultimate sense. It is the world itself, and the joyful understanding of the world, that ought to be admired, preserved, and cultivated. (AJ, 175)

Clark's religious way of putting the point seems to be that religion at its best encourages us to individually find our centers, each of which *is also* the center of all other life:

> Religion is not a matter of external judgements, descriptions of how the world is. . . . If we were truly nothing but placental mammals on a ball of grubby rock, in a universe that falls "as chance would have it," with no powers but those that served to spread genetic material, piety would be as insignificant as hunger or sexual desire or scholarship. (AJ, 194–95)

This emphasis on (human *and* divine) centeredness partially bridges the gap between Clark's particularism and conservativism, on the one hand, and his belief in the universal World Soul, on the other: "there is no I apart from my existence as a member of this family, household, clan, tribe, city, nation, kingdom, heavenly city" (AJ, 210–11). It is in the seeming absence of the divine from the outer world at large that we are reminded of its particular presence within, a presence that each individual conserves. Clark's poetic way of putting the point is that:

> We live, as it were, upon the outskirts of the (good) Empire, deep in the fog of chance and of despair: but there is . . . a door to enlightenment even amongst hungry ghosts. (AJ, 214–15)

Current physical theory cannot be understood in terms of the middle-sized bodies we normally encounter, hence for this reason alone we should be willing to at least consider the possibility that materialism is defective and the possibility that dualism is not the only alternative to materialism. Clark makes it clear, however, that his willingness to take both panpsychism and the World Soul seriously is an attempt to explain how the person is in the cells (once again, hurt my cells—say, with a knife—and you hurt *me*) and how the person partially transcends the cells (cut off my whole finger and I still have a full vote at the polling place).[8] It is also an attempt to explain how each of us human individuals is a cell in the world's body, which the World Soul animates, rather than in the political state conceived as an organism (CP, 10, 26, 99):

> The final context of our worldly activity is not our immediate nation-state, nor yet the socio-political nexus of suffering humanity, but the whole earth. . . . One of the many not-so-peculiar oddities of the present age is that the theologically inclined have shied away from any doctrine of God's activity in nature at the very same time as the Earth herself has come to be seen as a proper object of pious adoration and concern. (CP, 135)

Clark is skeptical of the supposed contrast between pantheistic or immanentist conceptions of the divine derived from Stoicism, on the one hand, and the monotheistic view, on the other. Nature is found in the Psalms as much as it is in Stoicism, in Plato's *Timaeus* as much as in pantheism. Theists in general should band together against the common enemy: the disenchantment of the world whereby an "objective gaze" (particularly on animals) is connected to obvious political, or better, ideological motives. Belief in the World Soul is at least partially meant to counteract the exploitation of nature, hence Clark's ecomysticism is not really subject to Regan's criticism to the effect that "deep" environmentalism is really an environmental fascism. First, Clark is not denying inherent value to individuals, but is rather placing such value in a theistic context and is questioning the extent to which ethical individuals are metaphysical ones. Second, Clark is attributing inherent value to things other than human beings and other sentient animals. Third, however, he is not attributing inherent value to nonsentient beings to the point where ants are viewed, as they might be in some "primitive" moralities, as ends in themselves (CP, 136, 141–43).

POLITICS

Lovelock's thesis, concerning which there is at least some biological evidence, that the living world is like a federation of interdependent organs, tissues, or cells, is convincing to Clark. Yet holding this thesis does not commit Clark to an ambitious plan to manage the whole earth; on the contrary, we cannot "put it all together" because it *is* together. We inhabit a cosmos, not a chaos. The religious way to express this, when Clark is in his oecumenical rather than in his particularist mode, is that the kingdom of God is what appears when our earthly passions subside or when we come to realize that Nirvana has been here all along. The "city of the wise" includes not only Christians and Buddhists, but also Hellenistic philosophers: the whole earth was "theirs" by virtue of their friendship with the gods. Aristippus' way of putting the point was to suggest that the philosopher was at ease everywhere and would not alter his behavior even if all local laws were repealed (CP, 144, 151–53). Scientists, and not only scientists who are convinced by Lovelock's Gaia hypothesis, should love the world (soul) once they come to see that they are "acolytes of something marvellous" (CP, 154). *Any* scholarly discipline is, or at least should be, governed by a vision of an intellectual brotherhood-sisterhood dedicated to the discovery of truth disdainful of local bias (again, in contrast to Clark's previously treated particularism), hence the grain of truth in the dictum that academic life has nothing to do with politics. In this view we would be betraying a vocation if we did not, qua our scholarly pursuits, view with equanimity the daily twists and turns of national (or international) life against the background of a cosmic epoch. However, in another sense of the term academic life is intensely "political" (and indebted to the Enlightenment) when it is considered that in order to live up to its (universal) mission it must be made open to members of all classes and conditions of humankind, with the only proviso that they be honest and capable seekers after truth (CP, 156–57).

Just as Clark is opposed to environmental fascism, so also is he opposed to the "international academy" appointing itself without qualification as the city of the wise that ought to have a check on the use of political power:

> The best thing to do with tyranny—unless we truly have the Mandate of Heaven—is to ignore it, and continue in good heart and conscience to make such connections, academic, economic, personal as will outlast the Caesars. (CP, 158)

Only some scholars really live up to their calling, according to Clark, only some of them are sages who identify themselves as (pious) citizens of the cosmos. Of course, we do not normally expect to encounter saints in academe, nor penniless wanderers who follow the lead of Diogenes the Cynic or the *sannyasin*. Neither do we expect one to explain away a scholar's personal indecencies by saying that they have no relationship whatsoever to his thought, as Richard Rorty does with respect to Heidegger's Nazism.[9] Heidegger's case, however, does illustrate some of the pitfalls involved when the city of the wise is identified with a political city rather than with a cosmic one (CP, 166, 169–71, 179–80).

Some may be skeptical of those who believe in the World Soul because of the supposed nonintellectual sources of such belief, as in Yeats's belief in the Anima Mundi as disclosed to him in a semitrance. Clark, never overly infatuated with human reason, responds by saying that there is more than random make-believe in fantasy literature, and by claiming that our more primitive ancestors, whose spirit is tapped by Yeats, were not wholly fools. Even convenient fictions regarding the World Soul are valuable to the extent that symbols of the World Soul evoke the ever-shifting borders of our minds, minds that in the seventeenth through the nineteenth centuries largely excluded a serious consideration of the World Soul due to an unquestioned faith in mechanism, but that now permit such a consideration due to mechanism's collapse. Fantasy is not so much telepathy as an opening of the mind's eye (again, phenomenologically, scientifically, and religiously) to a larger mind and to the possibility that "our" thoughts may not be entirely ours. Clark notices the strange intellectual schizophrenia that characterizes contemporary minds: most of us are absorbed in moods, visions, dreams, daydreams, and fantasies much of the day and night and yet we are supposed to attend to these with only an analytic and objectifying mind.[10]

A serious question faces Clark when he defends the World Soul itself and the city of the wise, whose members are believers in the World Soul: "Are the laws of the Great City such as to include the conventions of human society as special cases, or must the wise man despise all human law?" Or again, "To what extent does 'the City of the Wise' provide us with a useful moral norm?"[11] Clark's response to these questions is that the "city" of the wise is not a would-be city designed to accommodate ordinary humanity. It is a "city" of which the wise are *already* inhabitants, a "city" in which one's fellows are very often, but not necessarily, law-abiding citizens of political cities. In one sense Clark thinks that each of us is a citizen of the city of the wise, to the extent that each of us is rational, or at least sentient; in another sense one must actually see oneself as a citizen of this city in order to be so. Clark gives no indication of holding that in the future the city of the wise could, as Plotinus or Philo hoped, be realized in an outward, legal form. Further, Clark's concern for animals resurfaces when he implies that a use of the argument from "marginal cases" (again, Clark hates this designation) would make it possible to include nonrational yet sentient animals into the city of the wise, if nonrational yet sentient human beings are, in some sense, already in this city. The truly wise obey the laws of reason and of nature rather than the shifting customs and superstitions of any one little city, but even animals and the marginal cases of humanity are "wise" to the extent that they unknowingly obey the laws of nature, if not those of reason.[12] The higher citizens of the city of the wise are those who accept the existence of *nous*:

> To live by *nous* is to live in obedience to a vision of the world which transcends and explains the lesser realms of ordinary experience. Equivalently, it is to live as one would live who recognized that she must live by the same law as everyone else.[13]

Clark wonders why a sheer individualistic prudence must be considered more rational than a wider love, say, love of universal *nous*.

It is never made clear by Clark how his Aristotelian theory of politics arising out of tradition and family habits is compatible with the practical implications of belief in the World Soul. Perhaps ethics (from ethos, habit) gives way to (intellectualized) morality and politics, whereby what one is ashamed to do in public one should not do in private. This theory is meant to counteract the temptation to use Gyges' ring improperly and, in effect, to deny the category of "the private": all acts occur out in the open under the eyes of God. The intrinsic value of an action is not changed merely by retiring within or exiting a house, nor merely by crossing a state boundary, hence metephysically there is only one *patris* (fatherland): "The really radical conclusion was drawn by Diogenes: the laws of the land have no force at all."[14] By way of contrast, Pythagoras thought that the best education for his son would be to make him a citizen of a well-governed state. The wise one, he thought, was not only a citizen of the cosmos. The tension is clear: by siding with Diogenes rather than with Pythagoras, who is much closer to Aristotle regarding citizenship than is Diogenes, Clark undercuts the Aristotelian effort to promote not only good family membership but also good citizenship in the properly political sense of the term. Clark's efforts to show that Aristotle was more concerned with the World Soul than with citizenship per se are not, as his reviewers have indicated, too convincing. It is worth remembering that, according to Plutarch, all of the ancient philosophers, *except* Aristotle and the atomists, believed in the World Soul.[15] Or better, regarding ethologized politics Clark is very much in the tradition of Aristotle, but regarding politics in the usual sense of the term he is thoroughly neoplatonic. He seems to agree with Philo when he approves of those who flee society in order to search for solitude and the World Soul.

In some way or another, however, Clark is legitimately pointing to a link that must be established between immediate community and the wider world. Clark wistfully suggests that such a link could be established as it was in late antiquity: holy and wise men on the fringes of community were often brought in to regulate the constitutions of states because they were beyond reproach, because they burrowed down to that state of soul that united them with the World Soul. As a political program this idea is now more than wistful, it is positively antediluvian. Clark is on firmer ground when he has us consider seriously the Hellenistic and neoplatonic idea that the philosopher should be at home everywhere. One wonders, however, whether this literal cosmopolitanism has as its necessary condition a contempt for ordinary political activity, which Marcus Aurelius and Clark would seem to have us look on as something less than the squabbles of dogs over a bone, or children over a toy. This seems to denigrate political activity too much, such that the "philosopher" who flees (childish) politics may thereby be creating an intellectual vacuum to be filled by any number of hucksters or demagogues. A less extreme way of putting Clark's point here is to say that it is not necessarily a mark of maturity that one adjust one's beliefs to social norms and one's assigned role in political society. Clark is also on to something worthwhile when he suggests that if a modern state were to call on philosophical *cosmopolitai* for help we might not have many clear examples to offer because we have largely given up on the idea that a philosopher should strive to be a wise person or a sage.[16]

What is the relationship between "the city of the wise" and the actually existing communities (or, perhaps, societies) of scholars? Clark states that

> The international community of friends and fellow-scholars which is our nearest approach to the "city of the wise" or would-be wise is not marked by its tendency to encourage virtue, though we remember enough of the tradition to think that the academic world ought to be above national rivalries, and resistant to tyranny. Ideally, that community is one in which still-living scholars can have some correspondence with the dead, and partly transcend contemporary and local prejudice. My suspicion . . . is that the moral ideal of the academy only makes much sense if the city of the wise has a real and eternal existence there where Plotinus placed it. Otherwise it functions only as a hope.[17]

Because good people all over the world are friends in at least a weak sense of friendship, we understand ourselves as good when we see ourselves as citizens of a wider realm than that of our immediate city. In any event, the myth of the philosopher as a member of the city of the wise is no worse than our contemporary myth regarding the philosopher as a linguistic pedant or literary guru.[18] This "city" is what Berkeley meant by the whole created universe, as we will see, and, as we have seen already, what Aristotle meant by denying that human beings were the most important beings in the world (*Nicomachean Ethics* 1141a).[19] This "city" also refers to the existence of objective moral values in the universe, to the existence of values that have a real and continuing effect on the way things are; that is, to the sorts of value denied by someone like J. L. Mackie. To believe in the World Soul is to believe that the pattern we could uncover in our souls is the same as that which we could uncover in the world at large. These patterns were for the most part accepted for two millennia among philosophers, even empiricist ones, according to Clark:

> We may hope to find some acceptable synthesis of our assorted goals and readings of the universe. . . . But why on earth should we expect that our hope will be fulfilled unless there is indeed ONE world?[20]

In addition to the startling emphasis Clark places on Aristotle and the World Soul, he places a surprising amount of attention on one part of Berkeley's immaterialist enterprise, which Clark suggests was consciously adopted in order to subvert a fashionable version of the Enlightenment. Far from being solipsistic,

Berkeley, according to Clark, insisted that a person should not consider himself as an independent individual so much as a part of the whole, of the "great City."[21] Relying on Berkeley's *Philosophical Commentaries*, his sermons and essays, *Alciphron*, and *The Querist*, Clark alerts us to the Berkeley who, in an allusion to the Acts of the Apostles, believed in the free Spirit in whom we live and move and have our being:

> Generations of high-minded moralists have contended that "really moral" persons do not act for their own well-being, but for some other good, not their own. Berkeley was in the older (and sounder) tradition, in thinking that one could only have others' happiness as one's goal in so far as one identified oneself with the whole of which both one and others were parts.[22]

Inclusion in this free, divine Spirit has at least this political consequence: even if it is unlikely that we would set aside our own private interest for the sake of a government that is at least somewhat, if not largely, self-appointed, it is unlikely we would *not* do so once we become aware of ourselves as parts of a divine whole.

Both in his treatment of Berkeley, in particular, and in his philosophy, in general, Clark exemplifies his belief that philosophers should not *always* be explicit and precise. That is, *sometimes* they should use the methods at their disposal, including the telling of stories, to elicit an "awakened eye" in their readers (PS, 42). His fideism is such that the (Wittgensteinian) solution to theoretical puzzles is less important than thinking one's way to those truths that can inform the heart *as well as* the head. One of the stories Clark enjoys telling is that regarding contemporary scientists who fulfill the dream of ancient magicians by exercising power without reforming their hearts. This story deals with one of the great sources of divisiveness at work in our world, runaway technocracy, which is at odds with one of the great sources of unity: our growing awareness that "Courage, temperance, fidelity, civility, prudence are Aristotelian virtues over all the world, whatever we choose to call them" (PS, 97–99). Morality is not quite a ubiquitous phenomenon in the human species, even if it is much more prevalent than the heirs of positivism admit. Even the scientific enterprise consists of the pursuit of *valuable* truth:

> The occasional demand for absolute freedom of scientific enquiry from all other duties, or for the claim of individual researchers to follow their "own" conscience

(especially when that turns out to be the internalized prejudice of their particular clan or sect), amounts to . . . "right of clergy". . . as if "I want to know what broiled baby tastes like, or why it tastes like that" were a better excuse for cannibalism than "I want to enjoy the taste." (PS, 100)

Curiosity can be as great a source of evil as greed. Clark's point here seems to be that in the absence of the World Soul in general or of any particular notion of God we are bound to be left with some sort of antirealism in morality:

> Believing in God, amongst other things, just is believing that there is a discoverable truth that it must be our chief endeavor to find out and make our own. That discoverable truth may not be, probably is not, all the truth there is. . . . All our knowledge rests within an unbounded sea of ignorance. (PS, 103)

Clark quotes Duns Scotus to the effect that to know *any* being as a "this" is already to conceive of God in an indistinct way. He also often quotes Gerard Manley Hopkins in order to highlight the experience of Presence, or inscape, and of the realization that not all philosophical argument has to be abstract (PS, 106–7).

GENDER

There is significance in the fact that Hopkins's fascination stems not only from Scotus or from personal experience, but also from a reading of Parmenides. Clark infers from this reading that ancient belief in the World Soul is not that far from Christian belief in divine omnipresence. Parmenides saw that truth existed and that there was only One Truth, which Hopkins expresses as the presence of Christ. In this Parmenidean, Hopkins-like context, faith consists of the lived conviction that there is a way back to the center (PS, 106–13). By "faith" here is meant not only religious faith but also scientific faith: "Science and all scholarship, in short, rests upon the faith that there is a key" (PS, 114). Yet, Clark thinks, "If truth cannot be discovered in the religious realm, it cannot be discovered anywhere" (PS, 115). The link between Christianity and the World Soul is also seen in St. Paul, who uses marriage to make a statement about cosmic reality (MR, 185). The earliest testimonies of religion suggest the belief in a World Mother, in the notion of the world as a great living being. A decisive move occurred in primitive religion when the World Mother was replaced by Mother Earth, who was only one constituent in a dualistic view of religion. The other constituent was her superior, Father Heaven. The transcendent God of the monotheistic religions—and the philosophies of religion at least indirectly associated with these religions—grew out of the Father Heaven symbolism, such that when the mechanization of the earthly world through seventeenth-century science occurred, which extinguished any semblance of divine immanence, deism and then agnosticism and atheism were the logical results. That is, any effort to keep theism alive must be concomitant with the efforts to develop a sexually egalitarian theology and philosophy of God *and* to restore some legitimacy to the notion of divine immanence provided by the World Soul.

One of the difficulties connected with this latter effort is that since Spinoza it has been assumed by most that the only alternative to a transcendent, monotheistic God as father is the indifferent, immanent deity of pantheism. Hence the importance of the *tertium quid* provided by panentheism, whereby the natural world is included *in* God through divine knowledge and sympathy, but the natural world does not exhaust God. Pauline marriage and copulation metaphors are ways of saying that both traditionally male and traditionally female attributes stand for the divine, with the receptivity associated with the World Soul harkening back to the Great Mother tradition. In a patriarchal marriage the wife is required to see her husband as a representative of God, as in traditional versions of the Abrahamic religions. Belief in the World Soul, however, includes an attempt to balance the importance of God as transcendent (a traditional male trait) against the importance of God as embodied and immanent (traditional female traits). That is, Clark's attachment to the universal World Soul is not only in tension with his anti-Enlightenment political particularism, but also with his Abrahamic traditionalism, even if St. Paul, Origen, and Hopkins somewhat help to bridge the gap between orthodox Christianity and the Greek view of God as the soul of the world.

The patriarchal God of the Abrahamic religions *orders* the cosmos, but the World Soul (or the demiurgic function of the World Soul) exerts an influence over and a responsiveness to the cosmos, in that it is organically connected to it. In different texts Clark inconsistently defends these two conceptions of deity. In the present chapter, however, I am emphasizing Clark's pronounced commitment to the World Soul, to the second and third sorts of theology, not the first, mentioned in the following quotation:

> Even those of us who, rejecting patriarchy and the spurious feminism of romantic love alike, still hold to our marriages as friends and companions may appreciate

the sort of theological statement made by more communal institutions and rituals. We may even come to understand our own "nuclear families" as variations on the communal ideal rather than the atomic particles which go to make up society. Three competing stories about the building blocks of human society generate their own theologies. . . . The first, that society is made up of individual persons. . . . The second, that society is made up of cooperating nuclear families, which occasionally collapse to burden the air with rootless solitaries. The third, that society is the community network within which ancestral families and colleges and clans can sometimes be distinguished, and individual persons are late historical abstractions, not the first of things. Worshipping the One All Alone, we may find in our individual selves the proper image of the worshipful. . . . Worshipping the Twofold, we find once-married couples the real image, and resist all dissipation of monogamy. Worshipping the Manifold-in-Unity, we approach another ideal . . . They are all one flesh. This last ideal has not been unknown in tradition. . . . Our predecessors were more wary of allowing sexuality a place in their divine phalansteries. . . . Similar problems may yet bring us back to more stable couplings, but not to patriarchy. (MR, 190–91)

It is not the case that the attempt to give material attributes to deity forces us to sink back into a purely emotional, uncritical morass, as some critics might allege. The dipolar theologies of Whitehead and Hartshorne, which are more fully developed than Clark's, indicate what some of the possibilities might be here. The key Clarkian point regarding the connection between belief in the World Soul and gender issues is that *if* one accepts the traditional identification of immateriality, abstraction, and power with maleness, and of embodiment, concreteness, and receptivity with femaleness (traditional attributes that are, admittedly, problematic), then there is not sufficient reason to think of God solely in "male" terms (MR, 192–95).

A "maternal" concern for the fate of the earth is thus not unconnected to Clarkian religiosity, nor with Clarkian conservativism, in the sense of ecological conservationism. Once again, to have a sense of the cosmos as besouled is not to say that one has a detailed and coherent *plan* for the ecology of the cosmos. Our best approach, according to Clark, would be to conserve as much of the natural environment as possible without "managing" it as a natural "resource": "What would we think of early hunters who systematically slaughtered all wild horses to obtain some gastronomic delicacy or to remove a nuisance, without ever considering that there might be other 'uses' for the horses, other ways of relating to them?"[23] We care for children (another traditionally female trait) not merely—if at all—because they are resources or insurance policies. So also regarding our care for living nature. The analogy between individual human beings and the cosmos also has the following consequences regarding, for lack of a better word, lifestyle: if we need a whole chemistry industry (with its attendant experiments on animals) to keep us alive, we cannot be very healthy; likewise, a genuinely healthy nature is one that can get along quite well without us. However, when Clark deifies Nature and identifies it with the caring God of Abrahamic tradition, we should wonder whether it is legitimate for him to claim regarding Nature that: "It is the sheer indifference to us and to our projects displayed by the rest of the natural world that attracts us."[24] It would seem to be more consistent with Clark's traditionalism to say that the mature "climax" community (in ecological jargon), whereby a diverse number of species each find their niche, would actually contribute something to the divine enjoyment of the world. By this line of reasoning "self-sustaining" communities should be left alone because of their contribution to God rather than because of their contribution to us, say for our aesthetic (or touristic) enjoyment.

Clark merges Lovelock's Gaia hypothesis ("that the biosphere has operated as does a living organism, modifying its own environment and so maintaining conditions suitable for its own survival"[25]) with the design argument for God such that the survival mechanisms found in our biosphere are connected to divine decisions. Yet even without a divinized Gaia Clark could perhaps legitimately claim the following:

> If Gaia really did retreat into the dust and leave us as the managers of a planet-sized chemical laboratory we should not merely be hard-pressed to survive. It is doubtful that we could. . . . It would be so difficult, so Lovelock guesses, to wholly unravel the sinews of Gaia. . . . Gaia is adept at turning "pollutants" into necessary elements. Gaia would survive, most probably, even a nuclear spasm that eliminated us.[26]

Some animal species are key in a particular ecosystem, for example, alligators in the Everglades, whose digging operations are crucial for other species in that ecosystem. In a sense, human beings are a key species in every particular ecosystem (and sometimes they even improve a particular ecosystem, as in the traditional English countryside coming closer to a climax state due to human beings and their hedgerows), but not in the biosphere as a whole, which can at least *survive* either with or without us. The fact that Gaia, Nature, or God as soul of the world is not threatened by us should in some way energize our conservative conservationism, Clark thinks, in that it would be a mistake to develop a paralysis with respect to our interaction with nature:

> To lay down that we should not interfere at all, that we should never do anything to which another species might respond, lest we upset an accidental balance, would be both unrealistic and nonideal. . . . But we need not accept any absolute principle to the effect that no species ever be allowed to perish from the world. What matters is the maintenance of Gaia and her constituent ecosystems, not the preservation at all costs of any single line (even our own).[27]

There is something ironic about human existence on Clarkian grounds, because we are integral features of the natural world *as well as* alien and temporary inhabitants of it; as the Christian commonplace has it, we are in the world but not of it.

DEATH

We cannot seriously suppose that we are genuinely or fully independent beings, solid monads with only external relations with the rest of the world. Neither we nor God could truly be unmoved movers. We are temporal parts of a historical tradition and spatial parts of a cosmic system, once again a system that cannot be put together because it *is* together. The view that we are elements within a continuing cosmic community is, Clark thinks, the realistic analogue to Kant's idealistic kingdom of ends. Our prime duties qua our citizenship in the cosmic community are to avoid *pleonexia* (compulsive consumerism) and to reject any view that encourages us to consider only the present state of things: "we may yet have time to slow down our destruction of our kin, and rediscover that we share a commonwealth."[28] Because we are parts of a whole that survives us, it is easy to say, at least in the abstract, that only the misguided want to live forever: "Taking one's troubles philosophically, in ordinary speech, is still to take them as a good Stoic might" (PS, 116). Yet Clark correctly notes that dying or thinking about dying very often does not bring out the best in us; nor does poverty or oppression. If pain is an intimation of what death is—not because all deaths are painful but because all pains are deathly—then we can gradually come to understand our deaths as the natural phenomena that they are. Some solace is received in the Hebrew notion that we will continue after our deaths in our children, in others' memories, and in whatever monuments we leave behind us. However even greater solace is received when we realize that we contribute to, and will be remembered by, an omnibenevolent and all-remembering deity (PS, 197–99). In fact, as Hartshorne is fond of pointing out, the meaning to our lives largely consists of the degree to which we contribute to deity, including the contribution of our present happiness.

Even if it is true that the kind of person one is depends on the kind of center one identifies oneself with, identification with a divine center does not necessarily eliminate a fear of death:

> So the aphorism that death is not an event in life, not a thing we live through and so not a thing to be feared, is not entirely true. . . . To say that one should not rationally mind about death because one will not be there to complain can never be anything but a sophism: that one will not be there, that one will have been dissolved, "as if one had never been," is exactly what we mind about. (PS, 121)

Although we should "mind" about death, especially premature, ugly, or painful death, one should not develop a fetish for one's life, in that it is The One that remains. Some "many" or other remains as well, but this many or that shifts and passes:

> Even the thought or fear of death is only a passing colour on the surface of things, of the one thing that there really is. There are no "real" or "fundamental" differences between the living, the dead, and the inanimate. . . . We do not solve the emotional crisis occasioned by the prospect of dying by pretending that Stuff does not die; the horror of death just is that we are then assimilated to mere Stuff! (PS, 123)

The organizing principles that keep our cells working together only briefly maintain such unity against the dark, or against the light, as the case may be:

> Each of us is a colony organism, embedded in a biosphere and universe that has a larger program than just "ours." To put the matter rhetorically: just as my liver is an essential part of "me" because "I" cannot survive without it, so also are the algae on the shore without which I (and you) would die of sulfur loss. It is impossible to conceive of human beings that long inhabit an otherwise "dead" world,

just as we cannot conceive that they would long exist without their kidneys, lungs, or spinal cord. So to speak of "me here-now" is to imagine a boundary between Me and Not-me that we cannot seriously or exactly draw: some things, no doubt, are things that I can live well enough without, but the living earth is not one of them! (PS, 125–26)

CONCLUSION

Clark's philosophy will remain controversial. It may well be the case that he will not be able to render consistent all of the conflicting elements in his thought (e.g., regarding the World Soul itself, and regarding the tension between his belief in the World Soul, on the one hand, and his particularism, his Aristotelianism, his belief in God as omnipotent, and his individualism and anarchism in politics, on the other). Yet it is by no means clear that Roger Scruton is correct when he claims that the energy and variety of Clark's convictions, when combined with the supposed "sparseness" of his argumentation, will ensure that he will elicit agreement only from those who (like Scruton himself) already share his (largely conservative) sympathies.[29] I, at least, do *not* share those sympathies, yet I am repeatedly shaken out of complacency by Clark's arguments, exhortations, fantasies, non sequitur remarks, and historical citations. In the final analysis I think we must agree with Clark that how things are now is not how they must be. Things that now seem to have been true from everlasting are very often of recent origin, hence Clark's efforts to unsettle the present very often constitute a (literally) radical attempt to throw sand in the eyes of contemporary "conservatives." His defense of the World Soul is a notable example of this. Supposedly "fresh beginnings" are a trope in contemporary philosophy; they have been made by Derrida, Ayer, Heidegger, Wittgenstein, Moore, and so on. It is unlikely that all of these thinkers have refuted past pretenders. Clark's own fresh beginning is not so much an attempt to refute past pretenders as to restore them in his battle against several contemporary dogmas:

> Serious explorers must be more adventurous. It is not true that all human beings think the betterment of humankind is what matters most. It is not true that everybody thinks that being better off is being richer, or that "the better you live, the more oil you use." It is not true that individual human beings can be easily identified, through all the world, as autonomous agents having or deserving more rights than their fellow mammals, vertebrates or creatures. It is not true

that everyone agrees that children have fewer rights than adults do. It is not true that personal pleasure in the here-and-now is the only rational motive. It is not true that no-one nowadays believes in sin. It is not true that what has existed so far is all that could exist, or should.[30]

Clark cautions us against predicting the future, in general, or the future of philosophy, in particular. Nor would he have us wait for a God to save us, in that, on both sound Christian and Buddhist grounds, we are already "saved." Rather: "The point of reading ancient texts, consulting alien tribes, imagining strange futures, and detecting paradox is to destroy the obvious, and ready our tribes for what we don't expect."[31]

NOTES

PREFACE

1. See Lewis Ayres, review of *Limits and Renewals*, *Modern Theology* 10 (1994): 227–29; Oliver O'Donovan, review of *Civil Peace and Sacred Order*, *Journal of Theological Studies* 42 (1991): 441–44; and John Rist, review of *A Parliament of Souls*, *Journal of Theological Studies* 42 (1991): 819–21, and review of *God's World*, *Journal of Theological Studies* 43 (1992): 791–94. Also see Adam Morton, review of *How to Live Forever*, *British Journal for Philosophy of Science* 48 (1997): 310–12, who finds Clark "arresting," "profound," "amusing," and, paradoxically, "irritating."

CHAPTER ONE

1. Josiah Royce, *The Philosophy of Loyalty* (NewYork: Macmillan, 1908), 11. Cited in CP, 16.
2. See Fergus Kerr's review of AJ in *The Heythrop Journal* 29 (1988): 112–13. Also see Clark's "With Rationality and Love," *Times Literary Supplement*, 26 September 1986, 1047–49, where he criticizes Richard Dawkins for ignoring the intellectual basis for theism. Clark believes that atheists and unthinking media managers are unconsciously conspiring with fundamentalists to paint a ridiculous picture of theism.

3. See W. B. Yeats, *Autobiographies* (London: Macmillan, 1955), 78; and John Henry Newman, *An Essay in Aid of a Grammar of Assent* (Notre Dame, Ind.: University of Notre Dame Press, 1947), 286. Also see Clark's "How to Believe in Fairies," *Inquiry* 30 (1987): 337–38.

4. See J. D. G. Evans's review of AM in *The Philosophical Quarterly* 26 (1976): 168–69.

5. See Gerard Hughes's review of AM in *The Heythrop Journal* 18 (1977): 206–7.

6. See I. N. Robins's review of AM in *Philosophy* 51 (1976): 236–39.

7. See Aristotle, *Eudemian Ethics* 8.1248a.

8. William James, *The Will to Believe* (New York: Longmans, Green, 1897), 30. Clark finds it significant that many Hellenistic philosophers saw the Hebrews as a nation of philosophers, not because they asked questions but because they served God. That is, for Clark there is a spiritual significance to philosophy that we "sophists" in contemporary universities (to use Clark's own designation) often fail to notice. Some people still turn to philosophy as a consolation for their troubles, until they find out what most contemporary philosophy is about. See Stephen Clark, "The Spiritual Meaning of Philosophy," *Chronicles of Culture* 13, no. 9 (1989): 14–15.

9. See George Chryssides's review of MR in *Teaching Philosophy* 10 (1987): 159–60.

10. See Craig Staudenbauer's review of AJ in *Modern Schoolman* 64 (1987): 202–4.

11. Clark, "How to Believe in Fairies," 339.

12. Stephen Clark, "Cupitt and Divine Imagining," *Modern Theology* 5 (1988): 48, 50–51.

13. Ibid., 51–52, 53.

14. Ibid., 54–55.

15. Ibid., 55–57.

16. Ibid., 58–59.

17. Stephen Clark, "God, Good and Evil," *Proceedings of the Aristotelian Society* 77 (1977): 261.

18. Stephen Clark, "Retrospective (1988–1945)," *Between the Species* 5 (1989): 57, 60.

19. Stephen Clark, "Utility, Rights and the Domestic Virtues," *Between the Species* 4 (1988): 245. It should be noted, however, that among the arguments for the existence of God, Clark is most fond of the ontological, as opposed, say, to Swinburne's fascination with the argument from design. See Clark's "Limited Explanations," *Philosophy: Supplement* 27 (1990): 195–210.

20. Stephen Clark, "How to Reason about Value Judgments," *Philosophy: Supplement* 24 (1988): 176–78.

21. Ibid., 179–81. Also see Clark's "Philosophers and Popular Cosmology," *Journal of Applied Philosophy* 10 (1993): 115–22, regarding the need for philosophers to become

active critics of what Clark takes to be true: science is only the myth we have, and science is (unfortunately) the only myth we have.

CHAPTER TWO

1. Clark shows at least some awareness of process thought in his citation in MR, 245, of J. Cobb and C. Birch, *The Liberation of Life* (Cambridge: Cambridge University Press, 1981). Also see his treatment of process thought in *How to Think about the Earth* (London: Mobray, 1993). Further, in "Is the Universe a Put-up Job?" *Times Literary Supplement*, 26 June 1992, 6–7, Clark both reiterates his familiar defense of Peirce's "neglected argument" for God and considers the possibility that only process theism can accommodate the contingency of the world along with the necessary existence of God as articulated in the ontological argument (an accommodation that is a Hartshornian commonplace).

2. Stephen Clark, "How to Believe in Fairies," *Inquiry* 30 (1987): 347.

3. See C. Hartshorne and W. Reese, *Philosophers Speak of God* (Chicago: University of Chicago Press, 1953), 4.

4. Ibid., 2.

5. Ibid., 15.

6. Ibid., 3.

7. Ibid., 4. Also see Hartshorne's *Insights and Oversights of Great Thinkers* (Albany: State University of New York Press, 1983), 55.

8. Hartshorne and Reese, *Philosophers Speak of God*, 14–15.

9. Ibid., 24.

10. Hartshorne, *Insights and Oversights of Great Thinkers*, 366.

11. God must be as great as possible at any particular time or else God would not be the greatest conceivable being. Yet new moments bring with them new possibilities for greatness, which God must realize in the best way possible if God is the greatest, or better, the unsurpassable. This means that God is greater than any being that is not God, but God can always surpass Godself. It does not mean that God's earlier existence was inferior, because it was at that earlier time the greatest conceivable existence, the greatest existence logically possible, and greater than any other being.

12. Hartshorne, *Insights and Oversights of Great Thinkers*, 54.

13. *Meditations*, 11.1.

14. On John of the Cross see my *St. John of the Cross* (Albany: State University of New York Press, 1992).

15. See Aristotle, *Poetics* 1450b and *Meteorology* 351b.

16. The categories can be seen as a *tetractys*: *ousia*, a noun; *poson* and *poion*, adjectives; *pros ti*, *pou*, and *pote*, adverbs; and *keisthei*, *echein*, *poiein*, and *paschein*, verbs.

17. See Aristotle, *Physics* 4.218a. Clark's latest view regarding McTaggart is that the A-series is defective when describing God, as is the B-series. Clark favors the C-series, but it should be noted that the C-series is close to the B-series, in that it is timeless. The key concept here is inclusion, which offers us a model of the God-world relationship, an instance of inclusion that is sometimes misperceived as a temporal series. See J. T. McTaggart, *The Nature of Existence*, 2 vols. (Cambridge: Cambridge University Press, 1927).

18. See Aristotle, *Nicomachean Ethics* 6.1139b; and *De Caelo* 283b.

19. See Aristotle, *Metaphysics* 7.1039b; 13.1087a; *Posterior Analytics* 81b; and *Nicomachean Ethics* 2.1109b. Also see my Plato's *Philosophy of History* (Washington, D.C.: University Press of America, 1981).

20. Clark, "How to Believe in Fairies," 349.

21. Ibid., 350–51.

22. See Stephen Clark, "Mackie and the Moral Order," *Philosophical Quarterly* 39 (1989): 99.

23. Robert Gay's review of MR in *Philosophical Books* 28 (1987): 117, notes, however, that Clark's sympathetic account of polytheism can explain the role of belief in Aphrodite even if there is no such being: what one enters into imaginatively has real effects on one's life.

24. See my *Christian Pacifism* (Philadelphia: Temple University Press, 1991).

25. See Clark, "Mackie and the Moral Order," 109–10.

26. See Clark, "How to Believe in Fairies," 341–42.

27. Ibid., 346.

28. Ibid., 347–48.

29. See Stephen Clark, "Commentary on 'Multiple Personality and Moral Responsibility,'" *Philosophy, Psychiatry, and Psychology* 3 (1996): 55–57; idem, "Minds, Memes, and Multiples," *Philosophy, Psychiatry, and Psychology* 3 (1996): 21–28; and idem, "Substance: Or Chesterton's Abyss of Light," *Proceedings of the Aristotelian Society: Supplementary Volume* 69 (1995): 1–14.

30. Clark, "How to Believe in Fairies," 352–54. It should be noted that my use of Hartshorne in this chapter should not be interpreted to mean that Clark is extremely familiar with process thought. I do not think that he is (cf., note 1 above), as is evidenced in his "World Religions and World Orders," *Religious Studies* 26 (1990): 54, where he misleadingly claims that process thinkers such as Whitehead

or Hartshorne are saying that things are everlastingly changing for the better. Also see "Where Have All the Angels Gone?" *Religious Studies* 28 (1992): 221–34, where Clark traces belief in "angels," broadly conceived, from the time of ancient polytheism, to the denigration of angels in early Christianity (when monotheism was the overriding concern), to the rediscovery of angels in the Middle Ages. When we understand angels as moods or as modes of being we will cease to think that Gabriel and Mary once occupied a room together and we will begin to notice angels as "real essences."

31. The historical sources of Clark's preference for being over becoming include Philo, the Christian church fathers, and some of the ancients. See his "Ancient Philosophy," in *The Oxford Illustrated History of Western Philosophy*, ed. Anthony Kenny (Oxford: Oxford University Press, 1994), 1–53.

CHAPTER THREE

1. See Charles Hartshorne, *Creative Synthesis and Philosophic Method* (LaSalle, Ill.: Open Court, 1970), 239–40. Also see 30, 242, 292. Another edition of this work was published by SCM Press in London, also in 1970. A work of mine can also be consulted here: see *Christian Pacifism* (Philadelphia: Temple University Press, 1991) regarding the story of Jesus cleansing the temple.

2. See Clark's "God, Good and Evil," *Proceedings of the Aristotelian Society* 77 (1977): 247–49.

3. Ibid., 250–51.

4. See David Ray Griffin, *God, Power, and Evil: A Process Theodicy* (Philadelphia: Westminster, 1976).

5. See my "Hartshorne and Plato," in the Library of Living Philosophers Series, edited by Lewis Hahn, *The Philosophy of Charles Hartshorne* (LaSalle, Ill.: Open Court, 1991).

6. Clark, "God, Good and Evil," 252–57, esp. 256.

7. Ibid., 258–60.

8. Ibid.

9. Ibid., 262.

10. Ibid.

11. Ibid., 264.

12. Again, see my *Christian Pacifism* regarding the Judeo-Christian roots of both pacifism and just war theory.

13. See Clark's "God's Law and Morality," *Philosophical Quarterly* 32 (1982): 339–42, esp. 342.

14. Ibid., 344.

15. Ibid., 345.

16. Ibid., 346–47.

17. John Chandler, "Clark on God's Law and Morality," *Philosophical Quarterly* 35 (1985): 87–90, esp. 90.

18. Clark, "God's Law and Chandler," *Philosophical Quarterly* 37 (1987): 204.

19. Ibid., 205.

20. Ibid., 207.

21. Ibid., 208.

22. See Clark's "Cupitt and Divine Imagining," *Modern Theology* 5 (1988): 47.

23. Aristotle, *On the Parts of Animals* 681a and *History of Animals* 588b.

24. *On the Parts of Animals* 663b.

25. See Gerard Watson's review of AM in *Philosophical Studies* 23 (1975): 330–32.

26. See Clark's "Waking-up: A Neglected Model for the Afterlife," *Inquiry* 26 (1983): 212.

27. Ibid., 217.

28. Ibid., 219.

29. Ibid., 221–22.

30. Ibid., 224.

31. Ibid., 226.

32. Ibid., 227–28. It should be noted that Clark's traditional theodicy and his traditionalism in general put him in an ambivalent relationship with Descartes. See his "Descartes' Debt to Augustine," *Philosophy: Supplement* 32 (1992): 73–88, where Descartes is seen as offering a new way to secure old truths. It should also be noted that Clark's approach to religion and theodicy relies on his belief in the possible truth of metaphor. Even "literal" truths are metaphorical, as when we say that a claim "literally" *mirrors* reality. But Clark nonetheless adheres to some form of the correspondence theory of truth, as opposed to the deconstructionists. His view is that "literal" sentences are those where we come closer to identifying some finite set of implications of the sentence, whereas "metaphorical" ones are those where it is more difficult to draw a line around the class of implications. See Clark, "The Possible Truth of Metaphor," *International Journal of Philosophical Studies* 2 (1994): 19–30.

33. See Clark's *How to Live Forever: Science Fiction and Philosophy* (London: Routledge, 1995), 19, 30, 47–48, 61, 65, 83, 96, 108, 114, 145, 151, 162, 164, 178–79, 183–86. In

this work Clark argues that immortality is not one theme among others in the classics of science fiction, but the dominant theme of this genre. The immortality discussed in science fiction comes in many forms: anti-aging drugs, operations, cyborg-style prosthetics, being uploaded into a computer system, and so on. In all of these, problems of self-identity emerge. Also see Mason Cash, "Review of *How to Live Forever: Science Fiction and Philosophy*," *Philosophy in Review* 17 (1997): 396–98. In addition to providing options to us regarding how we can think about the possibility of immortality, the science fiction of a writer like Olaf Stapledon enables us to rethink apophatic theology or the via negativa. Fundamentalist preachers lead some reflective people to become unbelievers; likewise dogmatic agnostics and atheists lead some reflective people to feel a restless expectation of a "something more." See Stephen Clark, "Olaf Stapledon," *Chronicles of Culture* 10, no. 12 (1986): 18. Also see idem., "Robotic Morals," *Cogito* 2 (1988): 22. Finally, Clark's willingness to stay abreast not only with the latest fantasies regarding technology, but also with real world technological developments, can be seen in his "Philosophy," in *New Technologies for the Humanities*, ed. Christine Mullings, et al. (East Grinstead, U.K.: Bowker-Sauer, 1996).

CHAPTER FOUR

1. See Charles Hartshorne, *Born to Sing* (Bloomington: Indiana University Press, 1973). Also see my *Hartshorne and the Metaphysics of Animal Rights* (Albany: State University of New York Press, 1988).

2. Two authors who defend hunting on this basis, explicitly or implicitly, are Ann Causey, "On the Morality of Hunting," *Environmental Ethics* 11 (1989): 327–43, and Theodore Vitali, "Sport Hunting: Moral or Immoral," *Environmental Ethics* 12 (1990): 69–82. See a refutation by Evelyn Pluhar, "The Joy of Killing," *Between the Species* 7 (1991): 121–28.

3. Stephen Clark, "The Rights of Wild Things," *Inquiry* 22 (1979): 181. Also see 182–83, 188. Sources for Clark's views on ethology include C. J. Jolly, "The Seed-Eaters: A New Model of Hominid Differentiation Based on a Baboon Analogy," *Man* 5 (1970): 5–26; E. O. Wilson, *Sociobiology* (Cambridge: Harvard University Press, 1975); H. F. and M. K. Harlow, "The Affectional Systems," in *Non-Human Primates* (New York: Academic Press, 1965); Irenaus Eibl-Eibesfeldt, *The Biology of Peace and War* (London: Thames and Hudson, 1979); and Eugene Linden, *Apes, Men and Language* (New York: Dutton, 1975). Clark also relies on the well-known work of Lorenz and Tinbergen. See, e.g., Konrad Lorenz, *On Aggression* (London:

Methuen, 1966), and Nikolaas Tinbergen, "On War and Peace in Animals and Men," *Science* 160 (1968): 1411 ff. Also see the bibliography to NB.

4. See Robert Elliot's review of NB in *Australasian Journal of Philosophy* 61 (1983): 454–56.

5. See Patricia McAuliffe's review of NB in *Philosophical Books* 24 (1983): 125–26.

6. See the anonymous review of NB in *Philosophical Studies* 31 (1986–87): 523–25.

7. See Peter Miller's review of NB in *Environmental Ethics* 9 (1987): 277–79.

8. See Robert Gay's review of MR in *Philosophical Books* 28 (1987): 117.

9. See Stephen Clark, "Utility, Rights and the Domestic Virtues," *Between the Species* 4 (1988): 242.

10. See Gerard Hughes's review of AM in *The Heythrop Journal* 18 (1977): 206–7.

11. See Genevieve Lloyd, "Spinoza's Environmental Ethics," *Inquiry* 23 (1980): 293–311.

12. Stephen Clark, "Mackie and the Moral Order," *Philosophical Quarterly* 39 (1989): 104–6.

13. See Clark's "Notes on the Underground," *Inquiry* 33 (1990): 32–33.

14. Ibid., 35.

15. Ibid., 36.

16. Stephen Clark, "Aristotle's Woman," *History of Political Thought* 3 (1982): 177–88. Also see W. Cowling and N. Tuana, "Plato and Feminism: A Review of the Literature," *American Philosophical Association Newsletter* (1990): 110–15.

17. Clark, "Aristotle's Woman," 190.

18. Ibid., 191.

19. Stephen Clark, "Sexual Ontology and Group Marriage," *Philosophy* 58 (1983): 215–16.

20. Ibid., 217.

21. Ibid., 218.

22. Ibid., 219–20.

23. Ibid., 221.

24. Ibid., 222–23.

25. Ibid., 226.

26. Ibid., 227. It is not the case, as Mary-Catherine Geach alleges, that Clark's concept of group marriage refers to a "wife-sharing club." See her review of NB in *Philosophy* 59 (1984): 275–76.

27. Stephen Clark, "Hume, Animals and the Objectivity of Morals," *Philosophical Quarterly* 35 (1985): 117–23.

28. Ibid., 124.

29. Ibid., 127–29.

30. See David Hume, *Treatise concerning Human Nature*, 3.1.1, ed. by L. A. Selby-Bigge (Oxford, 1888).

31. Clark, "Hume, Animals and the Objectivity of Morals," 133.

32. Clark, "Utility, Rights and the Domestic Virtues," 242.

33. See William Eckhardt, "Primitive Militarism," *Journal of Peace Research* 6 (1975): 55–62, on the theories of Quincy Wright.

34. Again, see my *Christian Pacifism* (Philadelphia: Temple University Press, 1991).

35. Stephen Clark, "Humans, Animals and 'Animal Behavior,'" in *Ethics and Animals*, ed. Harlan Miller (Clifton, N.J.: Humana Press, 1983), 179.

36. Clark, "Hume, Animals and the Objectivity of Morals," 125.

37. Ibid.

38. Ibid., 126.

39. Ibid., 128.

40. Ibid., 131.

41. *Nicomachean Ethics* 7.1150a. Also *Politics* 2.1267a. An Aristotelian ethology is a longstanding interest of Clark's. See his "The Use of 'Man's Function' in Aristotle," *Ethics* 82 (1972): 269–83; as well as a forthcoming work of his to be published by Routledge titled *The Political Animal*.

CHAPTER FIVE

1. For an excellent article regarding what Aquinas's attitude toward animals should have been, in his own standards, see Judith Barad, "Aquinas' Inconsistency on the Nature and the Treatment of Animals," *Between the Species* 4 (1988): 102–11.

2. Vernon White, *The Fall of a Sparrow* (Exeter: Paternoster Press, 1985).

3. Aristotle, *De anima* 1.408b.

4. See, e.g., Patricia Churchland, *Neurophilosophy* (Cambridge: Harvard University Press, 1986).

5. Once again, see my *The Philosophy of Vegetarianism* (Amherst: University of Massachusetts Press, 1984).

6. Regarding this equation of *nous*, conscience, and guardian *daimon*, Clark is relying on Plutarch's appropriation of Aristotle. See *De Facie* 943a.

7. See Stephen Clark, "Reason as *Daimon*," in *The Person and the Human Mind*, ed. Christopher Gill (Oxford: Clarendon Press, 1990), 205.

8. See Stephen Clark, "Abstraction, Possession, Incarnation: Neo-Platonic Explorations," in *Being and Truth*, ed. Alastair Kee and Eugene Long (London: SCM Press,

1986), 297. Also see Peter Miller's review of NB in *Environmental Ethics* 9 (1987): 277.

9. Clark, "Abstraction, Possession, Incarnation," 298–99, 303.

10. Ibid., 304.

11. Among the critics of the argument see R. G. Frey, *Rights, Killing, and Suffering* (London: Basil Blackwell, 1983). Also see the bibliography to my *The Philosophy of Vegetarianism.*

12. Stephen Clark, "Utility, Rights and the Domestic Virtues," *Between the Species* 4 (1988): 239, 241.

13. See Peter Singer, *Animal Liberation* (NewYork: New York Review, 1975), 265. Also see Tom Regan, "Fox's Critique of Animal Liberation," *Ethics* 88 (1978): 126–33.

14. Stephen Clark,"Animal Wrongs," *Analysis* 38 (1978): 148–49.

15. See Stephen Clark, "The City of the Wise," *Apeiron* 20 (1987): 65, 67. Also see idem., "Riots at Brightlingsea," *Journal of Applied Philosophy* 13 (1996): 109–12, where Clark holds that a defensible view of animals will cause one to seek "the greatest change since the Neolothic."

16. See Stephen Clark, "Humans, Animals, and 'Animal Behavior,'" in *Ethics and Animals*, ed. Harlan Miller (Clifton, N.J.: Humana Press, 1983), 180.

17. Clark, "Utility, Rights and the Domestic Virtues," 239, 243.

18. Stephen Clark, "Is Humanity a Natural Kind?," in *What Is an Animal?*, ed. Tim Ingold (London: Unwin Hyman, 1988), 17–24.

19. Ibid., 26.

20. Ibid., 27.

21. Ibid., 28.

22. Ibid., 31.

23. Ibid. Also see "Genetic and Other Engineering," *Journal of Applied Philosophy* 11 (1994): 233–37, where Clark emphasizes that species are not fictions even if there are no rigid boundaries in nature; genetic engineering constitutes a serious distortion of natural order, he thinks.

24. See my "Vegetarianism and the Argument from Marginal Cases in Porphyry," *Journal of the History of Ideas* 45 (1984): 141–43. Also see my *Babies and Beasts: The Argument from Marginal Cases* (Champaign: University of Illinois Press, 1997).

25. Clark, "Is Humanity a Natural Kind?," 32.

26. Ibid.

27. See Tom Regan's review of MS in *Philosophical Books* 19 (1978): 118–19.

28. See Fergus Kerr's review of MS and NB in *The Heythrop Journal* 28 (1987): 498.

29. See Dale Jamieson's review of MS in *Nous* 15 (1981): 230–34.

30. See MS, 87, 89–90, 92–94, 106, 108–9, 182; AJ, 165; idem, "Animal Wrongs," 148–49; idem., "The City of the Wise," 65, 67; idem, "Utility, Rights and the Domestic Virtues," 239, 243; idem., "Humans, Animals, and 'Animal Behavior'," 180; and idem., "Is Humanity a Natural Kind?"

31. See L. W. Sumner's review of MS in *Dialogue* 17 (1978): 570–71.

32. Ibid., 571–72.

33. Ibid., 574.

34. Also see Dolores Dooley-Clarke's review of MS in *Philosophical Studies* 26 (1979): 341–42.

35. See Mary Midgley's review of MS in *The Philosophical Quarterly* 28 (1978): 177–78.

36. See, e.g., Patrick Sherry's review of MR in *Modern Theology* 6 (1989): 114–15.

37. See the unnamed reviewer of MS in *Ethics* 88 (1978): 186. In "The Reality of Shared Emotions," in *Interpretation and Explanation in the Study of Animal Behavior*, ed. Marc Bekoff and Dale Jamieson (Boulder, Colo.: Westview, 1990), Clark argues against both antirealism and eliminative materialism, and for several reasons. If antirealism is correct, then it seems we could eliminate animal and human suffering merely by revising our concepts. Likewise, eliminative materialism is defective because of the nastiness of pain as a direct and ineluctable given. Eliminative materialists, including a good number who experiment on animals, paradoxically appropriate such terms as "pain," "feeling," and the like, when it is to their advantage to do so. The appeal made by antirealists and eliminative materialists to Occam's razor (not to multiply entities beyond necessity) misrepresents what is needed in a morally defensible science: not postulation of extra entities, but a grasp of the nature of the ones immediately present to us, as in the fears and pains of animals. We have available to us the ability to share in the form of life of beings other than ourselves.

38. A recent critic who disagrees with both Clark's concern for animals and his realism is Keith Tester, *Animals and Society* (London: Routledge, 1991), 12, 159, 194. Tester thinks of animal rights as a fetish: there are no immutable, natural truths regarding animals; in fact, for Tester there are no truths at all "out there." Yet Tester surely errs here, especially when he says that for Clark the moral status of animals is precisely the same as our moral status, but Tester fails to support this claim with textual evidence. Further, and incredibly, Tester accuses Clark, again without textual evidence, of dishonesty in claiming that his theory applies to all animals equally, whereas it primarily applies to mammals. Also see Michael Leahy, *Against Liberation* (London: Routledge, 1991), 57, 143–45, 164, 258, who notes that Clark's style of argument, wherein science, literature, and religion are weaved into philosophy, is similar to that defended by Cora Diamond. Leahy, however, is not in agreement

with Clark's polemical stance with respect to our treatment of animals; specifically, he is not in agreement with the view that in animals we can see the prelinguistic beginnings of self-consciousness. In this regard Leahy has a view of Clark similar to that of Bernard Williams.

39. See Clark's "Enlarging the Community: Companion Animals," in *Applied Ethics*, ed. Brenda Almond (Oxford: Basil Blackwell, 1995), 318–30. Also see Clark's "Philosophical Anthropology," in *Encyclopedia of Ethics*, ed. Lawrence Becker and Charlotte Becker (New York: Garland, 1992), 963–64.

CHAPTER SIX

1. Stephen Clark, "Humans, Animals, and 'Animal Behavior,'" in *Ethics and Animals*, ed. Harlan Miller (Clifton, N.J.: Humana Press, 1983), 176.
2. See my "The Jesuits and the Zoophilists, Again," *Irish Theological Quarterly* 51 (1985): 232–41.
3. See several publications of mine listed in the bibliography. On St. Thomas and Kant also see selections in P. Singer and T. Regan, eds., *Animal Rights and Human Obligations* (Englewood Cliffs, N.J.: Prentice-Hall, 1976).
4. Clark, "Humans, Animals, and 'Animal Behavior,'" 172–75.
5. Ibid., 175.
6. Stephen Clark, "Animals, Ecosystems and the Liberal Ethic," *Monist* 70 (1987): 123. Also see 114–17, 119, 122.
7. Ibid., 130. Also see 128, 131.
8. See Stephen Clark, "Retrospective (1988–1945)," *Between the Species* 5 (1989): 57.
9. R. M. Hare, "What is Wrong with Slavery," *Philosophy and Public Affairs* 8 (1979): 103.
10. Stephen Clark, "Slaves and Citizens," *Philosophy* 60 (1985): 31–32. Also see 27–30.
11. Ibid., 33.
12. Ibid., 34–46.
13. Aristotle, *De Anima* 414b and 413b.
14. See "Higher Laws" in Thoreau's *Walden* and see my *Thoreau the Platonist* (New York: Peter Lang, 1986).
15. For a favorable review of MS see Charles Magel's review in *Environmental Ethics* 2 (1990): 179–85.
16. Clark, "Retrospective," 58–59.
17. Clark, "Humans, Animals, and 'Animal Behavior,'" 175, 178.
18. Clark, "Retrospective," 56.

19. See Stephen Clark, "Utility, Rights and the Domestic Virtues," *Between the Species* 4 (1988): 245. Also see 242–43. Finally, see idem., "Tools, Machines, and Marvels," *Philosophy: Supplement* 38 (1995): 159–76; and idem., "Natural Goods and Moral Beauty," in *Virtue and Taste*, ed. Dudley Knowles and John Skorupski (Oxford: Basil Blackwell, 1993), 83–97.

20. Once again, see Charles Hartshorne's *Born to Sing* (Bloomington: Indiana University Press, 1973).

21. See Clark, "Utility, Rights and the Domestic Virtues," 241.

22. Clark, "Humans, Animals, and 'Animal Behavior,'" 177, 181–82.

23. Stephen Clark, "The Rights of Wild Things," *Inquiry* 22 (1979): 172. Also see 171.

24. Ibid., 174. Also see 173, 175.

25. Ibid., 176.

26. Ibid., 179–80.

27. Ibid., 187. Also see 184, 186.

28. See John Benson, "Duty and the Beast," *Philosophy* 53 (1978): 542, 545–46, 548.

29. Stephen Clark, "Icons, Sacred Relics, Obsolescent Plant," *Journal of Applied Philosophy* 3 (1986): 203. Also see 202.

30. Ibid., 205.

31. Ibid., 206.

32. Ibid., 207–9. Further, Clark notices that environmentalists are often at odds with animal rightists, but animal rightists, he thinks, are more likely to achieve their goals through environmentalist policies than they are through advocacy of abstract animal rights. See "Animals," in *Concise Encyclopedia of Western Philosophy*, ed. J. O. Urmson and Jonathan Ree (London: Unwin Hyman, 1989), 16.

33. Clark, "Utility, Rights and the Domestic Virtues," 244.

34. Clark, "Animals, Ecosystems and the Liberal Ethic," 118. Also see 125.

35. Ibid., 120.

36. Ibid., 124. Also see 121.

37. Ibid., 126.

38. Ibid., 129. Also see 126. It should be noted that Clark did not start out a conservative; his parents voted Labour, as did he until the Falklands War, when he made a switch. Also, a final note regarding Clark's opposition to scientific experiments on animals or on "marginal" humans: these often infringe on the being's right to refuse. Some experiments (e.g., where a food reward is the result) animals "consent" to, but others (e.g., where pain is the result) they "refuse." Here Clark sounds like a liberal. See his "How to Calculate the Greater Good," in *Animals' Rights*, ed. David Paterson and Richard Ryder (London: Centaur, 1979).

39. See Stephen Clark, "Rights of the Wild and Tame," *Chronicles of Culture* 9, no. 8 (1985): 22.

40. Stephen Clark, "Substance: Or Chesterton's Abyss of Light," *Proceedings of the Aristotelian Society: Supplementary Volume* 69 (1995): 13.

CHAPTER SEVEN

1. Ferdinand Tonnies, *Community and Society* (East Lansing, Mich.: Michigan State University Press, 1957).

2. See my *Kazantzakis and God* (Albany: State University of New York Press, 1997).

3. On Aristotle's notion of friendship Clark relies on *Nicomachean Ethics* 8 and 9; *Eudemian Ethics* 7; and *Rhetoric* 1380b.

4. See Charles Hartshorne's *Man's Vision of God* (New York: Harper and Brothers, 1941).

5. See R. C. Morgan, "Non Angli sed Angeli," in *New Studies in Theology*, ed. S. Sykes and P. Holmes (London: Duckworth, 1980).

6. See my "Hartshorne and Plato," in *The Philosophy of Charles Hartshorne*, ed. Lewis Hahn (LaSalle, Ill.: Open Court, 1991), 465–87.

7. See the chapter on "The Romantic Reaction" in A. N. Whitehead's *Science and the Modern World* (New York: Macmillan, 1957).

8. Clark relies here on Oliver O'Donovan, *Resurrection and Moral Order* (Leicester: Intervarsity Press, 1986).

9. On right-wing anarchism see Lysander Spooner, *Let's Abolish Government* (New York: Arno, 1972); on left-wing anarchism see E. Capouya and K. Tomkins, eds., *The Essential Kropotkin* (London: Macmillan, 1976).

10. See G. Eaton, *King of the Castle* (London: Bodley Head, 1977).

11. Clark relies here on Wincenty Lutoslawski, *The Knowledge of Reality* (Cambridge: Cambridge University Press, 1930).

12. See Stephen Clark, "Morals, Moore, and MacIntyre," *Inquiry* 26 (1983): 426. Also see 425.

13. Ibid., 427.

14. Ibid., 429. Also see 428. Clark makes it clear in "Orwell and the Anti-Realists," *Philosophy* 67 (1992) that Wittgensteinian antirealism has disastrous, Orwellian consequences for politics; indeed it consists in a "collective solipsism" that avoids the reality of pain and death caused by politicians. Human beings are not infinitely malleable.

15. Clark, "Morals, Moore, and MacIntyre," 430.

16. Ibid., 432. Also see 431.

17. Ibid., 433.

18. Ibid., 436. Also see 432–35.

19. Ibid., 437–38.

20. Ibid., 439.

21. Ibid., 440.

22. Ibid., 441–44. Also see W. F. R. Hardie, "Aristotle on the Best Life for a Man," *Philosophy* 54 (1979): 35–50. Hardie sees in Clark himself the attainment of such a saintly point of view, but he is not convinced by Clark's attempt to unify the theoretical and the civic life in Aristotle's theory of human nature. Clark attempts such a unification by claiming that both facets of one's life are a service of the divine, a view that Hardie finds vague.

23. See Stephen Clark, "The City of the Wise," *Apeiron* 20 (1987): 68–69.

24. See Stephen Clark, "Abstract Morality, Concrete Cases," *Philosophy: Supplement* 22 (1987): 38–39. Also see my *Rawls and Religion*, forthcoming.

25. Clark, "Abstract Morality, Concrete Cases," 42.

26. Ibid., 48. Also see 40–41, 43. Kathleen Wilkes, "How Many Selves Make Me?" *Philosophy: Supplement* 29 (1991): 235–43, makes us realize, however, that it is difficult to found individualism in politics on a metaphysical self that is a will-o'-the-wisp. Clark agrees in his article "How Many Selves Make Me?" *Philosophy: Supplement* 29 (1991): 213–33, but the "polytheistic" self, he thinks, is unified in the One Self or *Nous* even if it is separated out as a one-in-many.

27. Clark, "Abstract Morality, Concrete Cases," 49.

28. Ibid., 52.

29. Stephen Clark, "How to Reason About Value Judgments," *Philosophy: Supplement* 24 (1988): 174–75.

30. Ibid., 176, 182.

31. Ibid., 184–85. Also see 183.

32. Ibid., 186.

33. Ibid., 187.

34. Ibid., 188.

35. Stephen Clark, "Mackie and the Moral Order," *Philosophical Quarterly* 39 (1989): 102, 107. Regarding the tension between the individual and the social, see Clark's "Social, Moral and Metaphysical Identities," *Personalist Forum* 8 (1992): 159–61. Here Clark urges that we do not need to travel outside of the Western tradition to find several different possible views of the individual and of personal identity.

36. See my "Adam Smith's The Theory of Moral Sentiments and Christianity," *American Benedictine Review* 35 (1984): 422–38.

37. See Stephen Clark, "Alien Dreams: Kipling," in *Anticipations*, ed. David Seed (Liverpool: Liverpool University Press, 1995), 172–94; idem., "Thinking About How and Why to Think," *Philosophy* 71 (1996): 385–403; and idem., "Nations and Empires," *European Journal of Philosophy* 4 (1996): 63–80. The conservative nature of Clark's politics is evidenced when he says that Moses was the best of all lawgivers, and that his laws truly came from God, because the laws he brought to us have endured. See Stephen Clark, "Herds of Free Bipeds," in *Reading the Statesman*, ed. Christopher Rowe (Sankt Augustin, Germany: Academia Verlag, 1995), 251.

CHAPTER EIGHT

1. Stephen Clark, "Good and Bad Ethology and the Decent Polis," in *Polis and Politics*, ed. Andros Loizou and Harry Lesser (Aldershot: Avebury, 1990), 18. It seems, however, that Clark's anarchism was a passing phase; his conservativism and traditionalism endure. Or better, if we cannot have a traditionalist state then anarchism may be a better response than liberalism, on Clarkian grounds.

2. See R. F. Atkinson's review of CP in *Philosophical Books* 32 (1991): 55–56.

3. Stephen Clark, "On Wishing There Were Unicorns," *Proceedings of the Aristotelian Society* 90 (1990): 251–52. Clark relies here on J. R. R. Tolkien, "On Fairy Stories," in *Tree and Leaf* (London: Allen and Unwin, 1961).

4. Clark, "On Wishing There Were Unicorns," 257. Clark relies here on G. K. Chesterton, *Tremendous Trifles* (London: Methuen, 1909), 97.

5. Clark, "On Wishing There Were Unicorns," 258–59.

6. Ibid., 261. Also see 254–55, 262, 270. It might seem that Clark's critique of those who downgrade political fiction is similar to Derrida's critique of Austin, but Clark is correct to emphasize that Derrida is far too obscure and coy to make such a comparison. See Jacques Derrida, *Margins of Philosophy* (Chicago: University of Chicago Press, 1982).

7. See Stephen Clark, "Children and the Mammalian Order," in *Children, Parents and Politics*, ed. Geoffrey Scarre (Cambridge: Cambridge University Press, 1989), 119. Also see 120–22.

8. Ibid., 123. Also see 124–25.

9. Ibid., 126. Also see 127–29.

10. Ibid., 130–31. Clark's anarchism is not violent; rather, by rejecting modern states he signals a return to a decent civil peace dependent on customary civilities; see

"Anarchists Against the Revolution," in *Terrorism, Protest and Power*, ed. M. Warner and R. Crisp (Brookfield, Vt.: Elgar, 1990).

11. Stephen Clark, "World Religions and World Orders," *Religious Studies* 26 (1990): 44. Also see 45–46.

12. Ibid., 47.

13. Ibid., 48. Also see 49.

14. Ibid., 50. Also see 51.

15. See, e.g., the work by Victor Farias that, even if not the best commentary, nonetheless lays out quotations from Heidegger and documentation regarding his Nazism that is damaging in the extreme: *Heidegger and Nazism* (Philadelphia: Temple University Press, 1989). Also see Sheldon Wolin's review of Gadamer's intellectual autobiography in *The New York Times Book Review*, 28 July 1985, 12.

16. Clark, "World Religions and World Orders," 52. Also see 53–55.

17. Ibid., 56.

18. Ibid., 57.

19. See Farias, *Heidegger and Nazism*, 285, 287. Also see Clark's "Taylor's Waking Dream," *Inquiry* 34 (1991): 198, 204, 208, 211, where he takes his strongest stand against the debased romanticism of Heidegger and the Nazis. By way of contrast, the great "romantic" poets were, because of their Platonism, also very much "classicists:" they articulated something greater than themselves as human beings. Debased romanticism is marked by the view that each person (or nation) has an original way of being wherein "courage" is supposed to save a world gone dry and wherein certain feelings allow us to touch the deepest cosmic truths.

20. John Benson, "Duty and the Beast," *Philosophy* 53 (1978): 537–38, 540–41.

21. Stephen Clark, "The Rights of Wild Things," *Inquiry* 22 (1979): 185.

22. See O'Neill's review of MS in *The Journal of Philosophy* 77 (1980): 442–43.

23. Ibid., 445.

24. See Fergus Kerr's reviews of MS and NB in *The Heythrop Journal* 28 (1987): 498.

25. Stephen Clark, "Retrospective (1988–1945)," *Between the Species* 5 (1989): 59–61.

26. Clark, "The Rights of Wild Things," 177–78.

27. Benson, "Duty and the Beast," 533. Also see 536–37.

28. Stephen Clark, "Humans, Animals, and 'Animal Behavior,'" in *Ethics and Animals*, ed. Harlan Miller (Clifton, N.J.: Humana Press, 1983), 169–71, 182.

29. Stephen Clark, "Utility, Rights and the Domestic Virtues," *Between the Species* 4 (1988): 240. Also see 235–38.

30. Stephen Clark, "Good Dogs and Other Animals," in *In Defence of Animals*, ed. Peter Singer (Oxford: Basil Blackwell, 1985), 47.

31. Ibid., 48.

32. Ibid., 51.

33. See Charles Hartshorne's *Anselm's Discovery* (LaSalle, Ill.: Open Court, 1965).

34. See Harry Wolfson, "Extradeical and Intradeical Interpretations of Platonic Ideas," *Journal of the History of Ideas* 22 (1961): 3–32.

35. Once again, see my *Plato's Philosophy of History* (Washington, D.C.: University Press of America, 1981).

36. See an excellent article by Robert Whittemore, "Panentheism in Neo-Platonism," *Tulane Studies in Philosophy* 15 (1966): 47–70, for a detailed interpretation of Plotinus similar to Clark's.

37. See J. J. O'Donnell, *Trinity and Temporality* (Oxford: Clarendon Press, 1983); and Schubert Ogden, *The Reality of God and Other Essays* (London: SCM Press, 1967).

38. See Paul Weiss, "God and the World," in *Science, Philosophy, and Religion* (New York: Conference on Science, Philosophy, and Religion, 1941).

39. Consult the excellent study by Lewis Ford, *The Lure of God: A Biblical Background for Process Theism* (Philadelphia: Fortress Press, 1978).

40. Once again, see my article "Hartshorne and Plato" (in *The Philosophy of Charles Hartshorne*, ed. Lewis Hahn [Lasalle, Ill.: Open Court, 1991]) on Plato as a panpsychist. Also see Clark's "Minds, Memes, and Rhetoric," *Inquiry* 36 (1993): 3–16, where Clark argues against Daniel Dennett's materialism and against his rhetorical use of computer metaphors for the human mind. Nonetheless, David Cooper is correct to highlight Clark's belief, to be treated in the following chapter, that the distinctive contribution of Christianity is the difficult identity between the *logos* and a particular, embodied being. Further, as a Christian, Clark is opposed to the pervasive belief in ethics and politics that God is, for all practical purposes, dead. In this regard, he thinks, liberal moralists are not as different from the Nazis as they normally suppose. See Clark, "Companions on the Way," *Philosophical Quarterly* 44 (1994): 90–100.

41. See Stephen Clark, "Dangerous Conservatives: A Reply to Daniel Dombrowski," forthcoming in *Sophia*.

42. See Stephen Clark "Environmental Ethics," in *Companion Encyclopedia of Theology*, ed. Peter Byrne and Leslie Houlden (London: Routledge, 1995), 7. Also see my "Do Critics of Heidegger Commit the *Ad Hominem* Fallacy?" *International Journal of Applied Philosophy* 10 (1996): 71–75.

43. See Stephen Clark, "Having Opinions," *Chronicles of Culture* 11, no. 4 (1987): 13–14.

44. See Stephen Clark, "Plotinus: Body and Soul," in *The Cambridge Companion to Plotinus*, ed. Lloyd Gerson (Cambridge: Cambridge University Press, 1996); and

Stephen Clark, "A Plotinian Account of Intellect," *American Catholic Philosophical Quarterly* 71 (1997): 421–32.

CHAPTER NINE

1. Erazim Kohak, *The Embers and the Stars* (Chicago: University of Chicago Press, 1984), 124–25.
2. James Lovelock, *Gaia* (Oxford: Oxford University Press, 1979).
3. See my *Analytic Theism, Hartshorne, and the Concept of God* (Albany: State University of New York Press, 1996).
4. See Martha Nussbaum's review of AM in *The Philosophical Review* 86 (1977): 241–44.
5. See Julia Annas's review of AM in *Mind* 86 (1977): 281–83.
6. See J. C. Dennett, *Brainstorms* (Hassocks: Harvester, 1978); and Thomas Nagel, *Mortal Questions* (Cambridge: Cambridge University Press, 1979).
7. See the review of AJ by Craig Staudenbauer (in *Modern Schoolman* 64 [1987]: 203), where the author distinguishes between functional consciousness and real consciousness; only the former can arise by adding together material parts.
8. See Christopher Stone, *Should Trees Have Standing?* (Los Altos, Calif.: William Kaufmann, 1974).
9. See Richard Rorty's review of the Farias book in *The New Republic*, 11 April 1988.
10. Stephen Clark, "How to Believe in Fairies," *Inquiry* 30 (1987): 343–45.
11. Stephen Clark, "The City of the Wise," *Apeiron* 20 (1987): 63.
12. Ibid., 64–67. Also see Stephen Clark, "Animals, Ecosystems and the Liberal Ethic," *Monist* 70 (1987): 125–27, 129. Clark finds it significant that animals are not generally individualists and that they generally take their lives seriously.
13. Clark, "The City of the Wise," 70.
14. Ibid., 72. Also see 71.
15. See William H. Goodwin, ed., *Plutarch's Morals* (Boston: Little, Brown, and Co., 1870), 3:133, "Whether the World Be an Animal."
16. Clark, "The City of the Wise," 73–77. Also see A. W. Levi, *Philosophy as Social Expression* (Chicago: University of Chicago Press, 1974), on the philosopher as sage or saint versus the philosopher as professional.
17. Clark, "The City of the Wise," 78.
18. Ibid., 78–79. Also see Clark, "Animals, Ecosystems and the Liberal Ethic," 124.
19. Another critic of Clark regarding the claim that Aristotle believed in the World Soul is I. N. Robins in his review of AM in *Philosophy* 51 (1976): 236–39.

20. See Stephen Clark, "Mackie and the Moral Order," *Philosophical Quarterly* 39 (1989): 112. Also see 98, 100, 111.

21. See Clark's "Introduction," in *Money, Obedience, and Affection: Essays on Berkeley's Moral and Political Thought*, ed. Stephen R. L. Clark (New York: Garland, 1989).

22. See Clark's "God-Appointed Berkeley and the General Good," in *Essays on Berkeley*, ed. John Foster and Howard Robinson (Oxford: Clarendon Press, 1985), 242. Also see 251. In "Soft as the Rustle of a Reed from Cloyne," in *Philosophers of the Enlightenment*, ed. Peter Gilmour (Edinburgh: Edinburgh University Press, 1989), 47–61, Clark emphasizes that Berkeley was not an Enlightenment free-thinker; rather his strategy was to begin from skeptical principles in order to subvert them and to make it possible to say that what is most reliable is what we are inclined to say most enthusiastically.

23. Stephen Clark, "Gaia and the Forms of Life," in *Environmental Philosophy*, ed. R. Elliot and A. Gare (University Park, Penn.: Penn State University Press, 1983), 183.

24. Ibid., 186.

25. Ibid., 188.

26. Ibid.

27. Ibid., 190.

28. Ibid., 196.

29. See Roger Scruton's review of CP in *History of Political Thought* 11 (1990): 546–47.

30. Stephen Clark, "Eradicating the Obvious," *Journal of Applied Philosophy* 8 (1991): 123.

31. Ibid., 125.

BIBLIOGRAPHY

PUBLICATIONS BY STEPHEN R. L. CLARK

"The Use of 'Man's Function' in Aristotle." *Ethics* 82 (1972): 269–83.

Aristotle's Man. Oxford: Clarendon Press, 1975.

The Moral Status of Animals. Oxford: Clarendon Press, 1977.

"God, Good and Evil." *Proceedings of the Aristotelian Society* 77 (1977): 247–64.

"Animal Wrongs." *Analysis* 38 (1978): 147–49.

"How to Calculate the Greater Good." In *Animals' Rights,* edited by David Paterson and Richard Ryder, 96–105. London: Centaur, 1979.

"The Rights of Wild Things." *Inquiry* 22 (1979): 171–88.

The Nature of the Beast. Oxford: Oxford University Press, 1982.

"Aristotle's Woman." *History of Political Thought* 3 (1982): 177–91.

"God's Law and Morality." *Philosophical Quarterly* 32 (1982): 339–47.

"Gaia and the Forms of Life." In *Environmental Philosophy,* edited by R. Elliot and A. Gare, 182–97. University Park: Penn State University Press, 1983.

"Humans, Animals, and 'Animal Behavior.'" In *Ethics and Animals,* edited by Harlan Miller, 169–82. Clifton, N.J.: Humana Press, 1983.

"Morals, Moore, and MacIntyre." *Inquiry* 26 (1983): 425–45.

"Sexual Ontology and Group Marriage." *Philosophy* 58 (1983): 215–27.

"Waking-up: A Neglected Model for the Afterlife." *Inquiry* 26 (1983): 209–30.

From Athens to Jerusalem. Oxford: Clarendon Press, 1984.

"God-Appointed Berkeley and the General Good." In *Essays on Berkeley,* edited by John Foster and Howard Robinson, 233–53. Oxford: Clarendon Press, 1985.

"Good Dogs and Other Animals." In *In Defence of Animals,* edited by Peter Singer, 41–51. Oxford: Basil Blackwell, 1985.

"Hume, Animals and the Objectivity of Morals." *Philosophical Quarterly* 35 (1985): 117–33.

"Rights of the Wild and Tame." *Chronicles of Culture* 9, no. 8 (1985): 20–22.

"Slaves and Citizens." *Philosophy* 60 (1985): 27–46.

The Mysteries of Religion. Oxford: Basil Blackwell, 1986.

"Abstraction, Possession, Incarnation: Neo-Platonic Explorations." In *Being and Truth,* edited by Alastair Kee and Eugene Long, 293–317. London: SCM Press, 1986.

"Icons, Sacred Relics, Obsolescent Plant." *Journal of Applied Philosophy* 3 (1986): 201–10.

"Olaf Stapledon." *Chronicles of Culture* 10, no. 12 (1986): 14–18.

"With Rationality and Love." *Times Literary Supplement,* 26 September 1986, 1047–49.

"Abstract Morality, Concrete Cases." *Philosophy: Supplement* 22 (1987): 35–53.

"Animals, Ecosystems, and the Liberal Ethic." *Monist* 70 (1987): 114–33.

"The City of the Wise." *Apeiron* 20 (1987): 63–80.

"God's Law and Chandler." *Philosophical Quarterly* 37 (1987): 203–8.

"Having Opinions." *Chronicles of Culture* 11, no. 4 (1987): 13–15.

"How to Believe in Fairies." *Inquiry* 30 (1987): 337–55.

"Cupitt and Divine Imagining." *Modern Theology* 5 (1988): 45–60.

"How to Reason about Value Judgments." *Philosophy: Supplement* 24 (1988): 173–90.

"Is Humanity a Natural Kind?." In *What Is an Animal?* edited by Tim Ingold, 17–34. London: Unwin Hyman, 1988.

"Robotic Morals." *Cogito* 2 (1988): 20–22.

"Utility, Rights and the Domestic Virtues." *Between the Species* 4 (1988): 235–46.

Limits and Renewals: I. Civil Peace and Sacred Order. Oxford: Clarendon Press, 1989.

"Animals." In *Concise Encyclopedia of Western Philosophy,* edited by J. O. Urmson and Jonathon Ree, 14–16. London: Unwin Hyman, 1989.

"Children and the Mammalian Order." In *Children, Parents and Politics,* edited by Geoffrey Scarre, 115–32. Cambridge: Cambridge University Press, 1989.

"Introduction." In *Money, Obedience, and Affection: Essays on Berkeley's Moral and Political Thought,* edited by Stephen R. L. Clark, vii–xxxi. New York: Garland, 1989.

"Mackie and the Moral Order." *Philosophical Quarterly* 39 (1989): 98–114.

"Retrospective (1988–1945)." *Between the Species* 5 (1989): 55–60.

"Soft as the Rustle of a Reed from Cloyne." In *Philosophers of the Enlightenment,* edited by Peter Gilmour, 47–62. Edinburgh: Edinburgh University Press, 1989.

"The Spiritual Meaning of Philosophy." *Chronicles of Culture* 13, no. 9 (1989): 14–19.

Limits and Renewals: II. A Parliament of Souls. Oxford: Clarendon Press, 1990.

"Anarchists against the Revolution." In *Terrorism, Protest and Power,* edited by M. Warner and R. Crisp, 123–37. Brookfield, Vt.: Elgar, 1990.

"Good and Bad Ethology and the Decent Polis." In *Polis and Politics,* edited by Andros Loizou and Harry Lesser, 12–22. Aldershot, U.K.: Avebury, 1990.

"Limited Explanations." *Philosophy: Supplement* 27 (1990): 195–210.

"Notes on the Underground." *Inquiry* 33 (1990): 27–37.

"On Wishing There Were Unicorns." *Proceedings of the Aristotelian Society* 90 (1990): 247–65.

"The Reality of Shared Emotions." In *Interpretation and Explanation in the Study of Animal Behavior,* edited by Marc Bekoff and Dale Jamieson, 449–72. Boulder, Colo.: Westview, 1990.

"Reason as Daimon." In *The Person and the Human Mind,* edited by Christopher Gill, 187–206. Oxford: Clarendon Press, 1990.

"World Religions and World Orders." *Religious Studies* 26 (1990): 43–57.

Limits and Renewals: III. God's World and the Great Awakening. Oxford: Clarendon Press, 1991.

"Eradicating the Obvious." *Journal of Applied Philosophy* 8 (1991): 121–25.

"How Many Selves Make Me?" *Philosophy: Supplement* 29 (1991): 213–33.

"Taylor's Waking Dream." *Inquiry* 34 (1991): 195–215.

"The Teaching of Ethics." *Humane Education Newsletter* 2, no. 1 (1991): 4–6.

"Descartes' Debt to Augustine." *Philosophy: Supplement* 32 (1992): 73–88.

"Is the Universe a Put-Up Job?" *Times Literary Supplement,* 26 June 1992, 6–7.

"Orwell and the Anti-Realists." *Philosophy* 67 (1992): 141–54.

"Philosophical Anthropology." In *Encyclopedia of Ethics,* edited by Lawrence Becker and Charlotte Becker, 963–64. New York: Garland, 1992.

"Social, Moral and Metaphysical Identities." *Personalist Forum* 8 (1992): 159–61.

"Where Have All the Angels Gone?" *Religious Studies* 28 (1992): 221–34.

How to Think about the Earth. London: Mobray, 1993.

"Apes and the Idea of Kindred." In *The Great Ape Project,* edited by Paola Cavalieri and Peter Singer, 113–25. New York: St. Martin's, 1993.

"The Better Part." *Philosophy: Supplement* 35 (1993): 29–49.

"Does the Burgess Shale have Moral Implications?" *Inquiry* 36 (1993): 357–80.

"Minds, Memes, and Rhetoric." *Inquiry* 36 (1993): 3–16.

"Natural Goods and Moral Beauty." In *Virtue and Taste,* edited by Dudley Knowles and John Skorupski, 83–97. Oxford: Basil Blackwell, 1993.

"Olaf Stapledon." *Interdisciplinary Science Reviews* 18 (1993): 112–19.

"Philosophers and Popular Cosmology." *Journal of Applied Philosophy* 10 (1993): 115–22.

"Ancient Philosophy." In *The Oxford History of Western Philosophy,* edited by Anthony Kenny, 1–53. Oxford: Oxford University Press, 1994.

"Companions on the Way." *Philosophical Quarterly* 44 (1994): 90–100.

"Genetic and Other Engineering." *Journal of Applied Philosophy* 11 (1994): 233–37.

"Global Religion." *Philosophy: Supplement* 36 (1994): 113–28.

"Modern Errors, Ancient Virtues." In *Ethics and Biotechnology,* edited by Anthony Dyson and John Harris, 13–32. London: Routledge, 1994.

"The Possible Truth of Metaphor." *International Journal of Philosophical Studies* 2 (1994): 19–30.

How to Live Forever: Science Fiction and Philosophy. London: Routledge, 1995.

"Alien Dreams: Kipling." In *Anticipations,* edited by David Seed, 172–94. Liverpool: Liverpool University Press, 1995.

"Enlarging the Community: Companion Animals." In *Applied Ethics,* edited by Brenda Almond, 318–30. Oxford: Basil Blackwell, 1995.

"Environmental Ethics." In *Companion Encyclopedia of Theology,* edited by Peter Byrne and Leslie Houlden, 843–70. London: Routledge, 1995.

"Herds of Free Bipeds." In *Reading the Statesman,* edited by Christopher Rowe, 236–52. Sankt Augustin, Germany: Academia Verlag, 1995.

"Substance: Or Chesterton's Abyss of Light." *Proceedings of the Aristotelian Society: Supplementary Volume* 69 (1995): 1–14.

"Tools, Machines, and Marvels." *Philosophy: Supplement* 38 (1995): 159–76.

"Commentary on 'Multiple Personality and Moral Responsibility.'" *Philosophy, Psychiatry, and Psychology* 3 (1996): 55–57.

"How Chesterton Read History." *Inquiry* 39 (1996): 343–58.

"Minds, Memes, and Multiples." *Philosophy, Psychiatry, and Psychology* 3 (1996): 21–28.

"Nations and Empires." *European Journal of Philosophy* 4 (1996): 63–80.

"Plotinus: Body and Soul." In *The Cambridge Companion to Plotinus,* edited by Lloyd Gerson, 275–91. Cambridge: Cambridge University Press, 1996.

"Philosophy." In *New Technologies for the Humanities,* edited by Christine Mullings, et al., 319–37. East Grinstead, U.K.: Bowker-Sauer, 1996.

"Riots at Brightlingsea." *Journal of Applied Philosophy* 13 (1996): 109–12.

"Thinking about How and Why to Think." *Philosophy* 71 (1996): 385–403.

Animals and Their Moral Standing. London: Routledge, 1997.

"Platonism and the Gods of Place." In *The Philosophy of the Enviornment,* edited by T. D. J. Chappell, 1937 (Edinburgh: Edinburgh University Press, 1997).

"A Plotinian Account of Intellect." *American Catholic Philosophical Quarterly* 71 (1997): 421–32.

"Natural Integrity and Biotechnology." In *Human Lives: Critical Essays on Consequentialist Bioethics,* edited by David Oderberg and Jacqueline Laing, 58–76. London: Macmillan, 1997.

"A New Stoicism." *Philosophy* 74 (1999): 126–28.

The Political Animal. London: Routledge. Forthcoming.

"Berkeley's Philosophy of Religion," Forthcoming.

"Dangerous Conservatives: A Reply to Daniel Dombrowski." Forthcoming in *Sophia.*

"Decent Conduct Toward Animals: A Traditional Approach," Forthcoming.

"How (and Why) to Be Virtuous," Forthcoming.

"Nothing without Mind," Forthcoming.

"Slaves, Servility, and Noble Deeds," Forthcoming.

"Unseen University," Forthcoming.

SECONDARY SOURCES

Alexander, R. D. "The Evolution of Social Behaviour." *Annual Review of Ecological Systems* 5 (1974): 325–83.

Annas, Julia. Review of *Aristotle's Man. Mind* 86 (1977): 281–83.

Atkinson, R. F. Review of *Civil Peace and Sacred Order. Philosophical Books* 32 (1991): 55–56.

———. Review of *A Parliament of Souls. Philosophical Books* 33 (1992): 94–96.

Ayres, Lewis. Review of *Limits and Renewals. Modern Theology* 10 (1994): 227–29.

Barad, Judith. "Aquinas' Inconsistency on the Nature and the Treatment of Animals." *Between the Species* 4 (1988): 102–11.

Benson, John. "Duty and the Beast." *Philosophy* 53 (1978): 529–49.

Bernard, Claude. *Introduction to the Study of Experimental Medicine.* New York: Macmillan, 1949.

Bostock, Stephen. Review of *Animals and their Moral Standing. Journal of Applied Philosophy* 15 (1998): 301–3.

Capouya, E., and K. Tompkins, eds. *The Essential Kropotkin.* London: Macmillan, 1976.

Cash, Mason. Review of *How to Live Forever. Philosophy in Review* 17 (1997): 396–98.

Causey, Ann. "On the Morality of Hunting." *Environmental Ethics* 11 (1989): 327–43.

Chandler, John. "Clark on God's Law and Morality." *Philosophical Quarterly* 35 (1985): 87–90.

Chesterton, G. K. *Tremendous Trifles.* London: Methuen, 1909.

Chomsky, Noam. *American Power and the New Mandarins.* Harmondsworth, U.K.: Pelican, 1969.

Chryssides, George. Review of *The Mysteries of Religion. Teaching Philosophy* 10 (1987): 159–60.

Churchland, Patricia. *Neurophilosophy.* Cambridge: Harvard University Press, 1986.

Clifford, W. K. *Lectures and Essays.* London: Macmillan, 1901.

Cobb, J., and C. Birch, *The Liberation of Life.* Cambridge: Cambridge University Press, 1981.

Cooper, David. *Review of Limits and Renewals. Philosophy* 68 (1993): 244–46.

Cowling, W., and N. Tuana, "Plato and Feminism: A Review of the Literature." *American Philosophical Association Newsletter* (1990): 110–15.

Dennett, J. C. *Brainstorms.* Hassocks, U.K.: Harvester, 1978.

Derrida, Jacques. *Margins of Philosophy.* Chicago: University of Chicago Press, 1982.

Diamond, Cora. "Anything but Argument." *Philosophical Investigations* 5 (1982): 23–41.

Dombrowski, Daniel. *Plato's Philosophy of History.* Washington, D.C.: University Press of America, 1981.

———. "Adam Smith's The Theory of Moral Sentiments and Christianity." *American Benedictine Review* 35 (1984): 422–38.

———. *The Philosophy of Vegetarianism.* Amherst: University of Massachusetts Press, 1984.

———. "Vegetarianism and the Argument from Marginal Cases in Porphyry." *Journal of the History of Ideas* 45 (1984): 141–43.

———. "The Jesuits and the Zoophilists, Again." *Irish Theological Quarterly* 51 (1985): 232–41.

———. *Thoreau the Platonist.* New York: Peter Lang, 1986.

———. *Hartshorne and the Metaphysics of Animal Rights.* Albany: State University of New York Press, 1988.

———. *Christian Pacifism.* Philadelphia: Temple University Press, 1991.

———. "Hartshorne and Plato." In *The Philosophy of Charles Hartshorne,* edited by Lewis Hahn, 465–87. LaSalle, Ill.: Open Court, 1991.

———. *St. John of the Cross.* Albany: State University of New York Press, 1992.

———. *Analytic Theism, Hartshorne, and the Concept of God.* Albany: State University of New York Press, 1996.

———. "Do Critics of Heidegger Commit the Ad Hominem Fallacy?" *International Journal of Applied Philosophy* 10 (1996): 71–75.

———. *Babies and Beasts: The Argument from Marginal Cases.* Champaign: University of Illinois Press, 1997.

———. *Kazantzakis and God.* Albany: State University of New York Press, 1997.

———. *Rawls and Religion.* Forthcoming.

Dooley-Clarke, Dolores. Review of *The Moral Status of Animals. Philosophical Studies* 26 (1979): 341–42.

Eaton, G. *King of the Castle.* London: Bodley Head, 1977.

Eckhardt, William. "Primitive Militarism." *Journal of Peace Research* 6 (1975): 55–62.

Eibl-Eibesfeldt, Irenaus. *The Biology of Peace and War.* London: Thames and Hudson, 1979.

Eliade, Mircea. *Cosmos and History.* New York: Harper and Row, 1959.

Elliot, Robert. Review of *The Nature of the Beast. Australasian Journal of Philosophy* 61 (1983): 454–56.

Ellul, Jacques. *The Meaning of the City.* Grand Rapids, Mich.: Eerdmans, 1970.

Evans, J. D. G. Review of *Aristotle's Man. Philosophical Quarterly* 26 (1976): 168–69.

Farias, Victor. *Heidegger and Nazism.* Philadelphia: Temple University Press, 1989.

Feyerabend, Paul. *Farewell to Reason.* New York: Verso, 1987.

Ford, Lewis. *The Lure of God: A Biblical Basis for Process Theism.* Philadelphia: Fortress Press, 1978.

Frey, R. G. *Rights, Killing, and Suffering.* London: Basil Blackwell, 1983.

Gay, Robert. Review of *The Mysteries of Religion. Philosophical Books* 28 (1987): 115–18.

Geach, Mary-Catherine. Review of *The Nature of the Beast. Philosophy* 59 (1984): 275–76.

Goodall, Jane. *In the Shadow of Man.* Boston: Houghton Miflin, 1971.

Godwin, William H., ed. *Plutarch's Morals.* Boston: Little, Brown, and Co., 1870.

Griffin, David Ray. *God, Power, and Evil: A Process Theodicy.* Philadelphia: Westminster, 1976.

Hardie, W. F. R. "Aristotle on the Best Life for Man." *Philosophy* 54 (1979): 35–50.

Hare, R. M. "What is Wrong with Slavery?" *Philosophy and Public Affairs* 8 (1979): 103–21.

Harlow, H. F. and M. K. Harlow. "The Affectional Systems." In *Non-Human Primates.* New York: Academic Press, 1965.

Hartshorne, Charles. *Man's Vision of God.* New York: Harper and Brothers, 1941.

———. *Reality as Social Process.* Glencoe, Ill.: Free Press, 1953.

———. *Creative Synthesis and Philosophic Method.* LaSalle, Ill.: Open Court, 1970.

———. *Born to Sing.* Bloomington: Indiana University Press, 1973.

———. *Insights and Oversights of Great Thinkers.* Albany: State University of New York Press, 1983.

Hartshorne, C. and W. Reese. *Philosophers Speak of God.* Chicago: University of Chicago Press, 1953.

Heidegger, Martin. *Being and Time*. Oxford: Basil Blackwell, 1962.

————. *What Is Called Thinking?* New York: Harper and Row, 1968.

————. *Early Greek Thinking*. New York: Harper and Row, 1984.

Hick, John. *Evil and the God of Love*. London: Fontana, 1968.

Hinde, R. A. *Ethology*. Oxford: Oxford University Press, 1982.

Howard, Len. *Birds as Individuals*. London: Collins, 1952.

Hudson, Liam. *Contrary Imaginations*. Harmondsworth: Pelican, 1967.

Hughes, Gerard. Review of *Aristotle's Man*. *The Heythrop Journal* 18 (1977): 206–7.

Inge, W. R. *The Platonic Tradition in English Religious Thought*. London: Longmans, Green, 1926.

James, William. *The Will to Believe*. New York: Longmans, Green, 1897.

Jamieson, Dale. Review of *The Moral Status of Animals*. *Nous* 15 (1981): 230–34.

Jolly, C. J. "The Seed-Eaters: A New Model of Hominid Differentiation Based on a Baboon Analogy." *Man* 5 (1970): 5–26.

Kerr, Fergus. Review of *The Moral Status of Animals* and *The Nature of the Beast*. *Heythrop Journal* 28 (1987): 497–98.

————. Review of *From Athens to Jerusalem*. In *The Heythrop Journal* 29 (1988): 112–13.

Kohak, Erazim. *The Embers and the Stars*. Chicago: University of Chicago Press, 1984.

Kummer, Hans. "On the Value of Social Relationships to Non-Human Primates." In *Human Ethology,* edited by Mario von Cranach, et al., 381–95. Cambridge: Cambridge University Press, 1979.

Leahy, Michael. *Against Liberation*. London: Routledge, 1991.

Levi, A. W. *Philosophy as Social Expression*. Chicago: University of Chicago Press, 1974.

Linden, Eugene. *Apes, Men and Language*. New York: Dutton, 1975.

Lloyd, Genevieve. "Spinoza's Environmental Ethics." *Inquiry* 23 (1980): 293–311.

Lorenz, Konrad. *On Aggression*. London: Methuen, 1966.

Lovelock, James. *Gaia*. Oxford: Oxford University Press, 1979.

Lutoslawski, Wincenty. *The Knowledge of Reality*. Cambridge: University Press, 1930.

MacIntyre, Alasdair. *After Virtue*. Notre Dame, Ind.: University of Notre Dame Press, 1981.

Mackie, J. L. *Ethics*. Harmondsworth, U.K.: Pelican, 1976.

Magel, Charles. Review of *The Moral Status of Animals*. *Environmental Ethics* 2 (1980): 179–85.

Maxwell, Gavin. *Ring of Bright Water*. London: Penguin, 1960.

McAuliffe, Patricia. Review of *The Nature of the Beast*. *Philosophical Books* 24 (1983): 125–26.

McCloskey, H. J. *Ecological Ethics and Politics.* Totowa, N.J.: Rowman and Littlefield, 1983.

McTaggart, J. T. *The Nature of Existence,* 2 vols. Cambridge: Cambridge University Press, 1927.

Midgley, Mary. Review of *The Moral Status of Animals. Philosophical Quarterly* 28 (1978): 177–78.

Miller, Peter. Review of *The Nature of the Beast. Environmental Ethics* 9 (1987): 277–79.

Monod, Jacques. *Chance and Necessity.* London: Collins, 1972.

Morgan, R. C. "Non Angli sed Angeli." In *New Studies in Theology,* edited by S. Sykes and D. Holmes, 1–30. London: Duckworth, 1980.

Morton, Adam. Review of *How to Live Forever.* In *British Journal for Philosophy of Science* 48 (1997): 310–12.

Mumford, L. "Closing Statement." In *Future Environments of North America,* edited by F. Darling and J. Milton, 718 ff. Garden City, N.Y.: Natural History Press, 1966.

Nagel, Thomas. *Mortal Questions.* Cambridge: Cambridge University Press, 1979.

Newman, John Henry. *An Essay in Aid of a Grammar of Assent.* Notre Dame, Ind.: University of Notre Dame Press, 1947.

Nozick, Robert. *Anarchy, State, and Utopia.* New York: Basic Books, 1974.

Nussbaum, Martha. Review of *Aristotle's Man. The Philosophical Review* 86 (1977): 241–44.

O'Donnell, J. J. *Trinity and Temporality.* Oxford: Clarendon Press, 1983.

O'Donovan, Oliver. *Resurrection and Moral Order.* Leicester: Intervarsity Press, 1986.

———. Review of *Civil Peace and Sacred Order. The Journal of Theological Studies* 42 (1991): 441–44.

Ogden, Schubert. *The Reality of God and Other Essays.* London: SCM Press, 1967.

O'Neill, Onora. Review of *The Moral Status of Animals.* In *The Journal of Philosophy* 77 (1980): 440–46.

Otto, W. F. *The Homeric Gods.* London: Thames and Hudson, 1954.

Pannenberg, Wolfhart. *Theology and the Kingdom of God.* Philadelphia: Westminster Press, 1979.

Pluhar, Evelyn. "The Joy of Killing." *Between the Species* 7 (1991): 121–28.

Rawls, John. *A Theory of Justice.* Cambridge: Harvard University Press, 1971.

———. *Political Liberalism.* New York: Columbia University Press, 1992.

Regan, Tom. "Fox's Critique of Animal Liberation." *Ethics* 88 (1978): 126–33.

———. Review of *The Moral Status of Animals. Philosophical Books* 19 (1978): 118–19.

"Review of *The Moral Status of Animals,*" *Ethics* 88 (1978): 186.

"Review of *The Nature of the Beast.*" *Philosophical Studies* 31 (1986–1987): 523–25.

Rist, John. Review of *A Parliament of Souls. Journal of Theological Studies* 42 (1991): 819–21.

———. Review of *God's World. Journal of Theological Studies* 43 (1992): 791–94.

Robins, I. N. Review of *Aristotle's Man.* In *Philosophy* 51 (1976): 236–39.

Rorty, Richard. *Philosophy and the Mirror of Nature.* Princeton: Princeton University Press, 1979.

———. "Taking Philosophy Seriously." *New Republic,* 11 April 1988, 31–34.

Roszak, Theodore. *Where the Wasteland Ends.* Berkeley, Calif.: Creative Arts, 1989.

Royce, Josiah. *The Philosophy of Loyalty.* New York: Macmillan, 1908.

Said, Edward. *Orientalism.* New York: Random House, 1978.

Salt, Henry. *Animals' Rights.* Clarks Summit, Penn.: Society for Animal Rights, 1980.

Schuon, Fritjof. *Spiritual Perspectives and Human Facts.* Bedfont, U.K.: Perennial Books, 1987.

Scruton, Roger. Review of *Civil Peace and Sacred Order. History of Political Thought* 11 (1990): 546–47.

Sherry, Patrick. Review of *The Mysteries of Religion. Modern Theology* 6 (1989): 114–15.

Shute, Sara. Review of *A Parliament of Souls. International Studies in Philosophy* 23 (1991): 101–2.

Singer, Peter. *Animal Liberation.* New York: New York Review, 1975.

Singer, P., and Regan, T., eds. *Animal Rights and Human Obligations.* Englewood Cliffs, N.J.: Prentice-Hall, 1976.

Spooner, Lysander. *Let's Abolish Government.* New York: Arno, 1972.

Staudenbauer, Craig. Review of *From Athens to Jerusalem. Modern Schoolman* 64 (1987): 202–5.

Stone, Christopher. *Should Trees Have Standing?* Los Altos, Calif.: William Kaufmann, 1974.

Sumner, L. W. Review of *The Moral Status of Animals. Dialogue* 17 (1978): 570–75.

Swinburne, Richard. "The Limits of Explanation." *Philosophy: Supplement* 27 (1990): 177–93.

Taylor, Charles. *Sources of the Self.* Cambridge: Harvard University Press, 1989.

Tester, Keith. *Animals and Society.* London: Routledge, 1991.

Thoreau, H. D. *Walden.* New York: New American Library, 1980.

Thorpe, W. H. *Animal Nature and Human Nature.* Garden City, N.Y.: Anchor Press, 1974.

Tinbergen, Nikolaas. "On War and Peace in Animals and Men." *Science* 160 (1968): 1411 ff.

Tolkien, J. R. R. "On Fairy-Stories." In *Tree and Leaf.* London: Allen and Unwin, 1961.

Tonnies, Ferdinand. *Community and Society.* East Lansing, Mich.: Michigan State University Press, 1957.

Torrance, T. F. *Space, Time and Incarnation.* Oxford: Oxford University Press, 1969.

———. *Theological Science.* Oxford: Oxford University Press, 1969.

Toynbee, Arnold. *A Study of History,* 12 vols. Oxford: Oxford University Press, 1954.

Vitali, Theodore. "Sport Hunting: Moral or Immoral." *Environmental Ethics* 12 (1990): 69–82.

Watson, Gerard. Review of *Aristotle's Man. Philosophical Studies* 23 (1975): 330–32.

Weil, Simone. *Notebooks.* London: Routledge and Kegan Paul, 1956.

Weiss, Paul. "God and the World." In *Science, Philosophy, and Religion.* New York: Conference on Science, Philosophy, and Religion, 1941.

White, Vernon. *The Fall of a Sparrow.* Exeter: Paternoster Press, 1985.

Whitehead, A. N. *Science and the Modern World.* New York: Macmillan, 1957.

Whittemore, Robert. "Panentheism in Neo-Platonism." *Tulane Studies in Philosophy* 15 (1966): 47–70.

Whorf, B. L. *Language, Thought and Reality.* Cambridge: MIT Press, 1956.

Wilkes, Kathleen. "How Many Selves Make Me?" *Philosophy: Supplement* 29 (1991): 235–43.

Williams, Bernard. *Ethics and the Limits of Philosophy.* London: Fontana Press, 1985.

Williams, Leonard. *Man and Monkey.* London: Deutsch, 1967.

Wilson, E. O. *Sociobiology.* Cambridge: Harvard University Press, 1975.

Wolfson, Harry. "Extradeical and Intradeical Interpretations of Platonic Ideas." *Journal of the History of Ideas* 22 (1961): 3–32.

Wolin, Sheldon. Review of *Philosophical Apprenticeships* by H. G. Gadamer. *New York Times Review of Books,* 28 July 1985, 12.

Yeats, W. B. *Autobiographies.* London: Macmillan, 1955.

INDEX

Bergson, Henri, 49, 61

Berkeley, George, 72, 116, 160, 181, 308–9, 338n. 22

Bernard, Claude, 116, 188

Bible (the Holy), 8, 9; animal rights in the, 209–20; on killing, 84–85, 86–87, 144; literalism, 237, 323n. 30; omnipotence in the, 105; omniscience in the, 88; truth in the, 19; vegetarianism in the, 210. *See also* interpretation; theodicy

biology, 169, 263

Blake, William, 145–46

body: and existence, 96–97, 125; sentiency and, 156–63

Boethius, 40, 55–56

Bohr, Niels, 16

Boswell, James, 83

Brown, Charlie, 280

Buddha, 76, 299. *See also* Buddhism

Buddhism, 19, 260; Clark influenced by, x, 19, 26, 52, 96, 97; dipolarity and, 64; objectivity and, 201; "passivity," 216; salvation in, 34, 277; time and, 61, 62; World Soul and, 299–300. *See also* Clark

Burke, Edmund, 12, 14, 264

C

Caesar, 52

capitalism, 250

Categories (Aristotle), 98

Causey, Ann, 325n. 2

ceremonial truth. *See* truth

Chalcedonian orthodoxy, 157, 279

Chaldean religion, 41

Chandler, John, 92–93

chaos: cosmos and, 304; God and, 80, 81, 89

Chesterton, G. K., 71, 221, 254, 281

Chisholm, R. M., 27

Chisholm's Rule, 27

Chomsky, Noam, 35, 203

Christianity, 7, 175, 240, 272; dipolar theism and, 64; infinite love in, 39; repentance in, 51. *See also* family; God; ritual; violence

Churchland, Paul and Patricia, 159

Cicero, 263

"city of the wise." *See* cosmos; World Soul

Civil Peace and Sacred Order (Clark), 14

Clark, Stephen R. L.: animals and, x–xi, 197; on animals and humans, 131–46, 151–53; as Aristotelian, 14–15, 23–29, 99–100, 105, 110–128, 211–12, 245; belief and, 14, 27–28; Clifford Principle of, 12; compared to James, 3–4, 11–12, 28, 138–39, 153, 171; compared to other philosophers, 12, 14; conservatism of, 145, 153–54, 187, 191, 213–221, 334n. 37; contradictions in, x, 76–77, 84, 88–89, 91–93, 154, 296; criticism of, 6–7, 11, 12; determinist, 153; as a dipolar theist, 40, 54, 64, 67; dualism of, 81–82; environmentalist, 213–21; ethics versus morals and, 111–12; ethology and, 109–46, 173; faith and, 9–10; feminism and, 77; fideism of, 84, 112, 114, 171, 309; foci of work by, x; humanism of, 190; hylomorphism and, 158, 159, 160; imagination of, 130; intellectuals and, 10;

interpretation, 14–15, 19; mistaken, 33.
See also philosophy
intuition and faith, 10
Irenaeus, 82
irreligion, 4, 48
Isaac, 84
Islam, 7, 39, 175, 238, 240, 260

J

James (Saint), 31
James, William: 28, 67, 138, 142, 153, 171,
181; and body, 158; Clark and religious views of, 3, 6, 11–12; consciousness and, 116; divinity recognized by,
31; dualism and, 181–82; as pacifist,
138–39, 142; religious reality and,
60–61, 67; science and, 199; service
and, 19. See also Clark
Jamieson, Dale, 179, 184
Jesus, 53, 64, 66, 73, 79, 90, 260, 272–73,
275, 279; pacifist, 138, 233; sparrow
and, xii, 88; vegetarianism and, 210
Job, 82, 83
John (Saint), 10, 272–73
John of the Cross (Saint), 52, 103, 210,
288, 290
Judaism, 7, 175; God in, 39
Julian of Norwich, 290
Jung, Karl, 19

K

Kant, Immanuel, 80, 97, 114, 181, 192,
209, 220, 245, 282; animals and,
188–90; autonomy and, 232; Clark
agrees with, 34; on destiny, 86;
divine command theory and, 93, 94,
105; existence and, 270, 314; freedom

types and, 151, 152–53, 154; on God
and value, 91; incest and, 121–22;
liberalism of, 129; libertarianism of,
247; on morality, 111–12, 132, 170,
288; rationality and, 259; reality and,
97; rights and, 143; speciesism and,
174; the state and, 238
Kazantzakis, Nikos, 52
Kerr, Fergus, 14, 178
Khomeyni, Ayatollah, 237
killing: Biblical, 144; Clark and, 92;
euthanasia, 166, 167; for food, 167,
176, 195; of innocents, 142–43;
research and, 163–64, 167, 177; rights
to, 84–85; soul and, 175–76. See also
Bible; war
King, Martin Luther, 54, 227, 232
kinship, 264–65
Kipling, Rudyard, 137, 251–52
Kohak, Erazim, 286
Koko, 132
Koran. See Islam
Kripke, Saul, 96

L

laboratory experiments. See animals
language: animal, 151–52, 207–8, 211;
Aristotle's use of, 100; Clark and,
15–20, 26; in community, 244–45;
Greek, 100, 271; and human existence, 15–20; literalism, 255. See also
communication
laws: civil, 234, 256; liberty and, 245–46;
natural, 234; permitting cruelty, 209.
See also animal "rights"
Laws (Plato), 70
Leahy, Michael, 330n. 38